WITHDRAWN
From Bertrand Library

S.N.D.T. WOMEN'S UNIVERSITY
BOMBAY

WOMEN IN A CHANGING SOCIETY

General Editors: Vina Mazumdar
                 Kumud Sharma

SYMBOLS OF POWER
Editor: Vina Mazumdar

S.N.D.T. Women's University, Bombay
Research Unit on Women's Studies

Forthcoming volumes in
Women in a Changing Society:-

—— The Invisible Gap: Studies on the Legal Status of Women in India.—
Editor: LOTIKA SARKAR.
—— The Social Fabric: Studies on Family and Kinship Systems:
Editor: VEENA DAS
—— The Trends of Change: Studies on Media Response to the Women's Movement
Editor: NEERA DESAI
—— The Challenge of Education: Studies on Issues in Women's Education
Editor: VINA MAZUMDAR

Other Publications of the Unit:

* 'Women in India' a handbook (1975)
  (revised edition in Press).
* "A select Bibliography of Women in India"
  (Allied Publishers 1976)
* "Widow remarriage" a movement (1800-1900)
  by S.G. Malshe and Nanda Apte (in Marathi) (1978)

Forthcoming:

* Translations in Gujarati and Marathi of the Synopsis of the Report of the National Committee on the Status of Women. (1971-74).

SYMBOLS OF POWER

STUDIES ON THE POLITICAL STATUS OF WOMEN IN INDIA

Editor
VINA MAZUMDAR

ALLIED PUBLISHERS PRIVATE LIMITED
BOMBAY ☐NEW DELHI ☐CALCUTTA ☐MADRAS ☐BANGALORE

ALLIED PUBLISHERS PRIVATE LIMITED
15 J.N. Heredia Marg Ballard Estate Bombay 400038
5th Main Road Gandhinagar Bangalore 560009
17 Chittaranjan Avenue Calcutta 700072
13/14 Asaf Ali Road New Delhi 110002
751 Mount Road Madras 600002

© S.N.D.T. Women's University, Bombay, 1979

PRINTED BY R.N. SACHDEV AT ALLIED PUBLISHERS PRIVATE LIMITED, PRINTING DIVISION, 4 SHIVAJI MARG, NEW DELHI 110015.

Foreword

I am indeed thankful to the ICSSR for giving the Research Unit on Women Studies, S.N.D.T. University, the responsibility for this publication. This volume is the first in a series, "Women in a Changing Society" inspired by the ICSSR. Mr. J.P. Naik, the then member-secretary, ICSSR, and Dr. Vina Mazumdar, Director, Women's Studies Programme, have provided the major initiative, effort and encouragement for the decision to publish under this series, the set of papers commissioned for the National Committee on the Status of Women.

The Research Unit on Women Studies, S.N.D.T. University, established in 1974, has all along been concerned with understanding and identifying problems of women and undertaking studies pertaining to women's status and role in society. As a collateral task, the Unit has consistently pursued dissemination of information made available through exploration and research. The two earlier publications of the Unit, *Women in India – A Handbook* (1975) and *A Select Bibliography on Women in India* (1977) have been well received. It is hoped that the present volume, published in collaboration with the ICSSR, will be useful to the general public and particularly to those interested in women.

In a way, it is fitting that *Symbols of Power* is the first publication in the planned series, "Women in a Changing Society" for there is a general self-congratulatory air about the fact that women in India have been granted political rights and that quite a few of them are occupying positions of power. An examination of the actual situation can be an eye-opener and jolt us out of some of the comfortable myths we have held on to.

I am confident this book will throw light on issues of concern not merely to women but to men also.

MADHURI SHAH
Vice-Chancellor
SNDT Women's University
Bombay 400 020

Contents

		Page
Foreword		vii
Editor's Note		xi

Part I: Women in National Politics

Votes For Women	G. Forbes	3
Women in the Electoral Process	S.D. Muni	24
Women Voters and the Mid-Term Poll (1971)	Nandini Upretti & D.B. Mathur	51

Part II: Politicization of Women in India—A Three-State Study

An Overview	V.M. Sirsikar	79
Gujarat	Dinesh M. Shukla	85
Maharashtra	P.N. Limaye	119
West Bengal	Nirmala Banerjee	140

Part III: Profiles of Women in State Politics

Andhra Pradesh	G.Y. Chandramani	173
Assam	K.M. Deka	191

Gujarat	Pravin N. Sheth	200
Karnataka	Amal Ray	221
Kerala	Lucy Jacob	226
Maharashtra	S.N. Tawale	246
Punjab	P. Rajput	265
Rajasthan	Bhagwant Rao Dubey	291
Uttar Pradesh	Indra Narayan Tewary	305
West Bengal	Bangendu Ganguly	319

Appendix 351

Index 365

Editor's Note

Modern western movements for women's rights, especially the one that developed in the latter half of the nineteenth and the first half of the twentieth century, sooner or later crystallized into a demand for "votes for women". The right of representation symbolized to many at that time "a place in the sun", at least a gateway to enter the all-male world of political decision-making. Earlier movements for women's liberation, which had sought to challenge the established definitions of women's roles and status as dependent functions of the family, were submerged by, or deliberately jettisoned in order to win greater support for a demand that could be strengthened by the logic of established political creeds of democracy through representative government.

While to the participants in the movement the prospect of returns from this right must have appeared as immense, radical feminists have tended to see the demand for the vote as only an attempt by the women of the elite classes to find some room for themselves in the established power-structure, thereby strengthening the monopolistic hold of the same groups on the political system. It is possible to make the same criticism of women's demand for the right of entry to higher education and the professions, which were also virtually monopolies of the same classes. But there is little doubt that to those who voiced these demands, they represented protests against a socio-political structure which *excluded women as women* from the sectors which dominated society of that period, classifying them as inferior beings and denying them the right of representation and access to political power.

Some anthropologists hold that women have always exercised considerable power through informal channels.[1] Such an observation is relevant only as long as we see power as an extended quality of an individual. In a man-woman relationship, there is always scope for a powerful personality to acquire a position of dominance. But this has little to do with a system of power-relations or generation and exercise of power through recognized channels. A few individual women might have commanded a lot of power through their hold on some men, but that could give little chance of power to women as a group.

With increasing formalization of power institutions, the effectiveness of such informal linkages were bound to weaken. Also the increasing role of the mass media and public scrutiny of persons in public office automatically tended to restrict the spheres of influence of "extra-constitutional authorities". The British factory girls who supported the suffragists certainly did not see the role of political hostesses or liaisons among the ruling classes as at all useful in their own struggles against wage discrimination, lack of health, education and welfare services, and perpetual insecurity and exploitation in employment.

A situation in which the right of representation came to symbolize access to political power in the same way as money and property symbolized economic power – the exclusion of women from both these spheres was bound to influence the perception of both men and women regarding the relative status and roles of the sexes in society. Most traditional societies which sharply differentiated the roles and worlds of men and women maintained a pluralist concept of social life. The value and status of individual men and women was defined by their performance of prescribed functions. Since the roles and functions of the sexes were regarded as complementary within the family and the community, the question of grading one group as superior to the other was not a major issue.

The classical Indian tradition, being a blend of highly sophisticed logical systems and primitive practices of heterogenous cultural groups, maintained a balance between the two sexes by permitting each culture group to maintain their own role differentiations, and protected statuses by functions. At the same time, religious symbols emphasized the bisexual basis of all reality, and various cults of the mother Goddess, as the source of energy, power, and fertility; as protection against evil, destructive, and cruel forces helped to maintain a myth that regarded women as potentially powerful, even dangerous beings. The persistence of this myth explains the easy acceptance by the people of a few women in positions of power.[2] The same people accepted – equally without challenge – widespread and institutionalized forms of oppression and subjugation of women as the natural order of things.

The nineteenth-century reformers, concerned by the impact of modernization – that increased the gap between men and women, and threatened the stability of the family – sought to strengthen women's position with education and limited rights to property. The question of

Editor's Note

women's political power or equality between the sexes was not on the reformer's agenda, though most of them shared the rising aspirations of the English-educated intelligentsia for a share in the governance of the country. Their urban middle-class origin and bias is evident from their perception of women's problems. Traditional attitudes and obscurantist customs such as *purdah*, child marriage, denial of divorce or remarriage, the oppressed condition of widows, ignorance and lack of property rights were seen as the main enemies. Education and removal of these oppressive customs, the reformers claimed, would allow women to develop to be better wives and mothers. There was no questioning of women's traditional familial roles or dependence on others. Instead, most reformers pleaded that increasing women's efficiency would strengthen the hold of the family and traditions in society, since women were – by temperament and convention – custodians of traditional culture and values. Reducing the communication gap between husband and wife and mother and son would help to insulate the younger men from the destructive influence of westernization.[3]

The reformers were very far removed from the problems that affected the majority of Indian women. A computation based on the Census of 1931 showed that at that date less than 10% of the population of the Indian sub-continent was affected by the ban on divorce and widow-marriage. Essentially the high caste Hindu customs, these bans did not extend to the rest of people. The upper class of some of the non-Hindu communities did imitate these norms to a certain extent, but for the majority, the non-elite groups, marriage laws were fairly flexible and permissive. Denial of education or property was hardly sex-discriminatory among the millions of illiterates who could claim little beyond their names as their own. *Purdah*, another upper-class norm, could not be practised by the working people, whose survival depended on their women's active participation in the labour force – in agriculture, industry, and services – as producers and sellers. Their problems stemmed from poverty, discriminatory and low wages, insecurity, and helplessness against exploitation of many kinds. The instruments of change advocated by the reformers – education and legal reform – could not have touched the lives of the vast masses of working women.

The demand for the vote, put forward in 1917 by a group of women to the Montague-Chelmsford Committee on Constitutional Reforms, was more on offshoot of the British suffragist movement than of any widespred awareness among Indian women. The women's organizations that developed a few years later voiced the needs of middle-class women – for education, reform of marriage and property laws, and the vote. Their perception of problems did not extend to women outside the middle-class or the aristocracy, even though there is some evidence to show that some small-town women's groups had started discussing the adverse impact of declining cottage industries on women's economic position. The leadership of the women's organizations came from well-to-do educated families, and had extensive contacts with different groups in the West. The men who supported their demands shared the attitudes of progressive liberals in the West, who saw the women's desire to play a role in public life as a reasonable outcome of the process of modernization and education.

The discordant, and perhaps unexpected, element in this picture of a gradual, smooth process of improving women's position by some concessions to their aspirations, provided they qualified for the privilege by birth, education and social status,[4] was introduced by Mahatma Gandhi, who brought completely new dimension into the debate on the women's question. Beginning from the basic premise that the subjugation and exploitation of women was the product of "man's interested teaching, and women's acceptance of them", he broke away from the reform tradition by preaching the philosophy not only of absolute equality of rights between the sexes, but of the pragmatic necessity of enrolling women's support to transform the nationalist struggle for the transfer of political power from British to Indian hands into a social revolution for abolishing social inequality of all kinds between the rich and the poor, the educated and the illiterates, the high castes and the untouchables, the workers and the non-workers, the industrial capitalist and the rural peasant, an authoritarian oppressive alien government and the masses of the people of the country.

The non-exploitative social order that he had visualized had to be achieved by participation of the masses of the people and the resolution of social conflicts by non-violent protests. Women, he claimed, were better than men in waging non-violent protests – because they had greater capacity for sacrifice and endurance, were less self-seeking, and had more moral courage. They must therefore become conscious of their historic role, reject the disgraceful role of being "man's plaything", and extend their capacity for love and sacrifice beyond their families – to "embrace the whole of

Editor's Note

humanity". Equality of legal and political rights, freedom from any coercion from the family or the society, and autonomy to choose her own way of moral and self-development, were only basic conditions, to enable the woman to play her destined role.[5]

One of the justifications for his economic policy of reviving the village economy and cottage industry was to restore to women their lost economic strength. The decline of village industry because of increasing competition from mass produced goods of modern technology and the capitalist mode of production had eroded women's productive roles considerably and increased their burden and problems. This process had to be arrested through the revival of village industries, and the restoration of women's economic base. Excessive burden of labour for no return and discrimination in wages demonstrated their exploited position.

Today the sole occupation of a woman amongst us is supposed to be to bear children, to look after her husband and otherwise to drudge for the household ... not only is the woman condemned to domestic slavery, but when she goes out as a labourer to earn wages, though she works harder than man she is paid less.[6]

The radical note struck by Gandhi found a close parallel in the ideas of Karl Marx which influenced socialists of different shades in India:

The emancipation of women and their equality with men are impossible and must remain so as long as women are excluded from socially productive work and restricted to house work, which is private.[7]

These two strains of social ideas were fused in the mind of Jawaharlal Nehru. As President of the Indian National Congress in 1931 he steered the resolution that pledged the nation to a policy of equality in law, political, and economic life after independence. As a leading member of the Constituent Assembly he incorporated the pledge into specific articles in the Constitution of the Indian Republic.* As Prime Minister he steered the laws improving the rights of Hindu women in marriage, guardianship and inheritance, and special labour laws for the protection of women workers in factories, mines, and plantations, making the passage of these laws a prestige

---

*See Appendix at the end of the book.

issue for the government. A new agency, the Central Social Welfare Board, was created to organize special measures to assist women, particularly in the rural areas:

We talk about a welfare State and direct our energies towards its realisation. That welfare must be the common property of everyone in India and not the monopoly of the privileged groups as it is today. If I may be allowed to lay greater stress on some, they would be the welfare of children, the status of women, and the welfare of the tribal and hilly people in our country. Women in India have a background of history and tradition behind them, which is inspiring. It is true, however, that they have suffered much from various kinds of suppression and all those have to go so that they can play their full part in the life of the nation.[8]

The First Five Year Plan admitted the significance of the new rights conferred on women, and held that they called for adequate provision of education and health services, including family planning. The implications of equality were clear in the statement of objectives for women's education:

The general purpose and objectives of women's education cannot, of course be different from the purpose and objective of men's education. At the secondary and even at the university stage women's education should have a vocational or occupational bias.[9]

The early fifties thus came to be regarded as the period of women's triumph – with middle-class women from a background of restricted lives confined to the roles of wives and mother entering administrative, professional, and political employment as equals of men. Institutions of professional education in law and technology, which had till then barred women's entry, were compelled to admit them. Women entered new occupations in the modern sector in increasing numbers. Women from aristocratic families, both Hindu and Muslim, began to abandon *purdah* and sought public offices. Women were elected to Parliament and State Legislatures, became Cabinet ministers, governors of States, ambassadors, vice-chancellors of universities, and judges, and exercised their vote in increasing numbers in successive general elections. Local self-governing bodies, in both urban and rural areas, were asked to include a few women on their panels by nomination, if they did not come through election channels.

All these could suggest, as they did to most people concerned with social policy in India, that "the revolution in the status of women" and

Editor's Note

the extension of their roles in society was well on the way. But the review undertaken in the early seventies by the Committee on the Status of Women in India reached a very different conclusion:

Though women do not constitute a minority numerically, they are acquiring the features of one by the inequality of class, status and political power.[10]

Three years after the Committee's Report a group of social scientists have drawn attention in an even sharper manner to what they call "the national neglect of women." The alarming deterioration in women's status, their research proves, began several decades ago, but has been accelerated in the past three decades. Demographic trends, with growing differentials between men and women in mortality, access to health care and medical services, literacy, education and vocational training, and accelerated decline in employment provide, in their view, "indisputable evidence of steady decline in the value of women in society." The best indicator of this trend is the persistent decline in the sex-ratio in the population.

Unless the economic and social utility of women is enhanced in the eyes of their families and the nation by opportunities to take part in socially and economically productive roles, the national neglect of women will continue. Erosion of productive roles emphasises women's position as consumers and bearers of children, makes their lives cheap and easily expendable through increasing malnutrition and mortality, reduces employability through inadequate training opportunities and increases economic discrimination and exploitation.[11]

Development plans and supportive services have tended to view women only as target groups for social services, ignoring their productive roles. In consequence, development itself has contributed to the massive displacement of women from agricultural, industrial, and trading occupations. The marginal increase of women in the service sector cannot offset this trend, but the visibility of middle-class women in white-collared occupations has helped to build an illusion of progress, hiding the stark reality of shrinking roles of the majority. Even in the service sector, much of the increased employment is in poverty-oriented occupations, i.e., personal and domestic services generated by population increase, especially in urban areas. Prostitution and traffic in women, the commercial use of females for career and business promotion, and illegal, even criminal activities – all point to growing use of women as commodities. The sex-specific roles prescribed by traditional society, even though limited, guaranteed greater dignity to the majority than its modern counterpart.

One traditional role that has expanded is the use of women as vehicles for display of wealth and status. Previously restricted to the feudal aristocracy whose status required keeping their women idle and bejewelled, this practice is now imitated by new or aspirant entrants to the middle class. The payment of dowry to obtain a husband for a young woman, which had become difficult during the thirties because of opposition from the Gandhian women's movement, has, in spite of a prohibitory law, increased in volume and incidence, affecting even communities which had followed the opposite practice of paying bride price till a few years back. There are many such examples of "regression from the norms developed during the freedom struggle". In politics, the emergence and fall of a woman Prime Minister has not succeeded in arresting the steady decline in the number of women in the legislative bodies, and in the parties' sponsorship of women for such positions. Gandhi's dream has indeed receded very far from the social horizon of contemporary India.

II

There is little doubt that it was the willing and spontaneous participation of women in the civil disobedience movements rather than the radical ideas of sexual equality that finally tilted the balance in favour of political equality between the sexes within the Congress Party and later in the Constituent Assembly. This explains the absence of any debate on this question or its implications.[12] that the majority of the Constitution fathers had not examined the social or political implications of this right is clear from the storm that erupted when the same body sitting as the Central Legislative Council had to consider the Hindu Code Bill. Nor was this body prepared to consider a suggestion of K.T. Shah (who had been a member of the National Planning Committee appointed by the Indian National Congress in the period before independence), that women's housework should find a place in the National accounting process.

The attitude of the women leaders also displayed an ambivalence and a failure to understand the varied nature of the constraints that operated on women at different levels. It is interesting to see how the controversy on whether women needed protective reservations on the

Editor's Note

same lines as the Scheduled Castes and Tribes resurrects itself periodically. Four decades after the defeat of the reservationists, this proved to be the only issue on which the Committee on the Status of Women in India failed to achieve unanimity.* Since then the falling representation of women in the State and Central Legislatures, added to the now indisputable evidence of "deterioration of their value, status and roles" unearthed by systematic research, have resulted in increasing support for reservation from different sections.

Jyotiba Phule and 'Lokahitawadi' Gopalhari Deshmukh – the most radical of the nineteenth century reformers – had seen the subjugation of women as an instrument for perpetuating brahminical domination in society. Gandhi believed that women, being an oppressed, unequal group, would be the best fighters against social inequalities of all kinds. The Kalelkar Commission on Backward Classes in the fifties observed that women should be regarded as a backward class for purposes of specially protective social policies. But the debate has never been seriously pursued – and the women's movement has shied away from it again and again.

There are three standard arguments against reservations. Many women leaders believe that it would be a retrograde step after the acceptance of equality. They also claim that such a step would isolate women from the main stream of political and social life, and relegate them to the protective custody of the government. Yet the same leaders have not hesitated to support the Planning Commission's belated recognition that without "special measures" it may be difficult to ensure to women a fair share of employment, without which no "improvement in their status" is possible.[13]

The proof of the pudding is in the eating. Would political commentators agree that the system of reservations for the Scheduled Castes and Tribes has totally "isolated" them from the main stream of politics or social life? Or has the system been the only pressure without which the issue would have remained outside the field of public debate? Would the women's question have faded out of the public area so easily, if reservation had been introduced in the Constitution? Or would the declining status of women have remained invisible and unattended to but for the historical accident of the appointment of a Committee, and the UN's decision to press for women's "integration in development"? Even now, three years after

---

*See Appendix at the end of the book.

the release of the Report of the Committee on the Status of Women in India, and the mounting evidence from empirical research, the facts of women's declining status are known to very few in this country. Can one say the same for the conditions of the Harijans?

The most important and substantial argument against reservations for women is the one offered by the Committee on the Status of Women – that women are not a category by themselves, that their problems and needs differ according to socio-economic classes. But the identical argument is offered by the opponents of existing reservations for Scheduled Castes, or proposed reservations for backward classes. They argue that the beneficiaries of reservations do not contribute to the uplift of their communities, that reservations develop vested interests in backwardness. Without belittling the strength of these arguments, one can ask the question – don't vested interests develop even without reservations? And isn't this what has happened to middle-class women, the *beneficiaries* of the equality principle?

III

The reservation controversy, like the earlier ones regarding the vote, higher education, rights to property, and entry into professions, represents attempts to grapple with a problem of basic inequality and growing imbalance in access to resources and power of different kinds. But the assumptions continue to be those extended by the founding fathers of the Constitution of the United States, that all *individuals* have equal opportunity to exercise power if they have a vote. Reservations seek to provide a little prop to a disadvantaged group, but cannot basically alter the power balance. It is now admitted that the cause of distributive justice requires *mobilization of the disadvantaged as groups* through organizations that can strengthen their voice and assertive power in the decision-making process. So far reservations have not contributed much to this process.

In the case of women this is particularly important because traditional values and behavioural norms, bred through thousands of years, inhibit them in asserting themselves as *individuals* except in very limited contexts. The more complex the process becomes, the greater is the communication gap, and difficulties in women's *effective* participation in the political process. This is borne out by the experience of women in the most developed countries – where in spite

Editor's Note

of higher educational levels and better developed communication systems, women's *effectiveness* in politics has remained limited.

The investigations of the Committee on the Status of Women in India demonstrated that many of our established assumptions about determinants of women's participation in the political process required empirical verification. Education, urbanization, family pressure, hitherto regarded as primary determinants of political awareness or participation have been sharply questioned by the Committee. Political scientists will have to answer the question posed by the Committee – why with increasing level of voting participation, women's representation and effectiveness in the political process has continued to decline?[14] Why is it that States like U.P., M.P. and Bihar – whose lack of concern for women's survival and development has now become proverbial and where women's mobilization as voters is minimal – continue to elect the largest number of women to State Assemblies and Parliament?

The Committee's recommendation of separate women's organizations at different levels of the political machinery – panchayats, municipalities, political parties, trade unions etc. – was an intuitive response to the problem of strengthening women's *effectiveness* through group strength. Do they reflect growing disillusionment with the existing political mechanisms which are male-defined, and display little interest in women's issues, or adaptability to women's requirements?

Gandhi, it is said, had wanted to *feminise* the political process by bringing women in on terms of equality.[15] Perhaps he had hoped that women would throw their influence on the side of the angels, for peaceful solutions of social or international conflicts. This is also the stated aim of some international women's organizations, and of the UN Decade. But the experience of the few women who have attained the highest positions of political power as individuals do not altogether support this. Competitive politics, as designed and defined by the male-dominated world, puts a premium on ruthlessness for survival, and it is hardly possible for individual women to manipulate these structures by alternative methods.[16]

The current global debate on how to increase women's role in development and in the process of decision making at all levels of society – as individual citizens and as *women* – has offered many explanations for the kind of trends now visible in India and in many other countries in both the developed and the developing world. The patriarchal ideology inherent in the capitalist path of development; the choice of technology and forms of economic organization imposed by international capital; blind imitation of western materialist values, life, and consumption styles to the detriment of indigenous cultural values; urban middle class and westernized bias in planning; over-concentration on economic growth and neglect of social development; increasing population and income disparity; and differential spread of the fruits of development between different classes of the population – one may select one or more of these explanations according to one's own ideological inclinations.

The questions that are bound to arise as the debate proceeds will inevitably shake the established values and perception of roles of both men and women. Does equality mean identity of rights and responsibilities? Does it necessarily involve replacing the complemental relations between the sexes by competitive ones? How will all this affect the family, children's development, and the social fabric as a whole? Does autonomy for women mean the end of marriage and family as basic social institutions? Is it necessary for women to define their lives and roles by the same concepts as men have done? Or, are the present concepts only products of a pattern of development which tend to put a monetized or achievement value on everything, even human relations and qualities? Are family relations really exploitative? Should women's child-bearing function be regarded as an asset or a liability from both the individual's and the society's point of view?

Do women have any special roles to play in the political process or must they adopt the practices as defined now and try to outbid men to be effective? Or, should they remain as docile and dependent members of a system in which they can function only by accepting the methods which others have introduced? A large number of politically active women told the Committee on the Status of Women in India that increasing violence, character assassinations, and unscrupulous competition for positions had become the greatest deterrents to women's participation in politics in any effective manner.

These are issues which must be considered by all who are concerned with the women's question, not only in India but in other countries as well. A frequently reported criticism from spokesmen of the western women's movement is that third world women at the World Conference at Mexico (1975) emphasized *dignity* and *justice* much more than *equality*. Is there then a contradiction between these

Editor's Note

three goals? Is it not necessary to examine their inter-relationship?

The social thinkers who contributed to the concept of sex-equality in India have invariably highlighted the similarities in women's position with that of the scheduled castes. But most women leaders have been reluctant to accept this equation, perhaps because they are apprehensive of the responsibility that they may have to shoulder as a concomitant of such a conviction. How many of us who are conscious of women's oppression would be prepared to identify ourselves wholeheartedly with the cause of other oppressed groups?

The Committee on the Status of Women saw its task primarily as a fact finding one. Taking the constitutional guarantees as the basic premise they sought to avoid raising value questions. In spite of their reluctance, however, they were compelled to face the realities of the social system which contain the roots of women's oppression and constraints as well as the values and role concepts that have enabled them to endure and survive in a world of unpleasant realities. The Committee, therefore, was forced to record its own set of values as guiding principles:

1. that equality of women is necessary, not merely on the grounds of social justice, but as a basic condition of social, economic and political development of the nation;
2. that in order to release women from their dependent and unequal status, improvement of their employment opportunities and earning power has to be given the highest priority;
3. that society owes a special responsibility to women because of their child-bearing function. Safe bearing and rearing of children is an obligation that has to be shared by the mother, the father and society;
4. that the contribution made by an active housewife to the running and management of the family should be admitted as economically and socially productive and contributing to national savings and development;
5. that marriage and motherhood should not become a disability in women's fulfilling their full and proper roles in the task of national development. Therefore, it is important that society, including women themselves, must accept their responsibility in this field;
6. that disabilities and inequalities imposed on women have to be seen in the total context of a society, where large sections of the population – male and female, adults and children – suffer under

the oppression of an exploitative system. It is not possible to remove these inequalities for women only. Any policy or movement for the emancipation and development of women has to form a part of a total movement for removal of inequalities and oppressive social institutions, if the benefits and privileges won by such action are to be shared by the entire women population and not be monopolised by a small minority;

7. that if our society is to move in the direction of the goals set by the Constitution, then special temporary measures will be necessary, to transform *de jure* into *de facto* equality.

Indian women have been more fortunate than many of their sisters in obtaining equal political rights without much struggle on their part. Unfortunately, the termination of the debate on the women's question has prevented realization of the implications and responsibilities that flow from these rights. One of the objectives of the programme of Women's Studies adopted by the ICSSR after the submission of the report of the Committee on the Status of Women in India is to revive the social debate on these vital issues which affect the prospects of Indian development.

IV

Most of the papers in this volume were prepared at great haste for consideration by the Committee on the Status of Women in India in 1974. They were described as "illustrative materials" by Prof. Iqbal Narain, who organized their preparation. They do not claim to be major or original studies, but offer many pointers for further enquiry, and focus attention on some hitherto unnoticed conundrums. The three studies in Part II were designed and coordinated by Prof. V.M. Sirsikar at the Committee's request, and provided added support for the Committee's growing doubts regarding some established assumptions about women's participation in politics.

Both the scholars drew the Committee's attention to the wide gap between "symbolism and actuality" and the failure of political rights to bring about the desired changes in women's status. My personal acknowledgements are due to them, not only for their prompt response to my request for help, but also for mobilizing the team of young scholars to investigate an area which had not so far attracted the attention of the academic profession. Some of them have

Editor's Note

continued their interest and I hope this volume will help to generate a similar interest among others.

Future studies on women's role in politics will, however, have to take note of the negative correlations and conundrums identified by this group, and consider carefully the need for alternative hypotheses and ways by which scientific scholarship can gain by learning from the perceptions of the subjects of study.

The editorial work for the entire series and most of the studies contained in these volumes were financed by the Indian Council of Social Science Research. The decision to assist their publication in a series was also the Council's. I must thank Mr. J.P. Naik, then Member-Secretary of the Council, for initiating the series and giving me and my colleagues the opportunity to be associated with the work.

I must thank Dr. Kumud Sharma and Anna Kuryan for shouldering the major responsibility in editing and preparing the manuscript, the SNDT Women's University for undertaking the publication with some support from the ICSSR, and Mr. W.H. Patwardhan for the immense patience in dealing with an editor who has little time to look after her editorial responsibilities.

VINA MAZUMDAR
Director
Programme of Women's Studies,
ICSSR.

7 May 1978

References

1. M.N. Srinivas: "Changing Position of Indian Women", *Man* (New Series), Vol. 12, No. 2, Aug. 1977.
2. Ashok Rudra: Culture and Religious Influences, In Devaki Jain (ed.), *Indian Women*, Publications Division, Ministry of Information and Broadcasting, Government of India, New Delhi, 1975.
3. Vina Mazumdar: "The Social Reform Movement from Ranade to Nehru", in B.R. Nanda (ed.), *Indian Women: from Purdah to Modernity*, Vikas, New Delhi, 1975.
4. The Constitutional Reforms of 1919 authorized the elected legislatures in the provinces to concede votes to women if they so desired. The Reforms Act of 1921 enfranchised a very small fraction of the Indian population, including women, if they possessed qualifications of wifehood, property, and education. The Government of India Act of 1935 increased the number of enfranchised Indians and relaxed some of the previous qualifications. Women over 21 could vote provided they fulfilled the conditions of property and education.
5. M.K. Gandhi: *Young India*, Dec. 15, 1921; *Young India*, Oct. 8, 1925; *Young India*, Mar. 21, 1927; *Young India*, Feb. 24, 1940; *Harijan:* Aug. 4, 1940.
6. M.K. Gandhi: *Young India*, Feb. 26, 1918, quoted in *Towards Equality – Report of the Committee on the Status of Women in India*, Department of Social Welfare, Ministry of Education and Social Welfare, New Delhi, 1975.
7. Karl Marx and Freidrich Engels: *Selected Works*, Vol. 2, Progress Publishers, Moscow, 1972.
8. Jawaharlal Nehru: Foreword to *Social Welfare in India*, Planning Commission, New Delhi, 1955.
9. *First Five Year Plan*, Chapter 33, Government of India, Planning Commission, New Delhi, 1952.
10. *Towards Equality*, etc., *op. cit.*, p. 372.
11. Indian Council of Social Science Research, Advisory Committee on Women's Studies: *Critical Issues on the Status of Women: Employment, Health, Education: Suggested Priorities for Action*, ICSSR, 1977.
12. Hansa Mehta, who was a member of the Fundamental Rights Committee of the Constituent Assembly, told me that the only discussions were of a frivolous nature which she had to snub. They were not recorded in the proceedings.
13. *Draft VI Five Year Plan*, Vol. II, para 3.39, p. 109, Planning Commission, Government of India, New Delhi, 1978.
14. It reached the lowest levels in the 1977 elections.
15. Sugata Das Gupta and I.N. Tewary: "Women's Emancipation in India – a sociological analysis," (unpublished).
16. Statements made to the Press by Indira Gandhi in the period before 1975 repeatedly emphasized that she did not particularly think of herself as a woman.

PART I

WOMEN IN NATIONAL POLITICS

VOTES FOR WOMEN

The Demand for Women's Franchise in India 1917-1937

Geraldine H. Forbes

In the space of less than 20 years India changed from a country with no women in political life to the third country in the world in terms of number of women legislators. India had 80 women legislators in 1937, exceeded only by the U.S.A. with 140 and the U.S.S.R. with 130.[1] Much of the credit for this change must go to the three national women's organizations which voiced women's demand for the vote and mobilized public opinion to support this demand. Begun between 1917 and 1927, these three organizations – Women's Indian Association, National Council of Women in India, and All-India Women's Conference – had developed branches all over India, annual and bi-annual meetings, journals and memberships which ran into thousands. Through their branches they had established contact with the majority of India's educated women. These organizations claimed the authority to speak for the women of India, followed up this claim with a steady stream of resolutions, reports and deputations, and were eventually accepted as the spokespersons for women.

The demand for 'votes for women', articulated by these organizations, was for equality with men. Referring to this, Tara Ali Baig has written:

Discrimination on the basis of sex has never happened in all India's modern political life, nor did women ever demand special reservation or preferential treatment.[2]

This paper traces the demand for 'votes for women' from 1917, the time of the first franchise delegation, up to 1937, when the first elections were held under the Government of India Act of 1935. Generally, gaining women's franchise has been termed the 'easy victory'. I intend to point out that there was considerable debate over the questions of who should have the vote, and that the right to vote was not 'granted' without pressure from organized women. It is my hypothesis that the firm insistence of organized women – that they be treated as the equals of men on the franchise issue – emerged not from their perception of the needs of women in India, but as a result of the influence of certain British women, in the case of the first demand for the franchise, 1917, and as a response to the nationalist movement, in the case of the second demand for franchise, 1927-1933.

From the beginning, the demand for 'votes for women' was based on the notion that women could bring something new and special to the political realm. Demands were not rooted in the concept of 'radical equality', that is, that all individuals are born equal and therefore deserve the same rights, but in notions of 'social equality', that stressed the difference between men and women, and insisted on the right to participate fully because of this difference. Women's true realm was admittedly the home, but it was argued that women voters and legislators could be a powerful force for social reform, morality in politics, and a world without war. Sarojini Naidu, one of India's leading personalities during the struggle for freedom, urged women to utilize their housekeeping skills to put the 'national house' in order.[3] Time and again, the spokespersons for women claimed that it was these special womanly talents that were needed if the country were to survive and progress.

The first franchise delegation of Indian women, which met the Montagu-Chelmsford committee on constitutional reform, was organized by the WIA in 1917. The WIA was itself a new organization, begun by the theosophist Dorothy Jinaragadasa in 1917 to advance the interests of women and encourage their development by bringing them together in service groups.[4] Annie Besant became its first president and remained (until her death in 1933) its guiding light. A long-standing advocate of women's role in politics,[5] Besant had urged women to join the Home Rule League and the *swadesi* movement. The members of the WIA had never debated whether or not the organization stood for *swaraj*, or whether members would be allowed to make patriotic statements – from the beginning they accepted the necessity of political freedom for concrete social reform.[6]

It was Margaret Cousins, another suffragette-cum-theosophist, who organized this first franchise delegation. Cousins had served with Mrs. Pankhurst in England and Ireland, gaining valuable experience in approaching government leaders and preparing memorials. Having read about Montagu's itinerary, she applied, on behalf of a group of women, for an audience, where social reform and education would be discussed. Montagu's secretary replied that only deputations on political subjects could be received. Mrs. Cousins sent a new application. Explaining how the first demand for women's franchise was born, she wrote:

I then circulated a couple of extra sentences about political rights or rather 'opportunities' in the draft of the memorandum. I know the women interested in the deputation believed in being citizens of their country and they wrote aggreeing to the addition, so the vote was claimed.[7]

Sarojini Naidu, well known as a political leader, was chosen to lead the deputation. The document presented has been written by Margaret Cousins, circulated for opinions, and then rewritten by her. The delegation included women 'prominently associated' with women's education: Lady Abala Bose, Mrs. Mazural Huque, Mrs. Nehru, Mrs. Chandrasekhar Aiyar, Mrs. Lazarus, Mrs. Herabai Tata, Dr. (Miss) Joshi (later Rani Rajwade), Mrs. Sanjiva Rao, Miss Gokhale, Annie Besant, Dorothy Jinaragadasa, and Mrs. Cousins.[8] The address claimed that women should have a say in political matters, that is, the vote, because they have their own independent opinion about the reforms that are necessary for the progress of India.[9]

The original intention was to request additional expenditure for female education. When the vote was requested, it was justified in terms of women's special needs and special talents. Women had a new outlook, claimed Sarojini Naidu, Miss Joshi, and Miss S. Naik in a private interview with Montagu; they were beginning to take part in public activities as a complement to men.[10] The lack of women in Legislative Councils was deplorable; when women's issues were considered, only men who could not understand the interests and feelings of women were present. Time and again it was argued that women could be extremely helpful in politics: 'for changing bad conditions into good conditions', to ensure that children grow up to be 'splendid, healthy, educated, efficient, and noble daughters and sons of India',[11] to bring peace between conflicting factions and to advise on vital issues such as sanitary conditions and morality.[12]

The Montagu-Chelmsford scheme suggested increasing the representation of Indians in the Legislative Council and widening the electorate, but it did not mention women. The Southborough Franchise Committee was appointed to investigate suggestions in the Montagu-Chelmsford scheme, and made plans to tour India. Women immediately prepared to show numerical support for their demands. In Bombay, the Committee was presented with a petition signed by 800 educated women and statements supporting women's suffrage from the all-India women's delegation to the Southborough Committee, the Women Graduates Union in Bombay, the 40 branches of the WIA, the women of the Home Rule League, and the Bharata Stree Mandal. Hopes were raised, and dashed. The Southborough Committee's report stated that extension of the vote to women would be premature in a society which continued to enforce *purdah* and prohibitions against female education.[13]

Indian women reacted by holding protest meetings and sending telegrams demanding the vote. They were supported by the nationalist parties. Provincial Congress Committees passed resolutions in favour of women's suffrage, while both the Home Rule League and the Muslim League asked that women be given the vote on the same basis as men. A special deputation, composed of Sarojini Naidu, Annie Besant, Mrs. Herabai Tata, and Mithan Tata, went to London in 1919 to give evidence before the joint Parliamentary Committee on the Government of India Bill.

They were able to gain the support of British women's organizations, particularly the Women's Freedom League and the Women's International League, who began to lobby on their behalf.[14] The politicking had its impact and the Joint Select Committee recommended that sex disqualification be removed. However, the initiative for this would have to come from the individual Legislative Councils, a provision which would allow the more conservative areas to retain an all-male electorate.[15] While Madras led the way and granted women the right to vote in 1920 and Bombay followed suit in 1921, other provinces lagged behind.[16] Bihar retained the sex disability for the Council of State and the Legislative Council until 1929, and even then the issue caused heated debate.

A reading of the debates in the various legislatures would lead one to agree with Mr. N.M. Dumasia, a member of the Legislative Assembly, that women's gaining the franchise had been a quite different process in India than in England. He said:

It is gratifying to find that in a country where men are accused of treating women as chattels the political progress of women has been more rapid than in England and free from the war of the sexes and the smashing of the heads and windows which preceded the enfranchisement of women in England.[17]

Generally, those opposed to women participating in politics spoke of their fear of family disintegration, and of the effect of rough-and-tumble politics on the 'tender' nature of women.[18] These solicitous statements rarely provoked anger, instead women who wanted the right to vote insisted that they would still be good wives and mothers. Smt. V. Kamalabai Ammal was almost alone in challenging the very method of granting women's franchise. She objected to leaving the right to grant women's franchise in the hands of men since this 'implies the monopoly of the male sex not only to enjoy the privilege but also to confer it upon others – women – as a matter of charity'.[19]

When the process was completed in 1929, all the Legislative Councils had extended the franchise to women on the same basis as to men. When the first elections were held in which women voted, it was found that their numbers were very small. Even male voters represented less than 14% of the male population, and females represented only 1.0% in Madras (men, 11.6%), 0.8% in Bombay (men, 13.4%), 0.3% in Bengal (men, 9.7%), and 0.5% in the Punjab (men, 11.96%).[20] The disparity could be traced to property laws, which prevented women from inheriting property, and a social setting where few women were economically independent.

Since the demand for the vote had been made partly in terms of 'no taxation without representation', there was little expressed concern with this disparity. Also, those who had requested the vote for women were concerned with the 'quality' of the newly enfranchised. When N.M. Joshi moved the resolution to remove sex disqualification from the Bombay Municipal Act, he spoke of women who were 'fit' to vote. Against opponents of women's franchise, he conceded that not all ladies were 'fit' to vote but argued that the restrictions should be removed even if Bombay had only one or two women with the right qualifications.[21] Even Dr. Muthulaksmi Reddy, later to become the first woman legislator, endorsed this view:

Only a few educated women of the land can speak on behalf of our sex, who have been denied for ages the freedom and opportunities to develop to their full moral, intellectual and physical height.[22]

Both the men and women, who supported 'votes for women' did so within the framework of social feminism. They accepted the idea that women could make a special contribution to debates on social issues affecting the welfare of women and children. Just as women had argued for political participation on the basis of their contribution to debates on social issues, so men accepted this as women's sphere. Supporting the case for admitting women to the Bombay Legislature, Dr. Paranjpye stressed that 'women would be of more help to the deliberations of the House in subjects like the Children's Act, temperance and laws of property.[23]

The right to sit in the Legislative Council followed the right to vote, given more easily in some provinces than others. In 1927, British India had its first female member of a Legislative Council – Dr. Muthulaksmi Reddy. When the elections were held in 1926, Kamaladevi Chattopadhyay and Mrs. Hannen Angelo contested the election for the Council. They were enthusiastically supported by the WIA, 'not because of their political views, for which the association is not responsible, but because of the necessity that the Association feels for the presence of women in the Council'.[24] Everyone was disappointed when these two lost, but they were pleased that the government then decided to nominate Muthulaksmi Reddy to the Council. At the meetings held to congratulate her, the speakers stressed the 'special' contribution she would make to the Council's proceedings: 'Now the presence of a lady doctor, of her position, in the Council would help the cause of women and children, in their education and physical welfare'.[25] That she had been nominated was inconsequential, important thing was that a woman – and a woman who was both well educated and socially aware – was now a member of the Madras Legislative Council.

The members of the Council showed their respect for Dr. Reddy by electing her Deputy President of the Council,[26] and Dr. Reddy lived up to the expectations of those who argued that women in politics would play a vital role in social reform. During the first session, she worked to improve the conditions of women and children: by introducing bills to abolish the *devadasi* system, and child marriage; making medical inspection compulsory in all schools and colleges; reducing secondary education fees for poor girls; establishing a children's hospital, and securing grants for institutions training destitute women.[27]

When the WIA compiled a list of women in public life (1927), it included five members of Legislative Councils (all nominated), 32 Municipal Councillors (six elected), four members of Taluk Boards (all nominated), 32 Honorary Magistrates and Justices of the Peace (all nominated), and four members of the University Senate (all elected).²⁸ Women were proud of their achievements, and there were no complaints because so many women had been nominated. Most of those nominated were prominent members of social organizations and their names had been presented to the respective governments by the organizations themselves. The issue seemed to be the input of women on social questions rather than their equality with men or any other group in Indian society. As Cousins insisted, even though the number of women voters was small,

> When the women's vote is well organized, as it will be by women's associations, for advancing specific interests relating to women's interests such as education, health, morality, prohibition, children's bills, etc., it may easily be the determining factor in an election result.

The vote would make it possible for women to bring about those reforms 'relating to the interests she has at heart.'²⁹

Before the second stage of the demand for 'votes for women' was launched, with the appointment of the Simon Commission in 1927, two additional women's organizations were formed. The NCWI was begun in 1925 by Lady Dorab Tata, a long-standing member of the WIA, as a branch of the International Council of Women. The aim of this organization was to bring the Indian women's movement into contact with international women's groups and, on the local scene, to band women together to promote the welfare of women and children. Primarily a coordinating organization, the National Council sought to mobilize women to improve their legal, economic and social status.³⁰ This organization was non-political, but joined the effort to secure the vote for women. The vote, they had decided, was important to ensure that women's voice – on laws which would influence them and their lives – would be heard.³¹

The All-India Women's Conference first met in Poona in January 1927. Organized by Margaret Cousins and the WIA, to bring women together to discuss female education, the AIWC decided that it would have to discuss general questions which affected the welfare of women and children.³² They had found it impossible to discuss female education without commenting on social customs, e.g., child marriage and *purdah*, which stood in the way of female education. When the Sarda Act, to set an age of marriage, was debated in 1928, the AIWC made its debut as a lobbying organization.³³ The Act was passed and the AIWC claimed a victory.³⁴ This early success convinced AIWC members that this was a profitable direction for their efforts and one which many of the members found challenging and personally satisfying. When the franchise again became an issue, they formed a franchise sub-committee and devoted serious attention to this topic. By the early 1930's, the important members of the AIWC were convinced that only political emancipation could release women from the 'shackles that have enchained them'.[35]

When the Simon Commission was announced, the WIA, the only women's organization then committed to women's franchise, asked that a woman be included. By the time the 'white seven' of the Commission arrived in India (February 1929), the WIA had joined the boycott against them. Patriotic from the very beginning, the WIA regarded political independence and women's problems as interwoven issues. Between 1930 and 1931, the WIA supported Congress action; encouraged participation in the salt marches; praised Mrs. Rukmini Laksmipathi, the first woman to court imprisonment; approved of Dr. Reddy's resignation from the Madras Legislative Council; and refused to take part in the first Round Table Conference.[36]

Even though the WIA would not cooperate with the Simon Commission, there were other educated women who decided to present women's demands. One of the deputations headed by the Dowager Rani of Mandhi, and included Mrs. Ahmen Shah and Mrs. Chitambar, complained about the low number of enfranchised women. Only 501,000 women had the vote, they complained, and blamed the low number on the application of the same standards to women and men. It was foolish to think, the leaders of the deputation argued, that women owned property, paid income tax and house rent. Mrs. Ahmen Shah argued against the application of the same franchise qualification for men and women. The deputation suggested that the problem be solved by giving the vote to property owners and literate women: and by ensuring actual participation through reservation of seats.[37]

The Round Table Conference was announced in November 1929, and once again the WIA was on the verge of cooperating: they asked that women be included in the Indian delegation and submitted the names of three women – Sarojini Naidu, Dr. Reddy, and Mrs. Brijlal Nehru.[38] But when the Congress decided to boycott it, the WIA also withdrew. This had been a difficult decision for them, because they drew their support from groups that held quite different views on the British presence and the Indian National Congress. But with Annie Besant as president, Dorothy Jinaragadasa and Muthulaksmi Reddy as vice-presidents, and Margaret Cousins and Ammu Swaminathan on the executive committee, there was little debate as to the stand the WIA should take. They recognized that by boycotting the Round Table Conference their impact on its decisions would be seriously diminished.[39] When it did meet in November 1930, Indian women were 'represented' by Begum Shah Nawaz and Smt. Radhabai Subbarayan, both long-standing members of women's organizations but deemed unacceptable by the WIA because they had been appointed by the British.

Begum Shah Nawaz and Mrs. Subbarayan asked for adult franchise. However, they weakened their demand in the eyes of the WIA, by adding that if this were not possible, there should be a special franchise for women as a temporary measure. Their proposals supported those of the Simon Commission, proposals which suggested increasing the number of enfranchised women by giving the vote to wives and widows of property owners over 25 years of age. Mrs. Subbarayan and Begum Shah Nawaz wanted the age lowered to 21 to make it consistent with the voting age for men.[40] This was not a new scheme, it had already been tried in Europe to achieve the same aim. But these suggestions were opposed by the WIA, who joined with the NCWI and the AIWC in formulating a joint memorandum demanding adult franchise and condemning any special franchise reservation or electorate.[41]

This first memorandum had been prepared in 1931, only one year after the famed 'awakening of Indian women' witnessed in connection with the salt march and Gandhi's new scheme for women's participation in the freedom struggle. Women were active on such a large scale which amazed Gandhi. He had called on his followers to be non-violent, to suffer without striking back, and to patiently return time and again to the scene of action. As one observer noted,

> Because the qualities which this new form of warfare is displaying are of the same nature usually characterized as feminine rather than masculine, we might rightly look on this life and death struggle of India to be free as women's war.[42]

No doubt, the entry of women into political life came with a startling suddenness, but the dramatic element has so far prevented or overshadowed a detailed analysis of women's involvement and the impact of their involvement on their own lives. Instead, we have many accounts describing their participation and claiming fantastic results: 'Ancient prejudices melted, walls of tradition cracked and rays of new hope came creeping in'.[43] Although it is difficult to assess the impact of this involvement on the demands for women's franchise, it is clear that many women who had previously been somewhat ambiguous about *swaraj*, now saw it as essential for the country's warfare; and women definitely gained respect for their efforts. Not only did they receive praise for their participation, but it inspired the Indian National Congress to pass the fundamental rights resolution at the Karachi session in 1931.[44] Thus, the move to demand equal franchise was strengthened.

The WIA was firm in its commitment to *swaraj*, but the other women's organizations wanted to remain 'apolitical' lest they alienate some of their members. Claiming to speak for all Indian women, regardless of their religion, party, or community, they hesitated to declare themselves in public for political independence. But this became a position which was increasingly difficult to maintain faced with the realities of the Indian situation. While they continued to declare themselves as 'non-political', many of their members charged them with supporting Congress, and even their staunchest members admitted that they had all become political when they first reacted to the Montagu-Chelmsford Council.[45]

By the time of the Second Round Table Conference, the women's organizations were willing to participate. Gandhi went as the sole representative of the Indian National Congress, Sarojini Naidu attended as a representative of women, and Begum Shah Nawaz and Mrs. Subbarayan attended as nominated members. Begum Shah Nawaz had by this time been convinced, by the arguments of the WIA, that special concessions and reserved seats were not the answer. Accordingly, she withdrew her proposals of the previous year.[46] Gandhi also argued against reserved seats and special franchise, demanding adult franchise and equality for women. He tried to convince Mrs. Subbarayan that she should follow the example of Begum Shah Nawaz, but she stood firm. Without reservation of seats, she insisted, Indian women would find it difficult to contest for seats.[47]

The Indian Franchise committee, appointed at the conclusion of the Second Round Table Conference, was to examine the whole question in detail and make concrete proposals for implementation. Mrs. Subbarayan was the only woman on the Committee, and she continued to ask for reserved seats for women. Although the Committee examined

311 witnesses and received 187 statements, the input from the organized women's groups was minimal. The WIA received a questionnaire, but re-submitted the joint memorandum in reply – a re-affirmation of their support for adult franchise and opposition to any kind of special franchise or concession. Dr. Muthulaksmi Reddy had been asked to give evidence before the Committee but she declined: she did not approve of the Government's stand and charged that the Round Table Conference had not been truly representative of all the people in India.[48] Once again, other women came forward to meet the Committee, and were united in the demand that the franchise be extended to include more women.[49]

The Lothian Committee accepted the premise that more women needed to be enfranchised to compel candidates to consider women's interests and opinions, awaken women politically, and to make women's votes effective, 'in providing reforms of special concern to women and children'. Ruling out the possibility of adult franchise, they proposed reservation of seats and special franchise. The report suggested that 2-5% of the seats in the provincial Councils be reserved for a period of 10 years, and that wives of property owners and women literates be enfranchised.[50]

While the women's organizations continued to demand adult franchise and oppose reservation, many women argued that it was difficult to contest against men. It was admitted by all the women's groups that registration procedures and voting arrangements had to be tailored to fit the needs of ladies who were unable to appear in public. In many cases, the same women who asked for absolute equality in terms of the provincial assembly asked for reserved seats in local bodies. Members of the Mangalore branch of the WIA insisted, in 1931, that there must be reservation of seats in the municipality. It was a 'well-known fact', they claimed, that women would not be able to serve the municipality without this special concession.[51] A number of women thought that the rigours of a campaign were just too much for women. When Mrs. Lekhwati Jain, member of the Punjab Legislative Council, moved to remove sex disqualification from the electoral rolls of municipalities and district boards, Mrs. Shave, also a member of the Council, said she would prefer to see women nominated because of the mud-slinging that took place before elections.[52] A former member of the Bangalore Legislative Council, M.K. Kamala Devi, stated that by making women contest elections with men, a great handicap had been created. The conditions of the country, she argued, made it difficult for women to run a race with men.[53] Men, said Lady Kailash Srivastava, another MLC, were not able to forget their prejudice against women. In these circumstances, reservation of seats, particularly on the local level, were invaluable.[54]

That this disparity in opinion existed is not strange. In the first place, the arguments as to why women should be in politics as voters and legislators had not changed. At the Punjab women's conference in 1935, Lady Shafi asked that provisions be made to involve women at all levels of government. Especially, women should be associated with education, health, and labour. She went on to request that one woman be nominated to each public service commission, that a women's and children's bureau be set up in each province, and that home science be provided in girls' schools.[55]

But these sentiments seemed incompatible with women's support for the nationalist movement. Gandhi had at first refused to allow women to participate in his salt march, because he feared police brutality and other complications. But women protested; they were as healthy and brave as most men, they claimed.[56] After Gandhi had changed his mind and given women an active part to play, he became a convert to the advantages of using women in processions and for picketing foreign cloth and liquor shops. He emerged as the champion of women's cause and they repaid his confidence with devotion. *Stri-Dharma*, the WIA organ, carried detailed reports of his activities, and urged women, at the time of his fast against untouchability, to give 'a practical demonstration of your great love for Gandhi'.[57] And Gandhi, in turn, let it be known that he was extremely pleased with the all-India women's organizations for their refusal to accept special favours and concessions.[58]

At this time, the desire of women to support Gandhi seems to have had considerable impact on their thinking on the franchise question. Between 1917 and 1930, they had not opposed the idea of reserved seats and nomination, and even after 1930, the plea for reservation for local bodies continued. Just prior to Gandhi's fast, the WIA stated that although adult franchise was the only answer,

> for a transition period it suggests the reservation of 20% of the seats in the new and enlarged legislatures and proposes that they be voted for by proportional representation by the newly elected members of Council from a panel of names sent forward by the officially recognized associations of women.[59]

But this was the last time such a possibility was entertained.

The Communal Award of August 1932 introduced separate electorates – a move that would affect women, because Muslim women would then be seen as a separate group. Also, 3% of the seats were to be reserved for women, to be determined on a communal basis. Gandhi's fast of 1932 (September) touched women; they condemned the Communal Award and dissociated themselves from this proposal. When various groups were demanding special concessions, women could either ask for the extension of these concessions to them, and side with the forces which seemingly weakened the nationalist movement, or repudiate these notions and support Gandhi. They chose the latter course. Many of these women were fully aware that adult franchise would not be granted and that women would find it difficult to contest elections. Yet, to ask for reserved seats or special concessions would make one a traitor to Gandhi. The nationalist struggle had affected the franchise question, and made it appear that the British were the enemy, opposed to the entry of Indian women into politics, and that Indian men were their allies and well-wishers.

In demanding adult franchise and opposing any special concessions, the women's organizations insisted that they were able to speak for all Indian women. However, communal electorates posed a problem. Begum Shah Nawaz dissented, but the members of the AIWC Franchise Committee decided to omit this from their final report, concluding that 'if she had wanted it included, she should have said so'.[60] Similarly, when the Muslim women of the Karachi branch of the AIWC sent a note of dissent, without any firm insistence that it be included in the memo, it was ignored.[61] It had been decided that only the majority vote counted, and when five Muslim women of Lucknow voiced their approval for separate electorates, it was disregarded as numerically unimportant.[62] But members of these organizations had always been aware that Muslim women were in a minority. The discounting of their opinion, at this point, caused ill feeling: Begum Shah Nawaz continued to object to their absolute rejection of the White Paper (1933),[63] and the Karachi ladies walked out.[64] Even after these expressions of dissent, the women's organizations insisted that they, unlike men, were completely untouched by the communal issue.

When the White Paper, including the conclusions of the Third Round Table Conference, was published in March 1933, it was found to be less favourable, in terms of women's franchise, than the Lothian Committee's views. It included reservation of seats, enfranchisement of wives of property owners and literates (passed matric), a different franchise for the Assembly, and stringent qualifications for election to the upper chamber. Whereas the Lothian Committee had urged that women's voting strength in relation to men be 4.5 : 1, the White Paper scheme would reduce the ratio to 10 : 1.

Two months before the White Paper was published, its contents were well known. The women's organizations suddenly found themselves in a difficult position – they wanted to maintain their credibility by retaining their stand, but they were faced with increased criticism from within the ranks. Rani Rajwade, Chairwoman of the AIWC Franchise Committee, and Muthulaksmi Reddy, Chairwoman of the AIWC Standing Committee and Honorary General Secretary of the WIA, were deeply committed to the principle of adult franchise. But, the rug had been pulled from under their feet. Dr. Reddy wrote,

> We cannot but accept the qualifications decided on by our men and accepted by them. As Gandhiji himself is justifying his cooperation with the Government for the sake of removing the evil of untouchability, the women social workers and educationists are eager to get the maximum for themselves, and they rightly feel that in the present backward condition of the country they cannot think of non-cooperation.[65]

At the same time, these women were accused of playing party politics and putting forth the pet schemes of the Congress.[66] They denied the charge, but became increasingly eager to have women appear united. Dr. Reddy wrote to Rani Rajwade, in February 1933,

> We should not on any account keep silent and allow individual women of our own constituencies to have their own say in this important question of women's franchise.[67]

By March, they had called for a joint committee of the WIA, AIWC, and NCWI to meet in Bombay. Presided over by Dr. Reddy, the membership included some of the women from the first 'votes for women' delegation (S. Naik and H. Tata), and many new members. Significantly, the committee did not include any of the former members of the AIWC Franchise Committee who had disagreed with Rani Rajwade and Dr. Reddy on special franchise and reservation of seats.[68]

Lord Linlithgow's Joint Select Committee, to discuss details of the White Paper, met in the spring of 1933. The women's organizations were ready with a memo which had been drafted by the WIA, and agreed to by the AIWC and NCWI. In addition, Dr. Reddy, WIA, Amrit Kaur, AIWC, and Mrs. Hamid Ali, NCWI, went to London (June 1933) to give evidence before the committee. In their statement, they claimed that these three organizations represented all the women of India, that their branches extended throughout the length and breadth of the land, and were organized on democratic lines. While they thanked the British women for the help they had given, they also made it clear that only Indian women could understand the problems and the 'measures most suited to ameliorate our conditions'.[69] This statement and others like it were intended for Miss Eleanor Rathbone, M.P., and her associates. Deeply interested in India and the problems of Indian women, Rathbone had written on Indian social problems, continually raised questions in the House of Commons about the implementation of social laws, and supported the extension of women's political participation through special franchise and reservation of seats.[70] While Miss Rathbone's concern with the problems of Indian women could not be denied, her support for Katherine Mayo of Mother India fame meant that her work to 'uplift' Indian women was related to her desire to see India remain within the British Empire.

Dr. Reddy, Amrit Kaur, and Mrs. Hamid Ali reiterated the demand of the women's organizations for adult franchise and protested against the indirect elections for the lower house of the Assembly and the stringent membership qualifications for the upper house. They proposed that all sex disqualification be removed and that the numbers of enfranchised women be increased by giving the vote to literate women and urban dwellers. Once again, they took their stand against communal seats, separate electorates, and reservation of seats for women. The problem was seen as increasing the number of women voters. Once that was done, they were certain that there would be no problem of having women returned to the provincial and central legislative bodies.[71]

While the women's organizations had been accepted as the spokespersons for women, the criticism against their stand was growing. On the one hand, their claim to represent all Indian women was challenged: the Madras Mail suggested that these 'few women' had no understanding of the needs or desires of the masses of women.[72] There were also organized groups of women, the Mahila Samiti of Bengal and an ad hoc group of Madras women, who prepared memos and sent them to the Joint Select Committee. They supported the Lothian Committee's plan of giving the franchise to the wives of property owners and reserving seats for women.[73] Mrs. Subbarayan, present at all the three sessions of the Round Table Conference, agreed with them and concentrated on the details of the literacy qualification and the franchise for the Central Assembly. She feared, and rightly so, that once again the question of women's franchise would be omitted from the Constitution and left to be worked out by the new Legislative Councils. Recognizing that women did have a number of supporters among Indian men, she criticized the women's organizations for underestimating the reactionary forces which would keep women's voice in political matters at an ineffectual level.[74]

At this time, a new element appeared in the demands of the women's groups, a demand for the enfranchisement of all urban women. It was obvious that adult franchise was a dead issue, and the problem had become one of deciding on a formula to increase women's political participation. Urban women were selected because they were likely to have had more education, polling and canvassing would be easier, the press was confined to cities, and urban women were more likely to have a desire to promote 'educational and social reform'.[75] Their objections to having the wives of property owners vote, were similar to those of men, of an earlier era, debating the 'fitness' of women to vote. Property owners, they claimed, were not enlightened and they were likely to have uneducated wives who would oppose changes in the social system.[76] Clearly, it was not numerical strength they desired, but women voters with enlightened ideas about social reform. After all, the prevalent argument as to why woman should have the vote was still based on the idea that she would be the prime mover in improving the conditions of women and children.[77]

The charge that these organizations could not, and did not, speak for all Indian women was disregarded. Women, the leading members argued, were all 'sisters under the sari', and the institutions and ideals that governed their lives were similar.[78] When Dr. Reddy made her plea for the enfranchisement of urban women, she claimed,

A further consideration of the subject will convince anyone that woman's needs and the women's interests are the same all over. Take any of the social reform measures such as child marriage, inheritance laws, property rights, marriage laws in which women are generally interested. These evils apply equally to both the town and village women. As the city woman learns to exercise and derive the full benefit from her political rights, her village sisters in course of time, with the spread of education and enlightenment into the village population, will follow in her footsteps.[79]

When Shudha Mazumdar wrote about communal electorates, she did so in the same way. They might make sense to men, she conceded, but 'as regards women, their problems are nearly the same for all communities'.[80]

When the time came for elections, the realities of getting women elected took precedence. The dream of having women elected who could represent the women's cause and who were supported in their work by enlightened women, could only remain a dream in the new circumstances. Hunnen Angelo, one of the first women to contest an election, and the first woman member of the Madras Municipal Council, had at first run as an Independent, and later switched to Congress. She insisted that it was impossible for a woman to seek election without party support – one needed financial backing, contacts, and sometimes physical protection. Moreover, social causes were not popular. Writing to Jawaharlal Nehru, Kamaladevi Chattopadhyay informed him that the fight against society and its rigid codes was harder than any political fight and also lacked the respectability attached to the political struggle.[81] Dr. Reddy, well known for the social legislation she had introduced in the Madras Legislative Council, readily admitted that while her medical and educational work was applauded, this was not true for her social reform legislation.[82] Party support was needed but social reform was unpopular; consequently, the same women who had claimed that women would be returned in any circumstances were faced with a situation where parties ignored the claims of women famous for their social work and were reluctant to run women in general constituencies.[83] This presented a serious problem.

...unless a certain number of our women are returned through the general constituencies in each province, all our statements against reservation of seats for women, both in our memoranda and in our oral evidence, would look impracticable propositions on the face of it.

The women's organizations became desperate, insisting that they must somehow have a few women returned to at least 'prove to the world' that Gandhi did not misrepresent the Indian situation when he opposed reserved seats for women.[84] It was found that the only women members of the women's organizations acceptable to the parties had also been staunch party members.[85]

Despite these difficulties, when the elections were over the women were pleased and looked upon the number of women in the legislatures as a victory for women's cause. Vijayalaksmi Pandit's appointment to the U.P. Cabinet was hailed by all, and other provinces were urged to appoint women ministers. At the same time, the organized women continued to ask that more women be nominated to councils, boards and commissions, since

...there are many things in public life in all Government Departments which could only be attended to by women, e.g., the administration of the Children's Act, child education, the problem of girls and women's education, the question of women and child labour, the suppression of traffic in women and children, the handling of women prisoners, etc.... No man was capable of satisfactorily solving the problems.[86]

The demand for women's votes and representation had consistently been justified in terms of 'social feminism': women needed to be in politics, because only they could adequately represent women's opinion and deal with the problems affecting women and children. The problems of women were seen as the same for all classes and communities, hence capable of articulation by the educated, urban women. At the same time, the actual demand was in the 'radical feminist' tradition: in voting and standing for election, women should be the equals of men. As this paper has pointed out, the first demand for 'votes for women' was greatly influenced by British suffragettes living in India, the second demand by women deeply committed to Gandhi and India's independence. In neither case was there an effort to work out a demand for representation which would be consistent with the reason; why organized women thought they should participate in the political life of the country.

References

1. M.E. Cousins, *Indian Womanhood Today*, (Allahabad, 1941), p. 85.
2. Tara Ali Baig, *India's Woman Power*, (New Delhi, 1976), pp. 213-4.
3. Manmohan Kaur, *Role of Women in the Freedom Movement, (1857-1947)*, (Delhi, 1968), p. 175.
4. 'A New Society for Indian Ladies', *New India*, (May 10, 1917), p. 9.

5. Annie Besant, 'The Political Status of Women' (1874), *The Annie Besant Centenary Book, 1847-1947*, (Adyar, Madras nd.).
6. *WIA Report*, 1931-1932, p. 4.
7. Cousins, *Indian Womanhood*, p. 33.
8. 'A Ladies Deputation to Mr. Montagu', *New India*, (October 25, 1917), p. 5; 'Women's Deputation to Mr. Montagu', *New India*, (December 13, 1917), p. 5. This list differs somewhat from that included in the selection of Mrs. Cousins' private papers published as *Mrs. Margaret Cousins and Her Work in India*, (Adyar, Madras, 1956). Her list also includes Mrs. Saralabai Naik, Mrs. Srirangamme, Begum Hazrat Mohari, Mrs. Dalvi, Lady Sadasiva, and Mrs. Guruswami Chetty.
9. J.H. and M.E. cousins, *We Two Together*, (Madras, nd.), p. 310.
10. 'All India Women's Deputation,' *New India*, (December 18, 1917).
11. *Stri-Dharma*, (May, 1928), p. 51.
12. File No. 28, Public of 1926, Home Department, Government of India.
13. *Cousins and Her Work*, p. 14.
14. Mrs. Besant and Indian Women's Franchise', *The Bombay Chronicle*, (March 18, 1920), p. 12.
15. 'Women's Franchise Rule', *Indian Quarterly Register (I.Q.R.)* II, (July-December, 1925), p. 166.
16. 'Burma Legislative Council', *I.Q.R.* I, (January–June, 1927), p. 390.
17. File No. 28, Public of 1926.
18. 'Women Suffrage and the Kitchen', *Modern Review*, XXX, 1921, p. 97.
19. File No. 212/1929. Public, Home Department, Government of India.
20. Kaur, *Role of Women*, pp. 162-3; S. Rajagopal, 'Indian Women in the New Age', in B.E. Ward, ed. *Women in New India*, (Paris, 1963), p. 209.
21. 'Bar Against Women', *The Bombay Chronicle*, (September 28, 1900), p. 8.
22. *Autobiography of Dr. (Mrs.) Muthulaksmi Reddy*, (Madras, 1964), p. 47.
23. *I.Q.R.*, I, (January-June, 1926), p. 243.
24. 'Women Candidates for the Legislative Council', *Cousins and Her Work*, p. 58.
25. 'A Congratulatory Meeting', *Stri-Dharma*, X, (January, 1927), p. 1.
26. *Autobiography of Dr. Reddy*, pp. 46-7.
27. *WIA Golden Jubilee Celebration*, p. 4.
28. *Stri-Dharma*, (December 1927).
29. M.E. Cousins, 'When Will Bengal Give Woman Suffrage?' *Modern Review*, XXX, 1921, pp. 328-30.
30. 'President's Speech', *NCWI Report* of 1926-28.
31. *NCWI*, 1932-34, p. 34.
32. *AIWC on Educational Reform*, (January, 1927), pp. 1-3.
33. *AIWC Report*, 1928, p. 40; 'Age of Consent', *The Social Reformer*, (August 27, 1927), p. 815.
34. *AIWC, 4th Session*, pp. 12-24.
35. *AIWC, 7th Session* (December 1932-January 1933), p. 30.
36. *Stri-Dharma*, XIII, (June, 1930).
37. 'Indian Statutory Commission', *I.Q.R.*, I, (January-June 1929), pp. 54-56.
38. *Cousins and Her Work*, p. 79.
39. *WIA Report, 1931-32*, pp. 3-4.
40. Mrs. P. Subbarayan, *The Political Status of Women Under the New Constitution*, (Madras, nd.), pp. 2-3.

41. *WIA Report*, 1931-32, pp. 6-7.
42. 'A Woman's War', *Stri-Dharma*, XIII, (June, 1930), p. 337.
43. Kamaladevi Chattopadhyay, *The Awakening of Indian Women*, (Madras, 1939), p. 13.
44. Pattabhi Sitaramayya, *The History of the Indian National Congress* I, (Bombay, 1946), pp. 463-65.
45. 'Indian Women's Power in Public Life', *The Bombay Chronicle*, (May 24, 1931).
46. Subbarayan, p. 16.
47. Letter from S.M. Reddy to Madam, (November 16, 1936). AIWC files, 315.
48. *WIA Report, 1931-32*, p. 18.
49. *Stri-Dharma*, (February-March, 1936), pp. 44-5.
50. 'Lothian Report', *Stri-Dharma*, (July, 1932), pp. 465-77.
51. *Stri-Dharma*, XIV, (May, 1931), p. 343.
52. 'Proceedings of the Punjab Council', *I.Q.R.*, I, (January-June, 1931), p. 209.
53. AIWC files.
54. 'Oudh Women's Conference', *I.Q.R.*, II, (July-December, 1935).
55. 'Punjab Women's Conference?', *I.Q.R.*, II, (July-December, 1935).
56. 'Gandhiji and Women', *Stri-Dharma*, (April, 1930), p. 247.
57. 'Gandhiji's Fast', *Stri-Dharma*, XV, (October, 1932), pp. 659-74.
58. *Stri-Dharma*, XV, (November, 1931) p. 66.
59. *WIA Report, 1930-31*.
60. Letter from Mrs. Huidekoper to Rani Rajwade, (May 20, 1933), AIWC files 37.
61. Letter from A. Khemsharar to Hon'ble Organizing Secretary of the AIWC, (May 31, 1933), AIWC files 34.
62. *I.Q.R.*, I, (January-June, 1934), p. 318.
63. *Stri-Dharma*, XVIII, (April, 1935), p. 228.
64. AIWC files 30.
65. Letter from Dr. Reddy. (February 13, 1933), AIWC files 95.
66. Letter from Rani Rajwade to Mrs. P.K. Sen, (January 2, 1933), AIWC files 37.
67. Letter from Dr. Reddy to Rani Rajwade, (February 15, 1933), AIWC files 35.
68. Notably Mrs. S.C. Mukherjee, Mrs. P.K. Ray, and Sushama Sen, Letter from Rani Rajwade to Madame, (January 7, 1933), AIWC files 95.
69. *Stri-Dharma*, XVI, (September, 1933), p. 549.
70. 'Reservation of Seats for Women', *The Hindu*, (February 19, 1932), p. 7.
71. *Stri-Dharma*, XVI, (September, 1933), pp. 551-5.
72. *Stri-Dharma*, XVI, (June, 1933), p. 367.
73. *Stri-Dharma*, XVI, (September, 1933), p. 556.
74. Subbarayan, pp. 3, 15-16.
75. *Stri-Dharma*, XVI, (June, 1933), 'Memorandum II'.
76. *Stri-Dharma*, XVI (June, 1933) p. 399.
77. 'Why Women Want the Vote?' *Stri-Dharma.*, pp. 223-4; Dr. Reddy, 'Paper on Franchise,' 1933 AIWC files; File No. 4/2/36 Public, 1936, Home Department, Government of India.
78. *Tamil Nadu Women's Conference,* Erode, 1931, p. 291.
79. Reddy, 'Paper on Franchise'.
80. Letter from Shudha Mazumdar to Mrs. S.N. Ray, (April 28, 1937) AIWC files 160.

81. Letter from Kamaladevi Chattopadhyay to J. Nehru, 11.7.36. Nehru papers, File No. G.48.36.
82. *Autobiography of Dr. Reddy*, p. 65.
83. Letter from M. Kamadani to Mrs. S.C. Mukherjee, nd. AIWC files 1191.
84. Letter from Dr. Reddy (November 16, 1936), AIWC files 135.
85. Letter from M. Kamalamma to President, Andhra Parliamentary Committee, nd. AIWC files 130; Letter from M. Kamalamma to Secretary, Madras Parliamentary Committee, (September 14, 1936) AIWC files 130.
86. *WIA Report, 1936-38*, p. 27.

WOMEN IN THE ELECTORAL PROCESS

A Statistical Analysis of the Lok Sabha Elections

S.D. Muni

Politics and governance of society in India have generally not been the area of female activity; women have seldom figured prominently in these fields. This is despite the fact that female deities like *Kali*, which symbolize power, strength and vitality, occupy a very important place in Hindu religious and social ethos. There have been instances in the various phases of Indian history where women actively participated in the 'game of power' through court cliques and conspiracies. But rarely did they play a decisive and significant role in this context, independent of male protection and dominance. The examples such as those of Begum Razia Sultana and Rani Lakshmi Bai were only exceptions.

The nationalist movement towards the close of the nineteenth century provided the necessary impetus and pull to draw an increasing number of women into the political mainstream. An atmosphere for such a breakthrough was created by the activities of the social reformers and nationalists, who raised demands for education and literacy among women. As the struggle for independence acquired a mass character, growing participation of women became necessary. Since then, political consciousness among women has shown a gradual increase, in both extent and depth. In India's fight against the British Raj women came forward in their thousands to sacrifice anything they could. They faced bullets, suffered imprisonment, and bore hardships along with their male comrades to win independence.

It is rather unfortunate that no comprehensive study or account is available on the nature and extent of women's participation in the struggle for independence. The historical accounts of some of the political parties, such as the Indian National Congress and the Communist Party of India, do mention about their women members, but such references appear to be incidental and are highly inadequate for the purpose of understanding women's role in politics. Similarly, the study of women in the politics of independent India has by and large remained an untouched subject.[1] Recently, some biographical accounts of prominent *political women* have come up, but they are very few in number. Moreover, they deal with only those women who constitute the top layer of the social and political hierarchy, ignoring the mass of women who constitute half of India and whose political behaviour, consciousness, aspirations, and involvement in/about politics constitute a vital segment of Indian political and social dynamics. A proble into this sector of Indian politics offers both incentives and challenges.

Election Statistics as a Source of Study

In a democratic system like that of India, participation in politics may be viewed at two levels: (i) acquisition and exercise of power; and (ii) awareness and assertion of citizenship (political) rights. In the absence of other reliable and adequate sources, the study of elections can be of great help in investigating the participation of people in politics at these two levels. While the analysis of *contestants*' behaviour would throw light on the various aspects of participation at the first level, that of the *voters*' behaviour may offer valuable insights into participation at the second level. In this paper women's participation in politics at these two levels is studied through an analysis of election statistics. Analysis and observations are confined to Lok Sabha elections from 1952 to 1971.

It may be of interest to know that no full-length study of women's electoral behaviour is available. All the election studies done so far in this country have largely neglected women. Through survey and empirical methods, women contestants and voters have been interviewed along with their male counterparts, but sex has not been included as an independent variable in the analysis, nor has its political impact been worked out in correlation with the other socio-economic indicators. Some researchers have devoted a paragraph or two on the mobilization and responses of women voters and the conduct of women candidates and party workers in their studies,[2] but they do not reveal much of the actual situation. With the exception of a couple of occasional brochures and pamphlets, such as *Women and Elections* (Indian National Congress, 1956), and *Why Women Should Vote Communist* (by Hajrah Begum, Communist Party publication, 1962), the political parties have also not given attention to this subject. There are, however, a small number of researched and reflective articles in journals and magazines, some of which offer viable hypotheses to work upon.[3] Others are analytically poor and factually inaccurate.

It is rather disappointing to note that in the statistics compiled and published by the Election Commission women candidates were not identified. Nor were the number of women electors and votes polled calculated and specified in the reports on the first two General Elections. In the subsequent reports, women candidates were identified by a (W) against their names, as was done in the case of constituencies reserved for Scheduled Castes (SC) and Scheduled Tribes (ST). Only in the report on the fifth General Elections (1971-72) have the percentage of women electorates and voters been calculated and recorded in a comparative perspective with the similar figures of men. The state and the party affiliations of the women candidates along with the votes polled by them and the results have been tabulated separately for the first time at the end of this paper. These inadequacies leave serious gaps and limitations in a study of the kind attempted here.

Mobilization of Women Voters

(a) *General*: The percentage of voter turnout for the first two General Elections is not available. For the third, fourth, and the fifth elections the figures are given in Appendix 1. The total voter turnout has fluctuated in the last three elections. The figure rose from 54.76% in 1962 to 61.33% in 1967, recording an increase of 6.57%. However, in 1971 it fell to 55.35%, which was 5.98% below the previous mark. See Table 1 (a).

As compared to the total voter turnout, the figures for female voters have always been less by approximately 6%. Looking at the trend in female voting, similar fluctuations as in the total voting are evident. In 1962, 46.63% women exercised their franchise; in 1967 this figure rose to 55.48%, marking a decrease of 6.33%. This decrease is somewhat equal to the fall in total voting percentage, which shows that in comparative terms, women's voting did not depict a discouraging trend.

A better comparative assessment can be had by looking at the difference in the percentage of male and female voter turnout. This difference has always been unfavourable to women. Strictly speaking, the difference also has shown similar fluctuations as evident in the

Women in the Electoral Process

TABLE 1a

Year	Total voting %	Turnout of female voters %	Difference between turnout of male and female voter %
1962	54.76	46.63	15.42
1967	61.33	55.48	11.25
1971	55.35	49.15	11.85

total and female voter turnout; however, the difference between the figures for 1967 and 1971 is insignificant – only 0.60%.

The general inferences of Table 1a are that women have shown a gradual increase in the exercise of their franchise and that this increase has been proportionate to the increase in the total turnout of voters. From the table, the fifth General Elections emerge as a deviation case, wherein the total and female voting has shown almost equal decrease, but the difference in male and female voting has remained unchanged as compared to 1967. The decrease in total and female voter mobilization may be explained by the fact that the fifth General Elections were held in 1971, a year earlier than scheduled. This was necessitated due to the dissolution of the Lok Sabha on 27 December 1970 – one year ahead of its normal life. Since the new Lok Sabha had to be elected by the middle of March 1971, it gave very little time to the Election Commission for the preparation of electoral rolls and the holding of elections. Similarly, the political parties also had to select their candidates and chalk out their election strategies within a very short time.

In addition to the shortage of time, there was widespread political confusion in the country – the split within the Congress party which had been in power ever since independence and dominated the political life in the country. The split had reduced the ruling party into a 'minority' in the Lok Sabha and for the common man the spectre of probable political instability – in case the Congress failed to secure absolute majority – appeared to be disturbing.

Both these factors proved detrimental to the mobilization of voters in the 1971 elections. However, the fact that the difference between male and female voting did not widen with the total fall in mobilization shows that perhaps mobilization of female voters was more than that of male voters as compared to the preceding elections. This becomes more evident if we compare the figures of 1962 and 1971. This comparison shows that whereas the total voter turnout increased only by

0.58% (54.76% to 55.35%), the increase in female voter turnout was 2.52% (46.63% to 49.15%). The greater activity among women could have been due to the Prime Minister, Mrs. Gandhi, who was the centre of all political debates and controversies in the country, and who had made special efforts through her addresses and party machinery to activize women. This, however, does not imply that women were necessarily activized in Mrs. Gandhi's favour. Tables 1b and 1c show the minimum and maximum turnout of total and female voters in the States and Union Territories. They have been arranged in descending order up to the fourth place, and the percentage figures have been recorded in brackets.

(b) *Statewise*: Orissa, Bihar, Madhya Pradesh, and Himachal Pradesh have changed positions (I to IV) among themselves in all the three General Elections since 1962 for minimum turnout of total and female voters. They also show the highest difference between male and female voters, i.e., the number of female electors exercising their voting rights has been much less than that of their male counterparts. In this table, Orissa presents an interesting deviation by maintaining its total voting percentage (43%), and improving the percentage of female voting though marginally (0.69%) in 1971 as compared to the previous election figures, and also against the other States in the same category which had shown a decline, in respect of both total and female voting. Except the four States mentioned above, Rajasthan, Uttar Pradesh, Assam, and Jammu & Kashmir have also marked their nominal presence in the table for greater difference in the percentage of male and female voting indicating lesser mobilization of female voters compared to male voters. It is interesting to note that they do not figure anywhere regarding the percentage of total and female voting.

The States showing minimum mobilization of female voters are generally known for their social, political, and economic backwardness. Feudal structures and forces have been fairly strong in Orissa, Rajasthan, Madhya Pradesh, and Himachal Pradesh. In Bihar, Assam, and Uttar Pradesh, also, land relationships have been by and large feudal. Except for Bihar and Uttar Pradesh (its appearance in the table is just nominal), these States were very late in participating in the struggle for independence. Socially extensive and severe restrictions on women's activities outside the family have been prevalent in these States. Economically, they are poor with comparatively less urbanization and industrialization. Female literacy has

TABLE 1b

Maximum Mobilization

Year		I	II	III	IV
1962	Total female difference	Orissa (23.00) Orissa (13.21) M.P. (32.00)	Himachal (33.00) Himachal (22.04) Bihar (23.00)	M.P. (44.79) M.P. (28.90) Rajasthan (21.00)	Bihar (44.88) Bihar (32.00) Orissa and U.P. (20.00)
1967	Total female difference	Orissa (43.70) Orissa (33.05) M.P. (22.00)	H.P. (51.20) Bihar (40.74) Bihar (21.00)	Bihar (51.53) M.P. (42.48) Orissa (20.00)	M.P. (53.47) H.P. (44.05) Assam (16.00)
1971	Total female difference	H.P. (41.18) H.P. (33.38) Bihar (23.00)	Orissa (43.20) Orissa (33.74) J & K and M.P. (21.00)	M.P. (48.00) Bihar (37.01) Orissa (18.00)	Bihar (49.10) M.P. (37.59) Assam (17.00)

TABLE 1c

Minimum Mobilization

Year		I	II	III	IV
1962	Total female difference	Kerala (70.55) Delhi (71.71) Delhi (+6)	Delhi (68.29) Kerala (67.08) Manipur (−1.83)	T. Nadu (68.77) T. Nadu (64.55) Kerala and Punjab (7.00)	Tripura (67.95) Manipur (64.44) Andhra, Gujrat, and T. Nadu (9.00)
1967	Total female difference	Goa (82.00) Laccadive (86.16) Goa, Diu Goa & Daman (+8)	Andaman (78.45) Andaman (76.77) Delhi (+2)	Dadra (70.29) Dadra (76.55) Chandigarh (−0.14)	T. Nadu (76.56) Kerala (74.22) Dadra Nagar (−1.93)
1971	Total female difference	T. Nadu (71.82) Andaman (72.33) Andaman Nicobar (+2.61)	Andaman (70.55) T. Nadu 69.17 Chandigarh (+0.32)	Pondicherry (70.10) Pondicherry (68.28) Kerala (−2.47)	Dadra (69.78) Goa (68.06) Delhi, Pondicherry, Goa, Dadra Nagar (−3)

also been the lowest in these States. These are some of the factors that account for low political consciousness and less enthusiasm for the exercise of franchise rights among women. According to a study of the first General Elections in Uttar Pradesh, the middle and upper-middle class women considered it below their dignity to go and vote in the open. The working class and backward caste women were inspired to imitate this attitude and refused to vote.[4] Such factors have also occasionally accounted for the low turnout of female voters.

Table 1c shows those States and Union Territories where the turnout of female voters has been the highest (up to the first four places); among these only Kerala and Tamil Nadu figure in the Table. Both have shown fluctuations, but the decline has been much too steep in the case of Kerala. If the figures for 1971 are compared with those of 1962, Tamil Nadu shows an increase of about 4.4% as against a decline of 3.6% in the case of Kerala. These variations are, however, difficult to explain in the absence of other indicators such as socio-economic variations, intensity of campaign, and other local factors.

Regarding Union Territories, the highest figure for mobilization of women since 1962 has never gone below 71.71%. In 1967, it was as high as 86.16% in Laccadive, Minicoy, and Amindivi Islands. In comparative terms, the territories showing the highest mobilization (I position) also indicate greater turnout of female voters than males.

In 1962, the difference was +6% in Delhi; where + indicates the difference in favour of women. In 1967, it was +8% in Goa, Daman and Diu. In 1971, it was 2.61% in Andaman and Nicobar Islands. The appearance of Chandigarh and Delhi in the case of higher mobilization of women is interesting since the female population in these territories is much less to the male number. For every 1,000 males, it is approximately 860 in these territories as against the average of 980 for the whole country. It would, however, be misleading to infer that less number of women leads to greater female voter turnout.

The States and Union Territories showing greater mobilization of women, socially and politically, are not backward and economically they are not deficient. Most of them being coastal areas, they were the first to be exposed to the Dutch, Portuguese, and British colonizers. Accordingly, some of the elements of western culture are generally dominant among them. Places such as Delhi and Chandigarh, though not falling into the above category, have a cosmopolitan cultural outlook, an industrial base, and urban character. The social structure of these States and Territories are not rigid and male-dominated. On the contrary, a State like Kerala has a matrilineal society which ensures a relatively dominant place to women.

Casting a vote is not a necessary indication of political consciousness and articulation in women. Through common experience and on the basis of available studies it is known that the great majority of women are less politically conscious, articulate, and active. In the first General Elections women, particularly in the rural areas, took polling as an occasion of festivity. They were hardly conscious of their right to franchise, nor its value in making or marring a government. Though the situation has since changed considerably, women seldom exercise their right to vote totally independent of their male family members such as the husband, father, brother, or son. Women are still largely mobilized through these relations, and once they have exercised their vote they by and large forget about politics and its processes. Issues particularly addressed to them, such as the Hindu Code Bill, hardly make any difference in this context.

Women in the Democratic Struggle for Power

(a) *General*: The number of women candidates contesting elections for the Lok Sabha has been highly discouraging. It has so far been less than 20% of the total seats contested and not more than 5% of the total number of male candidates contesting for the same number of seats. Table 2a shows the number of seats, women contestants, and women elected. The number of women candidates has increased since 1952 with the exception of 1957, when it fell down from 51 to 41. In 1967, the increase was negligible – from 65 to 66. The actual number of seats contested by women has been less than the number of women contestants since some of the seats were contested by more than one woman.

The number of seats in the first to fifth General Elections were 6, 5, 5, 5, and 9 respectively. In 1952 in Uttar Pradesh (Lucknow), in 1957 in Madhya Pradesh (Bhopal), and in 1962 in Rajasthan (Jaipur) such contests involved more than two women for the same seat.[5] The number and percentage of the successful women candidates increased in 1957 – from 19 to 25 and from 37% to 62%; but since then it has shown a decline. In 1971, only 21 candidates were successful out of a total of 86.

Women in the Electoral Process

TABLE 2a

Women Contestants

Year of General Election	Total seats contested	No. of women contestants	%	No. of women elected	Winners %
1952	487	51	10	19	37
1957	494	41	8	25	62
1962	491	65	13	33	50.6
1967	515	66	13	28	42.4
1971	518	86	17	21	25.9

The variations in the number of contestants and the percentage of successful candidates are not easily accountable. Much has depended upon the decision of the Congress party which always fielded the maximum number of women candidates, as will be seen subsequently. In 1971, a sudden spurt in the number of independent women candidates – from 10 in 1967 to 31 in 1971 – added to the total number. At the same time, the independent candidates performed very poorly – only one succeeded – and thus the overall percentage of successful candidates fell from 42.4 to 25.9, an all-time low. The increase in the number of independent women candidates and their failure perhaps resulted from the fact that Mrs. Gandhi was in the midst of a political controversy in 1971. More women entered the election fray since a lady was at the centre of politics. The decline in the total number of women contestants in 1957 was perhaps owing to their poor performance in the previous elections.

(b) *Statewise*: The number of women contesting for Lok Sabha seats in the States and Union Territories has roughly been in accordance with, though not in proportion to, the total number of Lok Sabha seats allocated to them. The maximum number of women entered the race in Uttar Pradesh except in 1957 and 1971, when Bihar, the next biggest State in terms of Lok Sabha seats, took the lead by one number. As compared to the total number of seats, however, some of the Union Territories such as Delhi and Goa, Daman and Diu, and Madhya Pradesh have put up greater percentage of women candidates. Madhya Pradesh needs a special mention in this context, since it has shown a poor turnout of female voters, and the number of total seats is also fairly high as against Delhi and Goa.

The number of women candidates in various States and Union Territories shows wide fluctuations from one election to another. The number of women centestants in Uttar Pradesh, for instance, was 15 in 1952, 6 in 1957, 14 in 1962, 13 in 1967, and 17 in 1971. The States that are an exception to these fluctuations are: Bihar, Madhya Pradesh, and Kerala. In Bihar and Madhya Pradesh, the number has gradually gone up. In Kerala, it remained constant at 1 for the first three elections, and then marked a slight increase to 3 in 1967 and 4 in 1971. Orissa may also be treated in the same category since for the first three elections no woman entered the election arena, but in 1967 one, and in 1971 two women contested for Lok Sabha seats. Most of the Union Territories along with Jammu and Kashmir, Haryana, and Mysore may also be clubbed into one category as the number of women contestants in them for all the five General Elections was either nill or just one. Here Mysore is on the other extreme of Madhya Pradesh, since it cannot be considered socially, politically, and economically a backward State. Nor have women performed too poor in terms of voting, which has always been more than 50% since 1962.

The number of successful candidates has naturally been greater in Uttar Pradesh, Bihar, Madhya Pradesh, and Andhra Pradesh, where the number of contestants has also been greater. Orissa, Haryana, Goa, Daman & Diu, and Manipur are the only areas where women contested, but were never returned. Percentage-wise, Mysore was the most successful State. It set up one candidate in 1962 and 1971, and returned the same. Uttar Pradesh, Bihar, Madhya Pradesh, Madras, and West Bengal were the only States which sent women to the Lok Sabha in every election. In terms of overall performance, however, Andhra Pradesh and Assam may also be termed as satisfactory.

The number of contesting or elected women candidates for Lok Sabha in a particular State or Union Territory does not appear to be decisively related with the literacy among women in that area. Laxmi N. Menon, while analysing the first General Elections, inferred that the number of women candidates was in inverse proportion to the percentage of literacy among them.[5] If we test this hypothesis with the figures of subsequent elections, Madhya Pradesh, Bihar, and Uttar Pradesh do intend to verify it. However, Bihar and Uttar Pradesh are big States and, therefore, only Madhya Pradesh may be taken to support the hypothesis. But then, Orissa, Rajasthan, Jammu and Kashmir do not conform with Madhya Pradesh in this respect. On the other hand, Kerala, West Bengal, Maharashtra, and Madras do not support the reverse of this hypothesis, i.e., with comparatively high literacy a,ong women, the number of women contestants in these

Women in the Electoral Process

States has not been comparatively less. It would, however, be safe to presume that literacy is not a single variable in this respect and it influences the number of contestants, but only in combination with other factors. The social ethos and taboos prevailing in the State and its particular constituency vis-a-vis women's role in politics, did influence the success or otherwise of its female contestants, but only in a small way. What mattered most were the personality of the contestants including their family background and involvement in politics, local conditions, campaign strategy, and the political party to which the candidates belonged.

Party affiliations of the Power-Seekers

As already noted, the maximum number of female candidates have been fielded by the Indian National Congress. From 25, in 1957, the number of Congress women contestants has increased gradually. It became 33 in 1962, and 36 in 1967. However, in 1962, the Congress had suffered a major split. As a result, in 1971, the Congress owing allegiance to Mrs. Gandhi fielded 21 women candidates as against 14 put up by the other Congress.

The number of women contestants put up by the Congress, however, always remained much below its stipulated target of 15% of the total candidates. This target of 15% was first officially fixed up by the party in 1957 and since then has been repeatedly reiterated.

Next to the Congress came the independents, though the difference between the two always remained substantial. The Communist Party of India (CPI), and the Praja Socialist Party (PSP) have been fielding women candidates since 1952. The other parties too have been fielding women in elections ever since their inception, with the exception of perhaps Bhartiya Jana Sangh (BJS) in 1952 and 1957. The CPI and BJS have kept the number of their female contestants fixed at 3 for all the elections. Whereas the Samyukt Socialist Party (SSP) has shown a decline, the Communist Party of India (Marxist) (CPM) has registered an increase in the respective numbers of their women contestants. The other smaller and unrecognized parties have shown fluctuations in this respect. An exceptionally large number of women candidates (14) fielded by the smaller parties in 1952, was mainly due to two parties, the Ram Rajya Parishad and Kisan Maidur Praja Party (KMPP), with accounted for six candidates each.[6]

TABLE 2b

Number of women contestants by States

States	Total No. of contestants				No. of contestants having women contestants					No. of women contestants					No. of women elected				
General Elections	I	II	III	IV	I	II	III	IV	V	I	II	III	IV	V	I	II	III	IV	V
Andhra Pradesh	21	25	43	41	N.A.	3	6	4	6	1	4	7	4	7	—	3	4	3	2
Assam	10	10	12	14	N.A.	2	3	1	3	2	2	3	1	3	—	2	2	N	1
Bihar	44	45	53	53	N.A.	7	8	10	14	3	7	8	12	18	2	5	6	4	1
Gujarat	—	—	22	24	N.A.	2	5	1	1	N	2	5	1	1	N	2	2	N	N
Haryana	—	—	—	9	N.A.	—	—	1	N	—	—	—	1	N	—	—	—	N	N
J & K	—	—	—	6	N.A.	—	—	N	N	—	—	—	N	N	—	—	—	N	N
Kerala	11	16	18	19	N.A.	1	1	3	3	—	1	1	3	4	—	—	N	1	—
M.P.	23	26	36	37	N.A.	5	9	10	8	4	7	11	11	8	1	N	7	5	3
Madras/T. Nadu	62	34	41	39	N.A.	2	4	4	2	7	2	4	5	2	2	4	1	1	—
Maharashtra	37	58	44	45	N.A.	3	2	4	5	5	3	2	4	5	3	1	1	1	—
Mysore	9	23	26	27	N.A.	N	1	N	1	N	N	1	N	1	N	N	—	N	N
Orissa	16	14	20	20	N.A.	N	N	1	2	N	N	N	1	2	N	N	N	N	—
Punjab	19	17	22	13	N.A.	1	N	2	1	4	1	N	3	1	—	—	N	2	N
Rajasthan	18	18	22	23	N.A.	N	3	2	4	2	N	6	2	4	—	1	N	2	2
U.P.	69	68	86	85	N.A.	4	13	11	15	15	6	14	13	17	5	3	6	7	6
West Bengal	26	28	36	40	N.A.	3	2	3	8	3	3	2	3	9	—	2	2	2	—
Nagaland	—	—	—	1	N.A.	—	—	N	N	—	—	—	N	N	—	—	—	N	N
Union Territories																			
Andaman etc.	—	—	—	1	N.A.	—	—	N	N	—	—	—	N	N	—	—	—	N	N
Chandigarh	—	—	—	1	N.A.	—	—	N	N	—	—	—	N	N	—	—	—	N	N
Dadra etc.	—	—	—	1	N.A.	—	—	N	N	—	—	—	N	N	—	—	—	N	N

Women in the Electoral Process

[Table continued from previous page — state/union territory data]

Delhi	3	4	5	7	N.A.	2	N	1	3	2	3	N	1	3	1	1	1	—	N	N	2
Goa, Daman etc.	—	—	—	2	N.A.	—	—	1	1	—	—	1	—	1	—	N	—	N	N	N	N
Himachal Pradesh	—	3	4	6	N.A.	N	1	N	N	1	—	—	—	N	1	N	N	N	N	N	N
Laccadive etc.	—	—	—	1	N.A.	—	—	N	N	—	—	N	—	N	N	N	N	N	N	N	N
Manipur	2	2	2	2	N.A.	N	—	N	N	1	—	—	—	N	N	N	N	N	N	N	N
Pondicherry	—	—	—	1	N.A.	—	—	N	N	—	—	N	—	N	N	N	N	N	N	N	N
Tripura	2	1	2	2	N.A.	N	—	N	N	—	—	N	—	N	N	N	N	N	N	N	N
Grand Total										51	41	65	66	86	19	25	33	28	21

Note: States and Union Territories as in the fourth General Elections have been following Himachal Pradesh, Manipur, and Tripura became States afterwards.

TABLE 3

Female contestants and their political parties

Year of the election		Cong.	Swat.	BJS	CPI	CPM	PSP	SSP	Ind.	Others	Total
1952	Total	N.A.	—	N.A.	N.A.	—	N.A.	—	N.A.	14	51
	Elected	14	—	N	1	—	N	—	N	2	19
1957	Total	25	—	N.A.	3	—	3	—	8	2	41
	Elected	22	—	N	1	—	N	—	N	2	25
1962	Total	33	9	3	3	—	1	3	8	5	65
	Elected	28	4	N	1	—	N	N	N	N	33
1967	Total	36	3	3	3	1	1	2	10	7	66
	Elected	21	3	1	N	1	1	N	2	N	28
1971	Total	21(14)*	3	3	3	2	1	1	31	7	86
	Elected	15(N)	1	2	1	1	N	N	1	N	21

*figures in parenthesis indicate 'Congress(O)'
N.A. = Not Available
N = Nil

As in number, the Congress also covered the maximum area. The Congress women candidates appeared in most of the States during all the General Elections except in 1971, when they were confined only to 8 States and one Union Territory. In fact, the Congress never fielded any women candidates in the Union Territories except in Delhi and there too only in 1957 and 1971. An interesting point to note regarding the weightage given to States by the Congress is that Madhya Pradesh always secured the maximum quota of tickets for women except in 1971. On the other hand, no Congress candidate was ever fielded from Orissa and Jammu and Kashmir from among the States. Rajasthan and Haryana had only one Congress female candidate each in 1962 and 1967.

The largest number of independent candidates has come from Uttar Pradesh, Rajasthan, and Bihar. The rest of the parties have put up women candidates largely in their strongholds: BJS in Uttar Pradesh and Madhya Pradesh; CPI in Andhra Pradesh, Madras, West Bengal; CPM in Kerala and West Bengal; and SSP in Bihar and Uttar Pradesh. Here again, Madhya Pradesh has often been favoured by most of these parties in terms of putting up a woman candidate.[7]

In terms of success, in both absolute numbers and percentage of women contestants, the Congress achieved the best results. Its success was the highest at 88% in 1957, and lowest in 1967 at about 61%. The Socialist Parties (PSP and SSP) have thus far not been able to secure the election of any of its female contestants. The CPI and CPM have maintained this figure at 1, except in 1967 when the CPI could not return any of its candidates. The number of winning candidates has been going down in the case of Swatantra Party as against that of BJS, which has shown a tiny but gradual increase. The independents and smaller parties have generally given poor performance.

Notwithstanding a few exceptions, the women contestants have been found poorly articulate in the overall political perspective and the issues pertaining to the particular contests. They have heavily depended upon either the party machine or a band of loyal men workers in conducting their respective election campaigns. They have normally taken recourse to emotional and sentimental appeals in order to establish rapport with the voters and seeking their support, and in this respect, they have often been successful.

Background of the Power-Seekers

Reliable statistics pertaining to the economic, social, and political background of the female contestants are not available. From whatever general and specific information is available, it appears that those women who enter the democratic race for power come from economically very well-off families. They themselves and/or their close relations, such as the father, husband, or brother, own either large land acreage, industrial units, big business, or other sources of substantial income. A number of women contestants belong to the old princely houses. The names of Vijaya Raje Scindhia of Gwalior and Gayatri Devi of Jaipur may be mentioned as examples. The affluent economic background facilatates them to finance their respective election expenses, which are huge, with ease.

Socially, the women contestants are Hindus belonging to the upper caste. Only the Congress has occasionally fielded women candidates from Scheduled Castes, Scheduled Tribes, and those having allegiance to Islam. This has been done respectively in the case of reserved constituencies for Scheduled Castes and Tribes and where Muslim electorates have been in majority. Most of the Scheduled Caste and Scheduled Tribe candidates put up by the Congress belonged to Madhya Pradesh, and this explains the large number of women contestants belonging to that State. However, here again the Congress was cautious in the selection of its candidates, and it gave tickets to those placed higher in the social hierarchy of Scheduled Castes and Scheduled Tribes. For instance, the party twice chose Rani Kesar Kumari Devi to contest from Raigarh ST constituency in Madhya Pradesh. From Jorhat, a Muslim-dominated constituency in Assam, Begum Mofida Ahmed has been given the Congress ticket since 1957.

The women contesting for Lok Sabha seats have been fairly well educated. Though many of them have had neither formal education nor received degrees, their family background and associations made them polished and highly 'cultured' in social outlook and behaviour. A substantial majority of them, about 70% to 80%, could read, understand, and speak English.

In terms of political socialization, the women contestants may be grouped into two categories. The first category comprised those whose families were in the thick of politics and thus, through experience and training, they were highly articulate and had a sharp perspective of politics. Such women were less in number. Most of these women belonged to the Congress. The names of Mrs. Sucheta Kripalani and Mrs. Tarakeshwari Sinha may be mentioned as examples. Those belonging to other parties, but in the same category such as Smt. Vijaya Raje Scindhia and Smt. Gayatri Devi, came from the old ruling princely houses. The majority of women contestants, however, belonged to the second category. They neither had a clearer and sharper political perspective nor were very articulate. They were drawn into politics through relations or close associates under whose protection and guidance they often worked.

A close look at the list of women contestants reveal an interesting fact, i.e., a great number of them, about 30 to 40, have stayed in politics for quite long. Many of them have contested thrice and some all the five elections. Most of these candidates belonged to the Congress, though the CPI and the Swatantra have also had their share. This shows that the circulation of women elites in the electoral processes and thus parliament and state legislatures has been slow and restricted. Their continuous success is only one factor behind their longer stay in the race for power. What has supported this trend, in fact, is their deep involvement in politics and substantial economic resources to meet election expenses.

Only a few of the women staying longer in electoral politics have changed their party affiliation. Most such changes took place outside the Congress.[8] Occasionally, outsiders joined the Congress ranks, but none left it up to the 1967 elections with the exception of Vijaya Raje Scindhia of Gwalior. It was only in the 1969 split that many Congress long-timers left the Congress led by Mrs. Indira Gandhi, which ultimately came to stay as the Indian National Congress. All these women, after a long, successful political career, lost the elections in 1971. This also indicates that the party machine is a decisive factor in election success.

Exercise of Power and Authority

Very few women have been able to reach the highest level of power and authority in this country. However, those who managed to reach the highest level have given an excellent account of their administrative capabilities and skill to manipulate and manage their affairs independently. Mrs. Indira Gandhi, Mrs. Sucheta Kripalani, Mrs. Tarakeshwari Sinha, Mrs. Laxmi Menon, and Mrs. Vijaya Laxmi

Pandit's names may be mentioned in support of the contention. But
below this layer, the picture is not very encouraging. A quick survey
of parliamentary debates, for instance, would show that hardly five or
six women have regularly participated in debates and other
proceedings. The statements of the female M.P.s have been by and
large ordinary in content and style. But this perhaps is also true for
most of the male M.P.s. The problem is that only party leaders, owing
to their position and personality, make the maximum use of
parliamentary forums. The rest follow their leaders and thus are, more
often than not, relegated into the background.

The issues raised by women, either during electoral contests
or in parliament, have seldom focussed on special problems related
only to women. They have been all-encompassing and general
in nature, in accordance with its national importance. Similarly, the
women ministers have also functioned as the representatives of both
men and women. This suggests that women as a class do not have
their specific politics; in other words, politics has no sex dimension.

Conclusions

It is dangerous to draw conclusions on the basis of limited election
statistics, yet one cannot escape some general impressions. It is misleading to assume that socio-economic indicators such as literacy,
urbanization, and industrialization are singly conducive to the greater
participation of women in politics. However, these indicators may be
related to social structures and values, and then analysed in a wider
and comprehensive perspective to find out their total impact on the
phenomena. The Election Commission and the census department
may be persuaded to coordinate and compile the relevant statistics,
and attempts made to bridge this vital gap.

Women in India have largely remained inactive and indifferent
towards politics. This is accounted for by the absence of such
traditions that encourage women in politics, the social backwardness
of women and, above all, heavy demands that home and family make
on a woman's time, attention, and energy.

The very few women who have been able to come to prominence in
politics are economically well-off and belong to the upper strata of
society. They entered politics through their relations or background,
and stayed there through the force of their resources and status, since

politics in this country is status and money-oriented. The Congress, having the longest experience of political struggle and extensive social base, could throw up the largest number of women political leaders. Besides, it has also been apt in manipulating the factors of 'status' and resources.

There is nothing wrong if women choose to involve themselves more in domestic affairs than anything else, as most of the women do. It is, however, definitely wrong if a society restricts women from participating actively in various fields including politics. Experience has shown that women are as good or as bad politicians as men. In most of the cases, they do better. The attack should be made on the social hindrances imposed upon women to relegate them into a subordinate position and perpetuate their status accordingly.

In Indian society, women suffered from many imposed hindrances in their effort to play a meaningful role in politics. They were economically dependent, illiterate, house and family bound, *purdah* clad, and subjected to a number of conservative, obscurant, and irrational taboos on their social freedom and mobility. Since independence, many of these hindrances are being removed. The process of 'liberating', and 'emancipating' women is going on, though it may not be as fast as desired. It is very difficult to exactly work out the implications of this on-going process on women's role and participation in politics, but generally the trend is encouraging. It is possible that the extent of women's participation in politics may reach a certain level and stop there; it may not increase even after complete removal of the imposed hindrances. That would mean that women choose not to participate in politics beyond a certain extent. Such a non-participation and indifference, if at all it be there, should be respected.

India may be backward and lagging in respect to women's participation in politics within itself. However, as compared to most of the developed and industrialized societies of the west, it is much ahead in this field. This is largely owing to the basically liberal, egalitarian, and tolerant socio-cultural ethos, so far as the sex differences are concerned. The expressed political well being in accordance with these ethos, as reflected in the constitution, adds further weight to these ethos.

APPENDIX I

Statement showing the percentage of votes polled by men and women voters, etc. in the last three General Elections to the House of the People

Name of State/Union Territory	1962			1967			1971		
	by men voters to men electors	by women voters to women electors	by total voters to total electors	by men voters to men electors	by women voters to women electors	by total voters to total electors	by men voters to men electors	by women voters to women electors	by total voters to total electors
1	2	3	4	5	6	7	8	9	10
1. Andhra Pradesh	69.03	60.34	64.72	72.08	65.26	68.67	64.39	54.71	59.57
2. Assam	51.50	37.23	45.09	66.50	50.83	59.28	58.37	41.57	50.69
3. Bihar	55.39	32.86	44.88	61.28	40.74	51.53	60.00	37.01	49.10
4. Gujarat	63.39	52.02	57.96	69.19	58.17	63.76	60.61	50.19	55.59
5. Haryana	—	—	—	75.41	69.44	72.62	67.78	60.48	64.34
6. Jammu and Kashmir	—	—	—	57.25	52.08	55.16	67.61	46.59	58.12
7. Kerala	74.10	67.08	70.55	77.13	74.20	75.64	65.77	63.30	64.53
8. Madhya Pradesh	60.36	28.90	44.79	64.35	42.48	53.47	58.24	37.59	48.00
9. Tamil Nadu	73.07	64.55	68.77	79.23	73.94	76.56	74.48	69.17	71.82
10. Maharashtra	66.02	54.29	60.43	68.82	60.49	64.75	63.54	56.12	59.94
11. Mysore	65.18	53.07	59.30	67.36	58.34	62.95	61.73	52.71	57.42
12. Nagaland	—	—	—	—	—	—	56.82	50.37	53.77
13. Orissa	33.07	13.21	23.56	53.56	33.05	43.70	51.85	33.74	43.20
14. Punjab	65.90	58.13	62.37	73.44	68.43	71.14	63.36	55.87	59.89
15. Rajasthan	62.63	41.35	52.44	64.96	51.02	58.27	60.07	47.50	54.04
16. Uttar Pradesh	59.42	39.46	50.35	59.27	48.96	54.51	52.23	38.84	46.10

Women in the Electoral Process

17. West Bengal	61.98	47.62	55.75	70.88	60.15	66.03	64.79	58.74	62.16
18. Himachal Pradesh	43.68	22.04	33.60	57.97	44.05	51.20	48.44	33.38	41.18
19. Manipur	66.27	64.44	65.34	68.73	65.80	67.23	53.37	43.55	48.35
20. Meghalaya	—	—	—	—	—	—	—	—	—
21. Tripura	73.33	61.77	67.95	76.45	72.98	74.84	65.00	55.91	60.84
22. Andaman & Nicobar Islands	—	—	—	79.22	76.77	78.45	69.72	72.33	70.55
23. Chandigarh	—	—	—	65.42	65.28	65.36	62.79	73.11	62.92
24. Dadra & Nagar Haveli	—	—	—	80.05	76.55	78.29	71.46	68.06	69.78
25. Goa, Daman & Diu	—	—	—	69.35	67.42	68.37	57.01	54.91	55.92
26. Laccadive, Minicoy, and Amindivi Islands	—	—	—	78.27	86.16	82.02		(Uncontested)	
27. Delhi	65.82	71.71	68.29	68.91	70.25	69.49	66.81	63.29	65.18
28. Pondicherry	—	—	—	76.01	73.72	74.85	71.93	68.28	70.10
29. Mizoram	—	—	—	—	—	—	—	—	—
Total	62.05	46.63	54.76	66.73	55.48	61.33	61.00	49.15	55.35

Source: Report on the fifth General Elections in India 1971-72.

APPENDIX II

Party affiliations of the women contestants

A: The Indian National Congress (Figures in ( ) for the Congress (O))

States	Total no. of contestants					No. of women contestants					Women contestants returned				
General Election	I	II	III	IV	V	I	II	III	IV	V	I	II	III	IV	V
A.P.	N.A.	43	43	40	—	N.A.	3	4	3	2(2)	N.A.	3	3	3	2(N)
Assam	N.A.	12	12	13	—	N.A.	2	3	1	1(1)	N.A.	2	2	1	1(N)
Bihar	N.A.	51	53	53	—	N.A.	4	4	5	2(1)	N.A.	3	4	2	1(N)
Gujarat	N.A.	—	22	24	—	N.A.	2	3	1	N(N)	N.A.	2	2	1	N(N)
Haryana	N.A.	—	—	9	—	N.A.	—	—	1	N(N)	N.A.	—	—	N	N(N)
Kerala	N.A.	17	14	19	—	N.A.	N	1	1	N(N)	N.A.	—	—	N	N(N)
M.P.	N.A.	36	35	37	—	N.A.	4	7	7	3(1)	N.A.	4	6	4	2(N)
Madras/T. Nadu	N.A.	41	40	39	—	N.A.	N	1	4	1(1)	N.A.	N	3	N	1(N)
Maharashtra	N.A.	66	44	45	—	N.A.	2	1	2	1(1)	N.A.	1	1	1	1(N)
Mysore	N.A.	26	26	27	—	N.A.	N	1	N	1(N)	N.A.	N	1	1	1(N)
Orissa	N.A.	20	19	20	—	N.A.	N	N	N	N(N)	N.A.	N	N	N	N(N)
Punjab	N.A.	22	22	13	—	N.A.	1	N	1	N(1)	N.A.	1	N	1	N(N)
Rajasthan	N.A.	22	21	22	—	N.A.	N	1	N	N(N)	N.A.	N	N	N	N(N)
U.P.	N.A.	86	85	86	—	N.A.	3	5	9	6(3)	N.A.	3	5	6	5(N)
West Bengal	N.A.	35	36	40	—	N.A.	3	2	2	3(2)	N.A.	2	2	1	N(N)
Delhi	N.A.	5	5	7	—	N.A.	1	N	N	2(1)	N.A.	1	N	N	2(N)
Total						N.A.	25	33	37	22(14)	N.A.	22	29	21	16(N)

Note: Only those states have been mentioned where there were women contestants. N = nil N.A. = not available

B: Other Parties: (i) Swatantra Party

State											
A.P.	—	—	28	19	—	1	1	—	N	N	N
Bihar	—	—	43	25	—	2	N	2	N	N	N
Gujarat	—	—	14	21	—	2	N	2	N	N	N
M.P.	—	—	5	2	—	N	1	N	—	1	—
Madras/T. Nadu	—	—	16	8	—	1	1	N	N	N	N
Orissa	—	—	1	7	—	N	N	—	—	—	—
Rajasthan	—	—	10	14	—	3	1	1	—	—	—
U.P.	—	—	33	38	—	1	N	N	N	N	N
H.P.	—	—	2	1	—	1	N	N	N	N	N
Total					—	9	3	3	—	4	3	1

(ii) Bharatiya Jana Sangh

State											
M.P.	N.A.	27	28	32	—	N.A.	N	1	2	N.A.	N	N	1
U.P.	N.A.	61	74	77	—	N.A.	N	3	1	—	N	1	1
West Bengal	N.A.	5	4	7	—	N.A.	N	N	1	—	N	N	—
Total						N	3	3	3	N	1	2

(Contd.)

Appendix II (*Contd.*) (iii) The Communist Parties of India (CPI and CPM)

	N.A.						1	2	1	—	—	N	1	N(N)	—
A.P.	—	15		20	22	(9)	1	2	1	—	—	N	1	N(N)	—
Kerala	—	1		14	3	(9)	N	N	(1)	1(1)	N	—	N	(1)	1(N)
M.P.	—	1		3	6	(N)	1	1	1(N)	N	—	—	—	N(N)	—
Madras/T. Nadu	—	13		14	7	(5)	1	1	N(N)	N	—	—	N	N(N)	—
West Bengal	—	14		24	11	(16)	N	1(N)	2	(1)	—	—	N	N(N)	N(1)
Total							3	3	3(1)	3(2)	1	1	1	N(1)	1(1)

(iv) Socialists (PSP and SSP)

A.P.	—	6	i(N)	i	(3)						
Assam	—	7	8(2)	4	(2)						
Bihar	—	4	32(24)	32	(34)	i	3/2	i(N)	N/i	N	N	N(N)
Gujarat	*		6(i)	3	(2)						
Haryana	—		(—)i		(5)						
J. & K.	—		(—)N		(N)						
Kerala	(9)		4(N)	i	(3)						
M.P.	—	22	19(14)		15(ii)	—	N(i)	N(i)		N	N(N)	N
Madras/T. Nadu	—	7	5(2)	—i	(N)	N	N	N	N		N(N)	
Maharashtra			13(N)	—8(5)				N(i)				
Mysore			12	12(N)	—5(2)							
Orissa		6	5(13)	—	5(2)			i(N)				
Punjab		3	N(i)		N(i)							
Rajasthan		2	N(6)	—	1(13)		N(i)	N(i)			N(N)	
U.P.		52	48(51)	—	27(43)	2	i	N	N		N(N)	
West Bengal		6	12(i)	—	2(3)			i(N)		N		
Total					N.A.	3	i(3)	i(2)	i(i)			

Women in the Electoral Process

(v) Independents

A.P.	*	44	61	—	N.A.	N	1	N	N	1	...
Assam	N.A.	13	18	—	—	N	N	N	N	N	...
Bihar		35	99	—	—	1	N	4	N	12	N
Kerala		9	12	—	—	N	N	N	N	2	N
M.P.		26	61	—	—	2	N	N	N	1	N
Madras		46	36	—	—	—	1	N	N	N	N
Maharashtra		50	62	—	—	1	N	1	N	3	N
Orissa		8	18	—	—	N	N	N	N	3	N
Punjab		39	25	—	—	N	3	1	N	N	N
Rajasthan		49	64	—	—	N	3	1	N	2	N
U.P.		86	90	—	—	1	—	2	N	7	N
West Bengal		14	44	—	—	N	N	1	N	1	N
Total						8	8	10		31	

(vi) Smaller, Regional, and the Rest

A.P.	N.A.					N.A.	
Bihar		2	2	2	2		1	N
Gujarat					1		—	N
Kerala			1	1			1	—
M.P.				1	1		1	—
Maharashtra					1		1	—
Punjab					1			N
Delhi					1			—
Goa, Daman, Diu								

References

1. There are very few articles on the subject which are referred to subsequently.
2. See for instance V.M. Sirsikar, *Political Behaviour in India: A Case Study of 1962 General Elections*, Manaktalas, 1965, pp. 93-95.
3. Mrs. Lakshmi N. Menon's two articles may be cited here: (i) 'Political Rights of Women in India', *UNESCO Seminar on the Status of Women in South Asia*, (New Delhi, 1952), ICWA Library; and (ii) 'From Constitutional Recognition of Public Officers', *The Annals of the American Academy of Political and Social Sciences*, Vol. 375, January, 1968.
4. Lakshmi N. Menon, 'Political Rights of Woman in India', *UNESCO Seminar*, n. 4.
5. Lakshmi N. Menon, 'Political Rights of Women in India', *UNESCO SEMINAR*, n. 4.
6. These are approximate numbers. For details see Appendix II.
7. See Appendix II.
8. Two cases of Bihar, Lalita Rajya Lakshmi of Hazaribagh and Vijaya Raje of Chatra constituencies, may be mentioned as examples. Both of them contested on CSP (Chhota Nagpur Santhal Paragana Party) ticket in 1957. They switched on to Swatantra in 1962, and to Janata Party in 1971. On 1967, the former contested on Jharkhand ticket and the latter as an independent candidate.

WOMEN VOTERS AND THE MID-TERM POLL (1971)

A Study of Attitudes, Awareness and Commitments

Nandini Upreti and *D.B. Mathur*

The contribution of women voters to the successful working of democracy in India, consequent upon the constitutional sanction, cannot be overemphasized. This is assuredly a step in the right direction, more so when one recalls that women in India were deprived of many egalitarian privileges and rights during the past centuries, after they had enjoyed a dignified status and respect in the earlier periods of recorded history. There are, however, discernible changes in the social fabric and consequently in the attitudes of and about women. By and large, they are neither an isolated nor an ignorant lot. This study seeks to look into their attitudes, awareness, and commitments with a view to identifying the status of women today. As shall be seen in detail later, our respondents were vocal in their assertions that they made their own decisions and were not influenced, one way or the other, by impositions or dictates from any quarter. This in some way, exposes the assumption that women voters lack individuality to identify their alternatives in politics.

For this study, 200 women voters were interviewed and questionnaires were administered to them. Of these, 195 questionnaires were utilized. The respondents belonged to two broad categories: housewives and working women, the former denoting those not employed and the latter in employment out of their homes. Altogether, they numbered 130 housewives and 65 working women. Our analyses treat the respondents in these two separate categories. The intention was to find out if there is some correlation between the different and respective backgrounds of the respondents, and their attitudes and reactions in the political context.

General Information about the Respondents

All the respondents belonged to an urban area – Jaipur. This study, therefore, does not claim to have gone into the corresponding analyses of the reactions of rural respondents. The largest number of respondents, 36.9%, belonged to the middle age-group, 31-40 years. Category-wise, 87.8% of the working women belonged to the age-group 21-30, which shows that more women from among the younger age-group are coming up for employment outside their homes. Cumulatively, a substantially large number of working women belonged to the age-group of 21-30 and 31-40, totalling up to 87.88%, whereas 60.8% housewives belonged to the age-group, 31-50.

With regard to educational level (Table 1), 46.2% of the housewives had virtually no formal education; and some were minimally literate.

TABLE 1

Educational break-up of respondents

	No formal education literate	Matric/ Inter	Graduate	Post-graduate	No Response	Total
H.W.	60	40	15	12	3	130
%	46.2	30.7	11.5	9.3	2.3	100
W.W.	6	12	17	30	—	65
%	9.2	18.5	26.1	46.2	—	100
Total	66	52	32	42	3	195

Note : H.W. = Housewives W.W. = Working women

Only 9.2% working women came under this classification. The table shows that as against 20.8% housewives 73.2% working women came under the cumulative category of educational level, graduate/post-graduate or above. This might also explain that women with higher education are more likely to opt for occupations outside their homes.

The main objectives of this study were to assess the attitude, awareness, and commitments of women respondents on the eve of the 1971 mid-term parliamentary election. The questionnaire, therefore, identified some major events and issues in the situational context, such as the Congress split, dissolution of the Lok Sabha, the four-party alliance, respondent's reactions to political leadership and parties, and attitudes governing voting behaviour. Yet another objective was to ascertain respondents' attitudes towards women's representation in parliament, etc.

Political Information

The first question, eliciting political information, was about the data of the previous Lok Sabha elections. Only 56.9% respondents gave the correct answer, of whom 64.7% were working women and 53.1% housewives. The lead of the former is understandable, owing to reasons of exposure to news media, educational attainments, and economic level. Again 15.3% housewives failed to respond to the question, and 18.6% housewives and 27.6% working women did not specifically have any information to mention.

Concerning the sitting MP from Jaipur in the dissolved Lok Sabha cumulatively, 66.2% respondents gave the correct answer and 33.8% either did not know or gave no response; 64.8% housewives and 69.3% working women gave the correct answer. However, housewives, though behind working women, were only 4.5% short of the level of the latter, and this was not a mean performance. Perhaps one reason might be that Gayatri Devi (former maharani) and her party workers had done some intensive house-to-house campaigning, and the urban housewife, generally speaking, knew about her representative. What is astonishing, therefore, is that 30.7% working women either expressed ignorance or failed to respond to this essential question.

Another question sought to ascertain public memory by asking the names of the candidate and the party respondents voted for at the previous parliamentary poll (Table 2). Significantly, 52.8% respondents did not exercise the right of franchise, of whom 64.7% were working women and 46.9% housewives. Of those voted, only 30.9% remembered both the party and the candidate: housewives (34.6%) were placed better than the working women (23.1%) in recalling the candidate and the party then voted for. Once again, Gayatri Devi was a significant factor, and her party seemed to have gained in popular estimation owing to the influence and appeal of the former maharani. Further, 11.5% housewives and 9.2% working women, who recalled the party they voted for but not the name of the candidate, voted for the Congress as such, and the candidate did not really matter to them.

TABLE 2
Voting behaviour of respondents and public memory

	Remembered party and candidate	Remembered candidate	Remembered party	Did not know	Total
H.W.	45	9	15	61	130
%	34.6	6.9	11.5	16.9	100
W.W.	15	2	6	42	65
%	23.1	3.0	9.2	64.7	100
Total	60	11	21	103	195
%	30.9	5.5	10.8	52.8	100

The inference that apart from the impact of a party, that of a tried leader cannot be minimized, is obvious.

The respondents were asked if they were aware that the Lok Sabha was dissolved at the instance of the Prime Minister: 56.9% housewives and 87.8% working women answered in the affirmative; 5.5% failed to respond; and 12.8% working women were ignorant of the fact. Another question asked the respondents about the incidents which led to the premature dissolution of the Lok Sabha. No respondent was aware of the political drama that preceded the dissolution of the Lok Sabha. The obvious inference is that women respondents, whatever their station in life, were not actually concerned about particulars of political events and issues.

TABLE 3
Information about dissolution of the fourth Lok Sabha

	Knew	Did not know	No response	Total
H.W.	74	45	11	130
%	56.9	34.6	8.5	100
W.W.	57	8	—	65
%	87.8	12.2	—	100
Total	131	53	11	195
%	67.2	27.4	5.5	100

When asked about the fifth Lok Sabha elections, and how it was different from the previous elections, the respondents failed to identify and pinpoint the difference. Though 65.3% housewives and 69.3% working women knew that the fifth Lok Sabha elections were different from the previous election, 4.6% housewives and 18.5% working women could not identify the difference; 30.1% housewives and 12.2% working women pleaded ignorance of the issues involved. This, once again, confirmed that the respondents were not concerned with the day-to-day happening and transformations in the political life around.

Respondents were provided with some specific factors which differentiated the fifth Lok Sabha elections: battle for issues, delinking of assembly, and parliamentary elections, four-party alliance against the ruling Congress, and, if the respondents felt, other factors. Maximum identification (48 housewives + 21 working women = 69) was given to 'four-party alliance', followed by 'battle for issues' (32 + 18, respectively = 50), and 'delinking of elections' (15 + 6, respectively = 21). Both, housewives (48) and working women (21) gave 'four-party alliance' maximum identification.

In view of the significance of the four-party alliance, the respondents were asked whether they were aware that such a political event had taken place. Cumulatively, 61.7% respondents answered in the affirmative and 24.1% in the negative, with working women leading at 78.3% affirmative responses followed by housewives with 65.3% affirmative responses. The high degree of awareness about this issue among housewives need to be noted. One might infer that the four-party alliance to oust the ruling Congress had, at that time, assumed such importance that even housewives were aware of its existence.

While an insignificant number of respondents could identify the constituent parties of the alliance, the response to the question about the purpose of the alliance was encouraging. (Two more current motivating factors for the alliance were specified in the questionnaire; that is, either the alliance aimed to defeat Indira Gandhi and the ruling Congress; or, it was a collaborative effort for gaining power and office.) Cumulatively, 54.4% respondents supported the former, 27.6% the latter, and 18% gave no response. Larger respondents (49.1% housewives and 64.7% working women) of both the categories thought that the alliance was forged to oust Indira Gandhi and her party. The response was in keeping with the generally held view at that time that the alliance had no ideological consensus and it was no more than a union of political convenience. The final question in this context dealt with some of the problems faced by the country, answers to be listed in order of their gravity.

TABLE 4

Major problems faced by the country

	Unemployment	Law and order	Poverty	Corruption	Rising prices	No response	Total
H.W.	51	15	51	18	39	24	198
W.W.	25	10	25	10	20	12	102
Total	76	25	76	28	59	36	300

The first two problems are: unemployment and poverty, and both received equal number of preferences (76 each). Rising prices (59 preferences), corruption (28 preferences), and law and order (25 preferences) were the others pointed out. During interviews with respondents, it was found that most of the respondents felt the pinch of economic hardship as their written responses identified unemployment, poverty and rising prices among the first three problems faced by the country. It might be recalled that no respondent gave any political problem to be causing concern. The importance of economic justice, therefore, was highlighted, political problems notwithstanding. With a view to assessing the reactions of respondents about ideological issues and commitments, a question was put whether India needed strong government or ideological fixation. Table 5 shows that cumulatively, 76.8% respondents believed that India needed a strong government, 12.9% preferred ideological fixation (all working women), and 10.13% pleaded ignorance on the matter. Significantly, 84.7% housewives wanted strong government, and none

TABLE 5

India needs strong government/ideological fixation

	Strong government	Ideology	Do not know	Total
H.W.	110	—	20	130
%	84.7	—	15.3	100
W.W.	40	25	—	65
%	62.6	37.4	—	100
Total	150	25	20	195
%	76.8	12.9	10.3	100

mentioned ideology as a relevant factor. In an underdeveloped society, this is not a very healthy sign in the sense that socio-economic challenges are more likely to assume grave proportions unless resolved by concerted efforts.

Respondents were asked whether democracy and socialism could go together. It is significant that while 39.2% housewives failed to give any answer, all the working women responded one way or the other. Thus 40.5% respondents felt that democracy and socialism could not go together and 33.4% answered otherwise. Another significant aspect was that larger number (37.6%) of housewives answered in the affirmative, whereas 53.8% working women thought that democracy and socialism could go together. The cumulative picture, as seen above, is, of course, different, as Table 6 shows.

TABLE 6

Democracy and socialism cannot go together

	Agree	Disagree	Do not know	Total
H.W.	49	30	51	130
%	37.6	23.2	39.2	100
W.W.	30	35	—	65
%	46.2	53.8	—	100
Total	79	65	51	195
%	40.5	33.4	26.1	100

Another question was whether India needs revolution for real progress and not the ritual of elections. Altogether 42% respondents supported revolution and 26.1% favoured elections; 31.9% failed to respond. It is significant that the balance was tilted in favour of

TABLE 7

India needs revolution not elections

	Revolution	Elections	Do not know	Total
H.W.	40	28	62	130
%	30.7	21.5	47.8	100
W.W.	42	23	—	65
%	64.7	35.3	—	100
Total	82	51	62	195
%	42	26.1	31.9	100

revolution in both the categories – 30.7% housewives and 64.7% working women rejecting the curative prospects of elections. This presents an interesting picture, because it is often assumed that women in India are, by and large, averse to revolution, and implied violence and instability. Another important aspect is that most of the housewives (47.8%) pleaded ignorance, whereas all the working women responded one way or the other, as seen in Table 7.

Further, a question was put whether India needed dictatorship or democracy. Cumulatively, 34.4% respondents preferred dictatorship and 44.1% chose democracy, whereas 21.5% did not know their choice. The preferences for dictatorship being less than those for democracy do not tally with the preceding response (Table 7), when larger number of respondents (42%) preferred revolution to elections (26.1%). However, housewives, in both the instances, were conspicuous in abstaining to identify their response (47.8% in the former case and 32.2% in the latter). Similarly, when 64.7% working women preferred revolution, (Table 7), it is surprising that 73.9% of the same category preferred democracy (Table 8). The housewives took a more consistent stand as we find that 30.7% voted for revolution, and 38.5% wanted dictatorship as opposed to respective preferences for 'election' (21.5%) and 'democracy' (29.3%).

TABLE 8

India needs dictatorship not democracy

	Dictatorship	Democracy	Do not know	Total
H.W.	50	38	42	130
%	38.5	29.3	32.2	100
W.W.	17	48	—	65
%	26.1	73.9		100
Total	67	86	42	195
%	34.4	44.1	21.5	

Two questions were put about the princes, especially in view of the issue of privy purses. The first asked respondents whether privy purses should be abolished: 53.8% housewives answered in the affirmative and 66.2% working women also responded likewise. Cumulatively also, larger number of respondents (57.9%) favoured the abolition of privy purses; 13.2% housewives failed to respond.

Another question was whether princes should take part in politics. It is interesting that 84.6% housewives and 90.8% working women preferred princes to taking part in politics. This might have some correlation with the popular image of the erstwhile maharani of Jaipur.

The foregoing analysis gives some indication of the level of political information of respondents. It is true that responses were forthcoming, but interviews with respondents brought out the fact that almost all of them betrayed ignorance of the nuances of political issues and events, and this was true for both categories of respondents.

Political Participation

The questionnaire also looked into the intensity of the respondents' political participation. The first question sought to find out if the respondents cast their vote for the fourth Lok Sabha elections. It is interesting that 47.2% respondents participated in the election whereas 52.8% abstained. On the other hand, more of housewives (54.5%) went for polling and more of working women (63.3%) abstained.

Perhaps one reason why 63.3% working women did not vote might be that they were preoccupied with their job. However, during interviews with respondents it was found that all of them expressed their willingness to cast their vote at the next parliamentary poll.

The next question concerned respondents' preferences for political parties. They were asked to specify four parties in order of preference.

It would be seen that of the first preferences, Congress (R) secured 102 out of 165, followed by Swatantra (30 out of 165), and Jana Sangh (20 out of 165). The big lead of Congress (R) is conspicuous, and it might be called a pointer to the mid-term poll verdict. However, it should be noted that the respondents gave second preference to Swatantra which, at that time at least, had considerable appeal among Jaipur's urban electorate.

One might, however, state that the respondents were perhaps more concerned with assigning preferences to political parties from the national angle, because from the Jaipur parliamentary constituency Gayatri Devi (Swatantra), and not the Congress (R) candidate, was elected subsequently, though Swatantra was given second place among first preferences.

Respondents were asked about the factors which determined their choice of a particular party. Three alternatives were provided in the questionnaire: liking for the leader; liking for the programme of the party; liking for both the leader and the programme.

Cumulatively, 44.1% respondents favoured a party because of its programme, 19.1% said they cared for both party programme and the leader, and 18.4% did not respond. It is interesting that a larger number of respondents of both categories – housewives (43%) and working women (46.1%) – expressed preference for a party's programme. But during informal conversations with respondents, it was found that only a handful of those respondents who had expressed preference for the programme of a party knew about its particulars and policy. This is not surprising, since the responses had given a low weightage to ideology.

Knowledge about the preferred party's candidate (78.6%) outnumbered the negative responses (13.8%); 7.6% respondents gave no response; working women (80%) had a slight lead over housewives (78.5%) in this context.

Respondents were asked if they knew the name of the candidate put up by the party of their preference.

It would be seen that 77.9% respondents answered in the affirmative and 22.1% did not recall the name of the candidate of the party of their preference. It is surprising that housewives (78.5%) stole a march over working women (76.9%), however small the margin might be. What is surprising is that 23.1% working women failed to recall the name of the candidate.

Women Representatives and Women Voters

With a view to assessing the respondents' attitude to the suitability and capacity of women to perform political assignments, they were asked a pointed question. The respondents answered in the affirmative. It was further put to the respondents whether women should vote for women candidates only. The responses show that the element of confidence, implied in the respondents' unanimous contention about the capacity of women to fulfil political assignments, did not preclude them from overwhelmingly denying that women should vote for women only (84.5%). Working women gave a 100% response in the negative, and housewives did likewise with 76.9% negative assertion. Only 10.7% housewives believed that women should vote for women.

However, when asked if women should vote on the basis of merit, 87.2% gave affirmative response. Working women, once again, gave a unanimous affirmative response, and 82.8% housewives did likewise.

Respondents were asked if they preferred to vote freely and independently, or would be willing to be guided by the decision of the family. Of the respondents 84.5% stood for freedom and discretion and 12.9% (all housewives) for following the advice of the family.

TABLE 9

Factors responsible for voting behaviour

	Faith in the party of the candidate.	Personal judgement	Ability of the candidate	Guided by others in family	Affiliation with former rulers.	Total
H.W.	25	58	18	11	18	130
%	19.2	44.6	13.9	8.4	13.9	100
W.W.	16	35	12		2	65
%	24.6	53.9	18.5		3.0	100
Total	41	93	30	11	20	195
%	21.0	47.8	15.4	5.5	10.3	100

Table 9 shows the respondents' reaction to a question about the most important and decisive factor for voting. The first two responses were: personal judgement (47.8%) and faith in the candidate's party (21.0%). This coincides with the separate response of housewives (personal judgement: 44.6% and faith in the candidate's party: 19.2%, followed by working women 53.9%, for the former, and 24.6% for the latter. Comparatively, while 19.2% housewives were agreeable to take the family's decision for voting, only 8.4%, housewives supported the factor of guidance of members of the family as a voting determinant. It would be seen that, the candidate's ability received only a 15.4% response (housewives: 13.9%, and working women 18.5%).

When asked if respondents were satisfied with women's representation in Parliament, 41.2% replied in the affirmative, 35.8% in the negative, and 23.9% did not respond. The distributive picture is entirely different: working women: 53.9% dissatisfied, 30.7% satisfied; and housewives: 46.2% satisfied, 26.9% dissatisfied. The dissatisfaction among working women is understandable owing to their exposure to life outside the household, and also a generally higher level of awareness expected of them.

Respondents who had expressed dissatisfaction with the representation of women were asked a follow-up question concerning reasons responsible for that. Six possible alternatives were provided, and multiple responses were expected in order of the respondents' preference. Maximum responses were given to the factor 'responsibilities of the household' (48), followed by 'political indifference' (42) and 'illiteracy' (40), in that order. Housewives also gave maximum response (28) to the factor 'responsibilities of the household', followed by 'social restrictions' (24). Working women gave maximum response equally to 'responsibilities of the household', and 'political indifference' (20 each).

A suggestion was put up in the questionnaire if reservation of seats for women is likely to ensure adequate representation of women in Parliament. Table 10 shows that both housewives (49.9%) and working women (53.8%) favoured reservation for women. This is surprising because earlier the respondents had disagreed that 'women should vote for women'. What is surprising, however, is the response of 53.8% working women who wanted reservation for women.

TABLE 10

Reservation of seats for women representatives

	Yes	No	Do not know	Total
H.W.	65	50	15	130
%	49.9	38.6	11.5	100
W.W.	35	30	—	65
%	53.8	46.2	—	100
Total	100	80	15	195
%	51.2	41.2	7.6	100

Respondents were asked if they were satisfied with the performance of women representatives in the State Assembly and Parliament, though during discussions it was found that none of them could give any reason for their satisfaction. What they repeated more than once was that women were as good as male representatives, which was not substantiated further.

Another question was whether the respondents favoured a lady

Prime Minister, consequent upon the fifth Lok Sabha election. Cumulatively, 83.1% respondents favoured the prospect, and only 17.9% gave a negative response. It should be noted that among the latter categories, 18.6% housewives and 16.9% working women gave no response.

Respondents were asked to state the causes as to why they either favoured or disfavoured a lady Prime Minister. Those who favoured it (54.1%) did so in the context of Indira Gandhi's previous record of performace. The next reason was 'better administrators' (25.3%). Distributively, both housewives (53.6%) and working women (54.7%) supported the issue on the basis of 'previous record'.

Respondents who did not favour a lady Prime Minister (41.5%), said that sex was an irrelevant factor; 28.5% thought that men were better administrators. Distributively, housewives gave equal weightage (33.3%) to two factors: 'men are better administrators' and 'Indira Gandhi's previous record', being instrumental in their disfavouring a lady Prime Minister; working women thought the sex of the candidate is an irrelevant factor. It is also to be noted that no working women referred to the factor of Indira Gandhi's previous record. Respondents were asked during the interview if, in their opinion, Indira Gandhi was likely to continue as Prime Minister and almost all of them answered in the affirmative.

In conclusion, we might collate the major trends emerging from this study of the attitudes, awareness, and commitments of urban women voters.

With growing opportunities of education, more women are taking to jobs outside the household, and a fairly large section prefers teaching. It was revealed that the choice of profession is rather limited for working women, most of whom choose a career to supplement the household income.

Since this study was undertaken on the eve of the 1971 mid-term parliamentary election, the trends of women voters' attitudes, awareness, and commitments need to be assessed in that context. The level of political information of respondents might be ascertained by the fact that working women were better placed than housewives. The former's exposure to mass media, educational attainments, and social contacts should explain their being better informed. It was found that 46.9% housewives and 64.7% working women did not vote in the 1967 Lok Sabha election. Of those who did, most had voted, not because of a particular person being the candidate, but primarily because that candidate belonged to the party of the respondents' preference. It was found that though the level of political information was fair, without being exceptionally high, a large number of respondents were neither acutely interested in, nor actually concerned about, particulars and nuances of political events and issues. However, working women were slightly better in their understanding. The respondents showed maximum concern for unemployment and poverty, as the problems faced by the country. Rising prices and corruption came next. By implication, it might be noted that they were found to be more concerned about ensuring economic justice. It is significant that respondents did not identify any political problem in this context. Similarly, they overwhelmingly favoured a strong government in India. While ideological fixation was mentioned by a few working women, no housewife thought it as a priority. A larger number of housewives failed to discern the meaning and significance of the query whether democracy and socialism could go together. However, a large number of respondents thought such an equation was an impossibility. On the other hand, it is interesting that more housewives considered it impossible, in keeping with the cumulative response, and more working women thought that democracy and socialism could go together. It seems an expected response since some working women had earlier favoured ideology.

Contrary to the generally held assumption, a large number in both the categories favoured revolution to elections in India. However, more respondents also favoured democracy to dictatorship. These two juxtaposed responses are interesting, because the emerging picture is that more respondents prefer revolution and democracy to go together. The variation of responses to these two questions was found to be more among working women.

A large number of respondents favoured abolition of privy purses and wanted princes to take part in politics, notwithstanding the fact that the erstwhile local ruling house had, at that time, enjoyed considerable influence in Jaipur. However, during interviews with respondents, it was found that almost all of them betrayed ignorance of the deeper implications of political issues and events. This was found true for housewives as well as working women.

Turning to political preferences, it was found that maximum responses went to the ruling Congress, followed by Swatantra and Jana Sangh. This does not explain the respondents' earlier preference for revolution, because the aforesaid political parties cannot be identified with either revolutionary concepts or goals. It is significant that the respondents did not consider socialist and Marxist parties as anywhere near plausible choices even when they had earlier expressed preference for revolution to elections.

Respondents were found to be overwhelmingly influenced by considerations of the programme of a political party, while liking for both leader and programme came next. This response should be evaluated in the light of the earlier response when respondents did not consider ideology to be acutely important. During interviews, it was found that almost all respondents failed to elaborate what they meant by their preference for programmes while rejecting ideology.

Respondents were found to be confident of the suitability and capacity of women to fulfil political roles. However, they overwhelmingly denied that women should vote for women only. Those who responded otherwise were all housewives. An overwhelming number of respondents felt that women should vote on the basis of merit of the candidate alone. This, however, has to be evaluated in the light of their earlier affirmative response that greater consideration be given to the programme of a political party. Whereas all the working women thought it imperative that voting is one's own discretion, 19.2% housewives thought that women should abide by the decision of the family. However, respondents overwhelmingly supported free and independent alternatives to be ensured. The earlier preference for a candidate's merit should be seen in the light of the response given about factors determining the ultimate voting behaviour of respondents. It was given out that the most important factor is 'personal judgement', followed by 'faith in the party'. 'Ability of the candidate' was relegated to third preference, whereas earlier respondents had overwhelmingly (87.2%) preferred merit of a candidate.

The respondents were satisfied with women's representation in the Lok Sabha (41.2% satisfied, 35.8% dissatisfied, and 23% gave no response). This is an interesting response considering the fact that most of the respondents were unaware of how many women were actually sitting members. Those who were dissatisfied with the representation of women gave 'responsibilities of the household' and 'political indifference' as the two more important factors for the existing situation. However, it was found that a larger number of both housewives and working women favoured reservations for women in the Lok Sabha. This is interesting, because earlier the respondents had disagreed that women should vote for women only. The implications of these two responses are obvious. The respondents were found satisfied with the performance of women legislators in the Assembly and the Lok Sabha, though they did not give the reason. Similarly, the respondents overwhelmingly supported the prospects of installing a lady Prime Minister after the elections. Among the reasons in support of this contention were: 'previous record' and 'better administrator'. Apparently, the respondents considered the question in the light of Indira Gandhi's earlier tenure. Among the reasons advanced disfavouring installation of a lady Prime Minister, the most important were: 'irrelevance of sex' and 'men are better administrators'. These responses are significant.

One might, therefore, say in summing up that the political attitudes, awareness, and commitments of women voters are gradually evolving in the context of a democratic political system. Given more opportunities, and with the growth of political articulation and involvement, women are likely to play a more effective and discerning role in politics than hitherto. However, this presumes a parallel maturing and viability of political socialization.

INDIAN WOMEN AS SEEN IN ELECTION STUDIES

Swaroop Rani Dubey and *S. Trikha*

With the attainment of independence in 1947 and the promulgation of the Constitution in 1950, women were brought on par with the traditionally dominant men, with equal rights to participate in the political process, and to enter high political offices such as those of President, Prime Minister, Governor, Chief Minister, Speaker, etc. Many of these offices have already been held by women successfully. Such achievements appear spectacular, when compared with the political status of women in many countries in both the developed and the Third World. This paper, however, attempts to examine not the legal position, but the empirical accounts of women's role in the political process.

Accounts of the General Elections agree that female electoral participation was not uniform throughout the country, and varied from State to State. In 1957, in ten States, the percentage of female votes cast was higher than the national average of 38.77%, the highest percentage being in Delhi, Tripura, and Kerala. It was lower than the national average in the remaining eight States, the lowest percentage being in Orissa, Himachal Pradesh, and Madhya Pradesh. In 1962, the female votes cast reached 46.63%. In 11 of the 18 States, the percentage was higher than the national average, being more than 60% in Tripura, Manipur, Delhi, Madras, Kerala, and Andhra Pradesh. It was less than the national average in seven States. The lowest percentage of 13.21 was recorded in Orissa, followed by 22.04% in Himachal Pradesh. The uneven distribution of electoral participation among the States suggests a possible correlation between the extent of literacy and electoral participation. High literacy States such as Delhi, Kerala, Tripura show a high voting percentage, while States with low literacy generally record a low percentage. The importance of adult education for raising the political status of women cannot thus be overemphasized.

As compared to the male contestants, the number of female contestants is very small, though it has been rising gradually. It is, however, remarkable that a large number of them have been elected. In 1971, the Congress put up 21 candidates; Congress (O) 14; Swatantra, Jana Sangh, and CPM two each; CPI three; and PSP one. A common complaint is that few serious women candidates of the right kind come forward to contest the elections.

With a view to getting suitable names of women candidates, Mrs. Indira Gandhi sent a circular through the women's wing of her party to all party units in States to suggest names of young and educated women workers from whom the party may select candidates for the ensuing elections. For reasons best known to the organizers, no woman candidate was put up in ten States, viz., Gujarat, Haryana, Himachal Pradesh, Jammu and Kashmir, Kerala, Maharashtra, Nagaland, Orissa, Punjab, and Rajasthan. It is difficult to believe that there were no competent women in any of these States. The Congress put up six women from Uttar Pradesh, three from West Bengal, three from Madhya Pradesh, two each from Andhra Pradesh, Bihar, and Delhi, and one each from Mysore, Assam, and Tamil Nadu. All selected women were in their forties and were either well-known social workers or former legislators.

Party Manifestos

The election manifestos issued by the parties are important documents, in that they contain the promises the parties would like to fulfil if they form the government. The items included in the manifestos are generally the ones on which there is consensus within the party.

Practically all the political parties agree that women constitute a backward section of the society, and that special privileges should be granted to them to bring them on par with men. The parties also agree that the existing gap between men and women should be reduced to the minimum possible. The Indian National Congress and the Congress (O) pledge themselves to the implementation of the directive principles laid down in the Constitution. Recent manifestos have emphasized education and employment opportunities for women.

The Communist Party of India stands for women in every sphere of national life. It demands equal pay for equal work for women, removal of all restrictions on employment of married women, and strict enforcement of the social legislation enacted to raise the status of women. The Communist Party appreciates the need for adequate financial allocations and extra facilities for education of women. It also wants employers to extend maternity benefits to married female employees.

The Praja Socialist Party felt that despite the talk of equality, women in India have continued to suffer under a variety of taboos and social inequalities. The inferior status of women is not compatible with our endeavour to establish a socialist society. PSP advocated free education to women at all stages, reservation of a substantial number of jobs for them in gram panchayats and municipalities, and preference in employment in fields such as education. For the PSP, raising the status of women is an essential step in the remaking of the nation.[1]

The Samyukta Socialist Party is of the view that because of indifference and lack of enthusiasm in the government, the laws are often not adequately utilized in matters such as widow marriage and property rights of woman. The party wants to arouse this consciousness among women. Harijan and Adivasi women have been backward for centuries and are, therefore, entitled to special opportunities. The progress of education of girls should get special encouragement.[2]

The Communist Party of India (Marxist) is thoroughly dissatisfied with the little the Congress government has done in the field of women's welfare. Women continue to be plagued by lack of education, poor opportunities for free development, and backward and obscurantist customs and prejudices. The party thinks that the Congress has done little to change this situation. No nation can progress if it allows its women to be enchained by backwardness, ignorance, superstitions, and does not give them equal treatment as citizens of the country. Therefore, the CPI(M) demands special facilities for promoting education among women, removal of social disabilities from which women suffer, equal rights in matters of marriage, admission to professions and services, and equal pay for equal work. In other words, the party is opposed to any kind of discrimination against women.[3]

The Jana Sangh, which cherishes old Indian values, stands for the advancement of women and advocates special steps to remove social and educational disabilities of women to enable them to discharge their responsibilities to the family, society, and nation. But such changes, it holds, must not destroy the age-old scientific principles of social organization. The Jana Sangh promises to enlarge and make more substantial property rights to women; she will be granted absolute rights as a member of her husband's family.[4]

The political parties, reflecting the aspirations of different sections of the society, agree that by and large women constitute a neglected section of the society. It is agreed that immediate steps should be taken to improve their status, because they represent nearly half of the population of the country and suffer from many social and economic disabilities.

Women's Role in Elections

Campaign

In the elections, women work both as instruments of campaign and as objects set forth for achievement (e.g., women's welfare). In the handbills, posters, and public meetings, the points already discussed above in the election manifestos pertaining to women, are emphasized. Several times, local problems are also emphasized in propaganda. For instance, in Bombay, it was promised that women will get copious water from the municipal taps and that prostitution will be abolished.[5]

Generally speaking, women are less interested in politics than men.[6] However, it is the endeavour of all the parties to reach the women voters in as effective a manner as possible. All the political parties engaged a sizable number of active women workers for campaigning in a constituency in Bombay; the Congress had 400; PSP 200; Jana Sangh 400; and SMS 100.[7]

In the Goa elections, girls were seen dancing and singing on on behalf of different parties.[8] One of the ways of aching the females was the kitchen to kitchen approach by more than a thousand housewives in the leisure hours of the afternoon.[9] Political wings of the parties also play an important role in impressing the female voters. Practically, all the parties have some kind of a women's wing; in the Congress, this is known as Mahila Mandal; that of PSP, Samajwadi Mahila Sabha; of Jana Sangh, Mahila Aghadi; and that of SMS, Mahila Samiti.[10]

Where there is no regular women's wing of the party, women workers are entrusted with propaganda work, and, if necessary, they are hired for campaign work. During the 1962 elections in Uttar

Pradesh, the Congress employed about 200 women for propaganda work in a constituency. In employing them, caste and religious considerations were also kept in mind. Most of them were drawn from the young age-groups. Of these workers, 12 were specially employed for door-to-door canvassing.[11] Similarly, the Swatantra Party employed about 100 workers for canvassing. Of these, six were paid women workers brought from outside.[12] However, aspersions were cast on the morals of the women, because, having been brought from outside, they were not known in the area and their credentials were doubted. The fact of hiring women was highlighted in private discussions in restaurants and pan shops.[13]

Since women are believed to be more religious, certain festive occasions were used to win their support by the political parties in Bombay. In Maharashtra, January 14 (the Makar Sankranti day) is always celebrated as *tilgur* ceremony. The election having fallen around this time, the Jana Sangh exploited this occasion for impressing women, particularly the illiterate ones.[14] Even parties such as Congress, PSP, and SMS which profess secularism also exploited this opportunity.[15]

An organization called the Stree Matdata Sanstha (Women Voters' Council) arranged a number of meetings to educate women on how to exercise their right to vote. Candidates were invited to address meetings and inform women about their programmes. The Consumer Guidance Society also arranged meetings, where the candidates addressed the voters and explained what they proposed to do for the voter as a consumer.[16]

Every voter is a valuable person to the candidates and the parties they represent. Obviously, therefore, attempts are made to approach all the voters. Since the *purdah*-observing Muslim women do not attend public meetings, in Maharashtra recorded appeals by leaders were played in the Muslim areas for the benefit of the Muslim ladies.[17]

Despite the fact that the candidates try to approach all the female voters, the usual practice is to approach the male, active head of the family, who wields authority over the younger members and the women in the family.[18] The ladies, who are economically dependant on men and are not very educated, look up to men for guidance.[19]

Though women constitute almost 50% of the voters, there has not been any organized bargaining on their part with the political parties for their support, except the stray demand for reservation of six seats in the Jammu and Kashmir Assembly by the Istri-Sabha in Jammu.

Political parties have also not yet appreciated the value of women's votes. In the estimate of some, if a party organizes half the nation, its chances of winning the election will improve considerably.[20]

In certain studies attempts have been made to find out the efficacy of different mass media. Regional differences apart, in case of women, public meetings are most effective and popular.[21] Similarly, women have been found to be more to interpersonal media than men. Radio has proved to be equally effective for both men and women.[22] In Bihar, however, the pattern of efficacy of mass media is slightly different. The public meetings were effective but more in case of men. Similarly, the interaction between friends and relatives was not as effective as the motivation offered by party workers.[23]

Awareness and Participation

A large number of women voters, at their own or at the instance of others, are participating in the elections. However, it is of considerable interest to know as to what the women think of elections. Are they aware of the parties and candidates? Are they aware of the objectives of the parties and problems facing the country? This depends mostly upon the level of political information obtaining among women. The observation in Rajasthan study,[24] that men have a higher level of political information than women, both quantitatively and qualitatively, is corroborated by other studies also.[25]

There is a general lack of awareness among women in the country. Illiteracy, social customs, and severe backwardness gave most of them few occasions to participate in public life. In the first General Elections, almost 2.8 million names of potential female electors were deleted from the electoral roles, because they did not give the name of their husbands. There was considerable improvement in the second General Elections, when about 94% females were registered reaching 100% in the third General Elections.[26] It may be pointed out that the Election Commission had to give up the idea of photographing the voters because some of the women were not prepared to be photographed, even by women photographers. Despite the significant changes taking place, difficulties in the political advancement of women continue in a very real sense.

In certain studies, awareness of the women about the election, i.e., the candidates, the parties, and issues for elections were tested. While the majority of male respondents were found to be highly aware of the contesting candidates and their principal rivals and political affiliations, the women lacked that awareness.[27] It was further observed that an absolute majority of males knew the MLA, MP, and their party affiliations, while the majority of women did not.[28]

A major conclusion emerging from the studies carried out in different parts of the country is that, by and large, women are in political agreement with their husbands. If not strictly the decision of the husband, the decision about electing a particular candidate or party rests with the head of the family or village headman.[29] The political parties are also to be blamed for this. Assuming that the turnout of women voters is less than that of men, and that men influence women's votes, they do not concentrate on mobilizing female voters, which leads to continued lack of political information among women.[30] If the parties and the candidates make greater efforts to mobilize women voters, the women will improve their level of political information resulting in a greater turnout at the polls.

Voting Intention and Non-Voting

There being a gap in political consciousness between men and women, the former tend to make a quicker decision about the voting, etc. than the latter.[31] In Rajasthan, a higher percentage of men voters were registered on the positive side of voting intention, while the women voters scored higher on the negative side.[32] There is one interesting observation about women voters who exhibit a degree of indecision in their voting intention as also the voting act. In Rajasthan, of 112 female voters who intended to vote in the first phase, only 42 continued to do so in the second phase, compared to 50%, 217 men voters in the first phase.[33] This has been corroborated by other studies also. It was also observed that this pattern was equally prevalent in both rural and urban areas.

Elections are regarded as festive occasions for the women.[34] In several instances, the women voters are extended the facility of tractors, jeeps, and other automobiles, making the visit to the polling booths an interesting diversion. In the urban areas, the behaviour of women voters is a bit different. Life in the urban areas is not corporate, and they are confronted with such problems as security of the home and the care of children, when the lady is out for polling.

Nevertheless, the women exhibit some distinctive features. At the Assembly level, they are more exercised about the problems that touch them personally such as water shortage, slums, etc. At the national level, men are more aware about political and administrative problems such as defence, corruption, boundary disputes, rather than economic difficulties such as food shortage, or rising prices over which higher percentage of women show concern.[35]

A higher percentage of women vote for independents,[36] which suggests that women are more candidate-oriented than party-oriented. Surprisingly, however, the analysis of votes cast for the Assembly and the Lok Sabha revealed that women voted at the two levels for the party, while the men did so for candidates.

Concluding Remarks

It sounds paradoxical that a country under the Prime Ministership of a woman has only a few women leaders. Though half the electorate of the country consists of females, they are not contributing their 50% share in returning the MLAs and MPs for the formation of the government. An overwhelming majority of the contestants are men on the face of it, the studies do not suggest that men are opposed to conceding equality to women. All the political parties agree on the principle of sex equality, though they may disagree on certain points of details. No body in the country, in or outside the Congress party, was opposed to the leadership of Mrs. Indira Gandhi because of her sex.

The majority of Indian women being illiterate, they are unlikely to fight for their right. Special efforts, therefore, will have to be made to bring them on par with men. Once women become educated and aware of their surroundings, they will have a definite role to play in shaping the destiny of the country. In 1960, the Kerala women exhibited unprecedented popular aggressive interest, and according to a correspondent, they were responsible for the defeat of the Communists.[37] Long before the elections, it was feared that the result of the election would depend on how the women votes.[38] Kerala women today represent a large number of literate and politically conscious women. If after some time the women in the rest of the country also become educated and politically conscious, for which concerted efforts will have to be made, the political status of women would undergo a sea change. As things stand today, despite the fact that a large number of women are taking interest in elections, they continue to be influenced, if not dictated, by men.

References

1. S.L. Poplai, *1962 General Elections in India*, Delhi, Allied Publishers, 1962, pp. 67 and 168.
2. M. Pattabhiram, *1967 General Elections in India*, Delhi, Allied Publishers, 1967, p. 246.
3. *Ibid.*
4. S.L. Poplai, *op. cit.*
5. Aloo J. Dastur *et al.*, *Parliamentary Elections in Bombay*, 1971, pp. 26 and 32.
6. V.M. Sirsikar, *Political Behaviour in India: A Case Study of the 1962 General Elections*, Bombay, Popular, 1963.
7. V.M. Sirsikar, *op. cit.*, p. 94.
8. G.S. Halappa *et al.*, *First General Elections in Goa.*
9. Aloo J. Dastur *et al.*, *op. cit.*, p. 79.
10. V.M. Sirsikar, *op. cit.*, p. 94.
11. Yogesh Atal, *Local Communities and National Politics*, Delhi, National, 1971, p. 173.
12. *Ibid.*
13. *Ibid.*, p. 183.
14. V.M. Sirsikar, *Sovereigns without Crowns – A Behavioural Analysis of the Indian Electoral Process*, Bombay, Popular, 1973, pp. 136 and 194.
15. V.M. Sirsikar, *op. cit.*
16. Aloo J. Dastur *et al.*, *op. cit.*, p. 65.
17. V.M. Sirsikar, *op. cit.*, p. 79.
18. B.S. Khanna and Satya Deva, 'Campaign and Voting in Punjab and Haryana', (Mimeographed), Department of Public Administration, Punjab University, Chandigarh.
19. *Ibid.*, p. 139.
20. V.M. Sirsikar, *op. cit.*, p. 94.
21. N. Srinivasan and V. Subramanian, 'Indian Voter: A Study of the General Elections of 1967', (Mimeographed), IIPA, New Delhi, p. 74.
22. Raj Narain, 'Voting Behaviour in Uttar Pradesh: A Study in the Fourth General Elections', (Mimeographed), Department of Psychology-Philosophy, University of Lucknow, 1970, p. 622.
23. V.P. Varma, 'A Study of the Voting Patterns and Behaviour in the Fourth General Elections in Bihar (1967)', (Mimeographed), Institute of Public Administration, Patna University, 1969, p. 62.
24. S.P. Varma and Iqbal Narain, *Voting Behaviour in a Changing Society*, Delhi, National, 1972, pp. 308.
25. N. Srinivasan und Subramanian, 'The Indian Voter: A Study of the General Elections of 1967, (Mimeographed), p. 186.
26. Shivlal, *op. cit.* part III, p. 86.

27. C.P. Bhambhri and P.S. Varma, *The Urban Voter*, Delhi, National, 1973, pp. 78-79.
28. *Ibid.*
29. S.P. Varma and Iqbal Narain, *op. cit.*, p. 308.
30. *Ibid.*, p. 20.
31. Aloo J. Dastur *et al.*, *op. cit.*, p. 98.
32. S.P. Varma and Iqbal Narain, *op. cit.*, p. 15.
33. *Ibid.*
34. Yogesh Atal, *op. cit.*, p. 259.
35. Aloo J. Dastur *et. al.*, *op. cit.*, p. 331.
36. Aloo J. Dastur *et. al.*, *op. cit.*, p. 191.
37. K.P. Bhagat, *The Kerala Mid-term Election of 1960: The Communist Party's Conquest of New Positions*, Bombay, Popular, p. 123.
38. *Ibid.*

PART II

POLITICIZATION OF WOMEN IN INDIA – A THREE/STATE SURVEY

POLITICIZATION OF WOMEN IN INDIA

An Overview

V.M. Sirsikar

These three pilot studies on the politicization and participation of women in India were carried out in Gujarat, Maharashtra, and West Bengal. The purpose of the studies was to test the influence of various factors on the politicization of women – by age, religion, caste, language, educational level, and economic status. Information was sought on the actual record of political activities, attitudes towards political participation, and reactions to the present political situation in the country.

The purposive sample for each study was limited to 150. West Bengal completed 150 interviews while Gujarat did 145. In the case of Maharashtra, in addition to the 150 interviews, there were 25 interviews of Scheduled Caste women. It was not possible to attempt a large State-wide survey based on statistically-determined random sample. The idea behind the pilot studies was to find out the variables affecting politicization and participation of women.

The three surveys exhibit not only different levels of sophistication, but also different interests of the three researchers. Nirmala Banerjee had competently used the statistical tests and tried to base her conclusions on a sounder footing. Her sample was well-balanced and was spread over five districts of West Bengal. Thus, the West Bengal study had been handled more carefully than the other two.

The Maharashtra study had in practice become an urban study. The sample was not balanced. In an effort to rectify the imbalance, additional interviews of 25 Scheduled Caste women were taken. Still, the sample was tilted in favour of educated women.

It was unfortunate that the Gujarat study did not mention, in the original draft, anything about the sample. On enquiry it was found that the study was based on 145 interviews possibly taken in Ahmedabad. There was no description of the sample anywhere. It thus also became an urban study.

With the regional modifications in the original questionnaire designed by me, it has become a little more difficult to draw generalizations based on all the three surveys. What follows is an attempt to hazard a few guesses without any statistical support. But the intention behind these pilot studies was to have a qualitative feel of the situation rather than a quantitative study. To that extent, the three studies have contributed enough material for the following conclusions.

Politicization and participation of women in a country will necessarily depend on the overall political situation. In our country, there are certain factors in the situation which favour politicization and participation of women in political life. The background of the freedom struggles, specially during the Gandhian era, was very conducive to this process. Thousands of women, all over the country, participated in the freedom struggle. Gandhiji's emphasis on the socio-political emancipation of women contributed to the process.

Levels of politicization and participation vary from region to region. The three States selected for study cannot be regarded as representative. These States have a higher level of modernization than most of the other States. Hence politicization is also higher.

After independence, different political parties, for reasons best known to themselves, did not continue this healthy trend. Politics became more and more a business for 'men only'. No doubt, a few seats were always given to women, but this was not in proportion to women's strength in the population. Even the party in power, which claims to be progressive, never thought of increasing the quota of women candidates from a mere 15% of the total seats. The blame for such a poor representation of half the adult population can be placed at the doors of the Congress. This does not mean that other parties were better. They also followed the policy of 'tokenism' in giving tickets to women aspirants.

It is not without comment that a former Chief Minister of Uttar Pradesh, Charan Singh, could publicly express his anti-women stand. This reflects to a certain extent the prevailing socio-political climate in the biggest State of the Union – Uttar Pradesh.

Other political leaders may be more discreet than Charan Singh. But this does not mean that they had any more liberal views on this issue. The traditional Indian social structure is heavily tilted in favour of men, giving them all the authority and prestige, and reducing women to the lowest status confining them to the kitchen. The process of modernization has not penetrated beyond the urban fringe. The rural masses still very much remain traditional in their attitude towards women.

In the context of Indian political culture, it can be expected that there should be a far greater participation of women in politics. But the reality is different. Muslim women have many more constraints on their participation than Hindu women. Though Scheduled Caste women exhibit a greater political awareness, their economic condition becomes a barrier against their active participation. Higher education and high socio-economic status do not necessarily induce high participation. On the other hand, they are sometimes reflected in greater apathy towards political life. It might be due to a cynical view of politics. These and other findings underline the fact that participation is low.

In the effort to probe into the political socialization process of women, it was found that women from political families exhibit not only greater political awareness but also greater participation. This suggests that family tradition and influence of individuals become significant agents of socialization. One of the obstacles to women's participation mentioned in all the three studies is societal attitudes. This has been mentioned by even those women who have been active in politics. Indian society, in the latter half of the 20th century, does not look upon women's participation with sympathy and understanding. From the point of view of early political socialization, this can be regarded as a very retarding factor. A change in societal attitudes has to be brought about by effective campaigning and, if necessary, by structural changes.

Political parties have a major responsibility in facilitating women's participation. Parties must make deliberate efforts to place their women members in both party organization and outside in positions of authority. This might need changes in the party constitutions in favour of women. Today women are there in all parties, but only as a token. This must change, and women should have their rightful place.

What is true of political parties is by and large true of other institutions also. 'Tokenism' is to be replaced by a genuine partnership of men and women in all socio-political organizations.

Women's organizations all over the country must take up the issue of securing their rightful place in the legislature. Unless women are able to reach the main decision-making centres in good strength, they might receive eloquent praise, but not power. It must be said that women's organizations are not very active in the political field. There is nothing like 'American Mothers' in India. Rights have a tendency to lapse if they are not asserted continuously. Therefore, Indian women must assert their right to an equal share in political power.

The influence of women's participation in politics will not remain confined to that sphere only. It will be felt in all walks of life. This will alter the very character of Indian society. We have committed ourselves to an egalitarian society. This ideal can never be achieved without the equal participation and partnership of women. All efforts must be directed towards this goal.

In view of the above studies and also the evidence available from other sources,* an attempt is made to make some suggestions for a greater participation of women in politics at all levels – local, State, and national.

1. A concerted effort through all the mass media about the importance of a greater role of women in public affairs is necessary.

2. The present statutory provisions regarding the cooption of women on the local bodies at different levels should be increased considerably, to at least 40%. This could be done at all levels: from grampanchayat to the zila parishad in rural areas, and municipal committees to corporations in urban areas. The problem of cooption raises the question of the system of coopting members. Unless certain safeguards are introduced to secure independent and competent women, the present practice of coopting women either as an adornment or as an innocent non-entity will continue.

Really speaking, it was very essential for the study undertaken by the Committee on the Status of Women to plan and undertake a sample survey of male political leaders regarding their attitudes towards women. No such empirical data is available. But everyone knows that, by and large, most political leaders are not very enthusiastic about the participation of women. This could be seen from the membership of the Constituent Assembly – women were there on sufferance. The Constitution-makers recognized the Scheduled Castes as weaker sections of the society and provided for them reserved seats, both in the legislatures and in the services. Their failure to recognize women as a weaker section was obviously a result of the predominant male composition of the Constituent Assembly. Women were given equal rights in voting. But, this did not mean much as it was next to impossible for women to compete for political power through elections.

*A group of 24 leading women in Poona public life were interviewed for the specific purpose of obtaining their views on securing adequate representation of women. See also V.M. Sirsikar, *Political Behaviour in India*, and *Sovereigns Without Crowns*, for details about women's voting behaviour.

3. A plea for reservation of seats for women may not be to the liking of many. It may appear to them as a retrograde step in this age of equality and women's liberation. But such reservation will introduce a structural change in Indian politics. Even a 30% reservation of seats in the country's legislature for women (who constitute nearly 50% of the population) will alter the very character of our legislatures. A real democratization will occur. The parties will be forced to change their strategies and tactics. Statutory provisions will induce them to give to the women their due.

Reservation of seats for women cannot be looked upon as if it is given for an underprivileged minority. It would not create, what is feared by the critics, isolated pockets, since women are not marginal to society as a minority group. They are not a dispensable part of the society – they are as essential as men for the very sustenance of the society. Participation may not be a function of statutes. But legal framework induces changes in the society. When 30% of the seats would be open to women, one could expect a considerable rise in their participation. This may make exacting demands on women – especially on those who contest. But this would motivate women to come forward to shoulder higher responsibilities.

Women, who occupy elective positions in the legislature or in the panchayati raj, may not be the only group of participants. A far larger group of party activists would be there. It is necessary to think of this group and understand their difficulties.

The state will have to accept some responsibilities to facilitate participation of women. For example, creation of day-centres, creches, nurseries, provision of maternity leave can be pointed out. Unless the woman is freed from her strenuous responsibilities of looking after the home and children, she cannot think of public life. In all the three pilot studies, women have referred to family and home responsibilities as obstacles in the way of their political participation. This has a relevance for those who want to be active in politics.

Another interesting case is that of wives of active political workers. These women bravely shouldered the burden of supporting the family. The political workers could participate actively, because they were not bothered about the maintenance of their families. Society has not given adequate recognition and support to such women. They are really participating indirectly.

Given proper leadership, women can be mobilized and this mobilization can bring about changes in the governmental structures and policies. The case in point is the way in which Bombay women have succeeded under the dynamic leadership of Mrs. Mrinal Gore. A significant development is the increasing participation of Muslim women in morchas and gheraoes. Probably the intensity of steep price rise and scarcity of commodities of daily consumption have aroused them equally as other women.

In conclusion, one could say that women's greater political participation has received only limited social acceptance. What is now needed is the active role of the government to force the change. If determined steps are taken, it would not take long to have women functioning as equal partners in the Indian democracy.

POLITICIZATION OF WOMEN IN GUJARAT

Dinesh M. Shukla

Introduction

Women are being increasingly viewed as an important segment of our political society. The way they perceive politics and the attitude they take on different political issues and on different political events deserve a careful analysis. However, the political impact of women has to be separated from their actual impact. In a traditional society, as the one in which we live, there are additional constraints on women besides their household duties. Therefore, a study of women in a society in transition like that of ours is called for. In India, with its highly differentiated and highly structured regional communities, it is likely that they might have developed a differential patterns of political behaviour on regional lines. Thus, a comparative as well as a comprehensive plan of the study of the Indian women is needed.

The study of women in Gujarat constitutes one such regional component of the overall study of the Indian women along political behaviour dimensions. Gujarat has witnessed a relatively liberal tradition in its social life. It is one of the first areas in the country which got exposed to western education. Gandhian movement had considerable impact on the women of Gujarat. Actually, the women in Gujarat had their first political socialization under Gandhiji.[1]

In the post-1947 period, women had generally remained dormant and even not interested in public and political life.[2] But, events such as 'Maha Gujarat' agitation and the recent 'Nav Nirman' movement have caused a notable degree of their political participation and mobilization.[3] Women participation was particularly widespread in Ahmedabad, Surat, and Baroda. So also at the time of voting a comparatively high degree of participation is generally noticed. For example, in the last (1972) Vidhan Sabha elections, out of the total votes (7,219,873), about 45% (3,238,507) votes were cast by female voters. It is, therefore, interesting to study some aspects of political behaviour of women in India's comparatively more developed State. In a limited study like this their behaviour is studied only within the modest frame provided by the conceptual nexus of politicization and political participation. The concept of political socialization of women is also woven in the frame to find if it is operative in the shaping of their political behaviour. The study is designed around certain assumptions on women, chief among which are:

1. The role an Indian women plays within her family or job may have correspondence with her political attitude and role.[4]

2. A husband and a wife in the Hindu society may not be equals in their experiences of political socialization and political participation. The husband plays his expected key role with regard to her politicization and participation.[5]

3. Apart from the husband, family and peer groups are considered to be the most significant political socialization agents.[6] However, the assumption 'family experiences are neither the only nor necessarily the most significant experiences that help prepare women for participation in the political world',[7] should also be open to our consideration as both males and females in a considerable degree are exposed to the modern instruments of politicization such as the audio visual media, particularly those of the radio and the press.

Also, the analysis of the data can be more indicative and perhaps meaningful if the relationship between certain aspects of the demographic profile of the women of Gujarat and their perceptual, attitudinal profile could be established with the help of the twin concepts of politicization and participation.

Concepts and their Operationalization

The political behaviour of women can be studied through certain basic concepts, viz., politicization, political participation, and political socialization.

Politicization is a process of drawing into political activity or other sort of participation – albeit temporarily – individuals or groups previously not interested in politics. Informal activities such as discussion of politics or political matters is an important process of politicization, particularly for an Indian woman. Now this concept or process is operationalized in different questions such as membership of political parties, discussion of 'politics' with members of family, etc.

Political participation is understood as voluntary, rather than coerced, activities of persons in political affairs such as voting, membership, and activities connected with political groups, e.g., political parties, political bodies such as local or State Assembly and poll campaigns. Now the concept is operationalized through attendance at public meeting arranged by political parties; membership of voluntary organizations; participation in agitational activities; and voting in elections.

Political socialization is a process by which a person acquires his/her views of the political world – its processes, events and phenomena, actors and structures – through the process of learning or knowing. Viewed from another perspective, political socialization is the way in which one generation passes on political standards and beliefs to succeeding generations. Through such process societies ensure intergenerational continuity in political attitudes and values. The indicators chosen in this study are relevant for the former meaning of this term.

Political socialization processes operate at both the individual and the community levels. We have also sought to relate the implications of political socialization of women to the social system of which they are a part.

We have operationalized the process of political socialization in the following questions: Which factors influenced your decision to participate in political movement or to join a political party? What are/were the sources of inspiration which influenced your decision to take part in political activity? The major factors such as (i) family tradition, (ii) specific political events, (iii) influence of an individual, (iv) influence of a book or literature, (v) influence of an ideology, were enumerated in the questionnaire.

We have asked certain questions to know the party orientations and attitudes of women – their party preference or rejection; their opinions and perceptions regarding the scope for women for political participation in the Indian social system; whether the difference between husband and wife in believing different parties or political opinions will effect their domestic happiness; whether there should be larger participation by women in political affairs; or whether women should keep away from politics and what do they think if they are deprived of their franchise.

A few questions of their perceptions regarding the leadership are also asked.

Data Analysis

Politicization of Women

Certain indicators were chosen to discern politicization of women. One such indicator is the membership of political parties of the family members of the respondents. Of the respondents 91% replied in the negative, 4.2% had their family members as members of Congress (O), 3.4% had Jana Sangh family members, and 1.4% had Congress (R) family members. Regarding the relationship of these members to the respondents who replied in affirmative, husbands of 4.2% women were party members, while 4.8% women stated that their brothers were party members. It is also found in other studies that the percentage of party membership of general population is below 10%. This reflects the low level of political institutionalization in India. The female population, which is generally confined to the four walls of the household, obviously falls in the pattern.

Discussion of politics with others gives some indication of the politicization, because it presupposes certain awareness or knowledge of political events, political phenomena, political parties, political leaders, or main political issues. Frequently they discuss 'politics' with their family members, neighbours, friends, and caste members. Of the respondents, 38.6% replied that they would not discuss 'politics' with their family members; 45.5% discuss 'politics' with their husbands; 5.5% with their fathers, and the rest with other relatives in the family. Regarding the frequency of discussion, the response pattern is interesting: 17.6% discuss 'politics' with their family members almost daily; 31.9% discuss it occasionally or sometimes; and 11.9% discuss it rarely.

Now, if we divide the women in non-discussing and discussing groups and compare their socio-economic status, we find interesting results.

Out of the total women belonging to non-discussing group, the tendency not to discuss politics is highest, i.e., 44.6% in the middle age-group (31-45 years). As compared to this, the tendency not to discuss politics is lower (33.9%) among the aged group (above 45 years), and the young age group (below 30 years).

In the group of discussing women, it is generally found that they discuss 'politics' with their husbands (62.1%). Here also, the middle aged women discuss politics with their husbands more than any other age-group.

Caste-wise, it is found that nearly 80% of the total non-discussing women belong to the upper castes (Brahmin, Bania, Patel, etc.). As compared to this, the tendency not to discuss politics with the family members is lower among the so-called lower castes (Kshatriyas, Scheduled Castes, Scheduled Tribes, etc.). Thus, only 20% of non-discussing women belong to lower castes.

In the group of discussing women, discussion of politics with husbands, more than any other relative in the family, is found in almost all the castes. But it is found that in lower castes the women discuss politics with their husbands only, barring a few Muslim women, who discuss politics with their sons and other relatives also. Kshatriya women are found to be discussing politics with their husbands only.

From the point of view of education of the respondents, it is found that nearly 50% of illiterate women are non-discussing women and 43% are educated up to primary level. Of the illiterate 40% discuss politics with their husbands only. Among more educated women, the tendency not to discuss politics with their family members is rather less.

Among the discussing group, women discussing politics with their husbands are found in all categories from illiterate to degree-holders and above. But women educated up to primary level discuss politics with their husbands more than any other category of educated women (30.3%), followed by degree-holders and above (25.8%). Thus, it can be said that the tendency to discuss politics with husbands is found more in educated women than in illiterate women (13.6%).

From the point of view of occupation of the respondents, it is found that nearly 70% of non-discussing women are housewives, and 14% are working women. The rest of non-discussing women include professionals, petty traders and hawkers, and labourers. More working women (44.4%) than housewives (38.6%) do not discuss politics with their family members.

Turning to the discussing women, it is found that housewives constitute the single largest group who discuss politics with their husbands (72.7%). Next comes the professional women (12.1%) who discuss politics with their husbands followed by the working women (9.1%).

From the point of view of economic status of the respondents, it is found that of the non-discussing women 71% have no income of their own, 16% fall in lower income group (up to Rs.2,500 p.a.), 8% fall in middle income group (up to Rs.7,500 p.a.), 2% fall in higher income group (above Rs.7,500 p.a.), and the rest have not answered the question.

Women discussing politics with their husbands are found in all the income groups, but the majority are in no-income group. Thus, of the women discussing politics with their husbands, 73% have no income of their own, 8% belong to lower income group, and 12% belong to higher income group.

It will be interesting to know whether exposure to the mass media has any impact on women discussing politics with their family members. It is found that of the non-discussing women, 28.6% do not read newspapers; 39.3% read soft-line newspapers (which are sympathetic to the government); and 16.1% read hard-line newspapers (which are critical of the government), and 14.3% read both soft-liners and hard-liners. From a comparison of the two types of readers, it is found that among the soft-liners the tendency not to discuss politics with their family members is more (42.3%) than among those, who read hard-line newspapers.

In the group of discussing women, women reading soft-line newspapers are discussing politics with their husbands more than any other reader-group. Thus, of the women discussing politics with their husbands, 31.8% read soft-line newspapers, 24.2% read hard-liners, 18.2% read both soft-line and hard-line newspapers, 25.8% women belong to the non-reading group.

It is found that of the non-discussing women, 23.2% do not hear radio at all, 42.9% hear it daily; 28.6% hear it sometimes, and 5.4% hear it rarely. It is rather surprising that nearly as many as 43% of the non-discussing women belong to the group who hear radio almost daily.

In the group of discussing women, women hearing radio almost daily are found discussing politics with their husbands more than any other hearing group. Thus, of the women discussing politics with their husbands, 59% hear radio daily, 18.2% hear it sometimes, 15.2% hear it rarely, and 7.6% do not hear it at all. It is also found that women discussing politics with other family members, for example, brothers and fathers, belong to the daily hearing group. Of the non-hearing group, nearly 62% belong to the non-discussing group. So, a positive correlationship with the exposure to mass media and the discussion of politics with family members is established.

The study also tried to find out whether discussion of politics with family members has any relationship to the attendance at public meetings organized by political parties, and, if any, of which parties. Of the non-discussing women, more than 85% have not attended any public meeting. Only Congress (R) is fortunate in the respect for it has attracted 8.9% of the non-discussing women to its meetings. Congress (O), the Jana Sangh, and other parties have each attracted only 1.8% of the women that belong to the non-discussing group.

Of the women discussing politics with their husbands, 22% have attended public meetings organized by the Congress (R); 15.2% have attended the meetings of the Jana Sangh, and 10.6% have attended those of the Congress (O). Here we find a very close correlation of non-discussion of politics with the family members to non-attendance of meetings organized by political parties.

A point of great interest will be to check up if discussion of politics with family members has any effect on the voting behaviour of the respondents. No positive correlation was found from the data between non-discussion of politics and voting behaviour, although the percentage of non-voters is higher in this group than in the discussing group: 26.8% have voted for the Jana Sangh in 1972 Vidhan Sabha elections; 21.4% for the Congress (R); 10.7% for the Congress (O); 1.8% for independent candidates, and 21.4% have not voted at all.

In the group of women discussing politics with their husbands, 45.5% have voted for the Congress (R); 21.2% for the Jana Sangh; 13.6% for the Congress (O). Here the non-voters are only 12.1%. We can say, therefore, that discussion of politics, especially with the husbands, does influence women to exercise their vote. Of the non-voters, 54.5% belong to the non-discussing group, and 36.4% belong to the discussing group.

As regards relationship between discussion of politics by women with their family members and their participation in election campaign, it is found that 87% women of the non-discussing group have not participated in election campaign and nearly 9% have taken part. Of these women who discuss politics with their husbands, more than 80% have not participated in election campaign, and 10% have participated in only one item. It may be concluded, therefore, that such discussion is not very crucial in influencing or otherwise to participate in election campaign.

In order to probe into women's orientations and attitudes towards different parties both the non-discussing and the discussing groups, it is found that of the total non-discussing women 32.1% do not know which party they feel close to; 21.4% do not feel themselves close to any of the parties; 26.8% feel that they are close to the Jana Sangh; 12.5% feel that they are close to Congress (R); 5.4% feel closeness to Congress (O), and 1.8% feel close to the Communist party. The Jana Sangh has a significant lead over other parties in terms of women voters' party orientation.

In the group of discussing women, especially those who discuss politics with their husbands, 21.2% do not feel themselves close to any party and 18.2% do not know about their closeness; 27.3% feel close to the Congress (R); 21.2% feel close to the Jana Sangh; the Congress (O) limps far behind (9.1%). At least it can be said that discussion with their husbands makes women more articulate regarding their perceptions towards parties.

In the non-discussing group, 35.7% feel that there is not a single party to which they shall never vote; 16.1% do not know to which party they shall never vote. The profile of party rejection is interesting: 19.6% have said that they shall never vote for the Congress (R); 8.9% have said that they shall never vote for the Jana Sangh; 7.1% have said that they shall never vote for the Communist party; 5.4% each have said that they shall never vote for the Swatantra Party and the Muslim League.

Among the discussing women, those who discuss politics with their husbands, 15.2% have said there is no party to which they shall never vote, and 10.6% do not know to which party they shall never vote. However, 27.3% have said that they shall never vote for the Jana Sangh; 19.7% have said that they shall never vote for the Congress (R); 18.2% have said that they shall never vote the Communist party; 4.5% each have said that they shall never vote for the Congress (O) and Muslim League each.

Discussion of politics especially with their husbands does help women in cultivating better understanding regarding parties – their feeling of closeness or rejection of the parties has been influenced by their discussion with their husbands.

Women, who discuss politics with other members of primary as well as secondary groups is taken as indicator of their politicization. 36.6% have replied that they do not discuss politics with their neighbours at all; 15.8% have said that they discuss it regularly; 34.4% discuss it occasionally or sometimes, and 11.1% discuss it rarely; and 2.1% have not answered the question.

Likewise, the question was asked whether and how frequently they discuss politics with their caste members. It is found that 46.9% do not discuss politics with their caste members at all; 2.6% discuss it regularly, 20.7% discuss occasionally or sometimes; and 27.2% discuss rarely; and 2.1% did not respond to the question.

With regard to discussion with friends, it is found that 44.8% do not discuss politics at all; 15.9% regularly, 22.1% occasionally, and 11.7% rarely discuss politics; 5.5% have not responded to the question.

Thus, it can be seen that women in Gujarat discuss politics very frequently with their family members, especially with their husbands more than any other family relations. But the interesting point to note is that they discuss politics more with their neighbours and friends than with their caste members. Whatever the reason, it is quite clear from the data that neighbourhood and friendship, the secular bases of social relationship, are playing a more important role in politicization of women through discussion of politics. More than 56% have found such discussion useful in forming opinion: 9% have stated that such a discussion of politics with others helps in forming opinion to a great extent; 47.9% have stated that it helps to some extent; and 11.7% have said that it does not help at all.

Political Participation of Women

Political participation is a process by which people take part in political activity with more or less clear choice or preference. Attendance at public meetings, taking part in agitational activities, attendance at study circles of political parties, voting in elections, participation in election campaign, membership of a political party, and membership in representative bodies are some of the important indicators of political participation.

Attendance at public meetings is an important indicator of political participation. Of the respondents, 63.4% have replied that they have not attended any public meeting organized by political parties; 15.3% attended meetings organized by the Congress (R); 11% have attended meetings of the Jana Sangh; 6.9% have attended meetings organized by the Congress (O); and the rest 3.5% have attended meetings organized by other parties.

The reasons given by the respondents for attending public meetings organized by political parties are important: 20% were attracted to the party and its programmes; 6.2% were attracted to the leaders of the party whose meetings they attended; 2.1% attended party meetings because of persuasion of others, e.g., friends, neighbours, etc; 4.8% attended for other reasons; and 3.5% did not give the reasons for their attendance.

This suggests that the degree of political participation of women through attending the public meetings organized by political parties is significant, if not very high. At least in 26% cases, the choice or preference for a particular party is conscious and deliberate, and is based on knowledge and awareness about the party's programme and the estimate of their leaders.

If we divide the respondents in categories of non-attending and attending women and compare with their socio-economic status, some interesting results emerge.

Of the total non-attending group, 51.1% belong to the middle age-group; 25% to the young age group, and 23.9% to the aged group. In other words, the women of middle age-group generally do not attend public meetings organized by political parties.

A look at the figures of attending women will suggest that of the women attending public meetings organized by the Congress (R), 54.5% belong to the middle age-group, while 36.4% belong to the higher age-group. Only 9.1% women belong to the young age-group. Of those attending the Jana Sangh meetings, 56.3% belong to the middle age-group, nearly 19% belong to the young age-group. Thus, in the attending group, women belonging to young age-group are more attracted to the Jana Sangh meetings than the Congress (R) meetings.

From the point of view of caste of the respondents, it is found that the non-attendance is higher in upper castes (Brahmin 21.7%, Bania 33.7%, and Patel 8.7%) than in the lower caste (Kshatriya 3.3%, Scheduled Caste 6.5%, and Scheduled Tribe 1.1%). The percentage of Muslim women is quite considerable (8.7%).

Of the women attending meetings organized by the Congress (R) the attendance of lower caste women is higher (45%) than that of upper caste women (41.1%). Attendance of the Muslim women in the Congress (R) meetings is also considerable (14%). In the meetings organized by the Congress (O), it is found that 90% who attend the Congress (O) meetings belong to the upper caste (40% Brahmin, 20% Bania, and 30% Patel); the remaining 10% belong to Scheduled Castes. In the case of the Jana Sangh also, more than 82% women belong to the upper castes (38% Brahmin, 44% Bania), and the remaining 18% belong to other castes.

Viewed from another angle, it is found that of the Muslim respondents, 72.7% do not attend any party meeting, and the remaining

27.3% attend meetings of the Congress (R) only. In the same way, of the Scheduled Castes women, 50% do not attend any party meeting, while 41.7% attend meetings of the Congress (R), and 8.3% attend the meetings of the Congress (O); and in case of Scheduled Tribes women, 50% do not attend party meetings at all, but the remaining 50% attend meetings of the Congress (R).

The women belonging to the lower castes and minority community, specially Muslims, attend more the Congress (R) meetings than of any other party.

It will be interesting to know whether there is any relationship between attendance at public meetings organized by a political party and the education of the respondents. Of the non-attending women, 39.1% are educated up to primary level; 22.8% are educated up to matriculation; 18.5% are highly educated (degree and above), and 14.1% are illiterate. Thus, the tendency not to attend party meetings is rather higher in educated and highly educated women than in illiterate women. Viewed from another angle, of the illiterate women, 59.1% do not attend party meetings at all; 31.8% attend the Congress (R) meetings; 10% attend the Congress (O) meetings. In the case of women educated up to primary level, out of the total such women 67.9% do not attend party meetings at all; 11.3% attend the meetings of the Congress (R); 13.2% attend the meetings of the Jana Sangh.

It is interesting to compare the educational status of the respondents attending the Congress (R) and the Jana Sangh meetings. Of the women attending the Congress (R) meetings 31.8% are illiterate; 27.3% are educated up to primary level; 13.6% are educated up to matriculation; and 27.3% are degree-holders and above. In the case of women who attended the Jana Sangh meetings, it is found that there are no illiterate women; 43.8% are educated up to primary level; 25.1% are educated up to matriculation; and 31.3% are degree-holders and above. So, a conclusion may be drawn that women of all the educational statuses are found attending the Congress (R) meetings with varying degrees. More educated women are attracted to the Jana Sangh meetings than to any other party meetings.

From the point of view of occupation of the respondents, it is found that nearly 70% of the non-attending women are housewives, while 15% are working women. The rest of the non-attending women include professionals (7.6%), petty traders and hawkers (4.3%), and others (2.2%). It is interesting to note that of the percentage of housewives, 63.4% do not attend any party meeting at all; 11.9% each attend the Congress (R) and the Jana Sangh meetings; 7.9% attend the Congress (O) meetings; and 5% attend the meetings of other parties. Of the working women 77.8% do not attend party meetings; 11.1% attend the Congress (R) meetings; 5.6% each attend the Congress (O) and the Jana Sangh meetings. But in the case of professionals, it is found that they attend the Jana Sangh meetings more than any other party meeting: 23.1% attend the Jana Sangh meetings; 15.4% attend the Congress (R) meetings; 7.7% attend the Congress (O) meetings, and 53.8% do not attend any party meeting. In the case of women engaged in petty trades and who are petty hawkers, it is found that 44.4% do not attend any party meeting; 55.6% attend Congress (R) meetings. The majority of the women attending Congress (R) meetings (54.5%) are housewives; in the Congress (O) meetings there as many as 80% are housewives; and in the Jana Sangh meetings 75% are housewives.

From the point of view of economic status of the respondents, it is found that of the women, 70.7% have no income of their own; 9.8% fall in the lower income group; 11.9% fall in the middle income group; and 5.4% fall in the higher income group. The rest of the non-attending women have not answered this question.

In the group of attending women, of those attending the Congress (R) meetings 54.4% belong to the no-income group; 31.8% belong to the lower income group; 9% belong to the middle income group; and 4.5% belong to the higher income group. Of women who attend the Congress (O) meetings, 80% belong to the no-income group; 10% each belong to the middle and the higher income groups. And in the case of women who attend the Jana Sangh meetings 75% belong to the no-income group; 12.5% each belong to the higher income and the middle income groups. More women belonging to the lower income and middle income groups are found attending the Congress (R) meetings then any other party.

If we classify our respondents according to total family income, we find that 21% belong to the lower income group; 45% belong to the middle income group; 26% belong to the higher income group; and 8% have not answered the question. Of the non-attending women, 28% belong to the lower income group; 46% belong to the middle income group; 18% belong to the higher income group; the remaining (8%) have not answered the question.

In the case of attending group, of the total women attending the Congress (R) meetings; 18.1% belong to the lower income group;

54.6% belong to the middle income group; 22.7% belong to the higher income group. Of those attending the Congress (O) meetings 40% belong to the middle income group, and 60% belong to the higher income group. Of those attending the Jana Sangh meetings; 12.5% belong to the lower income group; 31.3% belong to the middle income group; 56.3% belong to the higher income group.

It will be of interest to know whether exposure to mass media of communication has any impact on women attending the meetings of political parties. Of the non-attending women 28.3% do not read any newspaper; 38% read soft-liners; 17.4% read the hard-liners; and 14.1% read both soft-liners and hard-liners. If we compare the women reading soft-line and hard-line newspapers, we find that among soft-liner readers the tendency not to attend any party meeting is more (38%) than those who read hard-line newspapers (17.4%).

Of the women attending the Congress (R) meetings, 50% read only soft-line newspapers; 18.2% read only hard-line newspapers; and 31.8% do not read any newspaper. Of the women attending the Jana Sangh meetings, 37.5% read both soft-line and hard-line newspapers; 25% each read soft-line and hard-line newspapers; and 12.5% do not read any newspaper. And, of the women attending the Congress (O) meetings, 50% read both soft-line and hard-line newspapers; 30% read hard-liners, 10% read soft-liners; and 10% do not read any newspaper. Thus, one can say that readers of soft-line newspapers are more attracted to the Congress (R) meetings than to any other party meetings.

Regarding radio, it is found that of the total non-attending women, 16.3% do not hear radio at all; 45.7% hear it daily; 27.2% hear it sometimes; and 10.9% hear it rarely. In the group of women attending Congress (R) meetings 45.5% hear radio daily; 22.7% hear it sometimes; 13.6% hear it rarely; and 18.2% do not hear it at all. Of those attending the Congress (O) meetings, 90% hear radio daily and 10% hear it rarely. Of the women who attend the Jana Sangh meetings, 68.5% hear radio daily; 12.5% each hear it sometimes and rarely; 6.3% do not hear it at all.

It can therefore be concluded that those women who are more exposed to the mass media participate more in the meetings of opposition parties than those of the Congress (R).

It will be of interest to know whether attendance at party meetings has any relationship to their participation in agitational activities. It is found from the data that out of the total non-attending women 81.5%

have not participated in agitational activities; 12% have taken part in *morcha* and demonstrations; 4.3% have taken part in *dharna*; and 2.2% have taken part in *satyagraha*. So, one can say that there is a positive correlation between non-attendance at party meetings and non-participation in agitational activities.

In the attending group of the total women attending the Congress (R) meetings, 18.2% have taken part in *morcha* and demonstrations; 4.5% each have taken part in *dharna* and *satyagraha*; and 72.7% have not taken part in any agitational activity. Of those attending the Congress (O) meetings, 50% have taken part in *morcha* and demonstrations; 20% have participated in *satyagraha*; and 30% have not taken part in any agitational activity. Of the women attending the Jana Sangh meetings; 50% have taken part in *morcha* and demonstrations and an equal percentage have not taken part in any agitational activity. Women who attend the meetings of the Jana Sangh and the Congress (O) take more part in agitational activities especially in *morcha* and demonstrations. It is found from the data that out of those who have participated in *morcha* and demonstrations (19.3% of the total respondents), 28.6% attend the Jana Sangh meetings; 17.9% attend the Congress (O) meetings; 14.3% attend the Congress (R) meetings; and 39.3% have not attended any party meeting.

It is worthwhile to know if attendance at party meetings has any relation with the voting behaviour (1972 election) of the respondents. It is found from the data that of the non-attending women 35.9% have voted for the Congress(R); 20.7% have voted for the Jana Sangh; 8.7% have voted for the Congress(O); 2.2% have voted for independent candidates; 20.7% have not voted; and 12% either do not know whom they have voted for or have not answered the question. The fact that out of the total non-attending women nearly 68% have voted in the election clearly indicates that attendance at party meetings is not crucial for voting.

Nonetheless, it will be of interest to know whether attending the public meetings of a particular party has any relation to voting for that party. It is found from the data that of the women who have attended the Congress (R) meetings, 72.7% have voted for the same party; 9.1% have voted for the Jana Sangh; 4.5% have voted for the independent candidates; and 13.6% do not remember or have not answered the question. It is significant that not a single respondent who has attended the Congress (R) meetings has voted for the

Congress (O). But of the women who have attended the Congress (O) meetings, 90% have voted for the same party, and the remaining 10% have voted for the Congress (R). In the case of the Jana Sangh, 62.5% have voted for the Jana Sangh; 25% have voted for the Congress (R); 6.3% have not voted at all; and 6.3% do not know whom they have voted for or have not answered the question. In the case of those who have attended the meetings of other parties, 20% each have voted for the Congress (R), the Congress (O), and the Jana Sangh, and 40% have not voted at all. Thus, out of all the three important parties, the Congress (O) has the most faithful attendants.

Regarding the relationship between the attendance at party meetings and participation in election campaign, it is found that of the non-attending women, 88% have not participated in election campaign; 5.3% have participated in one item of election campaign – house to house campaign; 2.2% have participated in two items of election campaign – house to house campaign and election work at the polling booths; and 5.4% have not answered the question.

Of the respondents who have attended the Congress (R) meetings, nearly 91% have not participated in the election campaign, while 9% have participated only in house to house campaign. In the case of women who have attended the Jana Sangh meetings, 56.3% have not participated in election campaign; 37.5% have participated in election campaign (house to house campaign); and 6.3% have participated in three items of election campaign (election work at polling booths as volunteers and distribution of party literature along with house to house campaign). In the case of Congress (O), 20% have not participated; 40% have participated in three items of election campaign (election work at polling booths, distribution of party literature, house to house campaign); 30% have participated in one item (house to house campaign), and 10% have participated in four items of election campaign (financial contribution to the party funds along with the other three items mentioned above). Here also it is found that the Congress (O) has more sincere and faithful audience than any other party. Of the women who attend its party meetings, only 20% have not participated in election campaign while in case of the Jana Sangh and the Congress (R) the corresponding figures are 56% and 91% respectively.

Orientation and Attitudes Towards Political Parties

It will be interesting to know whether the attendance at party meetings has any relation to the feeling of closeness towards any party. From the data it is found that of the non-attending women, 35.9% do not know which party they feel close to, or have not answered the question; 18.5% do not feel close to any party. Thus, nearly 54.4% do not feel close to any party. While 20.7% feel that they are close to the Jana Sangh, 15.2% feel close to the Congress (R); 7.6% feel close to the Congress (O), and 1.1% each feel close to the Socialist party and the Communist party.

In the group of women attending the Congress (R) meetings, 18.2% women do not feel close to any party; 13.6% have not answered the question; 54.5% feel close to the Congress (R); 9.1% feel close to the Jana Sangh; and 4.5% feel close to the Communist party. On the other hand, of those attending the Jana Sangh meetings, 12.5% do not feel close to any party; 18.8% do not know their closeness or have not answered the question; and 68.8% feel close to the Jana Sangh. In the case of the Congress (O), as many as 80% do not feel close to any party, and 10% do not know or have not answered the question. From the data, one can say that women who attend the Congress (R) meetings and the Jana Sangh meetings do have a very high feeling of closeness to the party.

The data also reveal that of the total non-attending women, 16.3% feel that no party should be banned and 34.8% do not know or have not answered the question. Thus, nearly 51% women do not feel or have no idea as to which party may be banned. But 20.7% feel that the Congress (R) should be banned; 12% feel that the Jana Sangh should be banned; 12% feel that the Communist party should be banned; 3.3% feel that the Muslim League, and 1.1% feel that the Congress (O) should be banned.

Of the women respondents who attend the Congress (R) meetings 27.3% feel that no party should be banned; 31.8% do not know or have not answered the question; 27.3% feel that the Jana Sangh should be banned; 4.5% feel that the Communist party should be banned; and 4.5% want the Muslim League to be banned. Of those, who attend the Congress (O) meetings, 40% feel that no party should be banned, 20% want that the Jana Sangh should be banned; another 20% feel that the Muslim League should be banned; and 10% feel that the Congress (R) should be banned. Of those who attend the Jana

Sangh meetings, 25% feel that no party should be banned; 6.3% do not know or have not answered the question; 50% feel that the Communist party should be banned; 12.5% feel that the Jana Sangh should be banned. Thus, those who attend the Congress (R) and Congress (O) meetings feel very strongly against the Jana Sangh than against any other party; while the women who attend the Jana Sangh meetings feel very strongly against the Communist party.

The reasons given by the respondents that the Congress (R) should be banned are: the party is responsible for higher prices, shortage of essential commodities, corruption, lack of discipline, no moral scruples, etc. The women who believe that the Jana Sangh should be banned feel: it has a communal attitude towards minorities, responsible for riots, looting and burning of homes of the minority community (memory of the 1969 riots in Ahmedabad), hostile attitude towards Harijans and other low caste Hindus, etc. The women who say the Communist party should be banned have given reasons such as anti-national and anti-patriotic attitude, has roots in foreign land and takes inspiration from foreign country, and believes in class conflict and spreads violence. The women who want the Muslim League to be banned have stated as their reasons that such a party need not exist in India after the creation of Pakistan that it is a communal party and obstructs the process of national integration.

Another indicator of party perceptions and party attitudes is their negative preference for the party. From the data it is found that of the non-attending women, 26% say that there is not a single party for which they shall never vote; 15.2% do not know their minds or have not answered the question. Thus, nearly 59% non-attending women have a clear negative preference for a particular party. It also suggests that attendance at party meetings has no positive relation to the formation of a negative orientation towards political parties.

Of the women respondents who attend the Congress (R) meetings, 31.8% say that there is not a single party to which they shall never vote; 13.6% do not know or have not answered the question; 45.5% declare that they shall never vote for the Jana Sangh; 4.5% shall never vote for the Communist party; and the same percentage shall never vote for the Congress (R). Of those who have attended the Congress (O) meetings, 10% have stated that there is not a single party for which they shall never vote; 60% have declared that they shall never vote for the Congress (R); 20% shall never vote for the Communist party, and 10% shall never vote for the Muslim League. Of those who have attended the Jana Sangh meetings, 6.3% have said that there is no party for which they shall never vote; 6.3% do not know or have not answered the question. 37.5% each have declared that they shall never vote for the Congress (R) and the Communist party; 12.5% have said that they shall never vote for the Jana Sangh. Of the respondent who attend the Congress (R) meetings, the percentage against the Jana Sangh is the highest (45.5%). Of those who attend the Congress (O) meetings, the percentage who dislike the Congress (R) most is the highest (60%); and of the women who attended the Jana Sangh meetings, the percentage who dislike the Congress (R) and the Communist party most is the highest (37.5% for each).

Institutionalization

Institutionalization is another indication of participation in politics. Membership of the voluntary organizations is one aspect of institutionalization. Of the respondents, 76.6% have replied that they are not members of any voluntary organization; 11.3% are members of social reformist associations; 4.4% are members of caste and community associations; 3.5% are members of professional associations; and 4.2% are members of other women's organizations. Only 4.3% of the respondents are office-bearers of the associations of which they are members.

It can be said that the degree of institutionalization at the membership level is quite moderate among women considering their general status in Indian society. It may, however, be added that active participation in voluntary organizations in the form of holding office is rather very low. Their interest in social reformist associations is relatively higher.

The socio-economic background of the non-member respondents indicates that 21.6% belong to young age-group; 49.5% belong to middle age-group; and 28.8% belong to aged group. The percentage of women of the middle age-group in women's association is: 68.8% in social and reformist organizations; 60% in professional organizations, and 83% in caste and community organizations.

It will be interesting to know whether institutionalization of the respondents has any relation to their participation in agitational activities. Of the non-members, 79.3% have not taken part in agitational activities; 15.3% have taken part in *morcha* and

Politicization of Women in Gujarat 103

demonstrations; and 2.7% each have taken part in *satyagraha* and *dharna*. If we turn to the member group, we find that of those who are members of social and reformist organizations, 62.5% have not taken part in agitational activities, and 25% have taken part in *morcha* and demonstrations. Of those who are members of caste and community organizations, 66.7% have not taken part in agitational activities, and 33.3% have taken part in *morcha* and demonstrations.

It would be worthwhile to know whether institutionalization of the respondents has any relation to their voting behaviour. It is found from the data that of the non-member respondents, 40.5% have voted for the Congress (R); 19.8% have voted for the Jana Sangh; 7.2% have voted for the Congress (O); 17.1% have not voted; and 12.6% do not know or have not answered the question.

Regarding the member group of the women who are the members of social reformist organizations, 56.3% have voted for the Congress (O); 25% have voted for the Jana Sangh; 18.8% have voted for the Congress (R). But in the case of women who are members of professional organizations; 80% have voted for the Congress (R) and 20% have voted for the Jana Sangh. None of them voted for the Congress (O). In the case of those who are members of caste and community organizations, 16.7% have voted for the Jana Sangh; 33.3% have not voted; and 16.7% do not know or have not answered the question. Thus, among the members of caste and community organizations, the Jana Sangh is the most popular party, with the Congress (R) following.

It is also interesting to know whether institutionalization of women has any relation to their party orientations and attitudes. We find from the data that of the non-member women, 18.9% do not feel closeness to any party, and 35.1% do not know or have not answered the question. Regarding the remaining non-members, 20.7% feel closeness to the Jana Sangh, followed by Congress (R) (16.2%), Congress (O) (6.3%), and the Swatantra Party (1.8%) and the Communist party (0.9%).

Among the members of social and reformist organizations, 56.3% do not feel close to any party; 25% feel close to the Jana Sangh; 12.5% feel close to the Congress (O); and 6.3% feel close to the Congress (R). Among the women who are members of professional organizations, 60% feel close to the Congress (R); 20% each feel close to the Jana Sangh and the Socialist Party. And in the case of women who are members of caste and community organizations, 50% feel close to the Congress (R); 33.3% feel close to the Jana Sangh; and 16.7% either do not know or they have not answered the question. On the whole, institutionalized women feel more close to the Congress (R).

The pattern of party rejection among institutionalized women is interesting. In the case of those who are members of social and reformist organizations, 18.8% have stated that there is no party which they shall never vote for; 31.3% each have stated that they shall never vote for the Congress (R) and the Communist party; 12.5% have said that they shall never vote for the Muslim League. Thus, one can see that the so-called leftist parties are not very popular among the women who are members of social and reformist organizations. In the case of women who are members of professional organizations, 20% have said that there is no party which they shall never vote for, while 20% each say that they shall never vote for the Congress (R) and the Jana Sangh. On the other hand, 40% say that they shall never vote for the Communist party. Lastly, in the case of women who are members of caste and community organizations, 16.7% say that there is no party which they shall never vote for, 33.3% say that they shall never vote for the Congress (R), and 16.7% each say that they shall never vote for the Congress (O), the Swatantra, and the Communist party. Thus, in this group of institutionalized women, the Congress (R) is more unpopular than any other party.

Agitational Activities

The part taken in agitational activities by women indicates how they feel concerned about the issues in which they actively participate. From the answers we have found that 73.8% have not taken part in any agitational activities; 19.1% have taken part in *morcha* and demonstrations; 3.6% each have taken part in *dharna* and *satyagraha*. Thus, active participation in agitational activities is quite significant (more than 26% have taken part in such activities) for it belies the assumption that women are more confined to the four walls of the house.

Of women who participate in *satyagraha*, 60% belong to the aged group and 40% belong to the middle age-group. *Satyagraha* as a method of agitation, it seems, is not popular in the young age-group. In the case of women who participate in *morcha* and demonstrations, 67.9% belong to the middle age-group, 21.4% to the aged group; and

10.7% to the young age-group. This method of agitation is more popular in the middle age-group. Also in the case of women who participate in *dharna*, 60% belong to the middle age-group and 40% to the aged group. The majority of women who belong to the young age-group (89.7%) do not take part in agitational activities; only 10.3% women of young age take part in *morcha* and demonstrations, as compared to the middle age-group (68.8%) and the aged group (71.8%).

There seems to be no significant relationship between the caste of the respondents and their participation in agitation. We find the higher percentage of upper castes in both agitating and non-agitating women, in comparison with the so-called lower castes.

We should also know whether there is any relationship between participation in agitational activities and education of respondents.

Morcha and demonstrations are more popular among the highly educated women (50%) than among the less educated women (42.9%). In the case of *satyagraha*, the less educated women take more part (60%) than the highly educated women (40%). Also in the case of *dharna*, the less educated women take more part (80%) than the highly educated (20%).

Occupation-wise, of the women who take part in *morcha* and demonstrations, 57% are housewives, 28.6% are professional women; and 14.3% are working women. On the other hand, of the women who take part in *dharna*, 80% are housewives and 20% are professional women. Of all the occupational groups of the respondents including housewives, more women who belong to professional group are found to be participating in agitational activities than any other group. In the professional group, only 30.8% women do not take part in agitational activities while the corresponding figure for housewives and working women are 75.2% and 77.8% respectively; 61.5% of the professional women take part in *morcha* and demonstrations (in the case of housewives and working women the corresponding figures are 15.8% and 22.2% respectively); and 7.7% take part in *dharna*.

Of the women who take part in *morcha* and demonstrations, 57.1% have no income of their own; 7.1% fall in the lower income group; 17.8% fall in the middle income group; 17.8% fall in the higher income group. Therefore, one can say that the women who belong to the middle income and higher income groups take more part in *morcha* and demonstrations than the women of lower income group.

Of the respondents participating in *morcha* and demonstrations,

42.9% belong to the middle income group, 46.6% to the higher income group; and 3.6% to the lower income group. In the case of women who take part in *dharna,* 60% belong to the middle income group, 20% to the higher income group, and the remaining 20% do not have any income. Thus, more women belonging to the middle and higher income groups take more part in agitational activities than women who belong to the lower income group.

Another interesting finding is regarding the relationship between exposure to mass media and level of participation in agitational activities. Of the women who take part in *satyagraha,* 60% read soft-liners; 20% read hard-liners, and 20% read soft-liners and hard-liners. In the case of women who take part in *morcha* and demonstrations, 39.3% read soft-liners; 32.1% read hard-liners; and 25% read both types of newspaper. Of the total women who take part in *dharna,* 80% read soft-liners and 20% read hard-liners.

When the figures of hard-liner readers are compared with those of the soft-liner readers, it is found that of the respondents who read the hard-liners, 60.7% do not take part in agitational activities (the corresponding figures for the soft-liners is 65.4%); 32.1% take part in *morcha* and demonstrations (the corresponding figure for the soft-liners is 21.2%), and 3.6% each take part in *satyagraha* and *dharna* (the corresponding figures for the soft-liners are 5.8% and 7.7% respectively). Here one finds a correlation between participation in *morcha* and demonstrations and reading of hard-line newspaper.

Again, those who take part in *morcha* and demonstrations, hear radio more (85.7%) than any other agitating group (the corresponding figure for the *satyagraha* group is 60%, and for *dharna* group 60%). Of the daily listners, 58.9% do not take part in agitational activities, and the corresponding figure in the case of sometimes listeners is 79.4%. In the case of agitating women, it is found that of the daily listeners of radio, 32.9% take part in *morcha* and demonstration; 4.1% take part in *satyagraha*; 4.1% take part in *dharna*; and the corresponding figures of sometimes listeners are 8.8%, 5.9%, and 5.9% respectively. Thus, one can say that there is a correlation between listening to radio daily and participation in *morcha* and demonstrations.

Further, it may be of some interest to know if participation in a particular agitational activity has any relation to voting for a particular party. We have found that of the respondents who have taken part in *morcha* and demonstrations, 46.4% have voted for the

Congress (R); 28.6% for the Jana Sangh; 14.3% for the Congress (O), and 10.7% do not know or have not answered the question. Of the total women who take part in *satyagraha*, 40% have voted for the Congress (O); 20% for the Congress (R); 20% for the independent candidates; and 20% have not voted. All the women who take part in *dharna* have voted for the Jana Sangh.

Has participation in agitational activities any relation to the feeling of closeness towards any party? Of the women who take part in *morcha* and demonstrations, 32.1% feel close to the Jana Sangh; 28.6% feel close to the Congress (R); 3.6% feel close to the Congress (O). Of the women taking part in *dharna*, 80% feel close to the Jana Sangh.

Regarding the negative attitudes of agitating women towards parties, 20% feel that there is no party which they shall never vote for, 40% shall never vote for the Congress (R); and another 40% shall never vote for the Jana Sangh. In the case of women who take part in *morcha* and demonstrations, 35.7% shall never vote for the Congress (R); 21.4% shall never vote for the Communist party; and 17.9% shall never vote for the Jana Sangh.

The main issues for which the respondents (12.4%) agitated are: price rise and other economic issues such as non-availability of essential commodities. (Of the 26% who have participated in agitational activities, this figure comes to about nearly half of it.) Of those who have agitated, 5.5% have agitated on the issues of pay and wages and dearness allowances; 4.8% have participated in other agitations, mainly in the recent 'Nav Nirman' agitation in Gujarat; 3.5% have not responded to the question.

Another interesting point to know is whether there is any relationship between the nature of issues of agitations and the socio-economic status of the respondents. Of those who agitate on economic issues the majority, i.e. 61.1%, belong to the middle age-group, 27.8% belong to the aged group, and 11.1% belong to the young age-group. The same is true in the case of women who agitate on issues of pay and wages. Of the respondents who agitate on these issues 87.5% belong to middle age-group and 12.5% to the aged group, though on other issues – chief among these is the recent 'Nav Nirman' agitation – women belonging to both the age-groups, middle as well as aged, have participated in equal numbers.

Caste-wise, our data suggest that the upper caste women feel more strongly about the economic issues and about pay and wages than the lower caste women. Of the women who agitate on economic issues, 77.8% belong to the upper castes. In the same way, of the respondents who agitate on the issue of pay and wages, 87.5% belong to the upper castes. On other issues – notably the recent 'Nav Nirman' agitation – of the respondents who have taken part in this agitation, 71.7% belong to the upper castes.

Regarding the educational status of women who participate in agitations on different issues, nearly 50% of them are educated up to primary and secondary levels, while 38.9% are highly educated. On the other hand, of the women agitating on issue of pay and wages, 87.5% are highly educated and 12.5% are educated up to SSC level. Highly educated women agitate more on economic and other related issues than women with less education and women who are illiterate.

Regarding the occupation of women who participate in agitational activities on different issues, it is found from the data that the housewives are in the forefront in the agitations on economic issues. Of those who agitate on these issues, 88.9% belong to this group and 11.1% belong to the professional group. Also in the case of other issues specially the 'Nav Nirman' agitation, 71.4% women are housewives, 14.3% are working women, and 14.3% are professional women. On the other hand, of those who agitate on the issue of pay and wages, 62.5% are working women and 37.5% are professionals.

Regarding the voting pattern (1972 elections), we find that all those who take part in agitations on economic issues, 38.9% have voted for the Congress (R); 27.8% have voted for the Congress (O), and 27.8% have voted for the Jana Sangh. On the other hand, of the women who participate on the issue of pay and wages, 62.5% have voted for the Congress (R) and 37.5% have voted for the Jana Sangh. Thus, one can infer that the women participating in agitations on economic issues vote for the opposition parties more than the Congress (R), but the same is not true with the women who agitate for pay and wages.

Attendance at 'Study Circle'

Political parties and voluntary organizations conduct 'study circles' to attract and orient the new entrants to their organizations, and recruit them in their fold. These study circles not only provide important information regarding the positions they take on different social, political, and economic issues, but also reorient the participants to their ideologies and programmes, and thus provide important channels of recruitment. The attendance at these circles thus provides an indication of the political as well as the social institutional participation. Only 3.4% women have attended such study circles, and 2.1% women have benefited from them, while 1.3% have benefited less from the study circles. Here also the data suggest that the level of institutionalized participation, whether social or political, is rather low.

Participation in Elections

Participation in elections, whether through voting or through active election campaign, is an important indicator of political mobilization and political participation. Elections not only provide an opportunity to people for choosing their representatives but also give them scope for participation in the wider political process.

A study of their voting behaviour in the last three General Elections (1967, 1971, 1972) was done. From the responses it is found that nearly half of the respondents do not remember whom they had voted for in the 1967 elections, both in the Vidhan Sabha and in the Lok Sabha elections. Of the respondents, 21% had not voted in the General Elections; 20% had voted for the (Undivided) Congress party; 2% had voted for the Jana Sangh; and 7% had voted for the other parties including the independent candidates.

In the 1971 election for the Lok Sabha, 21.2% women do not remember for whom they have voted; 10.3% have not voted; 40% have voted for the Congress (R); 17.9% have voted the Congress (O); 0.8% have voted for the Jana Sangh; and the rest for other parties.

From the answers regarding 1972 Vidhan Sabha elections, it is found that only 10.7% do not remember whom they have voted in the elections; 15.2% women have not voted; 37.9% have voted for the Congress (R); 12.4% have voted for the Congress (O); 21.1% have voted for the Jana Sangh; and 2.7% have voted for the independents.

If we compare the party choices of the respondents of 1971 and 1972 elections, there are some important points which deserve our notice:

1. Both the Congress parties have lost their popularity with women voters, though with varying degrees. The Congress (O) has lost more in comparison to the Congress (R). The Congress (R) was able to retain only 51% of its 1971 voters.

2. The Jana Sangh is the main beneficiary from the losses of the Congress parties. In the 1971 Lok Sabha elections, only 0.8% women

respondents voted for it, while in the 1972 Vidhan Sabha elections more than 21% have voted for it.

3. Independent candidates have also lost their appeal to women voters. In the 1971 election, 9% women voted for them; in 1972 elections only 2.7% have voted for them. It confirms the general polarization of choice in different parties among voters as a whole.

4. The degree of electoral participation of women has also fluctuated. In the 1967 elections, 20.7% had not participated in voting. In the 1971 election, under the highly politicized and mobilized atmosphere of 'Indira wave', participation of women has increased; only 10.3% respondents had not participated in voting in the 1971 election. But in the 1972 election much of that vigour had worn off and the voters seem to have become a little disillusioned. A sense of alienation was also discernible. So the level of the electoral participation of women went down (more than 15% respondents did not participate in voting in the 1972 Vidhan Sabha elections).

An attempt has been made at finding the correlation between the party choice in the 1972 election and the occupation of the respondents. Of the total women who have voted for the Congress (R), 69.1% are housewives; 12.7% are professional women; 10.9% are working women. In the case of women who have voted for the Congress (O), 72.2% are housewives; 16.7% are professional women; and 11.1% are working women. And also in the case of women who have voted for the Jana Sangh, 75% are housewives; 9.4% each are professional women and working women. From the point of view of occupation of the respondents, we find that of the total housewives, 37.6% have voted for the Congress (R); 23.8% have voted for the Jana Sangh; 12.9% have voted for the Congress (O). Of the working women, 33.3% have voted for the Congress (R); 16.7% have voted for the Jana Sangh; 11.1% have voted for the Congress (O). Of the total professional women, 53% have voted for the Congress (R); 23% have voted for the Congress (O); and 23% have voted for the Jana Sangh.

It can be said that in all the occupational groups including housewives and professional women, more women have voted for the Congress (R) than any other group. The Jana Sangh is equally liked by housewives and professional women.

If economic status of the respondents is related with their voting behaviour, we get interesting findings. Of all those, who have voted for the Congress (R), 23.6% belong to the lower income group; 54.5% belong to the middle income group. On the other hand, of those who

Politicization of Women in Gujarat

have voted for the Congress (O), 5.6% belong to the lower income group; 38.9% belong to the middle income group; and 55.6% belong to the higher income group. In the case of women who have voted for the Jana Sangh, 15.6% belong to the lower income group; 37.6% of the middle income group; and 46.9% to the higher income group. The Congress (O) has the support more of higher income group voters than any other party. The Jana Sangh follows it. In the case of the middle and lower income group voters, we find that the Congress (R) is more popular.

Owning durable assets, such as building, etc., is taken as another indicator of one's economic status. It is found from the data that of all those who have voted for the Congress (R), 52.7% do not have buildings of their own; 3.6% have a building with value up to Rs.10,000; 23.6% have a building with value up to Rs.25,000; 12.7% have a building with value up to Rs.50,000; and 3.6% own a building worth above Rs.50,000. From those who have voted for the Congress (O), we find that 15.7% do not have a building of their own; 11.1% have a building of value up to Rs.10,000; 11.1% have a building worth up to Rs.25,000; 44.4% have a building with value up to Rs.50,000; and 16.4% have a building costing above Rs.50,000. In the case of those who have voted for the Jana Sangh, we find that 24.4% do not have a building of their own; 3.1% have one with value up to Rs.10,000; 18.9% have a house worth up to Rs.25,000; 34.4% have a building worth up to Rs.50,000; and 6.3% have a building with a value of above Rs.50,000. Of those who have not voted in the election, 45.5% do not have a building of their own, 18.2% have one with value up to Rs.10,000; 22.7% have a building with value up to Rs.50,000; and 4.5% have one with value above Rs.50,000. In the case of more affluent respondents (having a building valued above Rs.50,000), it is found that they like the Congress (O) and the Jana Sangh more than any other party.

It is interesting to know whether exposure to mass media has any impact on the voting behaviour of the respondents. Of the total respondents who do not read newspapers, 53.8% have voted for the Congress (R); 2.6% have cast their votes in favour of the Congress (O); 15.4% have voted for the Jana Sangh; and 15.4% have not exercised their right to vote. Now, of those, who read the soft-line newspapers 36.5% voted for the Congress (R); 15.4% for the Congress (O); 23.1% for the Jana Sangh; and 11.5% have not voted. Of the women who read the hard-line newspapers, 35.7% have voted for the Jana Sangh; 25% for the Congress (R); 14.3% for the Congress (O). Thus, the soft-line newspaper readers love more the Congress (R) than any other party, while the hard-line newspaper readers prefer the Jana Sangh to any other party.

Regarding the listening of radio, it is found that out of those who do not hear radio, 61.9% have voted for the Congress (R); 19.0% for the Jana Sangh; 9.5% have not voted; and 9.5% either do not know or have not answered the question. Of the daily listeners of the radio, 30% have voted for the Congress (R); 16.4% for the Congress (O); 30% for the Jana Sangh; and 13.7% have not voted. Of the 'sometime listeners' of the radio, 32.4% have voted for the Congress (R); 14.7% for the Congress (O); 8.8% for the Jana Sangh; 23.5% have not voted; and 17.6% do not know or have not answered the question. Of those, who listen the radio rarely, 52.9% have voted for the Congress (R); 5.9% for the Congress (O); 17.6% for the Jana Sangh; 11.8% have not voted; and another 11.8% have not answered the question. It seems that radio has a negligible impact on the voting behaviour.

It will be very interesting to compare the voting behaviour of the respondents in the 1971 Lok Sabha election.

Membership of Political Party

Nearly 92% respondents are not members of any political party, and 2% either do not know or have not answered the question. Only 6% are members of political parties: 4% are members of the Congress (O), and 1% each are members of the Congress (R) and the Jana Sangh. It is not surprising to know the low level of party membership of women because the level of party membership of general population is not more than 3 to 9% in India.

Participation of women in representative bodies such as legislative bodies, Municipalities, Panchayats etc., is also not high. It is known from the data that 95.8% of the respondents are not members of any representative body; 2.1% are members; of them one is a member of Municipal Corporation and one of village Panchayat.

Political Socialization

A useful concept in the frame of the study was political socialization. The respondents were asked as to which factors were responsible in influencing them in taking part in political movement or in joining a political party. Regarding the factors which have influenced their political socialization, 32.4% have stated that specific political events have influenced them to participate in political movement, 13.1% have been influenced by individuals; 9.7% have been influenced by ideology; another 9.7% have been influenced by family tradition; 6.7% have been influenced by books or literature; and 28.5% either do not know or they have not answered the question. Among the politically socialized respondents, the percentage of women who are socialized into politics by specific political events is higher than any other group. The influence of ideology, books or literature as an agent of political socialization is not very significant. The same is true with family tradition also. But influence of an individual as an agent of political socialization is significant.

Political Participation: Perceptions and Opinions

It would be interesting to know the perceptions and opinions of women regarding their political participation. From the analysis of the responses, it is found that 29% think there is scope for political participation of women in the Indian social system. This is quite significant from the point of view of women's dormant status in the Indian society. Of the respondents, 51.7% do not think that there is scope for political participation owing to domestic and household responsibilities; 6.9% feel this owing to the attitudes of relatives; 5.5% attribute this to social attitudes; and 2.1% think the lack of scope to less chances given to them by political parties; 4.8% do not know or have not answered the question.

Regarding the educational background of respondents, who think there is scope for political participation in Indian social system, 33.4% are highly educated (degree-holders and above); 28.6% are educated up to primary level; and 7.1% are illiterate. Thus, a correlation may be established between the education of the respondents and their opinion regarding the scope for political participation of women in the Indian social system.

Of the respondents who do not think there is scope for political participation owing to domestic responsibilities, 20% are illiterate; 56% are educated up to lower and middle level; and 21.3% are highly educated. Thus, lack of scope for political participation owing to domestic responsibilities is ascribed by women with middle and lower levels of education more than those who are highly educated. The same is the case with those who ascribed the lack of political participation to the attitudes of relatives: 80% of such respondents belong to the lower and middle level of education, while 20% belong to the higher level of education. Of the respondents who have ascribed social attitude as the reason for lack of political participation, 50% belong to the lower and middle level of education, and 25% are illiterate. Thus, the high level of education among women is a significant variable in forming opinion and increasing their confidence regarding the scope for political participation in the Indian social system.

If this perception of the respondents is correlated with their economic status, the following points emerge. Of the women who think there is scope for political participation in the Indian social system, 57% belong to the higher income group, and 30.9% belong to the lower and middle income groups. In the case of those women who have related the lack of political participation with domestic responsibilities, 62.7% belong to the lower and middle income groups, and 29.4% belong to the higher income group. The same is true with those who have attributed the lack of political participation to the attitudes of relatives and societal attitudes. Thus, economic status is also a significant variable in forming the opinion regarding the scope for political participation by women in the Indian social system.

Another question was asked to know the respondents' opinion regarding the effect on domestic happiness, if the husband and wife belong to different political parties or hold different political opinions. From the answers, it is found that 58.6% respondents do not think that domestic happiness will be affected if husband and wife belong to different parties or hold different political opinions; 30.9% have answered that such differences do affect domestic happiness; 10.5% do not know or have not answered the question. Those respondents who believe that such differences affect domestic happiness have also suggested the ways to nullify such influence: 22.1% have suggested that both husband and wife should show tolerance to each other and respect each other's opinion and belief; 6.2% have suggested that women should submit to the wishes of the husband, and act according to their wishes; 2.6% have suggested other ways.

If we correlate this opinion of the respondents with their education, again some interesting points are noticed. Of those women who have opined that such differences will not affect the domestic happiness, 61.2% are educated up to lower and middle levels of education, and

27.1% are highly educated; 10.6% are illiterate.

A third question was asked to know the respondents' perceptions regarding greater participation by women in political affairs. The responses show that 46.2% respondents have opined that there should not be greater participation by women in politics, 4.2% either do not know or they have not answered the question. The fact that nearly 50% of them have opined that there should be greater participation by women in politics is very significant. The reasons given by the respondents for greater participation of women in politics are interesting: 40% think that greater participation will generate awareness regarding their rights and status and lead to general progress in women's status. 4.3% believe that it will help in solving their problems; 4.3% think that there should be equal opportunity for males and females regarding participation in political affairs.

The respondents were also asked whether they think that women should keep away from politics. From the responses it is found that 36.6% believe that they should keep away from politics; 8.2% do not know or have not answered the question; 55.2% are categorical that women should not keep away from politics. The reasons given for such an opinion are: 37.9% respondents have opined that it will retard the development and progress of women; 9.7% feel that by keeping away from politics, women's problems will not be solved; 7.6% have given other reasons. However, 28.2% respondents think that participation in politics will hamper their domestic duties, which they consider to be their first commitment; 8.4% have opined that politics being a dirty game, women should keep away from it.

Two questions were asked to know about women's perceptions to political leadership: which political leader was liked most by the respondents in their young age, and which political leader is liked most by the respondents at present. From the responses interesting points emerge.

Gandhiji comes first among the political leaders who were liked most by respondents in their young age (61.4%). Next comes Jawaharlal Nehru (17.2%), followed by Sardar Patel (9.7%). Golvalkarji (Guruji) was liked most by 2.8% in their young age, while 3.4% have named other leaders as their most favourite leaders. (Indulal Yagnik, popularly known as 'Induchacha', is the most prominent among other leaders.) Only 0.7% have said that no body was liked by them in their young age; 4.8% do not know or have not answered the question.

For the second question, which political leader they like most at present, very interesting answers are received; 26.8% respondents say that they like Mrs. Indira Gandhi most; 18.6 like Morarji Desai; 8.3% have shown their preference for Atal Bihari Vajpayee; 2.8% have named Hitendra Desai as their most favourite political leader; and 7% have given other names as their favourite political leaders; 4.8% do not know or have not answered the question. But 31.7% respondents have stated that they do not like any political leader. The fact that as many as 31.7% dislike all the present political leaders shows how strongly they feel about the present leadership. If we compare the figures of perception of political leadership of their young age with that of the present, the difference becomes more sharper. Only 0.7% say that nobody was liked by them in their young age, while 31.7% say that no body is liked by them at present.

It also shows a feeling of alienation among the respondents towards the present political leadership.

The last question deals with the perception of women regarding the role of franchise. It is found that 10.3% think that they will not lose much if they are deprived of their franchise; 35.3% do not know or have not answered the question. But the remaining 54.4% have stated that if they are deprived of their franchise, they will lose very much. Of these, 15.2% think that without the right of franchise, they will remain unrepresented; 12.5% believe that they will remain in the darkness about politics; 8.8% have stated that without franchise no attention will be paid to their problems; 7.6% have asserted that on grounds of equality, it cannot be denied to females only; 4.8% have stated that without franchise, they will not be able to perform their duties as citizens; 5.5% have given other reasons. The fact that as many as 54.4% respondents feel very strongly about their franchise is encouraging; but at the same time as many as 45.6% do not attach much importance to it.

Conclusions

It is hazardous to construct any definitive formulations of women's political behaviour in this study. The inadequate nature of the data precludes such a formulation. However, certain patterns do emerge which help us either to substantiate some of our hypotheses around which the frame of our study is built or to prompt us to suggest certain projections.

Caste is not a very significant variable in a woman's calculus of politics; nor so much her education. Some of the important variables are: exposure to the mass media, attendance at party meetings, and participation in agitational activities.

In the politicization and participation continuum the husband plays an important role in shaping the political component of woman's behaviour. There is a positive relationship between woman's exposure to media and her discussion with her husband. The participation level of those women who discuss politics with their husbands is higher.

Thus, family provides an important setting for the woman, and the husband occupies a critical position in her political syndrome. The family performs an important role in her politicization, and it emerges as the most significant social institution in developing the political attitude of women in Gujarat.

It is the general economic issues of daily concern that agitate housewives most. The growing discontent and resentment against the authority are motivated by the deteriorating conditions on the economic front.

Among the various sections, the middle aged group of women seems to have developed the most definitive behaviour pattern (in terms of discussion of politics, discussion with husbands and family members, participation in agitation, and on economic issues).

A large number of women think that they should take part in public life. More than half of the respondents also underline the importance and role of the women's suffrage. A surprisingly high number (71%) perceive that the woman has the opportunity of participating in public life. Thus, a significant proportion of our sample, though disoriented towards party and leadership, is ready for a greater participation in public life.

References

1. This is also underlined by responses to our relevant question in the study.
2. Pravin Sheth, "Status of Women in Gujarat" a report submitted to ICSSR, New Delhi (April, 1974).
3. For details, *ibid*.
4. Observations of Almond and Verba, *Civil Culture* (pp. 327-328), are modified here to suit the Indian context.
5. Based on Dowson and Prewilt, *Political Socialisation* (1969).
6. *Ibid*.
7. *Ibid*.

POLITICIZATION OF WOMEN IN MAHARASHTRA

P.N. Limaye

Introduction

This survey was conducted mainly in Poona, with a sample of 150. Theoretically, it would have been advisable to have the respondents chosen on a random sample basis, but was not possible due to many practical difficulties of time and resources. Therefore, a purposive sample was taken to include women from various categories, classified according to age, religion, caste, educational attainments, and socio-economic status. A deliberate attempt was made to include also the highly politicized women, social workers, housewives, etc. The original survey did not include any Scheduled Caste respondents. Therefore, a special survey was carried out, interviewing 25 respondents from the Scheduled Caste. They have been analysed separately. All other groups are respresented in the sample, though the number of some groups is very small.

A questionnaire was finalized after pre-testing it on a group of 15 respondents of various categories.

The survey was conducted by five lady investigators who were oriented to the interview techniques. The respondents generally cooperated with the investigators, and there was hardly any deliberate evasion. Only in a few cases there was reluctance to disclose incomes of the family and the parties for which they had voted.

Limitations

As the number of respondents in some categories was too small, any valid comparison enabling us to make generalizations is not possible. The total number of respondents was also too small. These two factors severely limit the wider applicability of the findings of the survey.

Description of the Sample

Table 1 gives the composition of the sample. The sample is classified on the basis of religion, language, caste, occupation, and income.

TABLE 1.

The Sample N = 150

(a) Religion	
Hindus	123
Muslims	6
Christians	10
Jains	10
Parsis	1
(b) Mother-tongue	
Marathi	107
Hindi	7
Tamil	4
Telugu	2
Gujarati	10
Kannada	4
English	1
Sindhi	3
Bengali	2
Konkani	2
Marwari	1
Punjabi	1
Urdu	6
(c) Caste	
Brahmin	87
Intermediary	11
Maratha	23
Others	29
(d) Occupation	
Professionals	45
Government and private service	25
Manual labourers	6
Housewives	74
(e) Income	
Less than 5000	29
500-1000	43
1000-1500	29
1500-2500	32
2500 and above	14
Not mentioned	3

There is a predominance of the Hindu middle class Brahmin women. The respondents belonging to the other religions too are represented, but in a very small number. The mother-tongue of the majority is Marathi. Occupation-wise, the sample is divided equally between housewives and self-earning women.

Method of Analysis

The focus of the enquiry was on the assesment of the degree of political participation of women. The questionnaire included a set of questions which sought to extract information indicating the extent of participation. An attempt was made to give scales by attaching scores to each factor, so as to indicate the range of participation, the exposure to political communication, and also to determine their socio-

TABLE 2
Socio-economic status

Total income (Rs.)	Property (Rs.)	Things owned	Dependants
0- 5000	0- 5000	Nil	5 and above
5000-10000	5000-10000	1-2	2-3
10000 and above	10000 and above	2 and above	2-1

0- 8 = Low
8-16 = Middle
16-24 = High

TABLE 3
Political communication scores

Reading of newspapers		Attendance at public meetings		Discussing politics	
No reading	−0	No attendance	−0	No discussion	−0
Reads 2 daily	−1	Attending occasionally	−1	Discussion occasionally with family member	−1
Reads 3 or more	−2	Attending regularly	−2	Discussion regularly with family other groups	−2
Reads newspapers, magazine, weeklies	−3			Discussion with both	−3

0-3 = Low
3-5 = Medium
6-8 = High

TABLE 4

Political participation scores

Voting (1)	Volume organization membership (2)	Party membership (3)	Election campaign (4)	Member of political body (5)	Participation in political movements (6)	Attending study classes (7)
Not voted —0	Not member —0	Not member —0	Not participated —0	Not member —0	Not member —0	Not attended —0
Voted once —1	Less than 3 years —2	Less than 3 years —1	In one —1	In one —1	In one —1	Attended occasionally —1
Voted in all elections —2	More than 5 years —2	More than 5 years —2	More than one —2	More than one —2	More than one —2	Attended regularly —2

Low 0-7, 0-5.
Medium 7-14, 5-10, 20,
High 14-20, 10-14,

economic status. (Refer to Tables 2, 3 and 4.) There is bound to be some degree of arbitrariness in the construction of such scores, especially on the socio-economic status.

The four factors that were considered while scoring the socio-economic status are: (a) total income; (b) the number of dependants; (c) the total property owned; (d) the articles possessed (e.g., radio, television, car, etc.). Three broad categories of high, medium, and low level of socio-economic status were constructed.

The factors that have gone into scoring on political communication are: (a) attendance at public meetings; (b) reading of newspapers, magazines, etc.; (c) discussion on politics with family members or other groups.

For political participation, the following factors were considered: (a) voting in elections; (b) membership of voluntary organizations; (c) participation in political activities; (d) participation in election campaigns, and attendance at study circles.

On the basis of the above scores, the respondents were categorized into high, medium, and low levels. Other sets of questions try to assess the political awareness and political attitudes of the respondents.

A higher degree of political awareness, high score on political communication, and high perception may not necessarily lead to a higher degree of participation. But, normally, it is expected that a higher degree of involvement will necessarily presuppose the presence of the above-mentioned factors. Therefore, the relevant factors were scored, and an effort was made to establish such correlations.

Politicization and political participation may be affected by socio-economic factors. It is therefore necessary to find out the correlations of political participation with caste, religion, education, occupation, income, etc.

On the basis of the above correlations, profiles of women of different groups are attempted. They are: (a) highly politicized women; (b) profile according to education; (c) profile according to religion; (d) caste; (e) profile of self-earning women; and (f) profile according to language.

Profile of the Highly Politicized Women

Twenty-six respondents (17.33%) are politicized to a certain degree. The levels of politicization, of course, vary, but certain minimum criteria for politicization can be laid down: (a) regular reading of the newspaper; (b) attending public meetings; (c) discussing relevant political issues; (d) definite sympathies or hostilities towards political parties; (e) participation, occasional or continuous, in political movements; (f) attending study classes of parties or volunteer organizations. This may indicate the motivation, the cognitive and cognitive maps, and the degree and level of participation.

It is not easy to establish exact correlations between the levels or degree of politicization and variables which motivated the politicization process. The relation may be uni-causal such as educational attainments, class and caste consciousness, family tradition; or multi-causal (the result of a simultaneous operation of some of the above factors). There is another limitation for hazarding any kind of generalization regarding the causal relationship, because the sample may not be evenly distributed and, hence, may have a specific rather than a wider general application.

TABLE 5

Highly politicized women N = 26
SES scores

	High	Medium	Low
SES	11	7	8
Political communication	19	7	—
Political participation	17	9	—

TABLE 6

Highly politicized women: SES scores according to parties

Party	High	Medium	Low
Congress	4	0	0
Jana Sangh	2	1	0
Socialist	1	3	4
Communist	0	1	1
Hindu Maha Sabha	0	1	2
Non-party members	4	0	1
Political organization	0	0	1
Total	11	6	9

There are 26 cases of women who are politicized to a greater extent than the rest. Twenty of them were/are active members of political parties classified according to their party affiliations (see Table 7).

TABLE 7

Congress	4
Socialist	8
Jana Sangh	3
Hindu Maha Sabha	3
CPI	2
Total	20
Member of political volunteer organization	1
Non-party member but highly politicized	5

It is difficult to pin-point any particular factor which might have motivated the decision of the respondents for political participation or of becoming members of political parties or organizations.

A significant feature of this category is that only two are non-Brahmins, i.e., Marathas. The rest are all Brahmins coming from the middle class or the lower middle class. This might be due to the fact that Brahmins have a long political tradition and heritage in the political process of Maharashtra in general and Poona in particular, and it is likely that tradition was the chief motivation.

Considering educational attainments, two respondents have primary education, seven have secondary education, but the majority, 17, are either graduates or post-graduates. This, however, does not mean that it is only the highly educated women who are politicized. Some of them have in fact pursued their educational career even while they were active in politics. This suggests that while higher educational attainments may sharpen their analytical capacity and mature understanding of the complexities of the politicized processes, education as such cannot be considered as the prime factor responsible for their politicization.

Age-wise, most of them have crossed 40 years. Only three or four are below 30 years of age. Most of those in the former group started their political career before independence. Some of them participated in the *satyagraha* movements of 1930 and 1940. Their continuation in politics can be attributed to this.

It seems that there is no correlation between socio-economic status and party preferences. Those who are members of CPI do not necessarily come from the poor strata nor do the Jana Sangh adherents or supporters hail from the typical middle class.

This categorization is a very broad one. It is found that out of the

26, 11 belong to what may be termed rich, seven to upper middle class, and eight to lower middle class. The majority of the Congress and Jana Sangh workers in the sample belong to the rich and the majority of Socialists belong to middle and lower middle classes. Four out of five non-party women, who are radical in their views, however, belong to the rich class. Thus, no exact correlation between income and party alignment can be established (see Table 6).

Attitudes and opinions might be the functions of early socialization and participation rather than of socio-economic status.

It was found that the *most influential factor* in the motivation of politicization is *ideology*, followed closely by the influence of an individual and family tradition. Specific political events have relatively less influence than the above factors.

Generally, the women have followed the party lines of either their fathers or husbands. Their choice to participate actively in politics is not due to any single cause but due to a set of causes.

There is one case where the respondent is a member of the Jana Sangh, though her father was a Congress MLA, and she was a member of Rashtra Seva Dal (RSD) for eight years. She was previously a member of the Congress for four years. She accounts for her shift in her political preference for lack of sincere and devoted workers in the Congress. She had participated in the Goa *satyagraha* movement, voted for a Jana Sangh candidate in the 1972 elections to the State Assembly. She was attracted to the Jana Sangh, because of the ideology of the party and sincerity of the party workers.

Of the 26 respondents, more than half are of the opinion that Indian women have less scope in the political field due to societal attitudes, domestic responsibilities, attitudes of relatives, or due to lack of interest in women themselves.

Nine respondents, on the other hand, are of the opinion that there is plenty of scope in politics for women, and it is up to women to decide whether or not they desire participation.

Franchise is considered by most – twenty-four – of them as a fundamental right, and women would lose much if they are deprived of their right. The right may not have been used effectively, yet it is a means of expression and a way of participation, and hence women should not be deprived of it. Only two are of the opinion that deprivation of the voting right would not be much of a loss to women as it is not very effective.

It should be noted that out of these 26 respondents, two were members of Parliament and two were/are members of the Municipal Corporation.

Many of the respondents from this group, however, participate in socio-cultural activities. Some of them are also office-bearers of socio-cultural organizations.

Another matter of importance is that none of the respondents from the highly politicised group is a member of trade union.

There were different responses to the question whether allegiance to two different parties by husband and wife would affect domestic happiness. Eight (about 33%) are of the opinion that domestic happiness is in no way affected by political differences between husband and wife. They hold that the political and the domestic fields are totally different, and hence the question of affecting domestic happiness does not arise. Some are of the opinion, however, that political differences between husband and wife do affect domestic happiness, but they have a solution to offer, i.e., both should strive to accommodate each other's views and reach some kind of understanding. Two are of the opinion, however, that it being the tradition in the Indian society for the women to submit to the husband's opinion, the problem does not arise. This is, however, a perception of the prevailing Indian social custom. But no respondent from the highly politicized group suggests that in case of conflict the woman should submit to the will of the husband.

One respondent of this group may be considered separately, as she deviates in some respects from the normal pattern of politicized respondents described earlier. This is a Muslim lady, whose high degree of politicization is chiefly due to her membership of a radical Muslim voluntary organization (Muslim Satya Shodhak Samaj). This organization is recently established, and aims at reforming the Muslim community by radical social measures and bringing it into the political mainstream. Its policies and programmes are opposed by a sizable orthodox Muslims. The respondent is a graduate and a teacher, and has also a family background of politics as her father was a member of the SSP, providing another reason for her motivation to participate in a political movement. She is strongly opposed to communal parties, e.g., Muslim League, and thinks that they should be banned.

She has a clear perception of the political processes and strongly advocates larger participation by women in the political affairs of the country for their development. She thinks that in the Indian social system women have no scope for participation because of domestic responsibilities and attitudes of relatives. According to her, the societal attitude is much more hostile in the Muslim community as compared to the Hindu. It is a common observation that the degree of participation is much less in Muslim men, and almost negligible in Muslim women. This case, therefore, may be treated almost as an exception and may indicate the slow but definite trend of awakening in the newly socialized women in this part of the country.

Profile According to Education

An effort is being made here to analyse the political attitudes and participation of women and to correlate it with their educational attainments.

The respondents are classified into four classes: (a) graduates and above; (b) SSC and above (see Table 8); (c) up to SSC; and (d) illiterates. In all the four categories participation is low.

TABLE 8
Educational composition

Educational level	High	Medium	Low	Total
SES scores				
Illiterate	0	0	11	11
Up to SSC	8	21	21	50
Under-graduate	2	4	4	10
Graduate and post-graduate	35	41	3	79
Total	45	66	39	150
Political communication				
Illiterate	0	0	11	11
Up to SSC	11	13	26	50
Under-graduate	2	6	2	10
Graduate and post-graudate	35	29	15	79
Total	48	48	54	150
Political participation				
Illiterate	0	0	11	11
Up to SSC	5	5	40	50
Under-graduate	2	0	8	10
Graduate and post-graduate	10	8	61	79
Total	17	13	120	150

All the illiterates score low on participation, communication, and SES. In the second group of respondents, who have been educated up to SSC, the few that score high and medium high respectively come from the middle and lower classes. So also in the under-graduates group and the graduates and above group.

Here an attempt has been made to correlate not only education and participation but also SES. The relationship of SES to political participation is inverse. It can be summarized that higher the socio-economic status relatively lower is the degree of political involvement. While the scores of SES are on the descending level, the scores on participation are on the ascending level. The respondents belonging to higher economic status are relatively lower on participation score. No definite conclusion could be arrived at for those who score the lowest on the SES regarding their participation score, because of the inadequacy of the number of respondents in this group.

According to the data, political communication as such is not a determinant of political activity, as the communication scores for politically higher and middle SES groups are more or less similar.

We may therefore suggest that the level of political participation of Indian women does not seem to be the function of education per se or exposure to communication. Nevertheless, those who are politically more involved are educated to some extent, and education may sharpen their capacity for political awareness and political perceptions. It may also be suggested that higher SES score may have an inverse relationship with political participation.

Another significant feature that is discernible is that the majority of women in all the four groups – graduates and above, under-graduates, educated up to school, and illiterates – are of the opinion that there should be more participation by women. All the women belonging to the illiterate group, are of the opinion that there should be more participation by women. The perception of the importance of franchise seems to be similar in all the four groups. Only a small minority feel that they would not lose much if they are deprived of this right.

The majority of respondents are of the opinion that women have less scope in politics due to various factors such as domestic responsibilities, attitudes of relatives, and societal attitudes. The majority in two groups – graduates and above and under-graduates – feel that women do have scope. Here we may consider education as an effective factor affecting the perception of women. The majority of the respondents in all the groups feel that domestic happiness is in no way affected even if there are political differences between the husband and the wife. A small minority, however, feels that domestic happiness is affected by political differences between the husband and the wife.

Profile of the Self-Earning Women

Another line of enquiry was pursued to find out the relationship between the economic independence of women with their political attitudes, perceptions and involvement. In the sample, there are 76 self-earning respondents. They are classified into three categories: (a) professionals; (b) government and private service; and (c) manual labourers and artisans (see Table 9).

TABLE 9
Occupational composition

Occupation	High	Medium	Low	Total
		SES score		
Manual labourers	0	0	6	6
Government and private services	6	14	5	25
Professionals	19	24	2	45
Total	25	38	13	76
		Political communication		
Manual labourers	0	1	5	6
Government and private services	8	5	12	25
Professionals	21	16	8	45
Total	29	22	25	76
		Political participation		
Manual labourers	0	0	6	6
Government and private services	5	3	17	25
Professionals	4	10	31	45
Total	9	13	54	76

An effort was also made to ascribe scores on SES, communication, and participation. The professionals, as expected, revealed a high degree of educational attainment: 66.6% are post-graudates; 22.2% are graduates; and 11.12% are under-graduates. As regards their SES, all post-graduates score high on the SES. This is on the expected line as most of these are doctors, lawyers, etc. As seen in the education profile, the relationship between participation and higher educational attainment and SES is inverse.

Only nine of the respondents have a high degree of political participation. In fact, the majority of respondents score low on participation. This indicates negative relationship of high SES and participation.

It seems that the professionals were either reluctant or unwilling to participate in political affairs. It may be that because of their professional obligations and duties they do not find sufficient opportunity and leisure to participate. Along with this, there might be apathy and cynicism towards things that are political.

Ten of the respondents from the professional group who have medium score on participation come from middle classes and have lesser educational attainments than the first group. But their relatively higher participation score could be explained more by other reasons such as family tradition, ideology, specific political events, influence of an individual, rather than belonging to the category of professionals. Many of them belong to the group of highly politicized women, which is analysed separately.

Again, as anticipated, most of the respondents belonging to this category are aware of the political events around them, as most of them score high on communication. But again, as seen elsewhere, *communication* is not a significant factor affecting a higher degree of political participation.

As regards (a) perception of scope for participation; (b) perception of defranchisement; (c) perception of participation; and (d) perception of domestic happiness and political differences, there is no deviation from the general trend mentioned in the earlier sections.

Government and Private Service Group

The very nature of the government and private service group more or less imposes certain inherent limitations on the scope for participation for the employees. This may partially explain the high degree of low scores (17 out of 25) on participation. The remaining eight respondents who score medium and high on the participation scale mostly belong to private services, allowing them more freedom to take active part in politics. The earlier findings of relationships between the SES and participation is maintained in this category of respondents as well.

Manual Labourers

All the six respondents, who are manual labourers, have low scores on all the three. The nature of their livelihood explains their low scores on both participation and communication. It is quite likely that they might be desirous of larger political participation yet lack of education and leisure prevents them from doing so actively. A significant majority desires more participation for women in political activities and think that women will lose much if deprived of their right of franchise. Here, the low SES has a direct bearing on a low participation score. This is vividly seen from the statement expressed by some of the respondents, 'even though we desire more participation, the circumstances compel us to be away from actual involvement'.

From the above, it seems that the self-earning respondents as a group do not reveal any significant characteristics regarding politicization and participation, different from the general group. The fact that they are self-earning by itself, does not seem to have affected their perceptions and participation.

Profile According to Religion

A comparison of the degree of politicization and participation between Hindu and non-Hindu shows that there is a much higher degree of political participation among the Hindu respondents than among the non-Hindu. This may partially be due to a general trend in minority communities to stay away from the political mainstream, and also to more or less a tradition among Muslim women not to participate in political activities as compared to the women belonging to other religions.

If a comparison is made between these two groups regarding the SES scores, 40% of the non-Hindu respondents and 50% of the Hindu group are middle class women. It might have been expected that there would have been a corresponding percentage of women in both the groups on the participation score. But while 16% Hindu women are found on the middle range of the participation score, no respondent in the non-Hindu group occupies this position.

Though the percentage of women belonging to the higher SES more or less in both the groups (Hindu and non-Hindu) is the same, only one respondent from the non-Hindu group scores high on the

TABLE 10
Religious composition

Religion	High	Medium	Low	Total
		SES scores		
Hindu	33	60	30	123
Parsi	1	0	0	1
Muslim	1	3	2	6
Jain	4	3	3	10
Christian	0	5	5	10
Total	39	71	40	150
		Political communication		
Hindu	45	39	39	123
Parsi	0	1	0	1
Muslim	0	1	5	6
Jain	1	4	5	10
Christian	0	3	7	10
Total	46	48	56	150
		Political participation		
Hindu	16	18	89	123
Parsi	0	0	1	1
Muslim	1	0	5	6
Jain	0	0	10	10
Christian	0	0	10	10
Total	17	18	115	150

participation scale, in contrast to 12% of Hindu women who score high.

A comparison of educational attainments also reveals similar contrast between the two groups. Hindu respondents have generally higher educational attainments than the non-Hindus. This might also have affected the degree of participation on the part of non-Hindu women. The Hindu respondent group broadly conforms to the earlier findings that it is the middle class educated group which constitutes the bulk of politicized women. This finding, however, is not borne out in case of non-Hindu women, though the majority of them belong to the middle class. The overwhelming majority of women in both the groups think that women will lose much if they are deprived of franchise. Only 18% of the non-Hindu group and 10% in the Hindu group are of the opinion that they will not lose much if they are deprived of this right. It is significant that though there is very little participation, women in both the groups are conscious of the value of franchise. Very few of the respondents who are of the opinion that they will not lose much have adduced reasons for their answers, but some believe that the vote has no efficacy.

A total of 22% of both the groups say that domestic happiness is affected if the husband and the wife hold different political opinions. Moreover, there is a marked difference of opinion regarding this and the remedies suggested. The majority of the Muslim women suggest that to prevent such a situation the women should submit to the will of the husbands. The majority from the Christian group, however, feel that domestic happiness is not affected by political differences. Those who feel so express the view that both husband and wife should have a mutual understanding or an accommodative attitude.

Only two respondents belonging to the Hindu group were of the opinion that domestic happiness would not be affected. This clearly reveals the difference of attitude between the two dominant religious groups – the Muslim attitude seems to be more authoritarian, and the Hindu more liberal.

Regarding the perception of the scope for participation for Indian women and their attitude towards participation the opinion of the majority in both conforms to the earlier findings.

Profile According to Caste

One of the glaring limitations of the sample is the absence of a Scheduled Caste respondent. A special sample of 25, therefore, was taken and compared with the general sample. The respondents were divided into three major caste groups of Brahmins, Marathas, and intermediary castes. Here again, the overwhelming preponderance of Brahmins has unbalanced the sample. The Brahmins and intermediary caste respondents score high on both educational and SES scale as compared to respondents from the Maratha caste group. The majority of the Maratha respondents score low on participation as compared to Brahmin respondents. A significant correlationship can be seen between higher level of education, middle SES score, and higher degree of political participation. Here also, it is observed, that educated middle class respondents participate relatively more than the respondents with higher SES score. This again reinforces the finding that political participation among women is chiefly the function of middle class educated women, mostly coming from the Brahmin community. This can also be proved by correlating SES and education scores with political participation among the intermediary caste respondents. All the 11 respondents in this category score low on the participation scale in spite of their relatively high scores on education and SES scale as compared to the Marathas. The spread of education among Maratha women is less as compared to the Brahmins. The relatively higher level of participation among Brahmins as compared to Marathas in Maharashtra is because the Brahmins have a tradition of higher involvement in political activities. The Marathas as a community came to the political scene relatively later and the Maratha women have not yet established a tradition of participation. But with higher politicization and with the spread of education, it is expected that there will be a higher degree of political involvement among the Maratha community. The low degree of participation on the part of women belonging to the intermediary castes could not, however, be explained by the above facts as they have a higher level of education. Probably it might be due to their relatively higher SES, which has an inverse relationship with participation. Also, the women of lower SES score who have very little political awareness and low score on the communication scale are not oriented towards participation.

As regards (a) perception of scope of participation, (b) perception of defranchisement, (c) perception of participation, and (d) perception of political differences and domestic happiness, the views maintained by the respondents in this section are the same as mentioned earlier.

Profile of the Scheduled Caste Respondents

As the original sample did not contain any respondents from the Scheduled Castes, a special survey of 25 respondents from the Scheduled Castes was carried out. In conformity with the trend among the other groups, the degree of participation among this group also is low.

Of the twenty-five respondents, three score high and four medium high on political participation. This compares favourably with the scores of the castes in the general sample. From this survey it appears that the Scheduled Caste respondents' participation score is higher as compared to the Christian and Muslim respondents.

Of the three who score high on participation, one scores high on SES and two score low. One of them is a graduate, one has high

TABLE 11
Caste composition

Caste	High	Medium	Low	Total
SES scores				
Marathas	1	3	19	23
Intermediary caste group	5	3	5	13
Brahmins	25	54	8	87
Total	31	60	32	123
Political communication				
Marathas	3	3	17	23
Intermediary caste group	1	8	4	13
Brahmins	39	29	19	87
Total	43	40	40	123
Political participation				
Marathas	0	4	19	23
Intermediary caste group	0	2	11	11
Brahmins	14	15	58	89
Total	14	21	88	123

school education, and one is illiterate. The case of the illiterate respondent who scores high on participation is interesting. She is a self-earning woman with a monthly income of Rs.600 does not read newspapers, but attends public meetings (especially of socialist parties), has participated in anti-Shankaracharya *morchas* and has taken part in *dharnas*. She is a loyal party member from 1951, and voted consistently for the Socialist party. She wants the Congress to be banned, and would never vote for the Congress, Jana Sangh, and Shiv Sena.

It is also interesting to see that 11 out of 12 respondents who have high and medium scores on participation come from the low SES group.

All the respondents except one, who score high and medium are educated up to school level only; and the one is a graduate.

Five respondents feel that domestic happiness will be affected if there are political differences between husband and wife. The rest conform with the earlier findings. But not a single respondent suggests that women should conform to the opinions of the husbands. They suggest that both should reconcile their differences.

Politicization of Women in Maharashtra

In conformity with the earlier findings, the opinion regarding (a) perception of the scope of participation for women in Indian politics, (b) perception of defranchisement, (c) perception of participation, and (d) perception of political differences and domestic happiness is similar.

TABLE 12
Scheduled Caste group

	High	Medium	Low	Total
		SES scores		
Scheduled Caste	2	1	22	25
		Political communication score		
Scheduled Caste	5	8	12	25

Profile According to Language

A group of 43, 'a significant minority', constitutes the non-Marathi speaking segment of the respondents. This group has languages other than Marathi, such as Gujarati, Tamil, Telugu as their mother-tongue. This is an attempt to find out whether language is an important factor affecting political attitudes and participation.

TABLE 13
Language composition

Language	High	Middle	Low	Total
		SES score		
Marathi speaking	25	50	32	107
Non-Marathi speaking	15	21	7	43
Total	40	71	39	150
		Political communication		
Marathi speaking	40	34	33	107
Non-Marathi speaking	6	15	22	43
Total	46	49	55	150
		Political participation		
Marathi speaking	15	17	75	107
Non-Marathi speaking	2	1	40	43
Total	17	18	115	150

On the communication scale, a small minority scores high. About one-third have medium scores and one-half score low. The relative percentage in the Marathi language group of respondents are higher. The language might be one of the significant barriers for the low communication exposure of the non-Marathi group, which consequently might result in their relatively low level of participation.

As many as 40 out of the 43 non-Marathi group of respondents do not participate at all in politics except for voting. On the contrary, in the Marathi lanugage group, 60% do not participate in political process, and 40% have medium and high scores on participation.

Regarding the perception about larger scope for women's participation, a large majority in both Marathi and non-Marathi groups is of the opinion that there should be larger participation. Also, most of them think that women will lose much if they are deprived of franchise. Like other groups, both these groups agree that, (a) attitudes of relatives, (b) societal attitudes, and (c) domestic responsibilities are the main factors limiting effective participation of women in political activities in India.

Conclusion

Some general traits applicable to all sub-classifications can be discerned now:

1. The most obvious finding is that participation on the whole is low.

2. Participation does not increase with education. The claim that participation is a function of education alone is not substantiated by this study. Participation, on the other hand, seems to be affected and determined by the socio-economic status. Those belonging to higher socio-economic status seem to be reluctant to participate in politics. Those belonging to the lower socio-economic status participate less for other reasons. They are so deep in quagmire of poverty that all their time is spent in trying to improve their plight.

3. It is the middle class which participates more actively and effectively. Their economic position is much better than the poor. They have a tradition of participation and may have some leisure too.

4. Hindu middle class respondents seem to participate relatively more than those belonging to other religions. However, the participation score of Scheduled Castes is relatively higher than Christians and Muslims.

5. Participation seems to be more a function of other factors such as family tradition, influence of personalities, specific political events such as the independence struggle, etc., or a particular ideology. This contention was borne out of the profile of highly politicized women. Though the level of actual participation is low, an overwhelming majority of the respondents reveal a high degree of politicization. They seem to be aware of their political rights and also of political events. Most of them hold clear perceptions about various questions that were posed to them, for instance, the questions regarding scope in politics for women, franchise, or whether women should participate in politics, etc.

6. A large majority of respondents are of the opinion that women have less scope in politics. This is attributed mostly to factors such as domestic responsibilities, attitude of relatives, societal attitude, or little scope in parties or even the attitude of the women themselves. A significant majority desires more participation by women for a variety of reasons. Many feel that the present deteriorating economic conditions make it impossible for women to participate. Most women are of the opinion that domestic happiness is in no way affected by political differences between husband and wife: the two spheres being different, the question will not arise. A small minority is, however, of the opinion that women should stay away from politics as they attach more importance to domestic responsibilities.

7. An overwhelming majority values franchise and opposes the idea of disenfranchisement. Though it may not be effective, it gives women an equal status with men, and also is a means of expression and participation.

POLITICIZATION OF WOMEN IN WEST BENGAL

Nirmala Banerjee

Introduction

The West Bengal study covers a sample of 150 women. Besides the common broad categories of religion, caste, and class, the sample includes some highly politicized women, highly educated, social workers, working women, and housewives. Since the sample size was so small it was not possible to select respondents by random selection.

In West Bengal, caste as such makes little difference as regards the attitudes of women. More significant is the division between upper and lower castes. Except for the Scheduled Castes, there is considerable caste mobility among the Hindus, which makes finer distinctions irrelevant. On the other hand, it was thought important to consider the differences in attitudes of women, since there is a very large difference in the availability of social and physical infrastructure in rural and urban areas. Again, in the rural areas, attitudes may well differ between tribal women and other women because of the widely differing ideas about family pattern in the two groups.

In urban areas, while among the educated women there is a high degree of communication and exchange of ideas, the uneducated urban women live in their own small areas with little or no communication between these pockets. We considered a fairly large sample of the educated and vocal group of female population of urban areas, and also tried to include respondents from as many small groups of these uneducated urban women as possible in our sample.

It is worth emphasizing that the sample is much too small to draw any parametric conclusions regarding the female population in West Bengal. Second, for each group of women the places and numbers included in the sample are too small to make any generalizations regarding their categories in the entire West Bengal on the basis of case studies of group. However, within each group, we did try to select respondents as impersonally as possible in order to collect reactions with a minimum bias. To that extent, our conclusions regarding individual case studies claim some validity. Table 1 gives the socio-demographic characteristics of the sample.

TABLE 1
Description of the sample

Urban (91)

	Working women				Housewives	
	Hindu	Muslim	Christian		Hindu	Muslim
1. Teachers	11	1	1	Calcutta	9	3
2. Professionals	12	1	—	Industrial workers	6	7
3. Clerks	6	—	1			
4. Menials	6	5	—			
5. Students	9	2	—			
6. Professional political workers	1	1	1			
7 Industrial workers	7	1	—			
Total:	52	11	3		15	10

Rural (59)

	Working women			Housewives		
	Hindu	Santhal		Hindu	Santhal	Muslim
1. Agricultural Labour						
(a) Midnapur	1	10	Midnapur	2	3	—
(b) Birbhum	4	10	Birbhum	2	—	—
(c) Hooghly	2	—	Hooghly	3	—	2
(d) Sonarpur	1	—	Sonarpur	8	—	1
2. Menials	5	1				
3. Teachers	3	1				
Total:	16	22		15	3	3

Bengali speaking	=	110
Hindi speaking	=	12
Urdu speaking	=	10
Nepali speaking	=	2
Gujarati speaking	=	1
Santal speaking	=	15
		150

	Hindu	Muslim	Santhal
Social workers	22	2	1
Political workers	8	1	1

District	Illiterate	Primary	School final	Graduate	Higher qualification
Calcutta					
(a) Working women	8	4	15	14	16
(b) Housewives	3	1	2	6	1
(a) Industrial workers	8	—	—	—	—
(b) Housewives	8	3	2	—	—
Agricultural workers					
1. Midnapur	11	—	—	—	—
2. Birbhum	14	—	—	—	—
3. Hooghly	1	1	—	—	—
4. Sonarpur	1	—	—	—	—
Menials	4	—	1	—	—
Teachers	—	—	1	2	1
Housewives					
1. Midnapur	4	2	—	—	—
2. Birbhum	1	—	1	—	—
3. Hooghly	2	3	—	—	—
4. Sonarpur	5	2	1	1	—
Total:	70	16	23	23	18

District	Higher caste	Lower caste	Scheduled tribe	Muslim	Christian
Calcutta	44	21	—	21	3
Midnapur	2	4	15	—	—
Birbhum	2	9	10	—	—
Hooghly	1	5	—	2	—
Sonarpur	3	7	—	1	—
Total:	52	46	25	24	3

Questionnaire

In rural areas, four small case studies were conducted in Bolepur sub-division of the Birbhum district, Dhaniakhali sub-division of the Hooghly district, Midnapore district, and Sonarpur thana of the 24-Parganas district.

For West Bengal, we modified the questionnaire to a certain extent, because we felt that direct questions regarding women's reactions to present political conflicts – conflicts between personalities and parties – may give rise to resentment or fear, and hence to non-cooperation.

Information was collected regarding the extent of women's participation in politics and their attitude towards activities as well as on the changes in their attitudes towards politics over time. In addition, we added a small list of questions regarding women's attitude towards social progress with a view to evaluating the differences in social status and attitudes of women of different groups. We feel that such differences in social status may to some extent explain their degree of politicization.

Method of Analysis

The first part of the questionnaire, which is concerned with general information regarding the respondents lends itself to easy categorization. After completing the survey, all women were classified into groups according to their age, religion, mother-tongue, caste, whether working or unemployed, and family income.

The questionnaire had been so designed as to draw either positive or negative responses to most questions, although there were certain questions which allowed for a variety of answers, e.g., questions which asked what political party or leader was preferred by the respondent or to give reasons for certain of their attitudes. For purposes of tabulation, however, questions with such answers were re-formulated so that the answers could be divided into just two categories. Further differences were ignored for the sake of first tabulation, although towards the end we have tried to analyse these detailed answers.

The positive responses to each question were given marks. All questions did not show an equal degree of political awareness or participation and, therefore, they were divided into three categories – strong, medium, weak – and given separate weights. Responses to questions regarding trade union activities (question 12, 12a, 13, 14) and to questions in part III were also similarly grouped. The weight given to any question was entirely a value judgement on the part of the author.

Table 2 shows this categorization of questions by the weights given to each.

TABLE 2

Weight given to different questions

	Part I: Political qualities	Question No.
I Weak Yes = 1 No = 0	(a) Regularly participated in political discussion	2
	(b) Voted in at least the last election	6
	(c) Knows about political parties	7
	(d) Accepts importance of women franchise	19
II Medium Yes = 2 No = 0	(a) Has sometimes attended political meetings	3
	(b) Supports women's participation in political movements	16(c)
	(c) Feels that there is need for further political activities by women	21
	(d) Holds a definite opinion about present political leaders	18
III Strong Yes = 3 No = 0	(a) Has participated in *satyagraha, morcha, michil,* etc.	8
	(b) Has been a member of a political party	9(a)
	(c) Participated in electioneering campaign	10
	(d) Has been a member of a political party	11
	(e) Willing to hold political opinions opposed to those of husband	20
	Part II: Trade union activities	
I Weak Yes = 1 No = 0	(a) Considers that women are discriminated against	13
	(b) Feels that trade union helps in these matters	14
II Medium Yes = 2 No = 0	(a) Is a member of a trade union	12
	(b) Participates in trade union activities	12(a)
	Part III: Socially Progressive attitudes	
I Weak Yes = 1	(a) Was consulted about or arranged her own/daughter's marriage	1+2

Politicization of Women in West Bengal

No = 0	(b) Resisted dowry	3
	(c) Approves of daughter being educated like son	10
	(d) Knows about divorce law	6
II Medium	(a) Disapproves of accepting dowry for sons	4
Yes = 2	(b) Approves of inter-caste and	
No = 1	inter-religion marriages	5
	(c) Widows/divorcees remarrying	6(c)
	(d) Approves of practice family planning	7
	(e) Was a member of voluntary organization	4 (Part II)
	(f) Knows about abortion law	9
III Strong	(a) Decided on the family planning method	
Yest = 3	either singly or jointly	8
No = 0	(b) Approves of abortion law	9
	(c) Manages family funds	11

For measuring political attitudes, women were judged only by the scores for political questions, i.e., questions mentioned under Part I in Table 2. Similarly, for measuring attitudes towards trade union activities, their scores in response to questions in part II of Table 2 were considered. For social attitudes, scores in part III alone were considered. All statistical tests in the next part were conducted on the basis of these scores of the respondents.

Statistical Analysis

This section describes the tests conducted and the results obtained. Each of the hypothesis mentioned above is tested by a non-parametric test selected by considering the size of the sample, the nature of the hypothesis, and the number of categories considered relevant. It may be worth repeating here that the scores used in the tests, whether for political attitudes, social attitudes, or trade union activities were given according to the statement in Table 2.

Low Level of Political Awareness and Activity

The first hypothesis was that the level of political awareness and activity among women of West Bengal was fairly low. Graph I shows the frequency distribution of the sample by political marks earned by each. There is a high concentration of the frequencies of political scores in the class interval $3-5\frac{1}{2}$. Graph II, showing the cumulative

GRAPH I

Frequency Distribution of Political and Social Scores

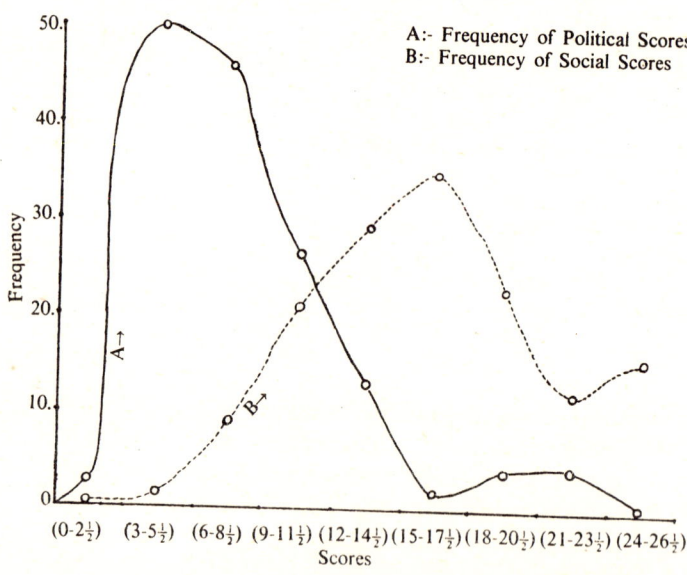

A:- Frequency of Political Scores
B:- Frequency of Social Scores

GRAPH II

Cumulative Frequency Distribution of Political and Social Scores

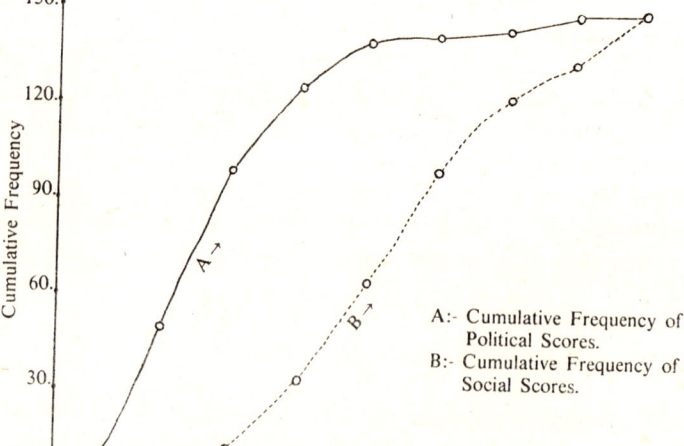

A:- Cumulative Frequency of Political Scores.
B:- Cumulative Frequency of Social Scores.

Politicization of Women in West Bengal

TABLE 3
Description of central tendencies of the Hindu, Muslim, and Scheduled Tribe samples

	Hindu	Muslim	Scheduled Tribes
Total	98	24	25
Arithmetic mean	9.04	6.91	7.20
Mode	7.25	4.25	7.25
Median	8.25	5.11	6.90

frequencies of the returns by class intervals of scores, shows a steep rise in the beginning and a flattening out of the curve later on. Nearly 100 respondents scored less than $8\frac{1}{2}$ marks, the maximum possible score being $27\frac{1}{2}$. Table 3 shows the mean, mode, and median political scores of Hindu, Muslim, and Scheduled Tribe women. It may be seen that the Hindu women score somewhat better than the other two.

Relationship Between Level of Education and Politicization

It seems reasonable to assume that better educated women will be more politically aware than less educated women.

Null hypothesis = H_0 = There is no difference in the proportions of women of different educational level among low and high political scores. H_1 = Women who score high on political awareness are better educated.

Test used: Since high and low scorers constitute two independent samples, the Kolomogorov-Smirnow one-tailed test for two independent large samples is chosen.

Level of significance = Let $\alpha = 0.01$ of the total 150 women in the sample, 76 scored less than the median score and 74 scored more than the median score.

Decision: Table 4 shows the cumulative frequencies of high and low scorers by education levels and the proportions of cumulative frequencies in each education level.

$n_1 = 76$ $n_2 = 74$ df = 2
   approximation = $4D^2$ $(n_1 n_2)/(n_1 + n_2)$
Calculated value of Max. D = 0.30
Calculated $\chi^2_{0.01,\ 2} = 13.77$
Tabulated value of $\chi^2_{0.01, 2} = 9.21$

TABLE 4
Cumulative frequencies of low scorer and high scorer returns by levels of education

Education level	Cumulative frequency of low scorer	Proportion of four in each group	Cumulative frequencies of high scorer	Proportion of two in each group	3 − 5
1	2	3	4	5	6
0	42	0.55	28	0.38	+0.17
1	55	0.72	33	0.45	+0.27
2	68	0.88	43	0.58	+0.30
3	74	0.96	59	0.79	+0.17
4	77	1.00	74	1.0	0

Max. D = +0.30

χ^2 approximation = $4D^2 \frac{(n_1 n_2)}{(n_1 + n_2)}$ = 13.77

f = 2

Hypothesis H_0 is rejected in favour of H_1. Women who score high on political awareness are in general better educated.

Relationship Between Family Income Levels and Degree of Politicization

Null hypothesis = H_0 = There is no difference in the proportion of women of different family income classes in different classes in political scores. H_1 = A greater proportion of women, who score high on politicization comes from the higher income than those who score low.

Statistical test: The χ^2 test for independent samples is chosen since the group of various levels of political scores are independent, and because the scores under study are in discrete categories.

Level of significance = α = 0.01   N = 150
df = (4 − 1) (3 − 1) = 6

Decision: Table 5 shows the observed and expected frequencies in different family income and political score classes.

Calculated $\chi^2_{0.01,6}$ = 21.04
Tabulated $\chi^2_{0.01,6}$ = 16.81

TABLE 5
Distribution of women by family income classes and political scores

Class	Less or equal to 7	Actual $7\frac{1}{2}-11\frac{1}{2}$	12 and Above	
0-200	30 (26)	21 (19.06)	1 (6.93)	52
201-500	23 (21)	15 (15.40)	4 (5.60)	42
501-1000	13 (11.5)	6 (8.43)	4 (3.06)	23
1001 and above	9 (16.5)	13 (12.10)	11 (4.40)	33
Total	75	55	20	150

$$\chi^2_{0.01,6} = \sum_{i=1}^{r} \sum_{i=j}^{k} \frac{(O_{ij} - E_{ij})^2}{(E_{ij})} = 21.04$$

Hypothesis H_0 is rejected in favour of hypothesis H_1. A larger proportion of high scorers comes from higher income groups than that of low scorers.

There is a significant relationship between family income levels and degree of politicization.

Relationship Between Religion and Politicization

The religions considered were Hindu and Muslim. Since Muslim respondents were mainly urban, the test considers only urban Hindu and Muslim returns. Null Hypothesis = H_0 = There is no difference in the median values of political scores amongst urban Hindus and Muslims. H_1 = Hindus are proportionately high scorers.

Statistical test: Since the sample sizes for Hindus and Muslims are widely different, and we are interested in testing the similarity between their central tendencies, the median test is used.

Significance Level = $\alpha = 0.05$; n_1 (Hindus) = 66; n_2 Muslims) = 21; $n_1 + n_2 = N = 87$.

It is to be noted that we have chosen a 5% level of significance here, because the Muslim sample is more biased towards better educated Muslim women than the Hindu sample on account of attempts to include all categories of Muslim women in the small sample.

Decision: Table 6 shows the frequencies of Hindus and Muslims below and above the combined median value of the two samples.

TABLE 6

Distribution of urban Hindu and Muslim returns around the combined median, for median test

	Hindu	Muslim	
Below combined median	A 29	B 14	43
Above combined median	C 37	D 7	44
Total	66	21	87

Combined median value = 7.4

$$\chi^2 = \frac{N|(AD - BC) - N/2|^2}{(A + B)(B + D)(C + D)(A + C)} = 4.263$$

Tabulated $\chi^2_{0.05,1} = 3.84$
Calculated $\chi^2_{0.05,1} = 4.263$

The hypothesis H_0 is rejected in favour of H_1. Hindu women score relatively high on politicization.

Relationship Between Urbanization and Politicization

We next attempted to evaluate the influence of urbanization on the political attitudes of women. Urban women, especially of Calcutta metropolitan region, living as they do in close and frequent contact with numerous political activities and movements, are likely to be politically more aware and active than the rural women. This presumption is being tested below.

Null hypothesis = H_0 = The proportion of women in the three political score categories, low, medium, and high, is the same for urban and rural women. H_1 = Larger proportion of urban women score medium or high political scores than those of rural women.

Statistical test: Since the groups under study are independent and number more than one, and the data are in discrete categories, the χ^2 test is an appropriate one.

Significance level = α = 0.01 N = 150
$$df = (k - 1)(r - 1) = (2 - 1)(3 - 1) = 2$$

Decision: Table 7 gives the frequencies of urban and rural women

TABLE 7
Distribution of urban and rural women by classes of political scores

Class	Rural	Urban	Total
Up to 7	33 (31)	45 (4.7)	78
$7\frac{1}{2} - 11\frac{1}{2}$	24 (19.5)	25 (29.5)	49
12 and Above	2 (9.5)	21 (14.5)	23
Total	59	91	150

$$\chi^2_{0.01,2} = \sum_{i=1}^{r} \sum_{j=1}^{k} \frac{(O_{ij} - E_{ij})^2}{E_{ij}} = 9.26$$

by the three categories. Figure in parenthesis shows the expected frequencies of each class.

$$\chi^2_{0.01,2} = 9.26$$

Tabulated $\chi^2_{0.01,2} = 9.21$

The calculated value of χ^2 is greater than the tabulated value; the null hypothesis H_0 is rejected in favour of hypothesis H_1. Urban women appear to be more politically inclined.

However, we felt that since political awareness is closely related with increase in level of education and income, the higher degree of political awareness of urban women may well be explained by the greater frequency of women of higher education and incomes in the urban areas.

Comparison Between Low Educated Urban and Rural Women

We therefore compared the performance of urban and rural women of low education (illiterate or primary education only) levels.

Null hypothesis = H_0 = There is no difference between urban and rural women of low education regarding politicization. H_1 = Urban low educated women score relatively high on political awareness.

Statistical Test: Since urban and rural women form independent samples and n_1 and n_2 are larger, the test used is the one-tailed Kolomogorov-Smirnov test, χ^2 approximation with df = 2.

TABLE 8

Distribution of urban and rural low educated women by classes of political scores

Class	Urban Cumulative frequency	(a)	Rural Cumulative frequency	(b)	a − b
0 = 2½	0	0	2	(0.04)	−0.04
3 = 5½	17	(0.47)	18	(0.35)	0.12
6 = 8½	29	(0.92)	36	(0.71)	0.21
9 = 11½	33	(0.92)	50	(0.98)	−0.06
12 = 14½	36	(1)	50	(0.98)	0.02
15 = 17½	36	(1)	50	(0.98)	0.02
18 = 20½	36	(1)	51	(1)	—
21 = 23½	36	(1)	51	(1)	—
24 = 26½	36	(1)	51	(1)	—
	36		51		

Max. D = 0.21
$\chi^2_{0.01,2} = 4D^2 (n_1 n_2)/(n_1 + n_2) = 3.8$

Significance level = α = 0.01, n_1 = 36, n_2 = 51.

Decision: Table 8 shows the cumulative frequencies of urban and rural women in each class of political scores and these cumulative frequencies as proportions of the total frequencies for urban and rural women. Max. D is the maximum difference between the proportionate cumulative frequencies in each class interval. Max. D = 0.21

Calculated $\chi^2_{0.01,2}$ = 3.8
Tabulated value of $\chi^2_{0.01,2}$ = 9.21
Therefore Hypothesis H_0 *cannot* be rejected in favour of H_1.

There is no difference in political awareness of urban and rural women of low education level.

Difference in Politicization Among Urban and Rural Low Income Women

Similarly, we also tested the null hypothesis H_0 = Urban women of low incomes (incomes of less than Rs.500 p.m.) do not score high on political awareness than rural women of the same income groups. H_1 = Low income urban women are politically more aware than their rural counterparts.

Test used: Once again the Kolomogorov-Smironov one-tailed test for independent large samples was used.
Level of significance $= \alpha = 0.01$
$$df = 2, n_1 = 44, n_2 = 49.$$

TABLE 9
Distribution of urban and rural women of family incomes less than Rs. 500 p.m. by classes of political scores

Political scores class	Urban		Rural	(b)	a – b
0 – $2\frac{1}{2}$	0	0	1	0.02	–0.02
3 – $5\frac{1}{2}$	18	0.41	17	0.35	+0.06
6 – $8\frac{1}{2}$	32	0.71	35	0.71	—
9 – $11\frac{1}{2}$	40	0.91	48	0.95	–0.04
12 – $14\frac{1}{2}$	43	0.98	48	0.98	—
15 – $17\frac{1}{2}$	44	1	48	0.98	–0.02
18 – $20\frac{1}{2}$	44	1	49	1	—

Max. D = 0.06

$$\chi^2_{0.01, 2} = 4 D^2 \frac{(n_1 n_2)}{(n_1 + n_2)} = 0.28$$

Decision: Table 9 shows that Max. D = 0.06

Calculated $\chi^2_{0.01,2} = 0.02$
Tabulated critical value of $\chi^2_{0.012} = 9.21$
Hypothesis H_0 *cannot* be rejected in favour of H_1.

There is no significant difference between urban and rural women of low income groups regarding their degree of political awareness.

We therefore do not think that there is any greater political awareness among urban women *as such*.

Relationship Between Economic Emancipation and Politicization of Women

Next we considered the effects of economic emancipation on women's political awareness. For this, we separated working women from housewives (students were altogether excluded).

Null hypothesis $= H_0 =$ There is no difference in the proportion in different classes of political awareness among working women and housewives.

H_1 = Working women score relatively high than housewives on political awareness.

Test used: Since there are two large independent samples of working women and housewives, we use the Kolomogorov-Smirnov one-tailed test for large samples where $n_1 = 47$, $n_2 = 91$.

Level of significance = $\alpha = 0.01$

TABLE 10
Distribution of working women and housewives by classes of political scores

Class	Housewives frequency (a)		Employed frequency (b)		a − b
0 – 2½	2	0.04	—	—	—
3 – 5½	21	0.44	28	0.30	0.14
6 – 8½	43	0.91	51	0.56	0.35
9 – 11½	46	0.97	70	0.76	0.21
12 – 14½	47	1.00	81	0.89	0.11
15 – 17½	47	1.00	83	0.91	0.09
18 – 20½	47	1.00	86	0.94	0.06
21 – 23½	47	1.00	90	0.98	0.02
24 – 26½	47	1.00	91	1.00	—
	47		91		

Max. D = 0.35

$$\chi^2_{0.01,2} = \frac{(n_1 \, n_2)}{(n_1 + n_2)} = 27.5$$

Decision: Table 10 shows the cumulative frequencies of working women and housewives in each class of political scores and the cumulative proportions to total in each class.

Calculated Max. D = 0.35
$\chi^2_{0.012} = 27.5$
Tabulated $\chi^2_{0.012} = 9.21$
Hypothesis H_0 is rejected in favour of H_1.

There is a significant difference between the degree of political awareness of working women and housewives. The former score more on an average.

Difference in Political Attitudes of Low Caste and Scheduled Tribe Women

Our survey had included a fairly large sample of tribal women from two rural centres. We thought that it would be worthwhile to examine whether there was any difference between rural Hindu women and rural tribal women. In order to eliminate the influence of higher incomes and education levels, which are found more frequently among Hindus, we thought that the comparison would be more worthwhile between Hindu women of lower castes and women of Scheduled Tribes. It is to be noted that women of both these groups are of low education and incomes and, if anything, it is more common among Scheduled Tribes women to do outside work than among Hindu women. Therefore, any difference between their political scores can be safely attributed to these women being tribal or not.

Null hypothesis $= H_0 =$ There is no significant difference in proportion of rural low caste Hindu and rural tribal women in different classes of political scores. $H_1 =$ Rural low caste Hindu women score proportionately better than rural tribal women.

Test used: Since rural tribal and rural low caste Hindu women form two independent small samples, the Kolomogorov-Smirnov one-tailed test for small samples is used.

Level of significance $= \alpha = 0.01$. $n_1 = n_2 = 24 = N$

Decision: Table 11 shows the cumulative frequencies of the two groups of women in different classes of political scores and their proportions of cumulative frequencies in each class.

When $N = 24$, the critical value Max. KD for one-tailed test $= 11$ at 0.01 level of significance.

Calculated Max. KD (numerator of D) $= 17$
Therefore, hypothesis H_0 is rejected in favour of H_1.

Rural Hindu low caste women are relatively more politically aware than rural tribal women.

Relative Political Scores Among Women of Different Language Groups

In West Bengal, the two most important language groups are Bengali and Hindi. We obtained a fair sample of Hindi speaking women.

TABLE 11
Distribution of rural low caste Hindu and tribal women by classes of political scores

	Rural Schedule Tribe		Rural Lower Caste		2 – 4
	Cumulative frequency	Proportion in each class	Cumulative frequency	Proportion in each class	
0 – 2½	0	—	1	0.04	0.04
3 – 5½	8	0.33	9	0.37	0.04
6 – 8½	18	0.75	14	0.58	0.17
9 – 11½	23	0.95	23	0.95	0.00
12 – 14½	23	0.95	24	1	0.05
15 – 17½	23	0.95	24	1	0.05
18 – 20½	24	1	24	1	—
21 – 23½	24	1	24	1	—
24 – 26½	24	1	24	1	—
			24		

Max. D = 0.17
Max. KD = 17

Since all of these women are urban and fall in the income group of below Rs.500 p.m., we compared their scores with those of urban Bengali speaking women of the same income group.

Null hypothesis $= H_0 =$ There is no difference in the proportion of Bengali speaking and Hindi speaking women among different classes of political scores. $H_1 =$ Bengali speaking women are politically more aware than Hindi speaking women.

Test chosen: Since Bengali speaking low income urban women and Hindi speaking low income urban women form two independent small samples of $n_1 = n_2$, the Kolomogorov-Smirnov χ^2 approximation test is used.

Level of significance $= \alpha = 0.01$

Decision: Table 12 shows the distribution of Bengali speaking and Hindi speaking women in classes of political scores.

Calculated value of $\chi^2_{0.01, 2} = 0.43$
Tabulated value of $\chi^2_{0.01, 2} = 9.21$
Hypothesis H_0 cannot be rejected. Therefore hypothesis H_1 is rejected.

Politicization of Women in West Bengal

TABLE 12
Cumulative frequency distribution of Bengali speaking and Hindi speaking low income urban women by classes of political scores

	Bengali speaking		Hindi speaking		
0 – 2½	0	0	0	0	
3 – 5½	11	0.44	7	0.37	+0.07
6 – 8½	17	0.68	15	0.78	−0.10
9 – 11½	22	0.88	18	0.94	−0.06
12 – 14½	24	0.96	19	1	−0.04
15 – 17½	25	1	19	1	0
18 – 20½	25	1	19	1	0
21 – 23½	25	1	19	1	0
24 – 26½	25	1	19	1	0
	25		19		

Max. D = − 0.10

$$\chi^2_{0.01,\,2} = 4 D^2 \frac{(n_1 n_2)}{(n_1 + n_2)} = 0.43$$

There is no difference in the relative degree of political awareness among low income urban Bengali speaking and Hindi speaking women.

Relationship Between Reading Habits and Politicization

One of the reasons why women are likely to be disinterested in politics is their relatively sheltered lives. For women staying at home, reading is one of the main channels of exposure to such interests. We therefore tested the hypothesis that women who read widely (i.e., those who read newspapers, magazines, serious and light books) are more politically conscious than women who read little or selectively. We have left out the illiterate or low educated women.

Null hypothesis: H_0 = There is no difference in the proportions of poorly read and well-read women among low and high political scorers. H_1 = well-read women are relatively more politically aware.

Test applied: Since low and high politically scorers form two independent samples, the χ^2 2 × 2 test is applied.

Level of significance = α = 0.01 or 0.05, df = 1, N = 61

Decision: Table 13 shows the distribution of educated women of poor reading habits and wide reading habits into low and high political scorers.

TABLE 13

Distribution of women by categories of low and high political scores against low and wide reading habits

Reading habit	Low political scores	High political scores	
Reads little	5(A)	12(C)	17
Reads widely	12(B)	32(D)	44
	17	44	61 = N

$$\chi^2_{0.01,1} = \frac{N[(AD-BC)-N/2]^2}{(A+B)(B+D)(C+D)(A+C)}$$

$$= \frac{1225'25}{5595'04}$$

$$= 0.023$$

$$= 0.02$$

Calculated $\chi^2_{0.01,2} = 0.02$
Tabulated $\chi^2_{0.01,1} = 6.64$, $\chi^2_{0.05,1} = 3.84$

The hypothesis H_0 is rejected. Better reading habits do not necessarily make women politically more active.

Degree of Political Awareness of Active Trade Unionists

Although trade union movement should generally be a stepping stone to greater political participation by citizens, this is not always supported by facts. Often trade union activities are based on the narrow economism of employed people. We, therefore, tried to analyse how far active trade unionism had led the employed women of West Bengal to greater participation in wider political activities by comparing relative distributions of trade union scorers and political scorers in low and high score groups. We considered only urban working women, since rural women and urban housewives are not familiar with trade union activities.

Null hypothesis = H_0 = There is no difference in the distribution of low and high trade union scorers among low and high political score groups. H_1 = Better trade union scorers generally also score better political marks.

Test applied: Since low and high trade union scorers form two independent groups, we applied the χ^2 2 × 2 test degree of significance = α = 0.01

TABLE 14

Distribution of urban working women of high and low political scores in classes of low and high trade union scores

	Low politicization	High politicization	
Low T.U.	A 20	B 12	32
High T.U.	C 7	D 15	22
	27	27	54

Low T.U. Scores $p \leqslant 1$ Low political scores $p \leqslant 7$

$N = 54$

$$\chi^2_{0.01,1} = \frac{N \left[(AD - BC) - N/2 \right]^2}{(A + B)(C + D)(A + C)(B + D)}$$

$$= \frac{54 \left[(300 - 87) - 27 \right]^2}{32 \times 22 \times 27 \times 27}$$

$$= \frac{1928934}{513216} = 3.758$$

Degree of significance $= \alpha = 0.01$

$df = 1,\ N = 54$

Decision: Table 14 shows the distribution of low-high trade union scorers between low and high political score categories.

Calculated $\chi^2_{0.01,1} = 3.76$
Tabulated $\chi^2_{0.01,1} = 6.64$

Hypothesis H_0 *cannot* be rejected even at 5% level of significance (tabulated $\chi^2_{0.05,\ 1} = 3.84$).

Therefore, greater trade union activities do not necessarily lead to greater political activities.

Relationship Between Socially Progressive Views and Political Activities

As mentioned before, we had included in the questionnaire a list of questions to ascertain the social attitudes of the respondents. These answers were also converted into positive and zero scores, with positive response to different questions being given different weights (see Table 2). Each respondent thus earned a total score of social marks lying between 0 and a maximum of 27. Below we test the hypothesis whether socially progressive attitudes of women necessarily mean greater political participation.

Null hypothesis: H_0 = There is no difference in the proportion of women with low and high social scores (median score being = $11\frac{1}{2}$) in categories of low and high political scores. H_1 = A larger proportion of high social scorers would earn high political scores than of low social scorers.

Test chosen: Since low and high political scorers form two independent samples, the χ^2 2 × 2 test was chosen.

Level of significance = α = 0.01, N = 147.

TABLE 15

Distribution of women by categories of low and high social scores and low and high political scores

Social scores	Political score		
	Low	High	
	A	B	
Low	17	58	75
	C	D	
High	16	56	72
	33	114	147

$$\chi^2_{0.01,\ 1} = \frac{N\,[(AD-BC)-N/2]^2}{(A+B)(B+D)(A+C)(C+D)}$$
$$= \frac{360186.75}{203148.00}$$
$$= 0.017$$
$$= 0.02$$

Decision: Table 15 shows the distribution of frequencies of low and high social scorers in low and high political scores categories.

Calculated $\chi^2_{0.01,\ 1} = 0.02$
Tabulated $\chi^2_{0.01,\ 1} = 6.64$, $\chi^2_{0.05,\ 1} = 3.84$

The hypothesis H_0 *cannot* be rejected. Socially progressive attitude of women do not necessarily lead them to greater political activities.

Some Qualitative Aspects

Why the Low Political Scores of Women?

As we saw above the West Bengal women were not very politicized as yet. This is all the more remarkable since they are socially quite progressive, but there is poor correlation between socially progressive attitudes and greater political awareness.

In trying to analyse the reasons for this we found three main trends:

1. Ignorance
2. Involvement in domestic duties
3. Disillusionment with present political leaders and parties.

1. *Ignorance*: Among the lesser educated women, a common feeling is that they cannot participate in politics because of their ignorance. Even though these women (illiterate or with primary education) generally accept the importance of economic emancipation and are usually compelled to work outside, they find that they cannot participate in politics because they do not understand the issues involved. Of the low educated 79 women in the sample, over one-half gave special weightage to lack of education as the main barrier to their participation in politics.

2. *Domestic pressures*: On the other hand, the better educated middle and upper caste women almost uniformly mention that the Indian woman's domestic and social obligations make it difficult for her to participate in political activities. Interestingly enough, very few poor women give any weightage to these difficulties, probably because they are already adjusted to managing both domestic and outside duties.

The fact that all middle and upper class women uniformly find domestic duties heavy may indicate that women are basically disinterested in politics. They merely use their domestic responsibilities as an excuse for their lack of political consciousness.

Another possibility is that in West Bengal the tradition of women participating in any activities outside their family and social circles is yet to develop. Although women are increasingly taking up jobs, there is less careerism among middle and upper class Calcutta women than those of other large Indian cities. Women in West Bengal do not seem to be interested in forming or joining voluntary groups for cultural or recreational purposes. We found that out of the 150 respondents only 37 belonged to a voluntary social organization.

3. *Political disillusionment*: A part of the reason for women's low level of politicization may be their widespread disillusionment with the present political atmosphere of the country. This has been clearly brought out by several points in the questionnaire.

(i) Lack of leadership: While only 17 of the respondents failed to mention the name of some political leader who had inspired them in their young age, there were very few who came forward with a positive preference for any of the present leaders.

Only 29 mentioned the name of a current leader whom they liked; of these eight are local social-cum-political workers, and twenty-one are national leaders. This is rather remarkable, since one would have thought that in a country with a popular and effective women Prime Minister, women would have shown a stronger approval of the present leadership.

(ii) Disillusionment with parties: In spite of the numerous shades of party politics operating in West Bengal, most women replied that no present political party could be said to have helped common people. Only 21 respondents mentioned a specific party.

(iii) Disillusionment with democracy in practice: About 64 of the respondents did not consider it important for women to have a vote. As a reason for holding this view, at least 40 replied that having a vote had not helped women or, for that matter, men. When asked whether they had voted in any of the last three elections, 12 respondents replied that they would not vote on principle, since voting did not help.

(iv) Lower degree of interest in politics among young women: Our survey did not include equal representation for all age groups and, therefore, hypotheses regarding older women scoring high on politicization could not be systematically tested. However, although our sample included only 27 women of 45 years of age and above, they accounted for 10 of the 25 high scorers (with political scores of 12 and above) of the total sample.

(v) Break with political family traditions: Our sample included 36 women whose near family members of last generation had been members of political parties. Only nine of them have carried on this family tradition by actively joining any party or movement.

Who are the Politically Active Women?

We saw above that, in general, West Bengal women are not politically

TABLE 16

No.	Level of education	Family income group per month (Rs.)	Religion	Whether working or not	Age	Caste	Social scores	Trade union act scores	Political score
1.	Graduate	above 1000	Hindu		30	Upper	11	1	22
2.	Graduate	500 to 1000	Hindu		40	Upper	17	1	18
3.	Higher qualification	above 1000	Brahmin		43	Upper	2	6	22½
4.	School final	above 1000	Brahmin		54	Upper	23	7	18
5.	Higher qualification	above 1000	Hindu	Not	57	Upper	20	1	20
6.	Graduate	above 1000	Hindu		48	Upper	22	×	22
7.	Higher qualification	200–500	Hindu		53	Upper	23	1	22
8.	Graduate	above 1000	Christian		45	—	16	1	24
9.	Higher qualification	501–1000	Muslim		52	—	17	2	22
10.	Primary education	501–1000	Santhal		60	—	4	—	10
11.	Illiterate	0–200	Santhal		50	—	11	4	20

very active. Nevertheless, our sample does include about 11 who have been members of political parties at some time or the other. In Table 13 we summarize some information about these women.

Table 13 in general confirms most of the conclusions regarding factors which influence politicization of women. Politically active women are in general highly educated, mostly belong to upper caste Hindu groups, come from high income families, and often are workers. An interesting point to note is that most of those women are above 45 or 50 years of age, i.e., at the time of independence, they were already old enough to participate in political activities. The absence of young women seems to indicate that the independence struggle acted as a stimulus to political activities since then such a force is lacking in West Bengal.

These women usually come from families with political backgrounds. The main reason for their political participation is the inspiration given by certain political events and/or persons. It is interesting to note that not even one of these actively politicized women at present unconditionally supports the claim of any party for having helped the common people.

Only two of these favour any of the present leaders. Most others reply that there is a lack of leadership in their party.

What Do the Students Think?

We had included in our sample 10 women students from colleges and universities. Some were from coeducational colleges, others from girls' colleges. Some were from arts faculties and others from science or engineering faculties.

These students also share the general disillusionment. None of them feels that any party has in recent times helped the people. Only one mentions her preference for a present leader. Of the rest, while some do mention names of the past leaders, none has faith in any of the present leaders.

Conclusions

The study generally indicates that women in West Bengal are at present not willing to take up a more active role in politics. It is not that they are not aware of the impact of political forces on their daily lives or of the political changes that are necessary to improve their situation; but, for various reasons, they do not feel that they could effectively intervene to change the situation.

1. *Education*: Education appears to be an important tool for encouraging further political participation by women. Not only are better educated women generally politically more active, but the uneducated women have repeatedly mentioned that in spite of their wishes, their lack of education prevents them from participating in political activities. The failure of the education and literacy programmes of the West Bengal Government, especially those meant for women, is likely to prove a great danger for the democratic institutions in this State.

2. *Economic emancipation*: Economic emancipation also seems to help women to develop a higher degree of political consciousness. Apart from bringing them in contact with groups outside their family and social structure, it also seems to give them confidence in their capacity to manage more than just their domestic responsibilities. The poorer women, who are already forced to work outside as well as manage their households, do not find their domestic responsibilities as binding as their upper class counterparts.

3. *Religion*: Hindu women because of their greater degree of economic and social emancipation seem to be somewhat more politicized than the Muslim or tribal women.

4. *Upper class*: A number of factors help the upper class women to take a more active part in politics. They are generally better educated and come from more liberal high caste families. A number of them are career women. The comparatively greater degree of leisure available to upper class women may also help their political inclinations.

5. *Urbanization*: Although, in general, urban people are a strong political force in our country, urbanization as such does not appear to make the West Bengal women politically more conscious. The poorer uneducated urban women are equally denied the common benefits of urbanization such as easy communication between groups, better living facilities, more opportunities for education, etc. as their rural counterparts. On the other hand, in a number of rural areas, there are to be found inspired local leaders working on political, social, and educational fronts who help even uneducated women to develop progressive attitudes. Rabindranath Tagore's work in Birbhum is a shining example of this, and is remembered even today by the older rural women of that area. A number of local leaders are even today

working in rural Bengal, with similar intentions. Surprisingly, most of such leaders do not belong to the hierarchy of any political party. In urban areas, on the other hand, no such local leader or social worker has been mentioned.

6. *Language groups*: Different language groups in our country represent different cultural and social attitudes, and such basic differences in attitudes would logically be aggravated by communication difficulties between different language groups. However, it appears that there is in our country an even wider culture of the poor – whether Hindi speaking or Bengali speaking. The poor share the same difficulties in making a living, and therefore react similarly to their situation.

7. *Disillusionment*: We have emphasized the general disillusionment about political parties and leaders which is very common among our respondents. There has not been any general political issue which has captured the imagination of all Indians – men and women, young and old – as did the independence movement. Hence, the growing apathy among young women even when they are highly educated and widely read. This may be one of the major reasons for the currently indifferent attitude towards politics among women. As an informed guess, the author would like to mention that this disillusionment is a product of the past two years and was probably much less common just after the December 1971 Bangla Desh incident.

8. *Trade unions*: Although trade unions are fairly active in West Bengal, there is complete ignorance about their role and activities outside the organized sector. Also, among the women working in the organized sector, trade unions have not always succeeded in helping them to link up their narrow economic activities with wider political issues.

Appendix

Social Status of Women

The questionnaire for West Bengal had included an additional small list of questions (Part III of the questionnaire) meant for assessing the social status of women today. In the main report, we have used only the overall indicators of relative social attitudes of the interviewed women. Here we attempt to give a somewhat detailed review of the findings.

Graphs 1 and 2 show that on the social front, the West Bengal women of our sample have much more progressive attitudes than on the political front. However, progressive attitudes as such do not always mean a higher social status since status depends on not just the reactions of the women themselves but of the rest of the family.

Table A gives a brief summary of these findings.

Social Position

1. *Marriage*: Of the sample only 24 women had arranged their own marriages. Of these, most were urban, highly educated women usually of the high income group. The only three rural women who fell in this group were career women – two teachers and one hospital worker.

2. *Dowry*: Ninety of the respondents claimed that they disapproved of taking dowry in son's marriages. The ones who candidly admitted that they would take dowry, were largely rural low income women. Only 45 admitted that dowry was given in their marriage and these were mostly of rural low income groups.

The question regarding dowry is somewhat delicate and it is likely that a number of women, especially of the urban educated middle class, have not told the truth. We have, however, no evidence that this is so from this sample.

3. *Family planning*: The record of family planning practices is very poor especially among the rural and urban illiterate low income women. The few urban women of this group belong to industrial worker families among whom there has been some spread of these practices. Among the 24 Muslim women interviewed, only seven practised family planning.

TABLE A

Social status and attitudes of women in West Bengal

Rural and Urban education groups by monthly family income	Total No.	Arranged own marriage	Dowry Given at own marriage	Disapproves of taking dowry	Practises family planning	Manages family funds	Knows about abortion law	Does not think it necessary to marry in own caste/religion	Approves of remarriage for women
1	2	3	4	5	6	7	8	9	10
A. Urban illiterate women									
1. less than 500	24	—	4	7	6	17	4	7	20
2. 500 to 1000	3	—	—	1	—	1	1	—	3
3. more than 1000	—	—	—	—	—	—	—	—	—
B. Rural illiterate women									
1. less than 500	41	—	25	29	3	16	6	5	33
2. 500 to 1000	2	—	2	2	—	0	—	—	2
3. more than 1000	—	—	—	—	—	—	—	—	—
C. Urban women with primary and secondary education									
1. less than 500	15	1	2	2	6	7	5	9	12
2. 500 to 1000	7	2	—	2	3	2	6	3	7
3. above 1000	4	1	—	—	1	1	1	6	4
D. Rural women with primary and secondary education									
1. less than 500	7	1	4	4	3	1	4	2	4
2. 500 to 1000	5	—	3	3	2	—	4	2	4

3. above 1000	—	—	—	—	—	—	—	—	—
E. Urban women graduate or professional									
1. less than 500	5	1	1	1	2	5	2	3	5
2. 500 to 1000	13	3	2	6	4	8	5	4	12
3. above 1000	26	13	1	2	15	15	19	20	25
F. Rural graduate or professional									
1. less than 500	2	1	1	1	—	2	—	—	2
2. 500 to 1000	2	1	—	—	1	2	2	2	2
3. above 1000	—	—	—	—	—	—	—	—	—

4. *Managing family funds*: Over one-half the respondents manage their family funds. This percentage is somewhat lower among low income uneducated women of both urban and rural areas. Among the Muslim women 14 did not manage their family funds.

5. *Abortion law*: Knowledge about passing of the abortion law is mainly limited to educated urban women. Since there is a greater resistance to other family planning methods among the manual worker families, it would be a help to these women if abortion facilities are made easily known and available to them.

Social Attitudes

1. Marriages within own religion/caste: Over one-half the respondents considered it essential that marriages should be within one's own religion and caste. Of the rest, eight were Muslims. Disregard for caste and religion is much more common among upper class, better educated urban women.

2. Remarriage of women: Except for 21, all respondents felt that divorcees and widows should re-marry, if they want to. Some felt that society would not approve of such marriages but it was necessary for women.

In general, therefore, it appears from our sample that women of all classes, regions, and areas are now developing socially progressive attitudes. However, among the low income uneducated women the status given by the society and families to women still leaves much to be desired. In some ways Muslim women face an even more restrictive social system.

PART III

PROFILES OF WOMEN IN STATE POLITICS

PROFILES OF WOMEN IN A.P.

G.Y. Chandramani

The Background

The pioneering social reform movement undertaken by Kandukuri Veeresalingam emphasized the urgent need to liberate women in general, and Andhra women in particular, from social and cultural taboos and restrictions of various types. Scores of men and women, inspired by his lead, crusaded for women's emancipation through meetings, writings, speeches, and organizations. He championed the cause of women's education by starting a school at Rajahmundry for girls. His wife Rajyalakshmi started a Prarthana Samaj where women of all castes were encouraged to come out and meet at a common place. Much encouragement was also given to women to participate in various activities, to contribute articles to Veeresalingam's weekly *Vivekavardhani*. This was really the beginning of the women's movement in Andhra.

The Women's Indian Association was started in 1917 with its headquarters at Madras, to tackle the educational and social problems of women. A number of women's organizations and educational institutions sprang up at various important centres in Andhra: (1) Vidyarthini Samaj was started by Balantrapu Seshamma at Kakinada. (2) Vaishya Seva Sadanam at Rajahmundry run by its secretary Bathula Kamakshamma. The Seva Sadanam started the first Sanskrit College for women in Andhra. (3) Penaka Kanakamma started the Kasturba Vidyalaya at Nellore. (4) Unnava Lakshmibayamma started the Sarada Niketan at Guntur to promote and spread basic education. (5) Duvvuri Subbamma and Kalagara Pichchamma were instrumental in starting Vidyalayas for girls which helped the spread of education among girls in Andhra.

The Andhra Mahila Sabha came into existence in 1937 as a small children's club – the group was known as the 'Little Ladies of Brindavan'. It started to arrange radio programmes and organized classes in classical music and dance. Children were backed up by mothers who also became members and it gradually grew in size and activity. By 1942, the Andhra Mahila Sabha had 500 members; later it became an independent organization; hitherto it was only a branch of the Andhra Maha Sabha. Many women of well-to-do families and maharanis contributed to its development through land and money When Andhra Pradesh was formed, the Andhra Mahila Sabha began its activities on lines similar to that of the government. Its aim is to train more women and harness their energies to build a new India. Its founder-president was the Rani of Mirjapur and founder-secretary Durgabai Deshmukh. As women's educational activities increased, a number of Telugu journals such as *Hindu Sundari, Grihalakshmi,* and *Telugutalli* exclusively for women came into existence.

Women leaders such as Durgabai, Jayanti Suramma, etc. participated in the freedom struggle and courted arrest. Many more women participated in the Civil Disobedience movement and Salt Satyagraha and also courted arrest.

After India became independent, greater opportunities to participate in the country's social and political life came to our women. There was in general a spurt in the activities of women's associations. The starting of social welfare boards gave an impetus to women's involvement in the task of reconstructing our society.

Women's Participation in Elections

In a democracy elections constitute a major political activity for the people, perhaps the only one for the illiterate people. Election to an office is an important process in the politics of the country. Propaganda, campaigning, etc. draw men and women into the vortex of elections.

Table 1 indicates that unlike most other States, in Andhra Pradesh the number of women electors were more than men electors, though the number of women who actually voted was less than men in spite of a slight increase in the number of actual voters, men and women; in the fifth General Elections, their percentage came down from 1967. This could be due to a lack of political awareness among newly enfranchised citizens. The total number of men voters in Andhra Pradesh alone was 8,433,154 out of 23,136,184 in the fifth General Elections. Among non-voters, women formed 55.44% and men 44.56%, indicating a higher percentage of abstention among women.

Table 2 shows variations in women's voting in some constituencies and indicates varying levels of awareness and participation of women

TABLE 1

Number of electors in the contested constituencies

Year	Men	Women	Total	Number of electors who voted		Percentage	
				Men	Women	Men	Women
1967	10,427,648	10,521,596	20,949,244	7,584,422	6,891,887	72.73	65.5
1972	11,545,411	11,580,773	23,126,184	7,787,412	6,905,618	67.45	59.6

TABLE 2

Electorate and votes polled in some of the Andhra Pradesh Assembly: constituencies (1967)

Constituency	Number of electors		Number of electors who voted		Percentage of actually voted	
	Men	Women	Men	Women	Men	Women
Tenali	41,666	43,821	31,862	32,480	76.47	74.12
Yellareddy	33,615	34,760	18,223	10,020	54.21	28.83
Wanaparthy	37,049	34,363	21,603	22,844	58.31	61.14
Vinukonda	43,081	42,300	30,095	28,009	69.86	66.22

in different Assembly constituencies. Similar variations can be found in the case of Parliamentary constituencies also.

TABLE 3

Electorate and votes polled in some of the Parliamentary constituencies in Andhra Pradesh (1967)

Consti-tuency	Number of electors in contested constituencies		Number of electors who voted		Percentage of electors voted	
	Men	Women	Men	Women	Men	Women
Srikakulam	230,559	260,108	174,538	174,616	75.70	67.13
Visakha-patnam	257,408	266,209	176,578	164,139	68.60	61.66
Tirupati	271,768	270,357	208,340	184,596	76.66	68.28

In 23 Parliamentary constituencies out of 41, the women electors outnumber men, but only in three Constituencies do they outstrip men in actual voting. In not even a single Parliamentary constituency is the percentage of women vote more than that of men.

TABLE 4

Fourth General Elections to the Lok Sabha and Legislative Assembly in Andhra Pradesh

	Number of electors who voted		The number of men voted more than women
	Men	Women	
Legislative Assembly	7,584,422	6,891,887	692,535
Lok Sabha	7,402,973	6,725,940	677,033

From Table 4, it is clear that the number of actual voters, both men and women, is higher in the elections to the State legislature than for Parliament. It can be inferred that though women are given equal voting rights, they are not exercising it to the required extent, and when compared with men, women are always in the minority.

There was an increase of women's vote by 6.76% over that of men in the 1972 General Elections to the State legislature. Generally interest, rather than ideology or issues, acts as a motivation for women to cast their vote. In the absence of such a motivation, women generally keep away from elections – local or State. It is found that women do not generally attach much importance to local elections. Apathy towards politics is common among women, but it is more in the case of elections to local bodies for various reasons:

1. Propaganda, publicity, slogans, and symbols, which generally excite the interest of the illiterate people in general elections, are not very much in evidence in local elections. Hence the illiterate people, especially women, are less involved in local elections than in general elections.
2. Propaganda is confined mostly to the male section of the electorate and the absence of women propagandists in elections is another reason for the abstention of women.
3. Males tend to discourage female participation in local politics. Tradition appears to be a significant factor here.

One can venture a generalization at this stage. Women are used occasionally as voters by men, but are not necessarily welcomed to a share in decision-making.

As women constitute half of the population, their vote can have a great influence if they exercise it effectively. Literacy enables a woman to properly exercise her political right, as she knows that her vote helps in electing a proper candidate and abstention results in the election of an undesirable candidate. But very few women are aware of this fact. Generally male members direct, but do not educate them. Evidence shows that women are encouraged to vote at convenient times, when men need their vote.

It is desirable that men educate and encourage their women to exercise their voting right without giving directions to them. Party workers should be instructed to contact women. If more women are used as propagandists at the time of elections, women's vote and participation can be mobilized extensively. Meetings held separately for women, in many places and at convenient times, can attract working women as well as housewives.

Women As Candidates

At the time of the first General Elections in 1951-52, Andhra Pradesh was not in existence. Circars and Rayalaseema formed an integral part of the Madras State. Four women, 2 from the Congress, 1 from the KLP and one independent contested for the Lok Sabha from Andhra, but none of them were elected though they had been active participants in the freedom struggle. Even the pioneer of women's movement in Andhra, Durgabai, could secure only 140,262 votes polled out of 900,175 votes. The Communist activity in certain important parts of Andhra and the demand for a separate Andhra State dominated the campaign in the first General Elections. Factions in the Congress were also a reason for the split in the Congress vote. These two factors explain the Congress failure to win the elections in 1952 in the Andhra area.

By the time of the second General Elections, Andhra Pradesh was formed, and four women contested for the Lok Sabha. All the three from the Congress party were successful. Sangam Lakshmibai was elected unopposed from Vikarabad. The other two secured nearly 50% of the votes polled in their constituencies.

In the third General Elections, seven women contested and four of them were elected. In the fourth and fifth General Elections, three women were elected each time to the Lok Sabha. One was nominated from the Anglo-Indian Community in the fifth General Elections. The number of women representatives in the Lok Sabha was never less than three after the 1957 elections.

TABLE 5

Election of women to the Andhra Pradesh Legislative Assembly

Year	Total number of women contestants	Number of successful candidates	% of successful candidates
1955*	6	2	33.30
1957	17	10**	58.82
1962	24	10	41.67
1967	N.A.	14	—
1972	50	25	50.00

*Mid-term poll to Andhra Assembly.
**In 1957, elections were conducted only in the newly added Telangana area. The members of the 1955 (mid-term poll) Legislative Assembly continued from Andhra area. So there were altogether 12 women legislators in the 1957-62 State Legislative Assembly.

If we consider the number of women in the State Legislature, the highest number of contestants and successful candidates among women was seen only in the fifth General Elections. This is due to the Congress party giving more opportunities to women to contest the elections and prove their competence in the State legislature. Out of 287 Assembly constituencies, women contested from 44 and 50% of them were successful. It should be mentioned here that women have begun to play an increasingly important role in the State legislature.

There are various types of women participants – some belonging to urban constituencies, some to the rural areas, some who enter politics with some idea of what they should do, and some without any idea. All of them can be broadly classified as the experienced and the inexperienced. For most of them, the only vehicle to take them into politics is the Congress party. Women were not much encouraged by the other parties in Andhra to contest elections. Moreover, women had been associated with the Congress party in the freedom struggle. After independence, till the first General Elections, women in Andhra were mainly attached to the Congress party. The emergence of the Communist party in Andhra politics resulted in a slight shift in the loyalties of some women. Many women belonging to the two Godavari districts, Krishna and Guntur, started leaning towards the Communists party. The ostensible reason for women's association with the Communist party in Guntur and Vijayawada was the fact that many women were employed in factories, particularly tobacco, in that area. The promise held out by the Communist party that each family would be given land if they came into power, attracted peasant classes as well – both women and men. In addition to this, caste was also a factor in the shift of loyalties. The Communist challenge was, however, beaten back in the 1955 bye-elections and the Congress came into power in Andhra. It has remained in power ever since.

Enquiries reveal that women have been more favourably inclined towards the Congress than the opposition parties. This could be attributed to the fact that the Congress, being in power, could be more helpful to the cause of women. They found that it would be more advantageous to support a party that has an all-India basis and has been in power in many States. It could also be said that it was partly due to the influence of the male members of their families. Their small number in the legislature and their limited role in the parties are responsible for the incapacity of women to voice their problems in these institutions.

Everything that is connected with elections such as reaching the voters, holding a meeting, setting an election office, etc. is expensive.

This is the reason for the inability of women to contest elections, as they are economically dependent they cannot foot the bill. Elections in India have become more competitive and financial investment by parties, individuals, and supporters have also increased. Out of 281 legislatures in the State Assembly in 1975, only 28 are women.

Studies of voting behaviour in India reveal that women vote according to the directive of the head of the family, who is invariably a male. Therefore, party workers and leaders approach mostly the male members during elections. Formal interviews with some women in Andhra Pradesh reveal that a greater number of them are unaware of issues involved in politics. At party and public meetings, the attendance of women is almost nil. This is due to various reasons, the most important one being women's attitude towards political meetings and their fear of violent disruption of meetings. It would certainly be more useful if political parties encourage women not only to join their ranks, but also to work in election propaganda in order to solve this problem. Some women respondents, when asked to offer a solution, said that they would like to attend meetings arranged by women's organizations and mahila mandals, where they could learn about politics in a congenial atmosphere. They would prefer to have a constant contact with the political system, more through women's associations than through the occasionally active political parties.

It is also revealed that there is great enthusiasm about politics, in both the literate and the illiterate circles. But to understand many issues, women take the advice of the male members of the family. Most women also feel it as their duty to obey the male members, and act accordingly in exercising their franchise. This is due to a lack of awareness of their rights.

Women in villages are more keen about the need to organize mahila mandals. In this regard, the impact of panchayat raj seems to be the real cause for the women's increased interest in social and political life. In addition to arranging meetings involving women, a nominal fee towards the membership of the parties could be collected from those women who can afford to subscribe. Each party should allocate some funds for the uplift of women.

There is no evidence of political parties showing a genuine interest to actively involve women in the political process. Several respondents expressed the view that women, half of the electorate, are being ignored by political parties. It was suggested by some that a political party should be recognized by the Election Commission only if it has at least 50% of women as members and workers.

Women and Politics

Interviews with some women legislators revealed certain difficulties they face in discharging their functions. A prominent woman politician, Roda Mistry, admitted in one of her articles: 'The life of a politician, especially of a woman politician, is not a bed of roses in any country. This is a whole time job and then they have to look to their family and responsibilities too. Usually, there is a clash and lot of unpleasantness.' To overcome this difficulty, '...in such cases they have to be very patient...they are known to be tactful and diplomatic'. She, however, expressed her confidence about women's capabilities in politics, as they 'take things seriously and mean business in whatever they wish to accomplish'. She felt that women 'go all-out to achieve their goals. With the qualities and gifts that God has blessed women with, they can make better politicians and diplomats.[1]

Another social worker and politician with nearly 40 years of experience in social work and local government said that the lack of incentives was a hindrance to women's participation in politics. She was of the view that politics was not a paying proposition to woman. For example, membership of a local body entails travel to and from the place of meeting. The allowance given for attending the meetings is just sufficient for travel. She was of the view that the cooperation of the husband and other members of the family was most essential for women's participation in public life.

An MLA from a rural constituency with moderate education said that uneducated or moderately educated women were generally afraid of politics and considered it as only men's business. But women once encouraged or made to enter politics, could learn many things in a short period. Participation, according to her, increased their enthusiasm and political knowledge. She also suggested that there was a greater necessity of imposing certain minimum educational qualifications for candidates for contesting elections. Although she knew little of politics and functions of the legislature, she began to learn quickly the functions of the legislative procedure by observation. Her enthusiasm began to grow gradually with her participation. In less than a year, she grew into an active participant of the Assembly, in addition to learning a good deal about the requirements of her constituency.

---

[1] 'Life of a Woman Politician'.

One urban educated legislator endorsed this view when she said that there was a greater need of educated women as legislators to adequately represent women. Educated women legislators could understand the problem of women and evince more interest in solving them. She also opined that women could do more for women and children at the legislative level than through social service. 'What I could not do', she said, 'to the women folk as a social worker, I could do from a more responsible and authoritative position as a legislator.' She was of the opinion that women at the lowest level of the society knew only to suffer, but could not find a way out. The middle classes are in between. They have greater enthusiasm and ideas, but lack money which prevent them from doing anything for the society or for the uplift of women.

Even before independence women showed their capabilities in the freedom movement and as members in the Provincial Legislatures. Rukmini Ammal was the Deputy Speaker of the Madras Legislative Assembly. In free India, their number has increased in legislatures. Now there are seven women in the Upper House and 28 in the Lower House of Andhra Pradesh.

Most of the present women legislators in Andhra Pradesh are educated. In the Assembly, there are three doctors, seven graduates, two studied up to intermediate, two are matriculates, and two with primary education. The details of others are not known. Their average age is about 43. In the Legislative Council, the average age of the women members is about 54. Of the seven women members of the Council, one is a scholar in Sanskrit, three passed school final. Two Members of the Council visited foreign countries as members of delegations. All but two of the 35 women (by 1975) of the State legislature are married, and all of them have domestic responsibilities. It must be mentioned here that in spite of domestic duties they have been playing a useful role in the legislature. In addition to being legislators, they are members of several non-political organizations such as the State and Central Social Welfare Advisory Boards and other bodies associated with women and children. There has generally been a woman member in the State Cabinet. Sangham Lakshmi Bai served the Hyderabad Legislative Assembly as Deputy Minister after the first General Elections. T.N. Sadalakshmi served the State as Minister for Religions and Charitable Endownments after the third General Elections. Roda Mistry was Minister for Women's Welfare and Tourism from 1969-1972. At present Lakshmi Devi is Minister for Women and Child Welfare. However, both numerically and in terms of portfolios much needs to be done in order to involve women more actively in politics. It is often felt that portfolios such as Women's Welfare and Child Welfare are highly innocuous, and women have not yet been given important portfolios. In view of their educational attainments and experience in the legislature, they deserve responsible positions. Women in the legislature are of the opinion that in capabilities they are not inferior to their male counterparts.

As an observer of the proceedings of the legislature, this writer has noticed that women members are more regular in attendance, though less active in participating in debates. When asked for their views regarding this aspect, women members said that though they were more regular, they did not actively participate in the proceedings because of two main reasons. First, new members, as in the case of male legislators, took a long time to adjust themselves to the legislative atmosphere. Second, some of the women members seemed to be oversensitive to criticism and caustic replies from the male legislators.

So, one often finds only a select few among the 35 women legislators taking an active part in the deliberations of the House. This is borne out by the fact that experienced women legislators such as Eswaribai, D. Indira, T. E. S. Anandabai, T. N. Sadalakshmi, and Roda Mistry are heard with rapt attention in the debates and proceedings. B. Jayaprada is the present Chairman of the Coastal District Development Board (Cabinet Rank). Three women served as Mayors of the Hyderabad Corporation also.

Women legislators are interested in participating on various subjects. Leading women members of the opposition make bold to attack the ruling party. For instance, when there was a debate in the Andhra Pradesh Assembly on 11 December 1963 over the Andhra Pradesh Municipality Bill 1963, K. Anandabai intervened in the debate and strongly criticized the government for the inconvenience caused to the Medak municipality regarding water supply, electricity, and the frequent transfer of executive officers. She criticized the government for being 'unhelpful' to a municipality led by the CPI. The effect of this participation has been that the new entrants to the legislature such as Bhanu Tilakam also have been enthused to participate in debates. It can be mentioned in this context that T. Lakshmikanthamma is among the active members of the Lok Sabha.

Committees are an integral part of the legislature. Since the legislature has to dispose of several matters and the available time is limited, the Committee system has acquired importance. As the Committee is a small body, it is possible to have detailed discussions. They are necessary for purposeful legislative actions. A number of women have served on important Committees. Two women served on the panel of Chairmen of the Committees.

TABLE 6

Women members of the Committee of Andhra Pradesh Legislature (1974-75)

Committee	Total number of members including Chairman	No. of women
Joint Committees		
Estimates Committee	20	3
Public Accounts Committee	20	1
Committee on public undertakings	16	4
Committee on Subordinate Legislation	16	4
House Committee	11	1
Committees of Legislative Assembly		
Business Advisory Committee	11	1
Rules Committee	14	2
Committee of privileges	16	6
Committee on petitions	5	2
Select committee on the A.P. land revenue bill	15	1
Select Committee on the A.P. Commercial Crops Bill 1974	15	1
Committee of Legislative Council		
Rules Committee	10	1
Committee on privileges	8	1
Committee on Petitions	—	1

Women in Municipal Councils

Though women have been represented on these bodies for a long time, the number of women contestants in elections to various offices in local government is generally low. In every municipality, a number of seats are reserved for weaker sections such as women, Scheduled Castes, and Scheduled Tribes. Women can also contest the non-reserved seats. In many municipalities only the reserved seats have been filled up by women. Women contesting for a general seat is a rare feature. Considering the increase in population, voting strength, active participation of women in the Councils, some municipalities have sent proposals to the Director of Municipal Administration to increase the number of reserved seats for women in municipalities.

However, in some cases political and other pressures were brought on women to withdraw from the contest. This, according to many women leaders, constitutes a denial of women's legitimate rights and negation of democratic principles, and they felt such practices should be curbed.

Urban politics being different from rural politics, the process of political socialization at the municipal level is generally quicker than at the rural level. In urban areas, the growth of literacy is quick, and social and cultural activities, coupled with the impact of mass media, have brought about a change in the outlook of women towards social and political issues. The urban women are more aware of their rights than the rural women. For instance Rani Kumudini Devi and Sarojini Pulla Reddy served as Mayors of the Corporation of Hyderabad. Very recently Sarojini Pulla Reddy was appointed as Chairman of the Urban Development Authority of Hyderabad. Many women have started to entertain the idea that they should contest the non-reserved seats also. Enthused by the success of women in Mattupalli panchayat where all posts are held by women, many women leaders seem to think that they should dominate municipal councils also. They argue that there should be an increase in the number of reserved seats for women for at least 10 years, so that women can have an adequate say in the affairs of municipal administration. The urge for reservation is mainly due to two reasons. First, women seem to feel, as stated earlier, that as long as they are economically dependent on men, their participation in municipal politics cannot be real or effective. Second, they think that elections are not 'fair' at the municipality level and are biased in favour of men.

A number of committees are constituted to run the municipal administration. Here again, women are discriminated against. Usually women are associated with a Committee of a less important nature such as the Committee on Women and Child Welfare. Table 7 shows the relative voting strength of men and women in 10 municipalities

TABLE 7

Population and voting strength of ten municipalities in Andhra Pradesh

Municipality	Population (excluding SC & ST)		Voting strength		Total no. of seats	Seats reserved for women
	Men	Women	Men	Women		
Kovvur	11,254	11,136	6,291	6,457	15	2
Palakol	18,079	18,138	10,151	10,725	20	2
Guntur	136,695	133,296	71,167	71,541	30	4
Proposed for the coming elections	As above	As above	As above	As above	(65)	(8)
Suryapet	11,416	10,107	1,273	1,249	16	2
Bodhan	19,370	18,171	9,441	9,460	20	2
Emmiganur	15,234	15,009	6,792	7,106	18	2
Kurnool	59,542	57,407	29,732	28,996	30	2
Srikakulam	22,979	22,194	11,756	12,387	24	2
Machilipatnam	57,669	54,987	26,978	27,290	32	3
Kakinada	62,132	60,477	30,435	31,192	36	5

belonging to the three regions of Andhra Pradesh – Andhra, Telangana, and Rayalaseema. In many cases, women voters outnumber men voters. But the number of seats reserved for women is disproportionately low.

Women councillors point out that women are inadequately represented in municipal council, though their participation in committee meetings and municipal government is quite satisfactory. In spite of their long-standing experience in municipal administration, they are not considered at the time of selecting candidates for elections to the Legislative Assembly. Women leaders of Kurnool complained that though women had been very active in municipal politics, no woman was given the Congress ticket to contest the General Elections. They put the blame on the ruling party and political leaders in general.

Women members of the municipal council are elected to the zilla parishad also as coopted members. But a comparison indicates that they are more active in the municipal council as they are directly concerned with the problems of their locality. The zilla parishad is concerned with the development of the villages and agriculture about which the coopted members seem to know little.

Women in Panchayat Organizations

Andhra Pradesh is among the earliest States to introduce panchayati raj, which seeks to involve the vast rural population in developmental programme. The Andhra Pradesh Panchayat Samithis and Zilla Parishads Act of 1959 introduced a three-tier system to promote the welfare of the local areas in Andhra Pradesh. This system provided representation to women at all levels. At the gram panchayat level, some seats according to the population is reserved for women. But for the zilla parishads, panchayat samithis and general bodies, the law provides that two women be coopted to each of the bodies.

Studies on panchayati raj leadership reveal that caste and land-ownership are the dominant factors which determine the position and status of leaders at the local level and decide the results of elections. In such a tradition-dominant environment, it is difficult for women to enter politics or get into positions of importance. In spite of their interest, they are not allowed to contest for a general seat, and sometimes even for a reserved seat contest is not forthcoming. It is observed in such cases that some close associates of the leaders and certain influential people are able to occupy the reserved seats.

However, the practice is of late slowly changing even at the village level. Women, once they enter public life through nomination or election to the gram panchayat or as coopted members of the panchayat samithis, are beginning to understand the changing circumstances and the patterns of an emerging society. Apart from holding the reserved seats in village panchayats, it is noticed that seven villages in Visakhapatnam district, which is considered to be a backward district, are headed by women sarpanches. In Kurnool district, which is even more backward, 15 villages are headed by women sarpanches, and in the villages the post of upa-sarpanch is occupied by women. Mattupalli village had an all-women panchayat. This particular aspect cannot of course be described as universal.

An important factor in this regard is the encouragement being given to women's participation by not only the non-governmental schemes and measures such as Jayanti village launched on Gandhiji's birth day, but by various measures and incentives provided through the District Women's Welfare Organization during the International Women's Year.

There is now greater rapport between the officials and the people at various levels. An effort is being made by the officials through programmes of educative value to make women conscious of their rights and responsibilities. Men also are being advised by these officials about the necessity of involving women in developmental activities. That women are taking keen interest in panchayati raj institutions is evidenced by the fact that in some villages they have been running the administration, as evidenced earlier.

However, group politics often obstructs women in the discharge of their functions. Where they are in power, women, inspite of pressure of group politics, have exercised their power independently and tried to push through certain measures. Even among the tribals enthusiasm is not found wanting. Illiteracy is no hurdle because with the help of literates they at times make representation to the authorities. An example in this regard is the way in which the illiterate tribal women of Anantagiri panchayat samithi of Vizag district made a representation to the Collector and succeeded in getting funds for a public building.

If that is the case at the village level where women members are generally elected, this activity seems much less at the samithi and zilla parishad levels where they are coopted. Comparatively, women members at the panchayat samithi level are a little more active than their counterparts at the zilla parishad level. Only one woman has become panchayat samithi president in the whole of Andhra Pradesh, i.e., in East Godavari district. No woman has attained that position at the zilla parishad level. The panchayat samithi president, cited above, came to occupy that office mainly by virtue of her family background. Her husband is the present zilla parishad chairman of East Godavari district, and his brother has been a top leader in State politics for a long period.

It is believed that women legislators of the district who are ex-officio members of the panchayat samithi and zilla parishad are so preoccupied with their work that they find little time to actively participate in the meetings and developmental programmes of these rural agencies.

A curious fact is that women at the samithi and parishad level seem less active than women at the village level. This is mostly because of the lack of opportunity for them. The meetings of the samithi and parishad are dominated by elected members, and the coopted women members depend on the officials for suggestions and guidance. This situation makes their role slightly formal. In some cases women members were unaware of the fact that they were members of a Committee. In a few cases the attendance registers were sent to them to obtain their signatures, days after such meetings. As such, women's representation appears to be nominal and formal in many cases at the zilla parishad level. Their participation in the meetings and as members of the Committees is almost nil. Perhaps their presence is essential for these bodies at the time of voting. Even here, there is no evidence to show that women are exercising this right willingly and independently. It is high time that the importance of women's participation in samithi and parishad affairs was realized so that their participation could become real and meaningful.

Conclusions

In view of the pioneering social reform movement undertaken by people such as Veeresalingam, the women's movement in Andhra began on more solid foundation than in many other States. Associations and organizations had sprung up, thanks to the dynamism of many women leaders. However, the enthusiasm and activity of women underwent a downward trend after India became Independent. If the pre-independence tempo were maintained after 1947, Andhra would perhaps have been foremost among the States in India in the movement for the uplift of women. This was largely due to the fact that outstanding women leaders such as Durgabai Deshmukh had to assume responsibilities at the national level.

The falling tempo of the women's movement has resulted in their failure to make use of the opportunities provided under the Constitution. There has not been any growth in institutions and organizations meant to serve women's interest. Nor has there been any significant change in the attitude of men or women regarding women's role in politics. The majority of women feel that they cannot and should not do anything that would displease the male members of the family. Most of the respondents informed that their participation in politics had the approval and encouragement of their husbands or fathers, as the case may be.

A solution for such a situation is not easy to offer. However, as suggested by a number of respondents, reservation of seats and positions for women on a large scale for at least 10 or 15 years should be considered. The need to give more opportunities for women's education cannot be over-emphasized. A woman who can stand on her own is bound to be an asset to the family and the country at large. Education and economic self-sufficiency are most vital for women's participation in social and political life. Only then will their participation in politics be real and meaningful.

PROFILES OF WOMEN IN ASSAM

K.M. Deka

Since independence, women in Assam have been contesting elections for the Lok Sabha and the Legislative Assembly. With the exception of a few independent candidates, all others contested on Congress ticket. None of the opposition political parties has been able to recruit female candidates for elections. The secretary of the Socialist Party (Assam branch) observes that women in Assam are not much involved in leftist politics. Similar views have been expressed by the spokesmen of the CPI and the CPI(M) (Assam branches). It appears that most women in the State are identifying themselves with the Congress, and hence the history of women's participation in politics in Assam is inseparable from the history of the Congress party before and since independence.

Available records on women's participation at the electoral level in general give the impression that women have been showing an increasing involvement in elections. However, a clear and exact picture of such involvement cannot be drawn in statistical terms since the data on the subject are incomplete.

The Congress manifesto (Assamese version) brought out in 1946 makes a broad but casual reference to the role of women in the building up of society and states that the Congress will strive for securing 'equal status, rights and privileges for every Indian citizen irrespective of sex'. The manifesto brought out on the eve of the first General Elections is more specific on the status of women, and emphasizes the necessity of removing their various 'social and other disabilities' and promises to make every effort 'to open out opportunities of service for them in the legislature and in social activities'. The 1962 Assam Pradesh Congress Committee (APCC) manifesto gives an account of special measures that have been taken up by the Congress government in Assam (the Ambar Charkha scheme), and promises to continue such efforts. The latter Congress manifestoes (APCC) are silent on this point.

The APCC has also taken other organizational measures to mobilize women voters. As early as in 1950, it opened a 'Mahila Front' as a part of its organizational structure, and since 1953 the

Mahila Front has been an integral part of the APCC organization at all levels. The objective of the Front is to (i) make the women conscious of their rights and status, (ii) help them in finding economic independence, (iii) to make their rights guaranteed by the constitution.

The CPI and the CPI(M) in their supplementary manifestos have not mentioned anything specific about their programmes relating to peculiar problems of women in the State. They have, however, adopted in toto the all-India policy of their parties in this regard. For instance, the 1952 and 1957 manifestos make no departure from the original all-India manifesto of the CPI. The Socialist Party is also not an exception to this. Other State level parties, such as the Ujani Asom Rajya Parishad, People's Democratic Party, and the Plains' Tribal Council which have entered the elections of late, also not specific on this point and have not so far focused on the problems of women and promised remedies.

The CPI, the CPI (M), and the Socialist Party are trying to gear up their organizational machinery to mobilize women. A CPI spokesman says that the Women's Front in the party has been activized and one woman member has been elected to the State Council in 1971. He claims that the party has with some degree of success organized women against different forms of social oppression, and for gradually drawing them into agitation on other political and economic issues. He further claims that the responses from women in such agitations is quite encouraging, and that more than 600 women actively participated in the recent *satyagraha* against the government on the issue of soaring prices of essential commodities. The CPI (M) and the Socialist Party are, however, not so optimistic about changing the attitude of women towards the left movement although both the parties have Women's Fronts. The fact thus remains undisputed that excepting the Congress, other parties in Assam have failed to attract women by providing them a clear and more comprehensive scheme of measures for their upliftment.

The register of Assam Acts has recorded since 1944 the following bills as passed by the Assembly:

A bill relating to conditions of female workers in Assam, (i) Act XVIII of 1944:

This Act regulates the employment of female workers on wage or salary basis in factories, plantations and any other establishment, which the State (Provincial) government may notify for the purpose of certain periods before and after child birth and to provide for the grant of maternity benefits to female workers. It prohibits employment of, or work by, a woman (i) during the four weeks immediately preceding the day of delivery except such light work which may be assigned to her as recommended by the medical practitioner, and (ii) during four weeks following the day of her delivery. It also prohibits the woman worker from taking a job elsewhere during the periods mentioned above. Besides, the Act specifies the rate of wages to be paid to a female worker in plantations and puts her on par with female workers in other establishments so far as leave and other maternity benefits are concerned.

In accordance with another provision of the Act, the employer is liable to render free medical treatment to such a worker, and must refrain from serving notice of dismissal on her during the period as specified above.

Contravention of the Act by an employer involves a penalty of Rs.500 which in full or a part of it may be paid to the worker as compensation.

This Act provides the basis for further welfare measures for female workers in Assam and is, in its modified form, still in operation. The following amendments to the Act have been made up-to-date.

(ii) Assam Act XVII of 1951:

It inserts a proviso which says that in case of a female worker in a plantation, she must not be engaged in work during a period of eight weeks preceding her delivery as well as during eight weeks following it. It is, however, not applicable in respect of miscarriage. The Act also enhances the rate of wage in general (in addition to usual food concession).

(iii) Assam Act V of 1952:

This Act, by effecting an amendment to the existing laws referred to in (i) and (ii) above, reduces the total period of maternity leave from 16 to 12 weeks in the case of workers in plantations.

(iv) Assam Act XII of 1964:

It makes two important amendments to the Central Act 53 of 1961 in its application to Assam, namely:

(a) the period of maternity leave has been increased from six weeks to eight weeks as provided in the Central Act, which shows the liberal attitude of the Government of Assam towards women workers;

(b) an employer, subject to the provisions of the Central Act, is made liable to extend maternity benefits to workers and to pay weekly in the case of wage-earners, and monthly in the case of others.

(v) Assam Act I of 1965:

This is the latest amendment to the Central Act 53 of 1961, which adds a proviso relating to the death of a worker on maternity leave. According to this Act, wages and other maternity benefits up to the day of her death shall be payable to the deceased's relatives in case she does not leave a child behind, and full benefits shall be payable in case the child survives.

(vi) Assam Act XX of 1953:

The Assam Nurses', Midwives' and Health Visitors' Regulation Act (Amendment) 1953 amends section IV of the Act of 1944 which now provides that the Council shall, in addition to other categories of members, include two nurses elected by the registered nurses, two midwives elected by registered midwives, two nursing superintendents and two matrons.

(vii) Assam Act IX of 1935:

It deals with Muslim marriages and divorces in Assam. According to this Act, registration of divorce of the 'Khula' system shall have to be signed by both husband and wife, thereby giving equal legal status to Muslim women in case of divorce. However, in other kinds of divorce the consent of the wife is not required.

The Assam Act IX of 1935 has been amended by the Assam Act XXI of 1953, which enhances the fees for registration. Since then the Act has not been suitably amended to give equal status to Muslim women in all matters relating to marriage and divorce.

Besides these Acts, the Assam Municipal Act 1956 and the Assam Panchayat Act 1959 also provide for nomination of women to Municipal Boards and Panchayats.

In an interview, Mrs. Anowara Taimur, a leading member in the Assam Assembly and convener of the Women's Front of the APCC, has told this author that adequate welfare measures for women in Assam have not been adopted by the government. She argues that unless the government removes economic disabilities from which the women in general today suffer, political and other rights given to them would carry little practical meaning. Asked as to why she and her female colleagues in the Assembly have not so far sponsored measures aimed at the welfare of women such as job-oriented schemes exclusively for women (as pointed out by Mrs. Taimur herself) in the State, she has said that women legislators constitute a microscopic minority in the Assembly and all such important legislation is to be brought forward by the government. Even if they are initiated by women, it would not be possible for them to carry them through the floor of the House without government's support.

Besides the Congress, which has been nominating the maximum number of women candidates to Lok Sabha and Assembly since the first General Elections, there were few women who contested elections as independent candidates and only one such candidate succeeded in getting herself elected. It is interesting to note that she belonged to the Congress till 1969, and when there was a split in the party she joined Congress (O). Before the fifth General Elections, she resigned from Congress (O), tried in vain to return to Congress (R) and finally contested the election as an independent candidate.

Table 1 shows the number of women candidates both elected and defeated according to their party affiliations, and the number of votes polled by them in the Lok Sabha elections since 1952.

TABLE 1

Lok Sabha election

Year	Constituency	Valid votes cast	Votes polled by women candidates	No. of women candidates and their party affiliation	Total candidates in the const.	Elected or defeated
1952	Goalpara	804,823	158,651	1, Ind.	6	Defeated
	Garo Hills Autonomous Hills Dist.	109,663	59,326	1, Cong.	3	Elected
1957	Goalpara	696,041	183,974	1, Cong.	3	Elected
	Golaghat	176,442	80,028	1, Cong.	4	Elected
1962	Cachar	196,100	72,086	1, Cong.	4	Elected
	Barapeta	221,598	86,691	1, Cong.	6	Elected
	Jorhat	185,615	77,184	1 Cong.	3	Defeated
1967	Cachar	196,152	89,713	1, Cong.	4	Elected
	Gauhati	261,339	88,658	1, Cong.	6	Defeated
1971	Cachar	—	—	1, Cong.	—	Elected
	Dibrugarh	197,279	11,009	1, Ind.	8	Defeated

An analysis of Table 2 shows that the average number of women contesting each of the five General Elections to the Assembly is about eight, and the total strength of the legislature varied between 108 and 114. Of the elected women candidates only one was an independent while the other 22 belonged to Congress. The average number of

TABLE 2

Legislative Assembly elections

Year	No. of women contestants	Total No. of valid votes cast in these constituencies	Total No. of votes polled by the women candidates	Party Affiliation of the WC		Total Candidates in the Contest	No. of women	
				Cong.	Ind.		Selected	Defeated
1952	5	88,143	25,862	4	1	37	1	4
1957	8	259,746	92,279	7	1	29	5	3
1962	4	89,910	38,826	4	0	20	4	-
1967	9	218,110	84,195	7	2	35	5	4
1972	13	351,647	181,973	9	4	13	8	5

female members in each of the five terms of the Legislative Assembly is less than five, which means that women MLAs constitute a microscopic minority in the legislature.

Mrs. Taimur told this author that the Election Committee, which did not have a woman member till 1972, appeared to be somewhat unsympathetic to women candidates. For instance, the Women's Front demanded 48 tickets for women candidates in 1972, but the APCC accepted the nominations of only nine of them. Sri Lalit Kumar Doley, President of the APCC, was, however, of the opinion that sufficient number of women of ability did not come forward to file nomination and commented that Congress had sometimes 'nominated women for the sake of commitment alone and not on consideration as to whether they had fair chances of winning the election'. A glance at the performance of female candidates (Congress), however, shows that their election casualties were comparatively less than those of their male counterparts. Hence, there is still a strong case for recruitment of larger numbers of women into the legislature.

As far as Anchalik panchayats were concerned, only two women, both belonging to Congress, were elected as vice-presidents in 1967. It may be mentioned that there were as many as 263 Anchalik panchayats under the Assam Panchayat Act, 1959. It is somewhat surprising that the performance of women in the State at the grass-root levels of Indian democracy is very poor.

Profiles of Women in Assam

The interest of women as a whole is not often seen to have been articulated by organized groups, which may be differentiated from political parties. In fact, the political parties, particularly the APCC, are concerned with carrying on the unfinished social movement for securing equal status for women in the society. This, however, does not mean that there are no politically oriented organized groups exclusively for women. The Assam Mahila Samiti having its organizational network throughout the State is the oldest women's organization in Assam. Some of its top office-bearers were devoted Congress workers (such as Smt. Chandra Prabha Saikiani), who also participated in the freedom movement. It was started as a social organization to rouse social and political consciousness among women, and to help them become independent in economic matters. Although apparently non-political, it actually had political links with the Congress. But after the death of its organizational alumni (C.P. Saikiani) the Samiti is now almost defunct.

The Northeast India Women's Association has its central office in Gauhati, and is primarily an organization of upper-middle class women apparently led by a lady belonging to the opposition. It is more a social club arranging flower shows and cooking competitions than an interest group.

The Kasturba Gandhi National Memorial Trust (Assam branch) is the one truly non-political organization in Assam, which has been doing commendable work since 1944, not only for women and children but also for bringing greater understanding among the various groups of people living in this region. It maintains a reasonable distance from political organizations.

(i) A glance through the newspapers of the period under review shows that women had displayed considerable interest in the two 'Refinery Movements'. They extended their support through various organizations, and participated in the mass *satyagraha* particularly in the second 'Refinery Movement'.

(ii) On the language issue which first cropped up in 1960 in connection with the Assam Official Language Bill, and then again in 1972 in connection with the medium of instruction in colleges, women played a very sober role. They expressed their anxiety at the grave situation which was being exploited by 'anti-social elements with a view to disintegrating the State', expressed sympathy for the families of those students who fell victims in the movement, and appealed to the public to respond favourably to the call given jointly by the political parties for finding a permanent solution by following a democratic method.[1]

(iii) During the Chinese aggression in 1962 the women in Assam with the help of the Women's Front of the APCC constituted 'the Mahila Defence Committee', with branches in all the districts, and sub-committees in the wards in towns. The committee collected money for the defence fund and coordinated the defence activities of women in Assam.

(iv) The contribution of women in rehabilitating the refugees from the erstwhile East Pakistan is also noteworthy.[2]

(v) From time to time women have been participating in agitations against price rise, hoarding, and food scarcity in Assam.

It is interesting to note that while women have been showing increasing interest in the general problems faced by the State, they have not shown much concern for removing their own disabilities. To give an example, no women's organization has so far voiced the demand for full implementation of the provisions of the Hindu succession laws, the implementation of which would certainly bring women on par with men in social and economic matters.

It is now not possible to determine whether the political parties used religion or religious symbols to mobilize women's votes. The scanty data collected from secondary sources tend to suggest that the elections were not free from religious influences. The symbols of the two Congress parties also have some bearing on religious-minded women in the rural areas. Besides, as has been pointed out by Sri Doley, APCC chief, the historical examples of Mula Gabhuru, Sati Jaimati, and the martyrs of the freedom movement who have secured a place in the history of Assam by their noble deeds were often cited to rouse the spirit of women and mobilize their votes. But it is difficult to measure its effects on voters.

Regarding the role of women members in the APCC, it may be noted that no woman so far has been elected as president, general secretary, or treasurer of the APCC. The composition of the Election Committee of the APCC reveals that a woman was included in it only twice – in 1957 and 1973. Taimur, the only woman in the Election Committee told this author that the APCC chief initially invited her to the Election Committee only as an observer, and it was on subsequent pressure from an influential Central leader (who also happens to be a woman) that she had to be included as a member of the Committee.

There are 23 District Congress Committees in Assam, and the average strength of the executive committee of the DCC varies between 22 and 23.

TABLE 3
District Congress Committees

Year	DCCs	No. of DCCs having women	Offices held					
			President	V.P.	Gen. Secy.	Secy.	Treasurer	Members, Ex. Committee
1952	23	2	1	—	—	—	—	1
1954	23	5	2	—	—	—	—	4
1957	23	3	1	—	—	—	—	3
1959	23	14	Nil	3	—	—	1	17
1963	23* one ad hoc	4	—	—	—	—	—	4
1967 1973*	23	4	—	2	—	—	—	3

*Complete figures are not available since some of the DCCs are yet to be reconstituted.

So far as the other parties are concerned, there is very little representation of women in their hierarchies. The CPI has elected one woman as member of its State council in 1971 (previously there was no woman in the council). Till today no woman has been elected to the State executive of the CPI. Only three district councils of the party have women (one each) as their members. The CPI(M) State committee or its executive has not included a single woman as its member. There is one woman as member of one of its district committees. The Socialist Party also has not recruited women to its hierarchies.

It was in 1970 that a woman had for the first time been inducted as a full cabinet member in the Chaudhury ministry. There were, however, two women in the earlier ministries, who were ministers of State. The present ministry also has a woman member who is the Minister of State for Social Welfare.

References

1. "Mahila Samajar Raijoloi Nibedan" brought out jointly by 13 women organizations in the State during the 'Language Movement' in 1972.
2. *Report of the Convener of the Women's Front*, APCC, 1964, p. 13.

PROFILES OF WOMEN IN GUJARAT

Pravin N. Sheth

One witnesses a relatively liberal tradition in the social life of Gujarat. However, this tradition is more observed in south, central, and urban Gujarat, and less in Saurashtra and north Gujarat. Gujarat is one of the first areas in the country which was exposed to western education, and its first female graduates came out at the beginning of this century.[1] The Gandhian movement had considerable impact on womenfolk who had their first political socialization process under Gandhiji, and its enduring effect could be seen even after independence when all the female MPs from the State belonged to the Gandhian era. This era brought out the women in urban Gujarat, most of them belonging to high castes and educated families. But as the first important *satyagraha* movements started in rural Gujarat were related to land and agricultural issues they caused considerable awakening among the agricultural Patidar women of Ras and Borsad (Kaira district) and Bardoli (Surat district). The significant impact of the Gandhian movement was seen on the backward class Koli women in Karadi-Matwad in Surat district. The post-1947 phenomenon till the mid-sixties bears the stamp of this impact, and most of the leading women in public life belonged to the Gandhian era. Democratic politics has not brought out many female leaders and only a handful of them have been able to make their presence felt at the State level.

It may be mentioned that the cause of freedom and the charismatic leadership of Mahatma Gandhi brought many more women to the fore in public life, and many more women workers faced the sufferings of agitation and undertook the rigorous task of nation-building than they did in post-1947 Gujarat.[2] He increased the efficacy of the programmes of national movement by involving in them the women of Gujarat.[3] It was a woman, Anasuyaben Sarabhai, the wife of a mill-owner, who initiated workers in one of the first and the most constructive yet efficient trade unions of industrial workers in Gujarat and India. Mithuben Petit worked for the uplift of the Adivasis. Scores of other women made excellent contribution in organizing effective picketing, fasting at the residences of mill-owners asking them to give relief to mill workers, organizing election campaign for the Provincial

Assembly (1937) and municipal councils, and for demanding women's rights in marriage and removal of untouchability, and all of them courting arrest.[4] A large mass of the women belonging to farmer's families in Ras and Bardoli and the backward Koli women of Karadi-Matwad showed awareness and action of a high degree. Gujarat became the citadel of the campaign. The women showed marvellous power of organization and they steered the movement successfully. Awakening of the woman, her liberty, her equality, and the courage the movement brought to her are the most important happenings in the social field of revolution in the Gandhian era.[5]

Political Parties and Women

Since the freedom movement, the Congress had provided for the constitution of women's wing as a part of Congress. This wing, familiar as the Mahila Congress, had done a commendable job in bringing out Gujarat women from their homes, helped women in organizing picketing before government offices and courts and near the *peetha* (liquor shops), prabhat ferries (morning freedom march), boycott of foreign goods, sale of khadi, and other such protests.

After 1947, many freedom fighters such as Mrinalini Sarabhai, Gangaben Jhaveri, and others could not adjust to the new type of Congress leadership who brought their own style and method of working in operating the party. Before 1947, activists belonged to the high castes and educated upper middle-class families. But after 1947, with few exceptions, such women turned to social welfare and women's entertainment activities. Some turned to spiritual life and the political mahila organizations at different levels went to less educated and intermediary caste groups. When the new Congress was formed women belonging to caste Hindus again got attracted to it, and they occupied important positions in the Mahila Congress (R).

The Congress has given special attention to the cause of women. Leaders of the undivided Congress since Mahatma Gandhi to Morarji Desai have never failed to stress the importance of women and the place that should be given to them in public life and the Congress organization. Congress (O) has lived up to this pledge by specially giving seats to women in the organization on the basis of one district-one seat to a woman candidate. The undivided Congress passed the anti-bigamy Act as early as 1948, and made bigamy a cognizable offence. This was followed throughout India in 1965.

In 1947 under the persuasion of women, the divorce law was liberalized and the Immoral Traffic Act was passed. Though the position of women is not yet satisfactory, the policy and the laws made by the Congress government have not been unsatisfactory so far as public provisions are concerned.[6]

In the Congress also, special mention has been made regarding uplift of women, giving equal wages to women, and bringing up the weaker sections of society including women and particularly the women belonging to the backward castes and tribes. Although no specific programmes have been organized, the Mahila Congress of both the Congresses have conducted 'shibirs' (training camps) for women workers. Congress (O) particularly has a record of more sustained programme of such activities.

Jana Sangh also has a wing specially run by and for women. This party has organized frequent *morchas* (protest rallies) against price rise and shortage of food and oil and articulated vociferously the problems of housewives in urban areas. On the whole, however, no party has articulated the problems of women in a noticeable way in their party literature and manifestoes, though in the party organs of Congress (O) and Congress (R), routine reports about their women's wings do appear. No party has cared to keep records of the activities of women. One can only find some improvised record of proceedings in the office of Mahila Congress (O).

Political Participation: Poll and Public Policy

Women in this context have been found active generally only at the time of elections for municipal councils, Vidhan Sabha, Lok Sabha and very insignificant for the panchayats. As a legacy of the Gandhian movement in Gujarat, the mahila branch of the Congress ruling party had continued to get cooperation from the women activists. Various city committees have therefore pressed them into party service and they have been found useful in the preparation of voters' cards, distribution of such cards and pamphlets, and mobilizing women voters to the polling booths. The same holds true for the Assembly and Lok Sabha elections. The women voters also have not lagged behind in voting. With successive elections, as politics became more competitive, social mobilization became greater and women voters also began to be the target of the competing parties. In the second General Elections of 1957, the women activists and voters showed considerable interest as a result of the consciousness aroused in the wake of the 'Maha Gujarat' movement in the State. However, this was more or less confined to Ahmedabad, Nadiad, and Mehsana. In 1967, when the Swatantra Party challenged the Congress party in a big way, considerable interest was evinced among women belonging to the farmer and trading class, and the Patidar and Kshatriya women polled in large numbers. A feature of the women's voting is their going to the poll en masse, and considerable bloc voting has been observed by political strategists and campaign managers belonging to the main parties of Gujarat. Rural women and women belonging to backward castes such as Thakardas, Kolis, Harijans and Adivasis, and a minority class such as the Muslims have been found particularly active in polling and voting on bloc basis.

The Congress split of 1969 and the mid-term elections of 1971 involved a female personality and considerable interest was shown in the leadership and policy drive provided by India's woman Prime Minister. Women belonging to rural as well as urban educated class veered round her. Many women thought that the challenge to Mrs. Gandhi was a challenge to women as such, her capacity to fight, and guide the nation. In the poll of 1971, therefore, women showed considerable interest in mobilizing voters and also by coming out in a big way to vote, largely for Mrs. Gandhi. The discussions throughout the State is evidenced from the newspaper reports, the women's periodicals such as *Stree* and *Shree*, and the weekly women's column that characterizes almost all the local dailies of Gujarat.[7]

Women generally do bloc voting in rural areas and areas belonging to Scheduled Castes and Tribes, and Muslims in cities. Their polling percentage are almost equal to men's. But except in 1971, and perhaps in the Assembly elections of 1972, women voters have not voted in a way markedly different from the men. On these two occasions a large proportion of women voted for Mrs. Gandhi as the Prime Minister, a leader who was looked upon as a symbol of India's great womanhood, one to whom they turned for bringing up the weaker sections of society, and the one who would usher into the society her promised socio-economic change.[8] In the queries regarding as to when and how they were first exposed to or interested in political events and matters, Mrs. Gandhi topped the list of items of political socialization.[9]

In big cities of the State, social workers and freedom fighters occasionally contested the municipal elections, particularly in Surat and

Ahmedabad. In many of the small and medium-sized towns, however, it was the women belonging to the local political and enonomic elite who contested these elections. Generally, it was the leading traditional elite family who would field its female members to contest the elections. Navsari, Nadiad, Broach, Gandevi and some erstwhile princely capitals in Saurashtra may be mentioned to substantiate this point.

In the panchayat few females would come forward to participate. This was not unnatural for a traditional rural community. However, the provisions of the Gujarat Panchayats Act have made it possible for the reservation of two seats for women in each panchayat. This has enabled women to participate in the panchayati process. Some female members even defeated male members as in the case of office of the president of taluka panchayats of Kapadvanj and Sanand. In some panchayats, they have become the sarpanch (e.g., Vallabh Vidyanagar) or deputy sarpanch (e.g., Gana, Kaira district). In one of the studies done by the author, it was found that panchayats in some areas had been found to function as an agent of socialization in public affairs.[10] But this is more an exception than a rule. On the whole, the women members hardly attend the meetings of the village panchayats (they are too busy in agricultural and family work) and the talati-cum-secretary goes to their home to get their signature in the minutes book for record.

So far as their participation in election campaign is concerned the active women generally do much of the routine work such as, door-to-door canvassing, distributing pamphlets and leaflets, pasting stamps on cards, etc. However, sometimes this work brings them into party headquarters and local election offices, and provides access to important party leaders. The Mahila Congress (undivided Organization) is found to be most active in this matter. Generally, during election time, it holds the meeting of its conveners and distributes work to its workers in talukas and branches in mofussil headquarters and city wards. They in turn treat the party volunteers and cater to them when engaged in election campaigns.

Participation in Voting

With regard to female voters in the whole State, the only empirical study made, completed and available, is in the case of the fourth General Elections of 1967. The Department of Political Science of the Gujarat University had undertaken one project of the study of three constituencies – urban, rural, and reserved and having differential competitive situations; the study covered the total sample pre-poll and post-poll investigations. Out of them, 554 were males and 144 were females. Out of the 144 females in the sample, 129 responded.

The following is the major finding with regard to women's voting and political behaviour as derived from this study.

As regards their perception of various issues, females assigned higher priority to price, food distribution, law and order; males gave more importance to corruption and leadership. Perhaps the type of problems that confronted female voters (prices of commodities rather than to deal with corrupt practices and persons) had something to offer as an explanation. Females scored highest (86.6%) on price problem and lowest (54.6%) on leadership issue. Candidate orientation was stronger among males (0.89 as score), and weak among females (0.50). Also, party identification was low among females (score 3.87) as compared to males (5.31). In all the constituencies, females displayed closer identification with parties, and it was more or less uniform in all the three constituencies, indicating the uniform position of females irrespective of their place of residence in regard to relationship with parties. Also, it was found that all the hree constituencies mostly had male members of political parties showing thereby that females were not actively associated with political life.

The exposure score of females (1.80) was almost half of that of males (3.65). Incidentally, both the sexes scored low on exposure item. Among the exposed section again, females were mostly confined to lower levels of exposure. There were 75% at low level, 22.50% at medium level and a meagre 2.50% at the high level.

Regarding the question as to how much political information women voters had in the 1967 poll campaign, they lagged behind the male score from 4 to 7 score points. Difference in the male-female score was the highest in the metropolitan area of Ahmedabad. Again, no woman voter belonged to the high information group.

As regards the various pressures that caused respondents to vote in a particular way, females were more exposed to the cross-pressures. Perhaps the fact that women generally stayed home and were more often and easily approachable by canvassers has something to offer as an explanation. This was also indicated by the finding that the gap between the male and female scores was higher in Ahmedabad than elsewhere. Males in the city were not available at home most of the time, while in rural areas gaps between the female and male scores were not so pronounced. Less women (7.3%) voted on account of party as against 19.8 of males. Females were more influenced by multiple (cross) pressures and issues.

Political participation is a process by which an individual in the system gets involved in politics. It is a cumulative process. The degree and level of participation also indicates acceptance of the system and his sense of political efficacy. Viewed from this point, participation scores of women (0.47) were uniformly lower than those of males (1.29) in all the three constituencies. Similarly, they also scored low on the item of participation in poll campaigns (0.43) than males (1.01).

In the Assembly election of 1967 in Ahmedabad city, 77.5% of female respondents voted the Janta Parishad (a regional leftist party), while only 10% reported that they had voted Congress; and only 7.5% voted the Swatantra. However, in the rural and the reserved constituencies, the Swatantra Party got greater support from females than from males. On the whole, the Congress got remarkably less support from women than from men. Only in the rural constituency of Matar could the Congress get majority of females votes. The reason might be the fact that the Congress had fielded a Harijan woman candidate backed by the popular panchayat leaders in the area. In 1971 and 1972 the situation had reversed when Mrs. Gandhi herself became a contender for leading the government and to fight on behalf of all the Congress candidates, most of whom depended for their success on her charisma.

Non-voter females were 8.46%, while 6.67% of male respondents turned out to be non-voters. As against 7.04% scored by males, less women (5.41%) showed perception of political efficacy. Political efficacy was lower among the women than among men in all the three constituencies.

Profile of Urban Participation

A study of political behaviour of women in Ahmedabad in the Assembly elections of 1972 made by Arvind Shah reveals certain important trends. The study covers women voters sampled from the Ellis Bridge constituency.[11] Being an area which can be characterized as urban, educated middle class, it is hardly representative of women of Gujarat. But in terms of SES, it represented a fairly good cross-section of women in terms of age, caste and religion, etc.

Of the sample, 8.5% was very much interested in politics, 67.5% had some interest, and 24% had none at all. Thus, 92.5% indicate little participation rate. Only 14% discuss politics with others and 39% never discuss politics. That a big majority of 86% never or hardly discusses politics tallies with the low participation rate.

As regards the mid-term poll of 1971 to the Lok Sabha, only 7% had shown good interest. This is significant because the low interest was evinced (though not in voting) by women in 1971 when Gujarat as well as India became a national constituency for Indira Gandhi.

Regarding voting in the Assembly election of 1972, 78.5% of the sample voted. This figure was remarkable, and it even surpassed the female voting rate of 1971. About their intention to vote in a future election, 97% answered in the affirmative. Thus, for them voting far outweighs their interest in politics.

It will be important here to note the pattern of political participation. In this educated, middle class suburb area 98.5% of women were not members of any political party; 79.5% did not join any political activity. In 60% of the families of the respondents, no political discussion took place. Out of the 40% families where such discussions did take place, 55% never participated or rarely participated. Only 11% had definite points to put before others and persuade them.

One interesting point is that while making the decision about voting, 66.5% made an independent decision. This is in contrast to the findings of a study on 'political behaviour of urban Gujarat' in general which observed that they consulted their peer-group or relations on voting.[12]

It is evident from the above analysis that though quite a large number of women vote and intend to vote in the future, their political participation ends at that level. 'It is not their interest that forms the basis of voting and half of them vote without intellectually getting involved in this vital act'.[13] In terms of interest in politics, discussion, and involvement they score low. They are active only at the time of elections. If this is the case with educated urban women, the case of the large mass or rural women may reveal a still lower level and rate of participation. However, the pattern is not different for male voters either.[14]

Performance in Elections

A very clear pattern about women in politics emerges in the case of their performance, election-wise and party-wise, in the State.

In the first general elections of 1952, five women candidates contested for Vidhan Sabha, of whom four were defeated. For the Lok Sabha, one contested and got elected. In 1957, 15 contested for the Vidhan Sabha and 11 were elected, while for the Lok Sabha six contested and two were elected. In 1962, 24 contested and 11 were elected to the Vidhan Sabha, and two contested and both won the Lok Sabha seats. In the fourth General Elections of 1967, 8 out of 17 got elected to the Vidhan Sabha. For the Lok Sabha one of the two contestants got the seat. In the mid-term poll of 1971 (Lok Sabha) only one candidate, an independent, contested and lost her deposit. The Congress (O) did not field any candidate. Curiously, Congress (O) asked the voters to vote for the 'spinning woman' as its symbol.[15] In the General Elections of 1972, 21 women appeared on the election scene, but only eight of them were elected, all belonging to Congress (R). Significantly, the pre-1969 position regarding the seats for women in the Assembly was more or less maintained by Congress (R); but Congress (O) women candidates (as opposition candidates) lost in all the six constituencies they contested.

A Note on Those Elected

All the Congress MLAs who contested won the elections. The Congress (O) when in opposition was defeated. The number of women MLAs, percentage-wise, decreased after every successive election. Is it devaluation? There were not many candidates except in 1962, and they were all from the Congress. The Vidhan Sabha revealed a better record of success than the Lok Sabha.

The Emerging Pattern

Of the 92 women candidates who contested the Assembly elections (1952-1972), about 49% belonged to the higher castes of Banias and Brahmins; 25% belonged to the Patidar community; 12% to the backward classes; 10% to other castes; and 4% Muslims. In the Lok Sabha poll, of the 12 women who contested between 1952-1973, half of the candidates belonged to the Patidar community and among them a Congress candidate, Maniben Patel (daughter of Sardar Vallabhbhai Patel) was elected thrice; while another, a Swatantra candidate (wife of the son of Sardar Patel) contested once from two places and lost in both. The same pattern of women legislators continued between 1952

Profiles of Women in Gujarat

and 1972. Thus, the large share in the power structure goes to women of three high castes – Brahmin, Bania (urban high caste), and Patidars (rural high-caste Hindus). But the significance of the presence of a good number of the Scheduled Caste women must not also be overlooked. The MLAs were Muslims. The dominance of the elite class can be traced to their education, public life, and ability to move and mix with those at the helm of affairs.

Another significant trend in elections is that since 1952 there has been a gradual but steady decline in the ratio of successful women candidates to total women contestants to the Assembly. There was a steady decline in the proportion of winning candidates, from 80% (1952), 69% (1957), 61% (1962), 48% (1967), to 34% (1972). The percentage with regard to the Lok Sabha was erratic, yet it has gone down from 100% (1952) to 66% (1971).

All the women MLAs belonged to the Congress till the 1967 elections and all belonged to Congress (R) in the Vidhan Sabha, which was constituted in the last Assembly election (1972). Not a single candidate fielded by opposition parties was returned to the Assembly. It was the same case with respect to the Lok Sabha poll. Even Congress (O), when in opposition, (1971 and 1972) contested and lost. There were not many women contestants except in 1962. The Congress candidates who won a good percentage of votes, and the performance of female candidates was better than that of the males.

Women Pressure Groups

Pressure groups in Gujarat are not many, neither are they active and effective, more so in the case of women. Only a few instances could be cited.

One such important group has been the Surat Grahak Mandal organized by women social workers in Surat in 1971. This was a milk consumers' movement started as a protest against price hike in milk of local dairies. The women workers under Dhrulata Parekh organized a consumers' resistance, prepared a cogent set of arguments, and articulated it in a sustained and systematic manner. It soon harnessed the cooperation of men and the support of the local newspapers such as the *Gujarat Mitra*. Though the movement did not succeed in its objective, it did create awareness about the problems of the common man particularly the housewives, and elicited a response of the authorities so that the quality of milk would not deteriorate. One of its more permanent results was the development of the Surat Consumers' Association. As one of the seven such units in the State recognized by the government, it is the best organized and the most active. The author was impressed by the commitment of its leaders as well as its good work, particularly in keeping the housewives informed of the problems of adulteration, faulty weights and measures of goods, and in keeping the authorities and traders on the defensive.

Another instance is that of the organization of Adivasi women for the welfare of this downtrodden community. In 1973, about 100 Adivasi demonstrators stopped the car of the Chief Minister in Dharmapur (backward area of south Gujarat) and asked for the distribution of foodgrains at fair price shops. The Chief Minister had soon to look into the matter. Also the Adivasi MLAs and other women workers staged a *dharna* at the doors of the bungalows of the Adivasis to get their grievances redressed.

Another active group of women is the mahila community of Khadia in Ahmedabad. In 1967-68, they took out a long procession angrily displaying empty tins of oil and heckled the authorities concerned. One of them (Madhuben) even contested a municipal by-election on the issue, though successfully. This group was supported earlier by the PSP and at present by the Jana Sangh. In the popular movement that rocked Gujarat in the winter of 1974, the women of this group in Khadia and Raipur formed one of the most active and agitated band of workers, challenging the police and the SRP asking them not to enter their poles (streets), and supporting men in organizing a non-cooperation programme so that the SRP guarding the areas could not get even a drop of water from the civic community. Similar instances could be cited in some other areas such as Shahpur in Ahmedabad, Wadi Falia, and Mahidharpura in Surat and Ahmedabadi poles, and Raopura in Baroda.

The farmers' lobby in Gujarat has a long tradition of sustained opposition to the government's agricultural policy, particularly against land reforms. The women of Bardoli in 1928 were not lagging behind in supporting the movement against the British government. In 1973, the women of this same farmers' community went with men to Gandhi Nagar when 50,000 farmers of the Khedut Sangh organized mass demonstration against the proposed land ceiling bill then being considered by the Chimanbhai Patel ministry. In Bardoli particularly, the women have become part of this agricultural pressure group and they have contributed to the powerful impact that the Khedut Sangh has created in such areas, and have come out to defend the property rights of their husbands and sons. Kamlaben Patel, one of its important office bearers, has stood in the forefront of this movement.

One of the most expressive and vigorous groups of women which emerged in the wake of the popular movement engulfed almost every section of society in the winter of 1974, was the movement against price rise, the shortage of food and other essential commodities, and corruption. The middle-class housewives, being the worst affected, bore the most resentment.

On 22 January 1974, when some of the girl students of the K. K. Arts College (Ahmedabad) were marching in a procession shouting slogans against the repressive measures of the government, the police used excessive force in dealing with them. This provoked the public and the press. In its wake, in the Paldi area of the city a Nav Nirman Yuvati Samiti was formed. This association of young girls soon caught the attention of the people by hijacking the municipal transport buses,[16] leading *morchas* to the office of the Pradesh Congress Committee. All India Radio protested against the latter's policy of giving news about local developments in a biased manner. The Yuvati Samiti vigorously put the case of the movement before the Union Ministers K. C. Pant and H. R. Gokhale who came to Gujarat as observers. The Yuvati Samiti members organized relay fasts, *dharnas*, and frequently organized programmes to persuade the local leaders to resign their posts. The Samiti became a pattern in other parts of the city and the State.

To a considerable extent, its leader Sonal Desai contributed to its effectiveness. At many public meetings, she became a star attraction as a powerful orator.[17] Ritivatsala Padia played a leading part in organizing programmes of mock trials for exposing corrupt practices.

Also a Nav Nirman Mahila Samiti of housewives and grown-up women was launched. Under the lead given by Indira Desai, the Samiti organized a protest march in which the housewives also participated. Hundreds of women in Narainpura moved in a procession with pots of water which they symbolically used to cleanse corrupt politicians.

The Mahila Samiti, like the Yuvati Samiti, presented the case of the harassed housewives before the Chief Minister and other authorities. These Samities helped widen the base of the movement on behalf of the women of Gujarat. The extent of widespread interest and appreciation which they created could be discerned from the fact that they figured in the talk of the common men in the street as well as in the reports and photographs which appeared in the daily press and women's periodicals.

Issues of Support and Opposition

Issues which have evoked remarkable opposition has been price rise, adulteration of food, and shortage of daily necessities. The women's deputations, independently formed or supported by opposition parties such as the PSP in Baroda and Khadia (Ahmedabad), Jana Sangh in Ahmedabad, Rajkot and other urban areas in Saurashtra, and Congress (O) in Surat, Ahmedabad and many other town have been a general form through which the agitated housewives have complained before the collector or the Minister for Supply.

In 1972, about 300 women organized a protest rally against the high rise in the milk price. In mid-February 1973, the Gujarat Mahila Congress (O) conference decided to observe a Mahila Mozavan Din (the day of anxiety of women) on 28 February 1973. This programme attracted widespread support in Bhavnagar, Surat, Godhra, Sanand, Ahmedabad, etc. where hundreds of women protested before the Collector's office against poor supply and adulteration of food in the fair price shops.

The issues which evoked support of women, though less dramatic, were more varied. In 1956, women and young girls of Ahmedabad had joined an agitation in support of the demand for the formation of a unilingual Maha Gujarat State. But much more phenomenal in depth and width was the support elicited from the women on the issue of resignation of Chimanbhai Patel and dissolution of the Vidhan Sabha.

Women also have come out quite effectively in supporting the consumers' resistance movement. Support given to the Surat Grahak Mandal organized by women is one instance. So also when the Mahila Congress approached the Minister for Supply in the Hitendra Desai government in 1968 and complained about adulteration of foodgrains, the Minister asked for their cooperation on this issue. The women responded fervently. They visited many shops in big cities such as Ahmedabad and listed the pricing or adulteration of the consumer commodities. The ministry then raided the shops, and in some cases took punitive action.[19]

Other issues which received support from women were suicide, immoral traffic in women, and murder of women. The Mahila Congress (O) had prepared a report on these problems. Once when some educated Muslim women demanded revision of talaq laws, quite a good number of women had assembled in the meeting held for this purpose, and the women's weeklies lent a big hand to this movement.

On the welfare and community front, the floods of 1958, 1968, and 1970, the scarcity year of 1973, and the communal riots of 1969 evoked great sympathy and action on the part of women who worked to mitigate the grievances of the persons affected by these calamities. They worked both individually and through a number of women's associations such as Mahila Mandals, All-India Women's Conference, Jyoti Sangh, Vikas Gruha, and Mahila Congress (both Congresses). The Mahila Congress (O) and the Jyoti Sangh served the Muslim women in distress during the communal riots of 1969. They distributed wheat to the Muslim families. Workers such as Kokila Vyas of Congress (R), Kamla Patel, Congress (O), Charumati Yodha and several ardent women workers of Jyoti Sangh and Vikas Gruha collected funds and food packets, and efficiently organized their distribution. The Jyoti Sangh and Parishad members went to far-off scarcity-stricken areas to distribute grain and cloth. The Mahila Congress (O) made a survey of the flood situation in 1968, and wrote a fine report with a set of recommendations. Thus, humanitarian issues where the women were particularly affected evoked not only sympathy but organized support from the women of Gujarat.[20]

In early 1971 the women's associations led by the Mahila Congress (O) in Ahmedabad met the Chief Minister Hitendra Desai and Gordhandas Chokhawala and persuaded them to make secondary education up to SSC free for girl students in the State. They also canvassed for this point in the Vidhan Sabha, and persuaded the women MLAs. This move helped the government in making a favourable decision on this point.

Though material welfare issues have not received enough support, two cases are worth mentioning. One is the Mahila Mudranalaya, the only press in Gujarat and few of its kind in western India, which is entirely run and efficiently managed by women compositors and printers. Founded by Indumatiben Sheth, it has not got the attention of the women that it deserves. Another undertaking is a mahila cooperative bank for women only, recently founded in Surat and managed by women.

Issues in the Legislature

Regarding participation of women MLAs and MPs in the legislative bodies, their record is far from satisfactory.

The most effective representation that can be said to have been made by a woman representative was by Pushpaben Mehta in the Lok Sabha with regard to the suicide of women in Gujarat. Contrary to popular belief, women's suicide rate in Gujarat is one of the highest in India (particularly in Saurashtra); besides, many incidents are suppressed. Pushpaben Mehta put this case before Parliament with facts and fervour, and asked the government to go deep into the matter. Accordingly, a committee was appointed and its findings revealed very grave aspects of this malaise. Maniben Patel and Jayaben Shah in the Lok Sabha took care of women's problems and their social welfare. Maniben Patel has frequently raised the issue of injustice done to Gujarat, particularly on the Narmada issue. Sumitra Kulkarni has similarly made representation on need of an atomic power station, Narmada, and other such issues of development.

In the Gujarat Assembly, women MLAs have put forward questions during the question hour in the Vidhan Sabha, and have touched upon issues of child marriages, women's suicide, Varli-matka, breach of the Antibigamy Act, and prohibition. The questions regarding wages for women labour have also been put forward to bring out disparities in wages between men and women. Shantaben Patel, Nirmala Gajawani, Kokila Vyas, and Hiraben Ninama have been some of the active female MLAs. A remarkable aspect of this is the performance of some women MLAs coming from reserved constituencies. Questions regarding the running of Ashram Shalas (tribal schools), plight of the Harijan and Adivasi men and women, untouchability, etc. were put forward frequently by Adivasi MLAs such as Hiraben Ninama, Shantaben Makwana, and Gangaben Vaghela. Few of them followed up the answer or 'commitment' given by the Ministers concerned in their chambers. However, on the whole, very few women MLAs have been found active on this front. During the two visits to the Vidhan Sabha sessions by this author (August 1972 and October 1973), few women MLAs (like many male MLAs) were found present in the Vidhan Sabha for a considerable part of the day, virtually no one raised a question or participated in a debate. Out of 60 to 90 questions asked generally during the question hour every day, only one or two were raised by a woman MLA.[21] Their record in

Profiles of Women in Gujarat

sponsoring bills relating to and sponsored by women in Parliament and Assembly is very poor except in the case of women deputy ministers such as Indumati Sheth and Urmilaben Bhat on whom fell the task of formally sponsoring a few bills with regard to girls' education, social welfare, and interests of women.

Position and Work in Party Organization and Government

Women found a good position in the organization of the pre-1969 Congress and later in Congress (O). But it was not the case with Congress (R). In the ad hoc committee of the GPOG (R) only one woman, Shantaben Patel, found a place. In the reconstituted committee, 4 out of 25 were women members, and one Kumudben Joshi was given the office of secretary. Women belonging to Scheduled Castes and Tribes were not found in the higher party hierarchy in spite of the avowed claim of the ruling Congress to work for and encourage the weaker sections of the society.

Kumudben Joshi had been very active in representing the case of her faction before the High Command. Comparatively quite a few women have been found in the party hierarchies, not so in the ministries. With the exception of the Congress (undivided) parties in Gujarat have not given woman her due place in their organization, (Two women, Smt. Mehta, and Niruben Patel at present, have so far been on the executive committee of the State unit of the CPI.) Even in Congress (R), there was only one woman in its first ad hoc committee (1969-72) and four in the outgoing (now dissolved in the wake of the popular Nav Nirman upsurge in the State). One of them, Kumudben Joshi, was actively associated with its president Jhinabhai Darji in the factional struggle in the Congress party at the State level, and in her home district (Chikhli and surrounding areas). The ruling Congress also has its Mahila Congress, a formally constituted women's wing. Arunaben Sanat Mehta (Baroda) was its convener. However, the Mahila Congress is very much faction-ridden. The record of the Mahila Congress (R) is on the whole poor if not dismal. Individually speaking, Kokila Vyas of Congress (R) has given an innovative programme – that of serving the slum areas in Ahmedabad city – and exhorted 100 well-off families to adopt one hut (zoopada) each from the slum area. Though her 'adoption idea' did not catch on,[22] it was a good effort in the realization of a progressive goal.

The Congress (O), however, has given a better place to women since 1950, and in the GPCC (undivided and Organization Congress), Manjulaben Patel (Ahmedabad), Manjulaben Patel (Sanand), Maniben Patel, and Kantaben Trivedi have held various offices. Smt. Trivedi had also been the vice-president. So also half of its coopted members are women. As mentioned elsewhere, a few branches (samities) of city, the *taluka*, and many city wards had women chairmen as well.

However, though the number of seats have increased in the state Vidhan Sabha (1952-1972), the corresponding number of women candidates has not increased. No candidate belonging to the non-Congress parties has been able to get elected. Only the Congress (undivided) and Congress (R) have been able to send a few women to the State legislature. Because of the policy adopted by the undivided Congress and Congress (O) that generally one seat from each district was to be given to a woman candidate, such women legislators ranged from 7% to 12%. In Parliament also, six women so far have represented Gujarat – among them Maniben Patel has already finished two terms. So far Congress (R) has sent two women to the Rajya Sabha.

With regard to ministries, the record of women ministers is neither outstanding nor poor. In all, there were only five women ministers since 1960 – in the erstwhile Bombay State, Indumatiben Sheth, Jayaben Shah (in the erstwhile Saurashtra State in the fifties), Urmilaben Bhatt (having the distinction of continuing in five ministries during 1960-1971, Kamlaben Patel, and Ayesha Begum (the last one being in two ministries formed by Congress (R).

With the break-up of the bilingual State of Bombay, Urmilaben Bhatt and Kamlaben Patel were given place in the Jivaraj ministry as Deputy Ministers. Smt. Bhatt continued in the Balwantrai Mehta ministry (1963-66), and in the Hitendra Desai ministry (1966-67, 1967-71, and April 1971) as Deputy Minister for Education, Social Welfare, and Public Works. In the first Congress (R) ministry led by Ghanshyambhai Shah (1972-73), Ayesha Begum was appointed as the Deputy Minister for Education. As a result of the political change that catapulated Chimanbhai Patel ministry (1973-74), she became Minister of State for Education. Except for a few weeks, their ranking never rose to the level of a Minister, and they were placed in the middle of the lower rungs in all the ministries. All of them have remained Deputy Ministers except Smt. Bhatt, who for a short while

Profiles of Women in Gujarat 217

became a Minister and Ayesha Begum who in the last ministry under Chimanbhai Patel was promoted to the status of Minister for State. It is very significant that all of them were given mainly the charge of either the education portfolio or social work.

The role and performance of most of the women ministers were mediocre. Almost all of them were in a ministry generally because they had been pushed upward by a politically influential personality and were given a medium or low position in the hierarchy of the government.

The Emerging Trends: Overview and Suggestions

After the Congress turned from a national movement into a political party, many women leaders and workers gradually turned away from public life – especially the political sphere. Many of them began working for associations of social welfare and there they have been doing excellent work.[23]

Some of them such as Vimala Thaker and Kantak turned to spiritual life. It is noteworthy that leaders such as Pushpaben Mehta and Maniben Patel who were active in political life and were known all over Gujarat in the post-1947 period were the product of the national movement. Few women, if any, emerged out of the new generation after 1947 who could claim to have made an impact on women throughout Gujarat. Like the Congressman of the dominant party in power, the woman leader working in the Congress organization and the government was also a different woman with different orientations, interests, and styles. In post-1947 Gujarat, therefore, comparatively speaking, in terms of time within the same region, the record of woman is satisfactory though not very brilliant.[24] She is found active at such times when price rise and other related problems agitate her. She becomes active generally only at the time of elections. The high degree of participation in terms of voting is not reflected in terms of political behaviour. But when the cause becomes emotional (such as issues of Maha Gujarat and Nav Nirman), she participates actively and effectively. Women politicians occasionally do show active concern in articulating the problems of women and make an effort to promote their cause. Women folk belonging to the farmers' community, particularly, and the Adivasi community to some extent, are the most active about the interest of their community. She has made insignificant impact in the Vidhan Sabha and much less in the ministry. At the organization level, however, she has a little more role to play. It is the woman politician belonging to undivided Congress, and particularly the Congress (R) at a point of time, who has been elected and has enjoyed some share in political power. Women activists belonging to the opposition are neglected by the voter. Congress (O) has continued the tradition of women's role and participation in public life more than the Congress (R). Anyway, those women who are known among the women in Gujarat and who have a record of sound and sustained work of community welfare are found more in the social and social welfare field than in political life, with greater commitment to the women's cause. Few women legislators would have been known but for the publicity given to them in the regional press which has the tendency to advertise the political aspect. Women political leaders are better situated to work as they have power and patronage as the resource-base of their activities; but their record is not equally appreciable. On the other hand, it may be noted that though many old women leaders blame their younger, politically more prominent counterparts for their being pushed in to the background, it is the unchanging attitude of these leaders which prevents them from adopting an orientation relevant for the needs of a changing political process which is mainly responsible for their reduced importance.

But compared to women in other States and judged by the same standard, women in Gujarat may perhaps fared better comparatively.

Certain points emerge from the foregoing description and analysis:

1. The post-1947 Gujarat has not encouraged the emergence of outstanding women leaders as during the period of the national movement. Also, leaders who have made their presence felt in the national forums have been those who had already been influenced during the Gandhian era.

2. At the State level no woman leader has emerged having a sustained dominance and State-wise impact. Many emerged, shone and faded from the power structure. However, some leaders did contribute to the development of a particular field of social welfare or the cause of women. Urmila Bhatt, Pushpaben Mehta, Hansa Mehta, Ninama may be mentioned in this regard.

3. More remarkable than the leaders was the emergence of an active band of women or a mass of women who articulated and sometimes became effective with respect to certain problems or events.

4. Participation of women has been quite good at the time of elections. But their activeness is reflected only in their voting behaviour.

5. Participation and share in the political power structure has remained the exclusive domain of females of the ruling party. Women candidates belonging to the opposition parties are denied this by the voters of Gujarat.

6. The general economic issues of the daily concerns of a housewife have particularly agitated the women, and was the mainstream of the expression of discontent against the government. In this the women's wing belonging to the ruling party remained as active as those belonging to the opposition.

7. To most of the women, politics has not remained a full-time occupation. The degree of their activeness has remained tied up with the career that they had during their position in the party in power or its government. For most of them, it was ascriptive or given under a specific favourable political situation. Their eminence did not correspond with the structure of support that should have been created in their constituency after a long and durable period of service to the women's cause and welfare.

8. Most of the able women opted to work in the women's social and welfare association; few were attracted to public life informed by politics.

9. Public life for women in the early fifties was more or less confined to the upper middle class. Since then the condition has progressively changed, but not very much. Also, they are more confined to the urban than to rural area, excepting a cluster of pockets of women belonging to the well-organized farmers' community in south Gujarat. So also the fruits of social reforms such as women's rights have yet to penetrate the lower strata of the society. The endeavours of urban educated women belonging to the higher castes to push forward these reforms have not been fruitful. On the whole, politics still remains an area left to men with women in public life dependent on and secondary to the former in pursuit of their activities in political matters.

References

1. For details, see Induben Mehta, "Stree Kelavani", in Congress AICC Souvenir (1961).
2. Jyotsana Shukla, "Swarajya Andolanman Mahilao", in Congress AICC

Souvenir (1961), A good article describing and analysing various issues and aspects of women's role in freedom movement in Gujarat.
3. Ammu Menon Majmundar, *Social Work in India*, p. 109.
4. Details in (i) Usha G. Bhatt, "Hindi Swatantra Ladatman Amdavadman Sri Netritvano Falo" (Ph. D. thesis, 1974; unpublished) (ii) Man Mohan Kaw, *Role of Women in the Freedom Movement*; (iii) Various issues of *Praja Bandhu* (like 25-4-1937 and 26-2-1939); *Congress Patrika* (13-9-42, 22-9-42, 28-9-42, Independence number 1942); and *Gujarat Samachar* (15-10-68, 11-5-69, 21-10-70, 11 and 18-3-73), and *Nav Jivan* (18-7-20 and 2-11-20).
5. Kaka Kalekar in Amritlal Yognik (ed.), *Gujarat man Gandhi Yog: Aitihasik and Sahityik Avalkan*, P. 44. The role of the Sabaramati Ashram in moulding women is specially noteworthy. see Usha Bhatt, *op. cit.*
6. Gunial Desai, *Gurjar Nari* (Thesis), Bombay Gujarat Granth Ratna (1962), Ch. 12.
7. Particularly *Gujarat Samachar, Jana Satta* (Ahmedabad) and *Gujarat Mitra* (Surat).
8. Based on preliminary frequencies obtained from the computed data under process in the Department of Political Science, Gujarat University.
9. *Ibid.*
10. Sheth, P.N.: "Panchayati Leadership: Politics of Participation" (mimeograph), to be published in D.N. Pathak (ed.) *Dynamics of Gujarat Politics* (Popular Prakashan), Bombay.
11. Arvind Shah, *Women and Politics in 1972* (Gujarati).
12. From the study of "Political Behaviour of Urban Gujarat" by the Department of Political Science, Gujarat University.
13. Arvind Shah, *op. cit.*, p. 6.
14. "Political Behaviour of Urban Gujarat". *op. cit.*
15. *Congress Patrika*, 13-2-1971.
16. *Jai Hind*, 28-1-1974
17. *Gujarat Samachar, Jai Hind, Jana Satta*, February 3, 4, 5, 6, and 7, 1974; *Gujarat Mitra*, 22 February 1974.
18. *Gujarat Samachar* and *Jai Hind*, February 3, 4, 5, 6, 7, 8, 1974.
19. Based on talks with Mrs. Kamlaben Patel, convener, Mahila Congress (O).
20. *Ibid.*
21. *Gujarat Vidhan Sabha Prashnottari* (Series for October 1973 Session). Only one question out of 69 was put by a woman MLA in the Vidhan Sabha session of 8, October, 1974.
22. From informal talks on this point with Professor Kokila Vyas, MLA. She also played an important role in initiating and activating the Ahmedabad Consumers' Resistance Association (Amdaved Grahak Pratikar Mandal), and distributed wheat to the urban poor in the city in the scarcity year 1972-73.
23. See for example, the Jyoti Sangh Souvenir 1973, and the record of the Vikas Gruha, and All India Women's Conference (Ahmedabad and Surat branches).
24. In the various studies on political behaviour in the State done by the author jointly in the department, the level of political participation and activeness of voters in general is also not found high. So women alone need not be blamed.

PROFILES OF WOMEN IN KARNATAKA

Amal Ray

In view of the important inter-regional variations in political development, there are several levels of political status and awareness for women in India as for other newly emergent groups. Actually, the concept of feminism in the political context has various shades. In some States, owing to early exposure to modernizing influences and the advent of radical politics, there has developed an organized feminist movement, and women in large numbers have been drawn into politics. But in a number of other States the myth of the natural division of labour between the sexes has persisted in some form even to this day. Thus, in terms of political status and involvement of women there are upper and lower margins, and the status of women in Karnataka lies in between the two.

The political status of women should be spelt out in terms of their ability to influence the decision-making of the State which in turn depends upon their role, perception and capacity for political organization. One should recall, in this connection, the sufferings of Yashodharamma Dasappa and others. Recently, the concept of feminism has acquired a certain organizational shape. Sudha Reddi, Dr. Anupama Niranjan, M.R. Lakshamma, etc. have set up associations to articulate the rights of the women of the State. However, the role of the associations as important pressure groups is negligible.

One of the best means of determining the political status of women is by identifying their position in several mass organizations and organs of political decision-making. In so far as the non-partisan mass organizations such as associations of white-collar workers are concerned, women have practically little position. Only in one or two such organizations have women assumed leadership. For instance, the President of the Secondary School Teachers' Association is a woman. Looking at the party organizations also, the overall situation appears disappointing. In the non-Congress (R) organizations, women are not very much represented in the State executive committee. Even in Congress (R) the situation is no better. The Executive Committee of the Karnataka Pradesh Congress Committee has a total strength of

25 members. But there is only one woman member (Addisaldhana)[1] in Bangalore city (urban); the Executive Committee has only one woman among 12 members: in Bangalore city (rural) the Executive Committee of Congress (R) has one woman among 14 members.

Let us now have a close look at electoral politics. In the 1972 State Assembly elections, while the male electors numbered 7,726,073, the female voters numbered 7,357,395. In terms of votes polled, the percentage for male voters was 65.92 and that for female voters was 57.00. Thus, the rate of participation for female voters was quite high. However, as Table 1 would show, the elections showed an extremely unfavourable ratio between the number of female electors and that of female contestants.

TABLE 1

Party	Nominated		Rejected		Withdrawn		Contested	
	M	F	M	F	M	F	M	F
Congress (R)	351	23	3	0	151	6	195	17
Congress (O)	311	12	2	1	140	5	170	6
Jana Sangh	166	1	1	0	63	1	102	0
Socialist Party	44	0	1	0	9	0	34	0
Swatantra	35	2	0	0	8	0	26	2
CPI (M)	20	0	2	0	2	0	16	0
CPI	7	0	0	0	3	0	4	0
Janata Paksha	15	0	0	0	9	0	6	0
Independents	522	7	12	0	273	4	247	3

M = Male, F = Female

Out of the 28 female candidates only 11 were elected, and all the elected candidates belonged to Congress (R). A second noteworthy feature was that none of them came from a purely urban constituency such as Bangalore or Mysore. Third, only one Scheduled Caste female candidate was elected, – from the Bagepalli constituency,[2] – although three contested.

A comparison of the fifth Legislative Assembly elections (1972) with earlier Assembly elections would show that except for the second and third Assemblies, the ratio of female to male representatives has always been extremely low. In the 1952 elections only three women were elected. However, two women came to the House through by-elections in 1956. Thus, the first Legislative Assembly contained five

Profiles of Women in Karnataka 223

women members. In the 1957 elections, the number of women MLAs rose to 18. In the 1962 elections also 18 female candidates were elected to the Assembly. But in the 1967 elections the number of women members of the Legislative Assembly was reduced to seven. In the 1972 elections, as we have already seen, the number increased marginally to 11 only. Table 2 provides a comparative analysis of seats won by women candidates in successive elections since 1932:

TABLE 2

Assembly	Women members
1st	5
2nd	18
3rd	18
4th	7
5th	11 + 1 (nominated)

The participation of women in the legislative process has also not been encouraging. Between 1967 and 1971, for instance, several special discussions took place on important subjects such as scarcity conditions, the Mysore-Maharashtra boundary dispute, the Krishna-Godavari water dispute, etc. But no motion on any such subject was moved by women members. Again, by and large, the women members did not participate in discussions.[3] During the same period, the number of Call Attention notices tabled by the members of the Assembly came to 893, but the notices tabled by women members numbered only five. The adjournment motions received during the same period totalled 115, but the share of the women members was nil.

However, this is not to say that they had no role. At times, they asked questions which were not necessarily confined to their natural spheres. A typical question put by a woman member was the following: Will the Government be pleased to state (a) whether a commission was set up to recommend amendments to the Hindu Women's Right Act 1933; (b) when the report of the Commission was received; (c) whether it is the intention of the government to amend the 1933 Act to give more rights to women.[4] They also question on general issues. Several times they put forward questions on a variety of subjects such as food and famine situation in the State, water facilities in rural areas, supply of electric power, education, land reforms, etc.[5]

Let us now look to the Committee system of the Assembly. It is found that the representation of women members has increased over years. The relevant data are given below:[6]

Committee on Public Accounts	1967-69	No lady member
	1972-74	One lady member
Committee on Government assurances	1967-69	No lady member
	1972-74	One lady member
Committee on the Welfare of Scheduled Castes and Scheduled Tribes	1967-69	No lady member
	1972-74	Two lady members
Committee on Private Members' Bills and Resolutions	1967-69	No lady member
	1972-74	Three lady members

It also, appears that the status of women has been enhanced by the election of K.S. Nagarathnamma as the Speaker of the fifth Legislative Assembly. She has earned a good reputation for her tact and impartiality.

In so far as membership of the Council of Ministers is concerned, women in Karnataka have never been adequately represented. The relevant data from 1966 onwards are presented in Table 3.

TABLE 3
Women's representation in the State Cabinet

Year	No. of ministers	Lady ministers
1966	19	1 (Deputy Minister)
1967	21	No
1968	27	1 (Deputy Minister)
1969	No change	No change
1970	No change	No change
1971	(Patil ministry resigned)	—
1972	23	1 (Minister of State)
1973	23	1 (Minister of State)
1974	20	1 (Minister of State)

It is thus found that during the past nine years there has been no woman Cabinet Minister in the State, with the exception of 1965 when Yashodhara Dasappa held the rank. Since then there has been no woman Cabinet Minister.

Very few women have been elected to the Lok Sabha from Karnataka. Among the notables may be mentioned Alva, Sudha Reddy, and Sarojini Mahishi (Union Minister of State till 1975).

A decision of the government which evoked widespread disapproval from women related to the withdrawal of prohibition. Yashodhara Dasappa resigned from the Council of Ministers on this issue in 1965. In recent months the issue of excessive price rise has aroused much protest. The women's wing of the Jana Sangh organized several demonstrations in the State.

From the foregoing it is evident that women in Karnataka do not enjoy much status in political life, in comparison to the women of Kerala, West Bengal, and Gujarat. The growth of female literacy (from 14.2% in 1961 to 20.8% in 1971) is not reflected in an improved status of women. The persistence of the traditional caste structure, late urbanization, and the near absence of radical politics are the main factors contributing to the existence of a relatively low status for women in Karnataka politics.

References

1. Interview.
2. *Mysore State Election Statistics, 1972.*
3. *The Mysore Legislative Assembly, 1967-71, a Review.*
4. *Mysore Legislative Assembly Debates.*
5. *Ibid.*
6. *The Mysore Legislative Assembly (1967-71): A Review and Interview.*

PROFILES OF WOMEN IN KERALA

Lucy Jacob

Role of Women in Politics: The Case of Kerala

The national liberation movement and the effort of Mahatma Gandhi, the Father of the Nation, led to the emancipation of Indian women in the 20th century. India's independence and the adoption of the Constitution paved the way for the concretization of the ideals set forward by Mahatma Gandhi. The Preamble of the Constitution assures all citizens of the Sovereign Democratic Republic equality of status and of opportunity, to usher in justice – social, economic and political. It is enshrined in the Fundamental Rights that the State shall not discriminate against any citizen inter alia on the grounds of sex, or subject them to any disability, liability, and restriction. The Directive Principles of State Policy empower the State to make special provisions for protecting women's rights to progress. Equality of women with men in the political set-up is guaranteed through the institution of adult franchise and article 15 which prohibits discrimination inter alia on the grounds of sex. Although constitutionally women enjoy equality with men, in actual practice their position is far from equal.

For the purpose of this paper, the role of women in politics is spelt out in terms of their ability to influence the decision-making of the State and their capacity for political organization and participation.

There is hardly any political writing about women in Kerala. There are only a couple of books (in English) in which one gets some idea about the political participation of women in Kerala in the pre-1947 period. One of the books (in two volumes) is P.K.K. Menon's *The History of Freedom Movement in Kerala, 1600-1885* (Vol. I) and *1885-1938* (Vol. II) in which one gets some references about the participation and role of women in Kerala during the national movement. Another book, though ready but not yet released, is *Who is Who of Freedom Fighters in Kerala* by K. Karunakaran Nair. Some of the Malayalam periodicals such as *Mathrubhumi* and *Vanitha* do reflect some concern for women's political views and participation. Recently *Janapatham* (a Government of Kerala publication), to mark the International Women's Year, brought out a special issue in Malayalam highlighting some prominent women in Kerala in the political, social, educational, and professional fields. *Mathrubhumi* (a popular and well-circulated Malayalam weekly) in its Onam (a festival in Kerala) issue of 1975 published about a dozen general articles on the role of women in the liberation movement, in education, in literature, etc. by such notable women as Lakshmi N. Menon, Parukutty, Leela Damodara Menon, and Justice P. Janaki Amma. It is interesting to note that much of the writing about women is by women themselves.

As no fullfledged study relating to the role of women in politics in Kerala has been conducted, it will be worthwhile to undertake a comprehensive study covering political awareness and role of women. Due to the short time which was available at my disposal for the preparation of this report, only the broad aspects of the political life of women could be covered.

The report is based on some periodicals, pamphlets, and a few administrative reports. But the information secured from these sources is supplemented by interviews with a few women who had been and are political leaders in Kerala belonging to different political parties, such as A.V. Kuttimalu Amma, O.K. Madhavi Amma, Mrs. Khallat, M. Kamalam, Lakshmi N. Menon, E. Ammukutty Amma, Annie Thayyil, K.R. Gouri, M.A. Sarojini, and Leela Damodara Menon.

Demographic Profile of Women in Kerala

During the seven decades from 1901 to 1971, Kerala has registered a sustained increase of population. The pattern of sex ratio in Kerala tells a different story from the rest of India. While the sex ratio in India is 930 females per 1,000 males, there are 1,016 females per 1,000 males in Kerala according to the 1971 census. There has been an excess of females in Kerala according to all the census from 1901 to 1971. Just as a low sex ratio has been the pattern in India as a whole, a high ratio has been the pattern in Kerala. The pattern of social life in Kerala, the high status given to women in society, and the system of female descent prevalent in the State had probably ruled out any tendency to ignore the existence of females.

Among the States in India, Kerala does not occupy an enviable position in urbanization. The slow progress in urbanization is reflected in the growth of the urban population. The percentage of urban population has increased from 15.11 to 16.24 in Kerala, whereas in India it has increased from 17.98 to 19.91. Nearly 84% of the total population of Kerala is rural. This is also true of the female population. Though the urban female population are in a minority forming only 16% of the female population of the State, they are more vociferous and influential, and supply most of the leaders in politics and administration.

In the matter of literacy, Kerala stands head and shoulders above the rest of India. According to the 1971 census, the rate of literacy in Kerala is 60.42% as against 29.45% in the whole country. In India, the males are twice as literate as females. But in Kerala 54.31% of the females are literate while 66.62% of the males are literate. More than anything else, it is this near equality in literacy between males and females that reflects the progressive outlook of the State. As is to be expected, the literacy rate is higher in the urban areas of the State than in the rural areas (66.31% in the urban areas and 59.28% in the rural areas). The same is true of the literacy rate among the male and female population: 53.10% and 60.62% of women in the rural and urban areas respectively are literate.

From very early days, women in Kerala enjoyed almost equal status with men and their education was not neglected. There were 49.8 lakhs of students attending schools during 1971-72, the bulk of them, i.e. 42.3 lakhs, were in primary schools. As much as 47% of the students were girls. The percentage of enrolment has increased from 17.5 of the population in 1956-57 to 22.5 in 1971-72. The per capita government expenditure on education has increased from Rs.6.30 in 1960-61 to Rs.27.45 in 1970-71.

Considering the sex ratio of the population as well as the high literacy percentage of women in Kerala, the performance of Kerala women in the occupational fields seems to be not very spectacular. The high rate of literacy among women has earned for them better representation in teaching, nursing, clerical, and administrative services than in other States of India. While women constituted 44% in the teaching profession, in nursing they constituted 62.5%.[1]

It may also be mentioned that 44.48% of those employed in household industry, 37.33% of agricultural labourers, 6.08% of the total number of cultivators, 29.27% of those engaged in other services, and 25.09% of those employed in industries excluding household industries are women.[2] In industries mostly uneducated women are employed in large numbers because the coir and cashew industries in Kerala are labour-intensive and women are particularly experts in them.

Among the workers, 84.95% live in rural areas and 15.05% in urban areas. Rural occupations absorb a comparatively higher proportion of female workers than urban occupations. In the rural areas the rate of participation in work by males is a little more than three times that of females, whereas in urban areas it is more than four times.

The condition of women workers in Kerala is no better than that of the women working force of India. While the percentage of workers in the total population in Kerala fell from 33.7 in 1961 to 28.91 in 1971, in the case of women workers the proportion fell from 19.11% in 1961 to 13.68% in 1971. The fact seems to be that job opportunities for women have not increased at the same rate as the increase of population during the past decades.

It is in this context of distinctive demographic characteristics of women in Kerala that one can understand the role they could play in the politics of Kerala.

Women in the National Movement in Kerala

In the pre-1947 years the present Kerala consisted of three distinct political entities – Malabar as part of Madras Presidency, and the Princely States of Cochin and Travancore. Till about the 1930s, there had been no organized political movement in the two Princely States as the Indian National Congress leaders were reluctant to interfere in State affairs.[3] But in Malabar where political conferences were held from time to time, men from all castes and creeds actively participated. Women – even educated from aristocratic and middle-class families – as a class never used to participate in public activities.[4]

The famous "Salt Satyagraha" and the inauguration of the "Civil Disobedience" movement under Gandhi's leadership gave a new impetus to the freedom movement in Kerala. Women in large numbers from all castes, religions, and classes came forward and participated in the movement. A.V. Kuttimula Amma, Kamala Prabha, C. Kunhikvu Amma, Kunhilakshmi Amma, M. Kartyayani Amma, Matilda Kallen, Gracy Aaron, Margret Pavamani, M.K. Janaki Amma, and Iswari Amma had been among the earliest to lead the *satyagraha* and non-violent movement in Kerala. Some women even resigned their jobs to join the *satyagraha* and national service.[5] The women had originally started their work with khadi and *swadeshi* propaganda, but many of them plunged headlong into the fray courting arrest and imprisonment in the salt satyagraha and the civil disobedience movement. The breaking of the forest laws, boycott of foreign cloth and liquor shops resulted in women suffering police repression. Scores of women poured out in defiance of government orders and police lathis. It was not only a display of courage and daring but more surprising was the organizational power they showed. Women political organizations such as the Rashtriya Stree Sabha (which organized classes in spinning, popularized Hindi, conducted propaganda for prohibition and *swadeshi* and picketed foreign cloth shops), the Kerala Mahila Desa Sevika Sangha which carried on national work and served the cause of women in the country, set up night schools and handicraft training centres for providing education and employment for poor women, and the Swadeshi Committee did excellent work in Kerala. Some very active women were elected/nominated to responsible positions, e.g., the President of Kerala Provincial Congress Committee, members of the Working Committee, Chairman of Khadi Pracharna Sangh, and also as 'dictators' who were to be in entire command of the *satyagraha* movement when the Kerala Provincial Congress Committee was dissolved during the emergency created by the Viceroy's ordinances in the early 1930s. Women not only did election campaign actively for elections to municipal councils and Provincial Assemblies but also got elected as members to those councils and Assemblies. A. V. Kuktimalu Amma and C. K. Leela Krishnan were some of the women who were elected to the Provincial Legislature.[6] In 1937-38, when the Cochin Congress, Cochin State Congress, and Travancore State Congress were formed to demand responsible governments in those two Princely States many more women such as Accamma Cherian, John Kuruvilla, Annie Mascarene joined the movement. Women's participation in the nationalist struggle reached its climax in the "Quit India" movement when several of them conducted underground political activities and courted arrest. With the achievement of independence, the national movement which had involved so many women of almost all castes and creeds came to an end. But in the post-1947 India, women in such large numbers fervent with the same idealism and commitment are not found participating in political activities in Kerala.

Women and the Legislature

Since 1947, many Kerala women including some of the freedom fighters have been active in politics. Some of them have held responsible positions not only at the State level but also at the national and international levels. Kuttimalu Amma from Malabar continued to be a member of the erstwhile Madras Legislative Assembly till 1952, had been a member of the Congress Working Committee (1958-1962), and is still a member of the KPCC.[7] Over the years, there has been one woman Deputy Speaker in the Kerala Assembly. Three women have held ministerial posts. Annie Mascarene who had been Congress General Secretary, member of KPCC, member of United Kerala Committee, and member of the Travancore Legislative Assembly, had the credit of being the first woman minister in the first ministry of T.K. Narayan Pillai (1949-51) in the erstwhile Travancore-Cochin State Assembly. After the formation of the Kerala State in 1956, K.R. Gouri has been minister twice – Revenue Minister and Food Minister in the first (1957-1959) and second (1967) Communist ministries respectively. The third woman who has held the post of Minister is Lakshmi Menon. She has been not only Deputy Minister (1957-62) and Minister of State (1962-66) at the Centre but also held the post of Parliamentary Secretary to the Prime Minister (1952-57) and has represented India in the U.N. General Assembly. Out of these three ministers, only K.R. Gouri continues to be active in politics. Except those years as a minister, she had been in the opposition actively participating in the deliberations of the Assembly. She is at present the Deputy Leader of the CPI(M) legislative party of the Kerala Legislative Assembly. All these three women attained their position not because of any political accident but because of their involvement and devoted work in politics.

Since independence, there had been only 25 MLAs in the erstwhile Travancore-Cochin, and Kerala State Assembly and three MPs in the Lok Sabha, and three MPs in the Rajya Sabha.

At the corporation, municipality, and panchayat levels, there has been one woman Deputy Mayor, a couple of Municipal Presidents, and one Panchayat President. The statutory provisions of the Kerala Municipalities Act have made it possible for the reservation of one seat for women for every 20 members in a municipal council. In 1971, out of 681 members in 29 municipalities, there were only 42 women members.[8]

Women and Elections

(a) *Elections to Vidhan Sabha:* Since independence, altogether eight elections have been held to the State Legislative Assembly – two general and one mid-term election to the erstwhile Travancore-Cochin State Assembly, two general elections and three mid-term elections to the Kerala Legislative Assembly. As the statistics for the first general election to the erstwhile Travancore-Cochin State Assembly could not be obtained, the comparison has to be limited to the 1952-1970 general elections.

Though there are no legal restrictions on women contesting elections, yet very few women have ventured to contest elections and enter the legislature. From Table 1 it is clear that over the years there have been variations in the total number of contestants according to the increase in the total number of seats for the Vidhan Sabha after several delimitations of the constituencies.

It is interesting to note that in the case of women contestants in the various general elections it has been inversely affected specially after the 1960 election. In 1957, there was a sudden increase of 1.2% in women contestants (Table 1, col. 6). This was because of the fact that in the formation of Kerala there was the integration of Malabar district of the erstwhile Madras State and Kasargode taluk of the erstwhile Mysore State with the Travancore-Cochin State. Hence the women who were politically active in those areas continued their activities in Kerala. In the 1960 mid-term election one saw a very encouraging increase in the percentage of women contestants by 2.4 than in 1957. Though the total number of contestants in the election was less than in 1957 election it was estimated that nearly 62.95% of women voters recorded their vote.[9] But in 1960 election, the Kerala women showed unprecedented popular and aggressive interest. In some constituencies women were reported to have outnumbered men by their massive turnout of about 4 million.[10] The notable feature of this election was that the women of Kerala had finally became conscious of their fundamental right to vote and exercised this right on a massive scale for the first time. But this enthusiasm did not seem to have remained in subsequent elections. From the 1965 election, there is a sharp fall by 2.3% in women contestants though the number of seats and the total number of contestants had increased. This small percentage of women contestants has almost remained the same in the two subsequent general elections.

TABLE 1
Women as a factor in the elections to Vidhan Sabha

Year	Nature of election	Territory covered	Total No. of candidates	Women candidates	% of women candidates	No. of successful candidates	% of successful candidates	Total seats	% of women representation
1	2	3	4	5	6	7	8	9	10
1952	General	Travancore Cochin	441	5	1.1	1	20.00	108	0.92
1954	Mid-term	-do-	265	4	1.4	1	25.00	117	1.17
1957	General	Kerala	389	10	2.6	7	70.00	126	5.5
1960	Mid-term	-do-	312	13	4.2	7	53.8	126	5.5
1965	Mid-term	-do-	557	11	1.9	3	27.2	133	2.3
1967	General	-do-	423	9	2.1	1	11.0	133	0.75
1970	Mid-term	-do-	504	10	1.9	2	20.0	133	1.50

Source: Reports of General Elections to Vidhan Sabha.

It would be worthwhile to compare the percentage of successful women candidates with the number of women contestants in the elections. Since 1952, the most noticeable change in the percentage was in 1957, when the percentage went up by 45 over the 1954 figure. (see Table 1, column 8) almost corresponding to the increase in the women contestants. But since 1957 a sharp downward trend is noticeable in the percentage of successful women candidates. Till 1970, in every election the percentage has gone down by 16 than in the preceding elections. This downward trend may be explained away by the fact that most of them were changed from their original constituencies from where they won in both 1957 and 1960, and were made to contest from new constituencies which were the stronghold of other political parties. For example, in the 1965 elections, five of the women sitting members contested and four of them were made to contest from new constituencies. Consequently three of them were defeated, and only one was returned.

With the increase in the total number of seats to the Vidhan Sabha as a result of delimitation of constituencies, the percentage of women representation has also shown an upward trend from 1952 to 1960 (see Table 1, column 10). But in 1965 the percentage of representation fell by 3.2%, and since then it has shown a still greater downward trend. This may be due to two reasons. First, the total number of candidates who contested the elections since 1965 has gone up by about 200 more than the earlier elections. The more the candidates, the less are the chances of winning. Second, most of the women who contested elections earlier did not contest in later elections and many new women entered the election arena. For example, in 1965 out of 11 women candidates, five were new; in 1967 out of nine, five were new; and in 1970 out of ten, six were new. Most of the new entrants who were without much political standing obviously could not win the election.

(b) *Elections to Lok Sabha:* As compared to the percentage of women candidates in the elections to the Vidhan Sabha, the percentage of women candidates to the Lok Sabha is quite encouraging. In spite of the formation of Kerala in 1957, and the increase by six in the total number of seats to Lok Sabha, the number of women candidates remained the same in the 1957 and 1962 elections (see Table 2, col. 4). The percentage went up by 2.91 in the 1967 elections, though there was only an increase of one seat in the total number of seats. This may be due to the rising of rebel groups from within the dominant political

Profiles of Women in Kerala

parties in Kerala like the Indian National Congress (splinter group Kerala Congress), and Communist Party (into CPM and CPI). Hence each splinter group set up women candidates for the Lok Sabha elections.

TABLE 2
Women as a factor in the elections to Lok Sabha – 1952-71

Year	Total seats	Total No. of candidates	Women candidates	Percentage of women candidates	No. of women elected	Percentage of elected women candidates
1	2	3	4	5	6	7
1952	12	47	1	2.12	1	100
1957	18	58	1	1.72	Nil	0
1962	18	50	1	2.00	Nil	0
1967	19	61	3	4.91	1	33.3
1971	19	67	4	5.97	1	25.0

The number of women participating as candidates at various elections to the Lok Sabha does not show much relationship to the number of seats allotted to the State. The most visible trend in Table 2, col. 7 is the stagnation in the number of contestants in the first three General Elections though it has shown a sudden increase in the last two General Elections (1967 and 1971). While the number of women contestants remained the same in the first three elections, the record of success at the elections showed a steep decline from 100% in 1952 to nil in 1957 and 1962. Then with the increase in the number of women contestants in the last two elections, there has been an increase in the number of successful candidates also. It is worth noting that there were no women representatives from Kerala in the Lok Sabha for a decade.

It will be worthwhile to compare the turnout of women voters in the various Lok Sabha elections. As statistics of the first two General Elections do not show any break-up of women voters, the comparison is limited to the last three General Elections.

It is clear from Table 3 (col. 4) that the difference between percentage turnout of men and women has been decreasing from 1962 onwards. Between 1962 and 1967, the women who voted has increased by 7.12% bringing down the difference between turnout of men to women voters from 7.02% to 2.73%. In 1971, there is a decline in the turnout of both men and women by 11.36% and 10.90% respectively. But the difference between the turnout of men to women voters has been reduced by 0.26%. Hence, one may infer that the participation of women as voters in the general elections is increasing and the difference in the percentage turnout of men to women voters is shrinking, and it can be hoped that the difference will be wiped out in the near future.

TABLE 3
Turnout of Women voters in Lok Sabha elections

Year	Percentage turnout of men voters	Percentage turnout of women voters	Difference between percentage turnout of men to women voters
1	2	3	4
1962	74.10	67.08	7.02
1967	77.13	74.20	2.73
1971	65.77	63.30	2.47

Source: *Towards equality – Report of the Committee on the status of women in India.*

The most visible trend that emerges from the participation of Kerala women in the elections to Vidhan Sabha and Lok Sabha is that their proportion in the population, literacy, economy, or society is not reflected in their poll participation.

Women and Political Parties

There have been altogether about 20 political parties which have participated in elections to the Vidhan Sabha since 1952 – five parties up to 1960, nine parties each in 1965 and 1967, and 20 parties in the 1970 elections. Out of these, only two political parties – the Congress and the Communist – have set up women candidates in most of the elections to Vidhan Sabha since 1952. In the 1948 Travancore-Cochin Assembly elections, out of five women who were returned, two belonged to the Travancore State Congress. The party affiliations of the other three could not be obtained.

From Table 4 it is quite clear that the Congress did not set up women candidates in the elections to Vidhan Sabha till 1957. Though the Congress set up seven candidates in the 1957 elections, by 1970

TABLE 4

Party-wise position of women candidates to Vidhan Sabha elections (1952-1970)

Parties	1952		1954		1957		1960		1965		1967		1970	
	Women candidates	Successful women	Women candidates	Successful women	Women candidates	Successful women	Women candidates	Successful women	Women candidates	Successful women	Women candidates	Successful women	Women candidates	Successful women
Congress	—	—	—	—	7	4	7	5	6	1	6	—	3	—
Communist	—	—	1	1	3	1	4	2	4	2	1	1	2	1
PSP	—	—	1	—	—	—	—	—	—	—	1	—	1	—
JS	—	—	—	—	—	—	—	—	—	—	1	—	—	—
Independents	4	1	2	—	—	—	4	—	—	—	1	—	4	1
Total	4	1	4	1	10	5	15	7	10	3	9	1	10	2

PSP: Praja Socialist Party
JS: Jana Sangh
Congress represents the combined strength of the Indian National Congress, Kerala Congress, and Congress (O)
Communists represent the combined strength of CPI, right CPI, and left CPI

the number had decreased to three. (The Congress represents the combined strength of the Indian National Congress, the Kerala Congress, and the Congress – O.) As compared to the number of men candidates the Congress has set up, the number of women is not very large; yet as a matter of policy, women have been accommodated by this party.

It is quite surprising to note that contrary to its policy in the Vidhan Sabha elections, the attitude of the Congress in giving tickets to women candidates to Lok Sabha has been very discouraging. It has set up only three women candidates in two out of five elections to the Lok Sabha. Women who have been very active in various elections since 1950 were not able to contest as Congress candidates. Annie Mascarene who had been very active in the political field had to contest as an independent in the 1952 Lok Sabha elections. Leela Damodara Menon, who had contested elections to the Vidhan Sabha on a Congress ticket in 1957, 1960, 1965, and 1970 seems to have failed to obtain a Congress ticket and hence contested the 1971 elections to the Lok Sabha as an independent. Another noticeable fact is that so far none of the women candidates from the Congress has been returned to the Lok Sabha, though two women from the Congress had been members of the Rajya Sabha.

For the Lok Sabha elections, the Communist Party started setting up women candidates as late as 1967. Again, as shown in Table 5, the Communist Party (CPI) and CPI (M) set up one woman candidate each in 1967 and 1971 elections. In both the elections, the Communist candidate has been returned.

The other parties which have set up women candidates to the Vidhan Sabha are the Praja Socialist Party and the Jana Sangh, their number and performance has been insignificant.

Interestingly enough, quite a few women have entered the election fray as independent candidates – in both Vidhan Sabha and Lok Sabha elections. But the success of such candidates has been insignificant. Out of 15 independent candidates (see Table 4), who contested various elections to Vidhan Sabha only two – one in 1952 and one in 1970 – have been returned. Out of four women who contested as independent candidates in Lok Sabha elections since 1952, none has been returned.

Thus, from 1948 to 1970, in the Vidhan Sabha elections altogether 44 women (the names for the 1948 elections are not available and hence only the names of elected women are considered) have con-

TABLE 5
Party-wise position of women candidates in Lok Sabha elections (1952-1971)

Parties	1952		1957		1962		1967		1971	
	Women candidates	Successful women	Women candidates	Successful women	Women candidates	Successful women	Women candidates	Successful women	Women candidates	Successful women
Congress	—	—	—	—	1	×	2	×	—	—
Communist	—	—	—	—	—	—	1	1	2	1
Independents	1	×	1	×	—	—	—	—	2	×
Total	1	×	1	×	1	×	3	1	4	1

Congress represents the combined strength of the Indian National Congress and Kerala Congress
Communist represents the combined strength of CPI and CPI(M)

tested. Out of these, only 15 had been returned – some only once and some more than once. Only 11 have contested the elections more than once. Out of the total candidates, 15 contested on behalf of Congress (INC, Congress – O, and Kerala Congress), and an equal number as independents.

Among all the women, K.R. Gouri from the Communist Party stands foremost as she is the only woman who has contested all the elections except the 1948 election, and has been always elected with a large margin of votes. She has been and is still very active, articulate, and also very popular. But there are some candidates from the Communist Party such as Rosamma Punnose who have been defeated in all the elections they contested. Leela Damodara Menon and K.R. Saraswati Amma, from the Congress party, have contested five and four elections respectively, but have not been successful more than twice. Devaki Krishnan and M. Kamlam are some of the Congress candidates who contested thrice and were always defeated. None of the Praja Socialist Party (altogehter three) and Jana Sangh (one) women candidates have ever been successful. Out of the 15 independents, the only successful candidate is the sitting member, Pennamma Jacob.

Thus, it is quite evident that women affiliated with the Communist or Congress parties have been more successful in the elections than all others. But unfortunately during the past decade these political parties have not been giving much encouragement even to active women in politics, not to talk of those who are inactive.

Women's Organizations

The political participation of women in Kerala has been more or less on party lines. All political parties admit that the party constitution has placed no bar to the enrolment of women as members. Almost all political parties have a women's wing attached to them in some way or other. The Indian National Congress Women's wing is called the Women's Front and the PSP women's wing is named the Socialist Mahila Sabha. But no separate rolls of women are maintained by any of the parties. These wings of almost all parties seem to be active generally at the time of elections to the municipalities, Vidhan Sabha, Lok Sabha and sometimes at panchayat elections.

But the interests of women in Kerala as a whole have been articulated by some organized groups which may be differentiated from political parties. Some of them are politically-oriented organizations exclusively of women and for the women, such as the Kerala Mahila Federation and the Muslim Educational Society. They are concerned with carrying on the unfinished social movement for securing equal status for women.

Kerala Mahila Federation

This organization was started in December 1968. Though it is not formally connected with the Communist Party, it is a Communist-dominated women's trade union front. Some of its office bearers are devoted Communist workers such as K.R. Gouri, who is the present secretary of the Federation. It has committees at the State as well as the district level. The committee at the State level consists of 29 members with one president, five vice-presidents, one secretary, and three joint secretaries. This committee meets once a year.

The Federation is composed of women from the lower working class mostly employed in mills, factories, small industries, agriculture, etc. Till now there are about a lakh of women on its rolls from all over the State. It is the contention of the Federation that though the principle of sex equality has been recognized by the Indian Constitution, in practice it does not exist because of the peculiar attitude of Indian society towards women. Society even among the well educated is still male-dominated and women are exploited by men. Due to some peculiar social norms, the fact remains that a very large section of women is confined to house-keeping. Those women who work in cashew factories, coir and textile mills, or at similar places occupy only unskilled jobs with very low wages. Hence the Mahila Federation aims at creating consciousness among women about their social as well as political rights, their social backwardness and their exclusion from the process of social production, which will ultimately lead women to a movement to liberate themselves from those inequalities.

Since its inception, the Federation has been very active. It has organized *satyagraha* by agricultural labourers, courted arrest, and participated in youth protest demonstrations. Thousands of women were in the forefront of the anti-price rise campaigns and the movement for the supply of wheat. They have also participated in all the activities of the Marxist party in Kerala.

The Federation has chalked out a programme for the year 1975-76.

The main points are:

1. To increase the membership to 1-1.5 lakhs.
2. To establish adult education institution, women's reading rooms, etc., and to organize reading groups in order to create political consciousness among women.
3. To take steps to encourage women to read party publications such as *Desabhmani* (newspaper), *Chintha* (weekly), etc.
4. To insist that women should be arrested only by women police and to keep the arrested women in sub-jails instead of in police custody.
5. To organize women security squads for the protection of women.
6. To demand establishment of seasonal creches at agricultural farms and also to give all amenities for women working in factories.
7. To fight for equal pay for equal work, and equal opportunities along with men.
8. To organize party classes to raise women cadres at both the State level and the district level.
9. To raise funds for the work of the Federation.
10. To encourage the enforcement of anti-dowry law.
11. To participate in all the issues concerning women in particular as well as issues in general.

The Federation is gaining strength under the able leadership of some very active women such as K.R. Gouri, though some claim that there is some lack of sympathy, understanding, and support among men to the Federation even among party members.

Muslim Educational Society

This Society, which was started in 1964, has taken up the cause of Muslim women. It has set up a women's section both at State and district levels – MES ladies' wing. Its state committee consists of one president, two vice-presidents, one secretary, one treasurer, one state organizer, and 15 members. Though girls' education has received great impetus in Kerala, compared to women in other communities, more than 90% Muslim girls are still illiterate or ignorant. It is surprising to note that not even 1% of Muslim women have completed secondary education. In some areas of Malabar, where the orthodox reactionary forces are dominant, a Muslim girl passing SSLC is still a nine days' wonder. Muslim women are not socially free or educationally equipped to play their role in society, though their position in other States is much worse than in Kerala. Economically, they depend on the earnings of their husbands. So Muslim women have many problems – social, educational and economic – some of which are the obscure forces within the Community. The main objectives of the MES Ladies' wing are to discuss, ventilate, and seek redress of their grievances. The most important objective is to spread education among Muslim women as education is considered to be the panacea for all ills in the social and economic sphere. To encourage education, MES distributes free books to poor students in schools and scholarships to deserving students in colleges. Since the advent of the MES, the community has established 13 colleges, many nurseries and other institutions where Muslim students – boys and girls – are being educated in increasing numbers.

Though this society claims to be a non-political association, many of its members are members of the Muslim League.

Emerging Trends

One may draw some conclusions regarding the trends in the role being played by some women in Kerala politics.

1. There was a kind of commitment among women who were involved in politics during the pre-independence period. Perhaps the political atmosphere during the national movement had taken such an idealistic turn that it permeated every part of one's existence and encouraged the emergence of an outstanding type of women leaders. But in the post-1947 period women – except those freedom fighters who continued in politics in the first few years after independence – entered politics more as a career made possible as constitutional right, and not with the same ideals which had made them enter the national movement.

2. The participation of women at the time of elections had been encouraging and not very far behind men.

3. Very few women have ventured to contest the elections and other political activities. So in Kerala, the proportion of population, literacy, economic or social position of women have no bearing on the participation of women at the polls.

4. No new woman leader has emerged at the State level out of the

many who have actively participated in politics.

5. Most of the women who have entered public life during the national movement and the early fifties belonged to upper middle class. Since then conditions have changed. The new trend is that it is the lower class (labour class) which has got organized and politically educated. In this the Communist parties have played an important part.

6. Most of the able women, especially those from the middle class, do not wish to involve themselves in political activities for many reasons.

(a) For a woman to enter politics is a very difficult thing. She has little opportunity for being trained in political organization and activity.
(b) Social tradition continues to look on women as part of the household and not as a part of the political system.
(c) When political activity means power, then women come into closer conflict with men who would prefer to keep women out of politics.

Notwithstanding the limitations that emerge from the social structure, there are many other factors such as economic dependence and some behavioural norms now current in political life, e.g. character assassination of opponents or rivals that restrain women from entering political life. One thing is quite clear. If proper dignity and decorum are maintained in the deliberations of the Vidhan Sabha, party meetings, election speeches, etc., far more women are likely to be attracted to politics. Or else, as one of the women leaders sarcastically put it, women politicians should develop the skin of a rhinoceros. There is no dearth of educated women or leadership among women. So, it would be worthwhile to probe deeper into the question why women, particularly educated women from the middle class, are becoming more and more indifferent to active participation in politics.

References

1. Calculated from 1971 Census and *Administrative Report 1974-75*, (Education Department, Government of Kerala).
2. K. Narayanan, *A Portrait of Population – Kerala*, p. 151.
3. P.K.K. Menon, *The History of Freedom Movement in Kerala*.
4. *Ibid.*, p. 232.
5. *Ibid.*, pp. 222 and 429.
6. *Ibid.* p. 400.

7. Information collected from interviews.
8. *Administration Report for the year 1972-73* (Department of Municipalities), p. 14.
9. K.P. Bhagat, *The Kerala Mid-term Election of 1960*, p. 123.
10. *Ibid.*
11. *Report of Kerala Mahila Federation*, 1974, p. 16.
12. Kerala Mahila Federation: *Oru Varshakala Paripadi.*

PROFILES OF WOMEN IN MAHARASHTRA

S.N. Tawale

During the period of renaissance in Maharashtra, there had been several first-rank social leaders and writers who persistently wrote about emancipation of women in its various ramifications. Through literary medium such as novels, plays, etc., the message of women's freedom was effectively conveyed. This process seems to have come to a halt by the middle of the present century. The contemporary fiction predominantly reflects individualistic trends. The happiness and sorrows, the hopes and disappointments of women as they appear in contemporary literary works do not generally possess social dimensions. A self-centred individualism of women is on the upsurge. "This individualism does not emerge from the life around us, but has its roots in copying foreign literature. . . . It is (for this reason) that the clarion call of the political ideology adopted by the nation of the 'socialist social order' has not filtered down to the majority of writers."[1]

In the post-independence period, there has been meagre political writing relating to women. Periodicals devoted to women's matters are good in number. But they hardly pay any attention to the political aspect of women's lives. As a rule, women's journals are content with domestic, emotional, educational, artistic, and cultural topics. Occasionally, personal interviews of women political leaders find a place in them. However, periodicals such as *Stri, Manohar,* and *Sadhana* do reflect some concern for women's political views and their political participation. Characteristically, much of the present political writing about women is by women themselves. Recently, quite a few autobiographical writings of women leaders in the social and political field have been published. Those of Godawari Parulekar and Usha Dange are notable contributions.

The present report is based mainly on information from periodicals, books, and pamphlets. The information is supplemented by personal talks with a few of the women political leaders in Poona – Sarojini Babar, Nalinibai Shinde, Indumati Kelkar, Maltibai Paranjape, Anasuya Limaye, Pramila Dandavate, and Kamalabai Bhagwat.

There is no fullfledged study about the political status and role of women in Maharashtra. As this trend report will indicate, a comprehensive study covering women's political awareness and role is worth undertaking. Owing to the short time available for preparing the report, only broad aspects of women's political life could be covered. In doing this, an attempt is made to minimize the male bias as far as possible.

Restricted Political Participation

It is a generally accepted view that women should participate in politics not only because it offers a challenging career but also because circumstances demand it. There has been a feeling among women leaders that if women devote themselves to politics in sufficient numbers and with dedication, it will greatly help remove much of the despicable character of the present-day politics. Chandrakala Hate, a sociologist, argues that in modern times the individual is increasingly giving way to the group as a unit of social action. Under the impact of ever widening state control and activity women have no alternative but to come together and evolved a joint non-party political front.[2]

The advocacy of a political role for women, however, does not mean that women in Maharashtra are in fact engaged in political activities on a large scale. They feel that the idealism which characterized politics during the nationalist struggle has largely decreased. It was expressed by women legislators in Maharashtra that politics being a dirty game women cannot identify with it.

As women are more reluctant than men to a public discussion of their personal life, they are in general prone to shun a political career. One of the factors which places severe limitations on women's participation in social and political affairs is their preoccupation with domestic responsibilities. Though at the public level men recognize the necessity and desirability of giving equal scope to women in social, economic, and political life of the community, their traditional attitude towards women's role has not changed much. The whole concept of men as the breadwinner and women discharging the functions of child-bearing and child-rearing, and other household work is more of an attitude than division of labour, because even when women work on farms, in factories, schools, hospitals, and offices, they are not relieved of household work. Domestic servants and kitchen gadgets may help those with well-paid jobs. But for the overwhelming majority of employed women with their meagre wages, work outside the home amounts to a rigorous double-shift routine.

Pre-Independence Years

The social liberation of women has been a vital segment of the reform movement in Maharashtra. The basis for this was laid during the 19th century and the persistent efforts of Lokahitawadi, Balshastri, Jambhekar, Mahadev Govind Ranade, Pandita Ramabai, Gopal Ganesh Agarkar, Dhondo Keshav Karve, and Mahatma Jyotirao Phule not only contributed towards eliminating the most glaring social inflictions on women, but also created a social environment in which, for the first time, women began to feel themselves capable of self-development and worthy of self-respect. This found its social expression when the nationalist movement passed into the hands of Mahatma Gandhi. In response to the clarion call of the Congress for civil disobedience at its Nagpur session (1921), thousands of women in Maharashtra threw themselves into the nationalist struggle. They not only displayed great enthusiasm in taking out *prabhat pheries* (morning marches), picketing at the liquor shops, adopting use of khadi and boycotting foreign goods, but also braved lathi-charges and imprisonment in the 'Salt Satyagraha' of 1930, and in the 'Civil Disobedience' and 'Non-Cooperation' movement of the early thirties. Avantikabai Gokhale, Yashodabai Bhat, Anusayabai Kale, Krishnakumari Sardesai, Prema Kantak, Maniben Kara, Kamala Devi Chattopadhyaya, Hansa Mehta, etc. had been among the earliest to lead the non-violent movement in Maharashtra. It is estimated that about 2,500 women were serving sentences in prison in 1931, in the Maharashtra area.[3] Women's political organizations such as Desh Sevika Sangh under the leadership of Hansa Mehta and Perin Captain, and Hindusthani Sevika Dal led by Ramiben Kamadar and Kusum Sovani did excellent work in Bombay. Dr. Malini Sukhtankar resigned from her post of J.P. in Bombay, and Anasuya Kala from her membership of the Legislative Council of the Central Province in protest against government repression. Women's participation in the nationalist struggle reached its climax with the "Quit India" movement of 1942 when several women successfully conducted underground political activities. With independence, the nationalist movement which had uniformly involved women of different castes, religions, and classes came to an end. The political participation of women after independence cannot be viewed in the same sense in which it was viewed before. The most striking fact about the present-day politics of women in Maharashtra is the almost inverse relationship between the caste and class status of women, and the degree of their politicization. This is so for the reason that post-independence politics has been the politics of democracy versus elitism, and equality versus privilege. Women in India have often been understood, and rightly so, as the most numerous "depressed caste". The phrase is very much pertinent in the context of male predominance in Indian society. And the fullest liberation of women in this sense will no doubt be an important stage in the evolution of society, not in this country alone but everywhere in the world.

This long-term perspective, however, should not distract us from the fact that the first battle which the low-caste and low-class women in Maharashtra have to wage today is not so much against the male-dominated social structure as against the economic and caste inequities which vertically divide the entire community of women themselves. Here, of course, for Muslim women the continuation of Shariyat laws relating to polygamy, oral divorce, etc. indicates a marked lag in the social evolution of that community. With the reform of the Hindu personal law in 1955 and 1956, the process of social emancipation of Hindu women which had begun almost a 150 years ago reached a high water-mark. The basic social equality of sex which has been attained by Hindu women has been still denied to their Muslim counterparts. This issue of reform of the Muslim personal law therefore has come to be a significant political theme in the Muslim Community, attracting some support as well as resistance to it.

Indifference of Upper-class Women

With the exception of this issue, women in Maharashtra present a political picture wherein those from the upper castes and classes, though presumably politically more literate, exhibit an indifferent attitude towards politics, while those from lower castes and classes show a relatively much higher degree of politicization. It should, however, be noted that the leadership role of women's struggles has been generally assumed by women of high castes and middle classes. But as a class, politics constitutes a peripheral interest from them. Recently, the St. Xavier's College of Bombay conducted a sample survey of political awareness among college and university students covering 4% of the total college and university students (69,000). The survey revealed that the percentage of politically aware female students is almost zero except among the Marathi-speaking female students in which case it is as low as 0.8%. If we consider the fact that college-going girls are by and large from the higher classes and castes, the survey findings confirm the fact of political indifference of women of this category. However, individual political contributions may be illustrated by the work of such prominent women leaders as Usha Dange, Ahilya Ranganekar, Roza Deshpande, Kamalabai Bhagwat, Indumati Kelkar, Sushila Patel, Mrinal Gore, and many others. The contributions which such women have made to politics in Maharashtra must be understood as instances of individual achievements irrespective of the caste or class to which they belong. Godawari Parulekar's work of politically arousing the Warlis in the Thana district[4] is an outstanding example of this phenomenon.

Social Work

The tradition of social and cooperative work for and among women has been strong in Maharashtra. Women's educational institutions such as Hingane Stri Shikshan Sanstha, Nathibai Damodardas Thakersey Institutions and Kasturba Mahila Ashram (at Sawad, near Poona) have been in existence for decades. Hundreds of Mahila Mandals which are organized in talukas and various localities in big cities such as Bombay, Nagpur, and Poona are generally engaged in cultural and social welfare activities. For instance, the Samyukta Stri Sanstha, a federation of 22 women's organizations in Poona, had an annual budget of over Rs.55,000 in the year 1971-72. The activities carried out by the SSS range from conducting kindergarten and primary schools to establishing cottage industries centres to provide work to needy women. There are also examples of outstanding social leadership among women. Kamalabai Hospet's name, for instance, has been associated for the past 50 years with women's welfare in the Vidarbha area. Individual attempts in the field of social welfare are illustrated by such women as Malatibai Chinchalikar, who, along with her husband, has set up a Maval Seva Mandal at Malavali (Bombay-Poona road), which through its handmade paper plant provides employment to the tribal community in the area. Dr. Indumati Patwardhan set up the Anand Gram Society in 1970, a colony of lepers at Alandi (near Poona).

Emancipation of Women – Different Perceptions

The political participation of women in Maharashtra has been more or less on party lines. All major political parties have women's wings attached to them in some way or the other. The party thinking, therefore, is naturally reflected in the views of the women leaders who are engaged in organizing these wings.

Congress Mahila Front

The thinking of the Congress women leaders is moulded by the fact that it is the party in power. As their party is in an advantageous position, a number of openings are available to them. Either they can secure an election ticket and more or less safely enter the legislature, a panchayat, or municipality; or they may be nominated on various advisory committees on health and education at the local level or be associated with the social welfare department at the State level. They may be appointed honorary magistrates or on the educational institutions such as universities. It is not just a matter of coincidence that the women who have already launched three cooperative banks belong to the Congress party.[5] For the Congress women, and particularly for women leaders, participation in agitational politics or even taking a public stand against the government deeds and policies amounts to anti-party activity.

Thus, they naturally content themselves with competing for small or big benefits (depending on their own ability and ambition) flowing from the State, and keep themselves away from the basic issues of the people. There appears to be some sort of complacency among them on general political issues as well as those relating to women. They justify this by laying stress on the constructive aspect of social life.

Jana Sangh Mahila Aghadi

The Jana Sangh Mahila Aghadi in Maharashtra, mostly of middle-class Brahmin composition, in keeping with the general political stand of the party does not recognize women as a separate social sector facing problems peculiar to it. In its opinion, women's problems are problems of the society as a whole and they cannot be solved by organizing women separately. There appears to be some confusion in the Jana Sangh view of women's equality. On the one hand it has to admit (however grudgingly) the inequality of women's social status; on the other it disapproves adoption of political means by women to attain the fullest realization of equality with men. In its view, women's demand for equality is misconceived in the sense that it puts a premium on a sectional view of society and loses sight of the relationship between men and women as something more than a contest for parochial and egoist interests. In so far as it recognizes the need for an honourable place for women in society, it adopts a kind of paternalistic attitude and declares its readiness to "give a fair deal" to women.

Jana Sangh women, like women of other parties, have from time to time participated in relief work and other social welfare activities. However, they are not known to have organized on an appreciable scale programmes providing work to needy women. Their argument is that such schemes are not likely to solve the stupendous problem of unemployment with which both men and women are confronted. The solution lies in changing the government which is responsible for such a state of affairs. It should be noted here that it is not systemic change which is implied as is the case of Communist parties.

Samajwadi Mahila Sabha

The Samajwadi Mahila Sabha is the most active political and social organization of women in Maharashtra. Though it is not connected in any formal manner with the Socialist Party, faith in democratic socialism is a necessary condition for its membership. It aims at arousing national spirit and creating consciousness about political and social rights and duties among women.

The Sabha is open to women over 18 years of age and has a membership of over 3,000 in 38 branches in western and northeastern Maharashtra. It is engaged in a variety of constructive programmes which include industrial cooperatives, propagation of family planning, organization of study circles, debates and symposia to educate women on the social and political situation, setting up of creches, kindergartens, etc. and occasional programmes such as drought relief work.[6]

Politically the Sabha operates at two levels. It perceives certain problems as peculiar to women, but at the same time it participates in the general political struggle for equality and justice for the masses in society.

Profiles of Women in Maharashtra

As to the first, it is the contention of the Sabha that though the principle of equality of sex has been recognized by the Constitution of India, much of it exists only in a formal sense, owing to the absence of a proper attitude in Indian society which still considers women as commodities. In spite of the grant of equal citizenship rights women are miles away from enjoying equal opportunity. It is true that law not only prohibits discrimination against women in employment but also provides for such facilities as maternity leave, creches, etc. for employed women. Yet the fact remains that a very large number of women are excluded from the process of social production and are confined to housekeeping due to conservative societal norms. Those women who work in factories, textile mills, or at similar places, mostly occupy due to their lack of technical skills and education, unskilled jobs or such jobs as require a very low level of tenhnical skill. Consequently, they cannot expect better wages. Much of the significance of the formal recognition of equal status for women is detracted by the age-long tendency of men to exclude women as far as possible from responsible positions.[7]

The Sabha has therefore thought it necessary to declare a charter of women's rights. The charter was framed under the guidance of Maniben Kara, the veteran trade unionist, and was adopted by the Sabha in 1969. The major demands contained in the charter are as follows:

1. Free education at all levels for girls.
2. Provision of vocational and technical courses for girls at the secondary school level.
3. Provision of part-time jobs for women.
4. Setting up of vocational guidance bureaus for women.
5. Provision of security arrangements and amenities for women working on night shifts and those employed as nurses, teachers, Gram Sevikas, and family planning canvassers in rural areas.
6. Promulgation of a uniform Civil Code for all the communities in the country.
7. Social mobilization against the dowry system which, though legally prohibited, is practised in a clandestine way.
8. Greater scope for women in the electoral contests and in the organization of parties.[8]

Joint Women's Action Committee

In recent years, the Samajwadi Mahila Sabha has begun to participate in a big way in mobilizing women against the government as well as against wholesale traders for their anti-social policies and activities. Though it also intends to direct its campaign against landlords, no marked activity is yet visible on that front probably because the Sabha's political influence is mostly in the urban areas.

During the past two years huge protest *morchas* and *gheraos* conducted by women in Bombay, Nagpur, and a few other places have startled the government and people of Maharashtra. The agitational campaign was organized and led by the Joint Action Committee of Women for the Resistance of Price Rise. The Joint Action Committee predominantly comprises leaders of the Samajwadi Mahila Sabha (Mrinal Gore, Pramila Dandavate, Kamal Desai, Vimal Paranjpe and Mangala Parikh), and those of the Communist Party (Ahilya Ranganekar, Sushila Patel, Manju Gandhi, etc.). The idea of a Joint Action Committee was mooted by the Bharatiya Mahila Federation[9] in an anti-price rise conference held in Bombay in September 1972.

The Joint Action Committee which was set up on 9 September 1973 started its vigorous campaign in Bombay. Its major demands include:

1. The government should take over wholesale trade in essential commodities and ensure their distribution at reasonable prices.
2. Manufacture of sugar, cloth, and pharmaceuticals should be nationalized.
3. The nationalized banks should be prohibited from extending credit to big traders.
4. Hundred-rupee notes should be demonetized to curb black money.
5. Black marketeers and hoarders should be sentenced to long-term rigorous imprisonment or should be flogged at public places.
6. Local vigilance committees should be appointed to supervise the dealings of the ration shops.
7. The network of ration shops should be widened.
8. The Land Ceiling Act should be amended to lower the ceiling, and land thus made available should be redistributed. The small and poor peasant should be provided with every possible assistance to increase the production of foodgrains.[10]

Maharashtra Rajya Shramik Mahila Samiti

Though declared to be a non-party organization, the Shramik Mahila Samiti, set up in 1964 and led by Roza Deshapande, Malini Tulpule, and Vimalabai Bangal, is a Communist-dominated women's trade union. Theoretically, the approach of the Communist Party towards the problem of emancipation of women is clear-cut. According to it, the male-dominated social structure is an integral feature of a capitalist society. The exploitation of women by men and exploitation of men by owners of property are the two links in the same chain. Any effort towards liberation of women, therefore, is not likely to succeed without transforming the economic basis of society.

To see the issue of women's emancipation primarily in the context of male chauvinism or patriarchalism is to lose perspective of the problem. With regard to the women of lower classes and lower castes, who constitute the great majority of the female population, it must be noted that traditional Hindu religious orthodoxy and patriarchalism did not apply to them so stringently as it did to higher class and higher caste women. It may, therefore, be said that the 'greatest barrier to the full liberation of Indian women today lies not so much in the survival of caste orthodoxy or patriarchalism as in the continuing socio-economic inequities that make it impossible for lower class women to capitalize on the democratising gains of the nationalist period'.[11]

The housework is highly exacting and completely absorbs women's energies; but it is never recognized in economic terms. A tremendous amount of labour is thus made available in the society without any cost. The sacrifices and hardships of women which economically sustain the family and which result in a complete denial of full development of their personalities are eulogised as the highest cultural values of the society. Under the impact of such a social atmosphere women have lost all ability to think and live except as appendages to men.

All this cannot be halted unless women are drawn into the process of production in a meaningful way. Economic slavery of women is the root cause of their stunted individual growth.

The Constitution of India recognizes equality of sex in employment. In reality, however, women do not adequately share along with men, the national income, and employment. According to the 1971 census, only 12% of the female population in the country are engaged in paid work, mostly of an unskilled and inferior nature. Most of the working women in Maharashtra are either landless labourers or wage-earners in textile mills, engineering and building projects. The share of women in the process of production which is already low, has shown a tendency to decline during 1961-71.[12] Employment opportunities are being denied to women by private employers to escape the inconvenient fact that women once employed, have to be provided with certain facilities (e.g. maternity leave) under the law. On account of this fact and partly due to mechanization, the proportion of women workers in mines has declined from 20% in 1952 to 12% in 1969.[13] The engineering and pharmaceutical industries did not admit married women as workers till 1964. It was under the impact of the Shramik Mahila Samiti's active campaign that this discriminatory rule was scrapped in that year.

This organization also strives for other important objectives such as provision of creches for the children of employed women; protection for Harijan women and women employees such as nurses, primary teachers, and Gram Sevikas in rural areas from local gangsterism.

The Samiti, along with the Samajwadi Mahila Sabha has been in the forefront of the anti-price rise campaigns.

Women in Bombay gave massive response to the call of the Joint Action Committee. In November 1973, 3,000 women staged a *satyagraha* and courted arrest. The Joint Action Committee directed its weapons of *gherao* and protest *morchas* against the Agriculture Minister, officers of the Waroli dairy, the Chief Minister, Ramnath Kilachand (wholesale dealer in edible oils), directors of the Hindustan Lever Company, Oberoi Sheraton Hotel, and the office of the Mill Owners' Association. The most striking event – the Pon Morcha – took place on 17 November 1973. On this day 5,000 women with rolling pins in their hands took out a *morcha* to the Legislative Assembly. The wooden implement has traditionally been regarded as a symbol of feminine weakness. The Joint Action Committee, however, converted it into a symbol of women's solidarity and strength.

Issues Which have Evoked Significant Support or Opposition from Women

During the post-independence period, women in Maharashtra have participated along with men, though this participation is numerically disproportionate to the number of women present in the two major political struggles – the Samyukta Maharashtra movement in the late fifties and the Goa Liberation struggle. There are, moreover, certain other issues which because of their direct bearing on women's lives have attracted significant attention from women.

Polygamy and Oral Divorce

Muslim women in Maharashtra, as in other parts of the country, have remained out of the process of modernization and liberation. They do not enjoy a place of security and honour in their own community. According to the Shariyat law of 1937 they suffer a discriminated social status. For instance, a Muslim woman can be divorced by her husband who merely pronounces *talaq* three times without giving reasons or providing for her maintenance except for a brief period of three months. But she, on the other hand, cannot secure a divorce without the consent of her husband. A Muslim can simultaneously have four wives. Similar discriminatory and unjust provisions exist in relation to property inheritance and guardianship over minors.

'With the purpose of mobilizing Muslim women against this unjust Muslim personal law, and to urge the government to reform it, the Muslim Satya Shodhak Mandal (a Poona-based Muslim reformist group) and the Indian Secular Society jointly convened a conference of Muslim women on 27th and 28th December 1971 in Poona. For the first time in the history of the Muslim community in India nearly 350 Muslim women hailing from Maharashtra, and to some extent from other parts of the country gathered in a conference and revolted against religious orthodoxy and obscurantism of Muslim society.

The conference which was inaugurated by Prof. A.A.A. Faizi and presided over by Sharifa Tayyabji passed the following major resolutions:[14]

1. The Government of India should enact at an early date the uniform civil code. Pending this, the Union and State Governments should take necessary executive or legislative action for immediate removal of the glaring inequities in the present Muslim personal law.
2. The Conference condemns opposition to family planning from obscurantist quarters in the name of religion or ideology. Facilities afforded by the Government should be curtailed or withdrawn in the case of those who either have more than three children or oppose family planning.

3. Government should encourage modern, professional and science-based education for Muslim children, and particularly for Muslim girls.
4. To secure economic independence for Muslim women, the Government as well as other organisations should institute programmes for imparting technical skills to them. Cooperative societies and other development agencies like banks, small scale and cottage industries corporations can provide important avenues for promoting economic independence of Muslim women.

The above resolutions of the Muslim Social Conference and the activities of the Muslim Satya Shodhak Mandal do not, however, constitute a mass movement, taking in its sweep the entire Muslim community. They are in the nature of the first stirrings of a somnolent society, which at present is confined to a tiny minority of educated and enlightened Muslims. It is interesting to note that the Muslim Social Conference was followed by several Muslim meetings in which not only men but also women of that community condemned the activities of the Muslim Satya Shodhak Mandal as obnoxious interference in Muslim Social life.

Dowry System, Outrages Committed on Harijan Women, etc.

In spite of legal prohibition, the dowry system shows no signs of abatement and has in fact become more widespread. With the intention of creating a social atmosphere against the dowry system, several women's conferences were held in different parts of Maharashtra. In March 1974 the Akhil Bharatiya Stri-Shakti Sammelan was held in Pawanar, the place of Vinoba Bhave's Ashram. The conference which was addressed by both Vinoba Bhave and Indira Gandhi, discussed several issues such as outrages on Harijan women, reform of Muslim personal law, etc.

An anti-dowry conference of women held at Faizpur, Khandesh district, in February 1973 passed several resolutions relating to extravagance and religious orthodoxy in marriage ceremonies and the dowry system. The conference recommended that girls should resolve not to marry those insisting on dowry.[15]

For the first time in Marathwada a conference on equality of women was held at Selu on 9 and 10 December 1972. The conference deprecated the inferior social status assigned to women by the society. It declared that women who observe castism are not entitled to expect a status of equality vis-a-vis men. The conference also condemned the dowry system, polygamy in the Muslim community, and outrages committed on Harijan women in the Marathwada region in 1972 and 1973.

Women's Participation in Legislature Party Hierarchy

In spite of the fact that women account for half the population of Maharashtra State as elsewhere and that there are no legal barriers to their political career in local government, State and Central governments, and party hierarchies, the proportion of women in these fields though not negligible, is marginal. The ministry in Maharashtra generally includes one or two women members. They are, however, assigned Deputy ministership, State ministership or Cabinet ministership with a simple portfolio such as Social Welfare. The Zilla Parishads Act provides for the nomination of one woman member to the gram panchayat if no woman is elected to it. Though there is a remarkable example of a gram panchayat at Nimbut (Baramati taluka, Poona district), where women won all the seats some years ago, the above legal provision indicates that women's initiative in contesting the elections and their success in elections is not thought to be a likely prospect. As illiteracy among women is widespread in the rural areas, women's participation in zilla parishads is bound to be extremely low. It is a significant fact that there is only one woman president of the zilla parishad (Thana district) out of the 25 zilla parishads in Maharashtra. In the urban areas, however, female membership of the municipal councils and municipal corporations is relatively larger. Though women's participation in voting in general elections is not much lower as compared to men (see Table 1), they play a minor role as candidates in the elections. There have not been more than one or two women members from Maharashtra to the Lok Sabha or Rajya Sabha.

The marginal nature of women's representation is reflected in the party hierarchies. Out of 41 members of the Jana Sangh, there are four women members in its Maharashtra executive, and one woman from Maharashtra sits on the all-India executive of that party.

The total membership of the Maharashtra Pradesh Congress Committee (MPCC), a State level general body composed of Pradesh Pratinidhis (i.e. delegates elected from the District Congress Committees and from the legislature); presidents and vice-presidents of all the

25 zilla parishads; and all the former presidents of the MPCC is 442, but of these the number of women delegates is only 19. Thirteen District Congress Committees have not sent a single woman delegate to the MPCC. At the district level, not a single woman happens to be a president of any of the 28 District Congress Committees (which include three City Congress Committees) in Maharashtra.

TABLE 1

Women's participation in voting (Lok Sabha)

	1962	1967	1971
1. Average percentage of voting	60.43%	76.56%	71.82%
2. Ratio of male voting to total male voters	66.02%	79.23%	74.48%
3. Ratio of female voting to total female voters	54.29%	73.94%	69.17%
4. *Ratio of women voters to the total number of voters	47.82%	50.42%	50.02%
5. *Ratio of men voters to the total number of voters	52.18%	49.58%	49.98%

Source: *Election Commission of India, *Report on the Fifth General Election in India 1971-72*, New Delhi, pp. 120-21.

Note: Ratios in columns 4 and 5 are calculated on the basis of other percentages in the table.

Out of the total membership of 54 of the MPCC executive, there are only three women members one of whom is an ex officio member by virtue of her being the convener of the Congress Mahila Front.

The picture of the Bombay Pradesh Congress Committee is a little better. The BPCC executive with a total membership of 37 has three women members. Of these three, one is a vice-president and another is a joint secretary. (There are seven vice-presidents and six joint secretaries in the BPCC executive.)

The Maharashtra Pradesh Congress Committee has elected 58 delegates to the All-India Congress Committee, which include four women members.

Thus, so far as the Congress party hierarchy is concerned, it appears that women's representation is the lowest at the lower rungs of the party organization, and that it improves slightly as we go up the ladder. It appears that numerically women in the Congress, as in other parties, do not constitute a large force at the level of ordinary membership; and that the presence of several women either at the

Profiles of Women in Maharashtra

higher levels of party organization or in the legislature is not due to the political base or support structure which in their case does not exist. In their upward journey of the political career, they do not have to wade through an intense and at times cruel competition for power. Either they owe their success to their family background or they are handpicked by the leadership in appreciation of their intellectual abilities and social work.

TABLE 2

Women's participation/elections (Assembly)

Party	1952 (264)		1957 (264)		1962 (264)		1967 (269)	
	Contested	Won	Contested	Won	Contested	Won	Contested	Won
Congress	7	5	29	13	19	13	**11	9
Socialist	4	Nil	—	—	*2	Nil	—	—
Peasants and Workers Party	—	—	—	—	1	Nil	1	Nil
Communist Party	—	—	1	Nil	***4	Nil	—	—
Scheduled Castes federation	1	Nil	—	—	—	—	—	—
Ram Rajya Parishad	2	Nil	1	Nil	—	—	—	—
Krishi Majdoor Praja Party	—	—	—	—	—	—	—	—
Kamgar Kisan Party	1	Nil	—	—	—	—	—	—
Hindu Maha Sabha	—	—	—	—	—	—	—	—
Jana Sangh	—	—	—	—	—	Nil	—	—
Republican Party of India	—	—	—	—	—	—	2	Nil
Swatantra Party	—	—	—	—	—	—	1	Nil
Independents	1	Nil	4	1	10	Nil	4	Nil
Total	16	5	35	14	37	13	19	9

*Praja Samajwadi Party **Indian National Congress ***CPI

Figures in the bracket indicate the total number of elective seats in the Assembly.
Figures in the 1952 and 1957 columns relate to the constituencies in the Maharashtra region only and, thus, exclude Karnataka and Gujarat constituencies respectively in the then existing Bombay State.

As regards the opposition parties, it becomes difficult to get women either to work as party office-bearers or to contest elections. The situation in the Congress party is of course slightly different. As Congress party ticket means an almost certain entry into the legislature, women are likely to show relatively greater enthusiasm in the matter. Since exact information regarding the number of women applicants for nomination was not made available by the Congress party office, one cannot say the ratio between the applicants and the nominations. In the 1972 Assembly etections, the MPCC had asked for 15% nominations for women. Actually, 24 women contested elections on the Congress ticket. The ratio of Congress women candidates to the total number of elective seats of the Assembly (27) works out to 12%. Commenting on this low percentage, Kamalatai Vicharay, the Convener of the Congress Mahila Front, has asked whether women are really capable of discharging the legislative responsibilities in order to deserve a much higher representation.

TABLE 3
Women's participation in elections (Lok Sabha)

Party	1952-57		1957-62		1962-67		1967-71	
	Contested	Won	Contested	Won	Contested	Won	Contested	Won
Congress	2	2	2	1	1	1	2	1
Independent	1	Nil	1	—	—	—	—	—
Republican Party	—	—	—	—	1	—	—	—
PWP	1	Nil	—	—	—	—	1	1
SSP	—	—	—	—	—	—	—	Nil

This brings us to the question of women's participation in the legislature. Meaningful participation in the business of the House requires a full grasp of the rules of legislative procedure, a grip over the facts, and capacity for articulate expression. If the extent and quality of women's participation in the Maharashtra Legislative Assembly is any guide, it must be said that they have in general not evinced these abilities in an appreciable degree. As most of the women members belong to the ruling party, their silence may partly, but only partly be attributed to party discipline.

Use of Religious Symbols

For the most part political parties have refrained from playing on the religious susceptibilities of women in Maharashtra. It is true that the election symbol of the Indian National Congress (cow with a calf) basically carries an emotional appeal for women. But, as the studies of electoral behaviour carried but in Maharashtra have revealed that women do not exercise their vote independently but according to the wishes of the male members of the family, such an appeal is not likely to be reflected in the pattern of female voting.

For the purpose of establishing rapport with women voters, 'haldi-kumku' ceremonies were held by the Jana Sangh and the Congress. As 'haldi-kumku' stands for long life and health of the husband, it is a symbol of security, prestige, and happiness for women. With all this, it is problematic whether these ceremonies have produced any political results for the parties concerned.

References

1. D.K. Sant, cited in Chandrakala A. Hate, *Changing Status of Women*.
2. Chandrakala Hate, *Changing Status of Women*, Allied Publishers, Bombay, 1969, p. 231
3. *Griha Lakshmi* (Ed. V.B. Marathe), Bombay, January, 1931. p. 81.
4. An excellent account of this remarkable story is found in her *Jeva Manus Jaga Hote*, Mouj Prakashan, 1970.
5. Shalinibai Patel, the wife of the Irrigation Minister, recently set up the Laxmi Cooperative Bank in Sangli and Indira Cooperative Bank in Bombay in 1972, Dr. Sarojini Babar set up the Bhagini Nivedita Bank in Poona in this year. Nalinibai Shinde, a senior woman leader of the Congress party, is engaged in promoting the Jijamata Cooperative Bank in Poona.
6. *Biennial Report 1972-73*, Samajwadi Mahila Sabha (Maharashtra), Poona.
7. It is interesting to note here that the managing committees (Life-Member's Boards, as they are locally known) of several renowned colleges in Poona do not yet have women members.
8. *Charter of Modern Women's Rights* (Marathi) Published by Smt. Anasuya Limaye, President of the Samajwadi Mahila Sabha (Maharashtra), Poona, 1969.
9. The Bharatiya Mahila Federation was set up in 1954 by women leaders such as Aruna Asaf Ali, Manju Gandhi, Ahilya Ranganekar, and Tara Reddi who had formerly worked in the All-India Women's Conference. The latter organization made an outstanding contribution under Sarojini Naidu's leadership during the freedom struggle. Later, however, it degenerated into a highbrow association.
10. *Yugantar*, Bombay, 11 November 1973. p. 14.
11. Gail Omvedt "Caste Class and Women's Liberation", paper read at the annual meeting of the Association for Asian Studies, March 30. The paper is based on Miss Ombedit's study of the status of women in Maharashtra.
12. *Ibid.*, p. 5.
13. *Ibid.*, p. 6 (figures on all-India basis).

14. Muslim Social Conference held in Poona on 27 and 28 December 1971 under the auspices of Indian Secular Society, Bombay, and Muslim Satya Shodhak Mandal, Poona.
15. *Sadhana*, 3 March 1973, p. 22.

PROFILES OF WOMEN IN PUNJAB

P. Rajput

The present report on the political role and status of women has been limited to the State of Punjab, the total population of which are 46% women.[1] It has its main focus on: women and elections; women and political parties; women as legislators and ministers; legislation concerning women; and the women's organisations.

Since the enquiry covers a number of aspects related to the political role of women, the data have been collected through two main sources, namely, the secondary sources and the personal interviews. The descriptive material has been drawn from secondary sources such as census documents, election statistical records and other official records, newspapers, and analytical accounts prepared by historians and political scientists. Most of the data are collected through personal interviews of the available women political leaders, leaders of women's organizations, etc. through unstructured questionnaires.

It may, however, be added at the outset that the present report is not aimed at testing any hypothesis, hence no such postulation has been done.

Women and Elections

Review of Literature

Investigations carried out by social scientists in Punjab in the field of politics and political behaviour have been conducted in a number of ways. In general, however, most of the social scientists have taken into account either the total population of a given area or a particular group therein. Some of the investigations have also taken into account the 'sex' factor for analysing the results, but these investigations do not provide a deep insight into the political role of women.

A report on the first General Elections in Punjab first appeared in the *Reports on the Indian General Elections*, compiled by S. V. Kogekar and Richard L. Park.[2] The report prepared by Bodh Raj

Sharma reveals that women played 'no insignificant part' in the first General Elections. They actively participated in mobilizing the voters for their respective parties. The women speakers of the Congress party, Jana Sangh, Socialist Party, and the Communist Party addressed combined meetings of men and women as well as meetings organized specially for women. In groups of four or five the women workers also helped in approaching the individual voter. The campaign by women workers was not restricted to urban areas only. The study reveals that groups of women workers went from village to village canvassing among the women and thus making sure of 50% of the vote. How far they were successful in their attempt, the study does not make any analysis to that effect.

The report in question has no focus and is too descriptive. The author seems to have mainly relied upon the newspaper clippings, and thus even the narration of facts is neither complete nor consistent. For instance, the information in regard to the turnout of women voters is not supplied about all the constituencies, and it also fails to point out why the women voters were more enthusiastic in some constituencies and not in others, thus affecting the percentage of women votes polled in the elections. Again, at one place the report says that in the Kangra district most of the Rajput women who are in *purdah* did not vote. Women of the agricultural class, however, did vote. What correlation the author wanted to arrive at is not clear.

A number of studies have been conducted by J.C. Anand on elections in Punjab.[3] Though he has contributed significantly to the study of the State politics through his various articles on elections and trends in State politics, none of his studies even remotely touches upon the role and participation of women in elections.

The study of the third General Elections conducted by B. S. Khanna[4] refers to the decline of women contestants between 1957 and 1962. In 1957, 17 women contested elections to the Vidhan Sabha, and only 14 contested in 1962. Again, in the case of Lok Sabha, where one woman contested in 1957 and got elected, no woman candidate was there in the field in 1962. It is observed that either many women did not apply for the ticket or their claims did not receive consideration. Whatever may be the reason, the author observes that it would have been more useful to have more women legislators to bring about social change in Punjab. The author, however, does not deal at length with the factors responsible for the decline and the scanty representation of women in the Punjab legislature.

The study on election campaign and voting behaviour in the fourth General Elections to the State Assemblies of Punjab and Haryana, conducted by B. S. Khanna and Satya Deva, makes significant reference to the women's participation in the fourth General Elections.[5] The constituencies selected from Punjab for the present study were two, one urban and one rural, namely, Ludhiana (South) and Dakha.

The study reveals that difficulties were confronted by the investigators in seeking answers to the questions from women voters. It is, however, not clear as to why they were not inclined or were reluctant to give answers. One thing, however, is clear as is pointed out in the study, that women being less educated and less exposed to the media of political communication do not give much thought to political questions and depend upon men for advice and directions whenever needed.[6]

Further, sociological analysis indicates that men were better informed than women. The maximum possible score being 26, the average score for the electoral information in Ludhiana for men was 11.06 and for women 5.40 and in Dakha for men it was 8.88 and for women 3.99.[7]

It is generally assumed that male participation in the elections is greater than that of women. In Ludhiana, in the fourth General Elections, the difference was negligible, whereas in Dakha the difference was of 17%.[8]

In the election campaign also, the study reveals that men were more actively involved than women. In Ludhiana the percentage of participation for men was 13, whereas it was only 3 in the case of women. In Dakha, participation of men and women was 4% and 1% respectively.

Another significant observation made by this study is that a higher percentage of women tends to support the religio-political parties. In 1967 elections, the Akali Dal and Jana Sangh both got more support from women than from men. In Ludhiana, one-fourth of the women voters supported Jana Sangh, whereas only one-eighth of male voters supported this party.

Again five out of every 36 women were for Akali Dal, whereas only three out of every 36 men were for this party.

Statistical Analysis of Elections

The right of franchise was granted to women in Punjab in 1926 by the Provincial government. But this right was subject to certain qualifications in British India, namely, that a voter must have certain amount of property and that one should be a graduate of seven years standing. Since very few women were educated at the time and even less had property, a large section of women were excluded from the exercise of this right. These conditions were, however, relaxed under the Government of India Act, 1935. In the first election to the Legislative Assembly of Punjab held under the Act of 1935, the position of women voters was as shown in Table 1.

TABLE 1

No. enrolled	No. of voters	No. voted	Percentage of column 3 to column 2
1	2	3	4
1,89,105	1,73,459	58,216	33.56%

The women voters in NWFP was 71.4%, Bombay 42.4%, Sind 34.7%, followed by Punjab with 33.56%.[9]

Since the adoption of the Constitution in 1950, there have been five General Elections and one mid-term poll in Punjab. It has been seen that during the elections in both urban and rural constituencies, women are equally enthusiastic, if not more than their male counterparts. They participate in canvassing from door to door, attend election meetings (though their attendance is comparatively less than men), address election meetings, take out processions, hold kirtans (a new style of canvassing noticed at the recent Amritsar bye-election to the Punjab Assembly) to mobilize the voters; especially the women voters.

The turnout of women voters is also significant. It is said that men vote more than women, but in the case of urban areas of Punjab in the elections to the Vidhan Sabha, it is significant to note that the percentage of women voters is higher than that of men (see Table 2).

In 1957, whereas 63.03% votes were polled, the percentage in the case of women was 63.40. In 1967 also the votes polled by men and women was 72.70% and 74.68% respectively. In 1969, it was 73.04% and 74.20% and in 1972, it was 67.78% and 67.54%. In 1962 and 1972, the trend was otherwise as the men votes polled were higher than those of women.

Profiles of Women in Punjab

TABLE 2
Percentage of votes polled in Vidhan Sabha elections (1952-1972)

Year	Urban			Rural		
	M %	W %	Diff. %	M %	W %	Diff. %
1952	Figures are not available					
1957	63.03	63.40	−0.37	63.80	53.46	+10.34
1962	70.10	69.03	+1.07	69.10	62.94	+ 6.16
1967	72.70	74.68	−1.98	73.74	67.82	+ 5.92
1969	73.04	74.20	−1.16	74.70	69.14	+ 5.56
1972	67.78	67.24	+0.24	70.95	67.38	+ 3.57

An important thing to be noted is that the difference in the voting percentage was the highest in 1967 and 1969, and in both the elections the Congress could not secure the majority. But in 1972, when again more men voted than women (though the difference was negligible (+ 0.24%), the Congress captured the majority. It is, however, difficult to say if there is a correlation.

In rural constituencies, however, the trend is the same as for India as a whole: men vote more than women. For 1952 the figures are not available. In 1957, 63.80% men and 53.46% women voted. In 1962, men votes polled were 69.10%, and women votes polled were 62.94%; In 1967, the percentage were 73.74 and 67.82; in 1969, they were 74.70 and 69.14; and in 1972 they were 70.95 and 67.88. But it may be noted that the gap in the percentages of the men and women votes polled has been narrowing down. In 1957, it was 10.34%, in 1962 it came down to 6.16%, in 1967 it was 5.92%, in 1969 it was 5.56%, and in 1972 it was only 3.57%.

Here again it can be noted from Table 3 that there is a gradual increase in the percentage of rural women voters from 1957 to 1969. It increased from 53.46% to 69.14%, but in 1972, it fell from 69.14% to 67.38%, a figure close to the one in 1967, i.e., 67.82%.

It is significant to note that the difference in the percentage of women voters from urban and rural constituencies has also been gradually narrowing down.

In 1957, the difference was 9.94%. It fell to 6.09% in 1962. It increased slightly in 1967, as compared to 1962. In 1967, the difference was 6.86%. It was 5.06% in 1969, and in 1972 the difference was only 0.16%.

TABLE 3

Difference in the percentage of votes polled by women in the urban and rural constituencies

Year	W/U%	W/R%	Diff. %
1952	Figures are not available		
1957	63.40	53.46	9.94
1962	69.03	62.94	6.09
1967	74.68	67.82	6.86
1969	74.20	69.14	5.03
1972	67.54	67.38	0.16

W: Women;   U: Urban;   R: Rural

There have been five General Elections to the Lok Sabha, and there is a gradual increase in the percentage of votes polled by women. In 1957, in the rural areas 59.06% men voted. In 1962, against 68.50% men voters, women voters numbered 60.80% and in 1967, men voters were 73.22% and women 68%. Thus, the difference between men and women voters had fallen from 8.75% (1957) to 5.22% (1967). It is interesting to note that in the urban areas, in the 1967 General Elections to the Vidhan Sabha, where the percentage of women voters was higher than that of men, the percentage of men voters polled in the Lok Sabha elections was higher than that of the percentage of women votes polled. The percentage of men voters was 75.24 as against 73.24 of women voters with the difference of 1.50%.

In general, it may, however, be observed that women voters are sensitive to the personality of the candidate or the leader of this party. The president of the Punjab Pradesh Jana Sangh disclosed to the interviewer that women belonging even to staunch Jana Sangh families voted for the Congress because of the charismatic personality of Indira Gandhi. Women being less exposed to the corrupt practices of elections, by and large there is stability of women's votes.

Women Contestants and Successful Candidates

Though there are no legal restrictions on women contesting elections, very few women have ventured to contest elections and enter the legislature. From Table 4, it is obvious that the number of women contestants in the elections to the Vidhan Sabha has been rather small. Consequently, the representation in the Assembly has been too scanty. It is clear from the table that to begin with, in 1952 the percentage of women contestants (0.70) was the lowest. It rose to 2.90% in 1957, but again there was a continuous decline in the percentage of contestants till 1967. In 1962, of the total contestants only 1.85% were women. The percentage further fell to 1.33 in 1967. From 1969 onwards, however, the percentage has been on the increase. In 1969, it was 1.70%, and it increased further to 3% in 1972.

TABLE 4
Percentage of women contestants and successful women candidates in the Vidhan Sabha elections

Year	Total candidates	Women candidates and % to total candidates	Successful women candidates and % to total women candidates
1952	842	6 (0.70)	3 (50.00)
1957	586	17 (2.90)	9 (52.94)
1962	756	14 (1.85)	8 (57.14)
1967	602	8 (1.33)	2 (25.00)
1969	471	8 (1.70)	—
1972	467	14 (3.00)	6 (42.86)

Note: Figures within brackets denote percentages.

The percentage of successful women candidates as against the women contestants has been fairly good. In 1952, 50% women contestants were successful. In 1957, the percentage was 52.94, and in 1962 it was 57. In 1967, however, only 25% women were successful, whereas in 1969, no women candidate could succeed. Only in a bye-election from Dakala a woman candidate got elected to the Assembly and thus became the lone woman member of the House. In 1972, however, the successful women increased once again to 42.86% – out of 14 women contestants, six were successful at the polls.

The position of women contestants in the elections to the Lok Sabha is not very different from that of the Vidhan Sabha. The highest percentage of women contestants has been four in 1967. It was 3.96% in 1952, and 1.28% in 1957. In 1962, no woman contested the elections (Table 5).

Again the position of successful women candidates to the Lok Sabha is not very happy. From Table 5, it will be seen that in 1952

TABLE 5

Percentage of successful women candidates in the elections to the Lok Sabha (1952-1967)

Year	Total candidates	Total women candidates	% of women candidates	Successful women	% of successful women to total women candidates
1952	101	4	3.96	1	25
1957	78	1	1.28	1	100
1962	107	—	0.00	—	—
1967	75	3	4.00	2	67

only one woman was successful out of four contestants. In 1957, only one candidate (Congress) was elected. In 1962, the position was the worst as there was no woman candidate. In 1967, however, the percentage of successful candidates can be rated as 67, for two women (one Congress, one Akali Dal), out of three contestants were successful.

Party-wise position of women candidates in Vidhan Sabha and Lok Sabha is given in Tables 6 & 7. It is, however, important to note that most of the women contestants in the Lok Sabha elections either have belonged to the Congress party or have been independent candidates. The Jana Sangh set up two women candidates only once in the 1967 elections to the Vidhan Sabha. Even the Communist Party of India has set up only one woman candidate so far in 1962. In the Lok Sabha elections, both the parties have never set up a woman candidate.

The Akali Dal set up one woman candidate in 1962 in the General Elections to the Vidhan Sabha and it was a decade later in 1972, when a candidate was given the ticket. As already mentioned, in a bye-election, a candidate was set up by the Akali Dal. The party set up a candidate in the 1967 Lok Sabha elections also.

The Congress, however, is the only party which has consistently put up women candidates in every election. Though the number of women who got the Congress ticket has not been very high as compared to men, as a matter of policy women have been accommodated. In the Vidhan Sabha elections in 1952, four women contested on the Congress ticket. In 1957, 13 were given tickets and in 1962 the number was nine. In 1967, only two women contested on Congress ticket and in 1969 also only three got the ticket. In 1972, however, seven women candidates were set up by the Congress. Thus,

TABLE 6
Party-wise position of women contestants and successful candidates in the Vidhan Sabha elections (1952-1972)

Party	1952 (N=126)				1957 (N=154)				1962 (N=154)			
	Contestants		Successful		Contestants		Successful		Contestants		Successful	
	T	W	T	W	T	W	T	W	T	W	T	W
Congress	125	4	98	3	154	13	120	8	154	9	90	8
Akali Dal	55	—	13	—	—	—	—	—	46	1	19	—
Jana Sangh	66	—	—	—	64	—	9	—	80	—	8	—
CPI	27	—	5	—	69	—	6	—	47	1	9	—
Independent and others	569	2	10	—	299	4	19	1	429	3	28	—
Total	842	6	126	3	586	17	154	9	756	14	154	8

Party	1967 (N=104)				1969 (N=104)				1972 (N=104)			
	Contestants		Successful		Contestants		Successful		Contestants		Successful	
	T	W	T	W	T	W	T	W	T	W	T	W
Congress	102	3	48	2	103	3	38	—	88	7	68	5
Akali Dal	58 (S)	—	24(S)	—								
	62 (M)	—	2 (M)	—	55	—	43	—	72	1	25	1
Jana Sangh	49	2	9	—	30	—	8	—	33	—	0	—
CPI	12	—	5	—	28	—	4	—	13	—	10	—
Independent and others	312	3	16	—	255	5	11	—	261	6	1	—
Total	602	8	104	2	471	8	104	—	467	14	104	6

N = Total number of seats;   T = Total;   W = Women.

TABLE 7

Party-wise position of women contestants and successful candidates in the Lok Sabha elections (1952-1967)

Party	1952 (N = 18) Contestants		1952 Successful		1957 (N = 22) Contestants		1957 Successful		1962 (N = 22) Contestants		1962 Successful		1967 (N = 13) Contestants		1967 Successful	
	T	W	T	W	T	W	T	W	T	W	T	W	T	W	T	W
Congress	18	2	16	1	22	1	21	1	22	—	14	—	13	1	9	1
Akali Dal	8	—	2	—	—	—	—	—	7	—	3	—	8	1	3	1
Jana Sangh	9	—	—	—	16	—	—	—	17	—	3	—	8	—	1	—
CPI	4	—	—	—	11	—	1	—	4	—	—	—	3	—	—	—
Independent and others	62	2	—	—	29	—	—	—	57	—	2	—	43	1	—	—
Total	101	4	18	1	78	1	22	1	107	—	22	—	75	3	13	2

the highest number of women candidates (13) set up by Congress was in 1957. From 1962 to 1969, the number was on the decline. It is only in 1972, in pursuance of the policy laid down by the Congress high command to give a certain quota of tickets to the women, that the number has again increased to seven.

In the Lok Sabha elections also, the Congress party has been setting up women candidates consistently except in the 1962 elections, when no woman candidate was given the ticket. In 1952, two women contested; in 1957 one woman contested; and in 1967 again a woman candidate contested on the Congress ticket.

Interestingly, quite a few women candidates have entered the election fray independently, both to the Vidhan Sabha and to the Lok Sabha. In the 1952 General Elections, two women contested for the Vidhan Sabha and two for the Lok Sabha. In 1957, four women contested the Vidhan Sabha elections. In the 1962 and 1967 elections, the number of contestants was the same, i.e., for Vidhan Sabha it was three. But for the Lok Sabha, there was no independent woman candidate in 1962; in 1967 there was only one woman independent candidate. In the 1969 mid-term poll to the Punjab Vidhan Sabha, there were again five independent women candidates and in the 1972 General Elections six women contested as independents. It is significant to note that in almost all the elections, the unsuccessful independent women candidates lost their security deposits.

It may be noted that though women candidates have contested the election as independents, the success of such candidates has been insignificant. Only in 1957 one independent candidate, Mrs. Jagdish Kaur, was successful for the Assembly seat from Jaitu constituency by polling 44.86% of votes.[10] It is mostly the women contestants backed by the Congress who have been successful at the elections. In the 1952 elections, all the three successful women belonged to the Congress party. In 1957, out of nine successful women, eight belonged to the Congress. In 1962, all the eight members belonged to the Congress. In 1967 also, the only two successful women members belonged to the Congress. In 1972 again, five out of six successful women were Congress candidates (see Table 4).

The only other party in the State whose women candidates have been successful at the polls is the Akali Dal (Sant). So far, out of three candidates for the Vidhan Sabha, its two women candidates have been successful, one at the General Elections (1972) and the other in a bye-election. A Lok Sabha seat was also captured by its woman candidate in 1967.

On the whole, it may be said that the independent candidates have little chance of success. From the facts stated above, it will not be wrong to say that the women candidates have been successful not because of their personality and capability but mainly because of the party supporting them.

Use of Religious and Other Symbols to Mobilize Women Voters

Though India is a secular State, some of the parties invariably resort to religious appeals to mobilize the voters, especially women voters who are thought to be more religious minded. In Punjab this has been true particularly of the Akali Dal and the Jana Sangh. This is supported by the observation made by B.S. Khanna in his study on the fourth General Elections that women tend to vote for religio-political parties.[11]

According to the tenets of the Sikh religion, assert the leaders of the Akali Dal, politics cannot be separated from religion. The late Master Tara Singh, the unquestioned leader of Akalis for a number of years, always raised the banner of 'Panth khatre mein hai', that is 'religion is in danger'. Consequently, the demand of Punjabi Subha, the main issue with the Akali Dal at all elections till the separate States of Punjab and Haryana were formed in 1966, though based on linguistic principle, nevertheless had religious and communal undertones. Women being more prone to religious and regional feelings than men are easily influenced by such slogans.

Likewise, the Jana Sangh has always appealed to women voters with the issue of cow protection. Thus, at every election this issue has the main appeal to women voters.

Another significant thing noted during the recent bye-election to the Punjab Legislative Assembly from Amritsar constituency (March 1974) was that though the Akali Dal and the Jana Sangh had joined hands to defeat the Congress candidate, the interviewer found from informal interviews with some of the voters that the Jana Sangh workers would make the voters, particularly the women voters, commit themselves in favour of the Jana Sangh candidate by an oath on *Gita*. This was, however, denied by the Jana Sangh leaders when put across to them.

In the bye-election in Amritsar, the posters which appeared on the walls and the pamphlets which were distributed had a direct appeal to women voters. But there were no religious slogans, instead the issues such as rising prices, long queues for essential commodities, and other hardships faced particularly by women were focused. Even the songs sung at the 'Kirtans' arranged by the Jana Sangh women supporters related to such issues as shortage of essential commodities.

The Congress, which has been in power almost all through since the first General Elections, except during 1967-1972, has never appealed to women voters on religious grounds. It has always approached the women voters with the argument that it was the Congress party which got them the right to equality, equal status, right to vote, equal wages with men for the same labour, etc.

Women and the Legislature

From the election results analysed above, it is clear that in all the General Elections to the Assembly, women's representation has been rather poor. The share of women members in the Assembly has never been more than 5.85%. In 1952, it was 2.38%; in 1957, it touched 5.85%; and in 1962 it was 5.2%. But in 1967 it fell to 1.9% as there were only two women members in a House of 104 members. Further, as already mentioned, in 1969 women's representation was nil in the Assembly till the selection of a woman candidate in a bye-election and thus the representation became 0.96%. In 1972, however, the women's representation increased to 5.77%.

The reason for inadequate representation of women in the House is that very few women contest elections and most of the parties avoid setting up women candidates. Since 1952 there have been 29 women members[12] and of them 26, i.e. 89.3%, occupied the Congress benches.

It is also maintained that there is shortage of suitable women candidates. In an interview, most of the male political leaders argued that this was the major factor, besides others, for the poor representation of women. On the other hand, women leaders have denied that there is a dearth of suitable women candidates. In fact in the Amritsar bye-election, even the active workers of the Congress party were resentful about the fact that a woman candidate had not been set up.

The viewpoints of men political leaders belonging to different political parties were sought through interview. At least all of those whom the writer met, spoke in favour of women representation in the Assembly and not taking the blame on themselves. They felt that it was the social structure of our society and its value system that had been primarily responsible for it. Also, they felt that women lacked courage, initiative, and independent thinking.

On the other hand, women political leaders such as the Late Sita Devi, Om Prabha Jain, Shauno Devi, Pritpal Kaur Wasu, Sarla Prashar, dispute about the latter contention. It is felt by these leaders that granting the limitations of the social structure of society, its value system (which is fast changing) and also the domestic responsibilities, women are not given proper opportunities and proper atmosphere to contest elections and work in the Assembly. To quote a leader, the 'gunda-gardi' and other mean and corrupt measures, resorted to by their male counterparts to win the elections or retain/gain power in the House, do restrain women belonging to good families and particularly the educated women from entering the political field.

It may further be pointed out that earlier the women members used to speak and actively participate in the deliberations of the House. To name a few, the late Sita Devi, Om Prabha Jain, Shauno Devi, and Sarla Devi, were known for participating confidently in the proceedings of the House. But lately, it has been seen that very few women legislators speak in the House. Women, no doubt, devote more time than men and attend the sessions of the Assembly seriously and regularly, but their contribution to the deliberations is negligible. When questioned about this strange development, all the present legislators answered in the same vein that they would not speak for fear of undesirable retorts from their male counterparts. Conceding this, it has to be admitted that women do hesitate to participate in the discussions, and then they are very sensitive to criticism.

Notwithstanding all this, women have occupied the ministerial posts and have worked on the Committees of the House. The present ministry of 17 members includes two women Ministers of State. Sarla Prashar, who was at first the Deputy Minister of Education till November 1973, was promoted to Minister of State for Social Welfare. Also in November 1973, another woman Minister of State for Housing, Gurbrinder Kaur Brar, was inducted into the ministry. Thus, one-third of the women legislators (two out of six) have been accommodated in the ministry.

Earlier also, women legislators have been in the ministry, Parkash

Kaur, a surgeon by profession, remained Deputy Minister of Health from November 1956 to March 1957, and a Minister of State from March 1962 to December 1962. Chandrawati, a law graduate, served as Parliamentary Secretary from March 1962 to December 1962 and as Deputy Minister of Food and Supplies from June 1965 till Haryana was separated from Punjab.

Om Prabha Jain, a law graduate and with a master's degree in English, is another distinguished legislator, who became Deputy Minister for Education in 1962 (March 1962 to January 1963), and from June 1965 to July 1966, she held the portfolio of Health. After Haryana came into existence, she became the first Finance Minister of Haryana.

There is a feeling, however, among the women legislators that being ladies they suffer a handicap in securing ministerial positions or in gaining it, to retain the position for it is difficult.

The women legislators have also served on most of the Committees of the House. Their representation has been mostly on the Public Accounts Committee, Estimates Committee, House Committee, and to some extent on the Committee of Government Assurances, Library Committee, and the Committee of Privileges. The Business Advisory Committee had only one woman member in 1963-64, Shauno Devi, the then Deputy Speaker of the Assembly. From 1969 to 1971, no Committee had a woman member on it. In 1972, however, Kulwant Kaur, an opposition member belonging to the Akali Dal, was included in the Public Undertakings Committee.

The Public Accounts Committee, which consists of 12 members, did not have a woman member in 1960, 1964, 1967, and 1968. In 1959 and 1961-63, each year it had one woman member. In 1965 and 1966, however, there were two women members on this Committee.

In the Estimates Committee, there was no women represented in 1962 and 1965. Excepting for 1960 and 1964, when the Committee had two members, each year the Committee had one woman member. The House Committee (except in 1950, 1960, 1961) had three women members each time in 1962 and 1963, and one member each year from 1964 to 1968.

The Committee on Government Assurances had a woman member in 1959, 1963, 1965, and 1967, and the Library Committee also had a woman member in 1959, 1960, 1964, and 1965. The Committee of Privileges also had representation of one woman in 1960, 1961, 1963, and 1965.

It is thus evident that women have served on the Committees fairly well. From the records available, it has also been noticed that the women members attended the meetings of the Committees very regularly.

Women and Legislation

Since independence, Parliament has enacted quite a few laws for the welfare and uplift of women with a view to bringing about their social and political progress.[13]

But there has not been any significant piece of legislation enacted by the Punjab Vidhan Sabha for women. Only through regulations has women's representation been secured in the local bodies such as municipalities and panchayats. It is provided that each municipal committee must have two women members through either election or cooption. Likewise, if a woman is not elected to the panchayat of a village, then one must be coopted.

Further, the widows and old women are given pension by the government. The pension has been increased from Rs.20 to Rs.50 per month.

Again, except the two non-official bills which were moved by the late Sita Devi, no bill has ever been introduced by a woman legislator. Sita Devi had introduced the famous Punjab Restraint on Dowry and Other Expenses on Marriage Bill in 1952. It could not, however, be passed and it lapsed on Pepsu's merger with Punjab in 1956. The other bill, the Punjab Prevention of Hindu Bigamous Marriage Bill, 1952, also met the same fate.

A move was made in the Assembly during Kairon's regime in 1960 to approach the Union Government to amend the Hindu Succession Act, 1956, in such a way that the daughter instead of becoming a share-holder in the property of her father, be made a share-holder in the property of her father-in-law after her marriage, to save the social and economic structure of the State. It was feared that the daughter's share in her father's property would not only lead to excessive fragmentation of lands but to feuds as well. The resolution which was moved by Bhupinder Singh Mann was carried out at the sitting of the House on 21 April, 1960. However, on the intervention of Om Prabha Jain, on 27 April 1960, the Chief Minister moved that the resolution be rescinded and the motion was passed. However, a Committee under the chairmanship of the Revenue Minister Giani Kartar Singh was appointed to consider what changes were required in the provisions of the Hindu Succession Act, 1956.

The Committee was composed of 21 members including four women MLAs and one woman MLC. The Committee in principle agreed that since the matter fell in the Concurrent List of the Constitution, the State government could amend the Act. But in regard to the amendment of the Act, Om Prabha Jain and Pritpal Kaur Wasu had a difference of opinion. Om Prabha Jain wrote a letter to the Chairman through which she suggested a compromise formula, but before it could be taken up by the Committee for discussion, it was withdrawn. Pritpal Kaur Wasu, however, dissented from the Draft Report of the Committee. In her note of dissent, she observed that it would be unjust and unfair to snatch the rights conferred on the females under the Hindu Succession Act 1956, the rights which were secured after a prolonged struggle for the upgrading of the social status of women. It is all the more unfortunate, she opined, that this should happen in the State of Punjab which has always been known for its advanced and progressive ideas.

While arguing at length in favour of the rights given to the daughter under the Hindu Succession Act, 1956, she contested the arguments on the basis of which the Draft Report was prepared by the Committee. She further cautioned that if a legislation were to be enacted on the basis of the Report of the Committee, that is, if the female off spring were to be excluded from succeeding to the landed property, whereas the male off spring would be entitled, it would be unconstitutional and violative of the right to equality. The discrimination would be highlighted particularly when she succeeds to the non-landed property of her father equally with her brothers under the provisions of the said Act. Consequently, she strongly urged that the Amendment be not made to the Succession Act, and as a result of these efforts the proposal to amend the Act was shelved. The move was revived again during the regimes of the late Gurnam Singh and Lachman Singh Gill but the women's organizations, especially the All-India Women's Conference, Punjab branch(es), and the Punjab Istree Sabha exerted pressure on the government and resisted the move. Thus, the rights secured to the daughter under the Act are intact so far.

Women and Political Parties

Each political party admits women members to its fold as there is no bar to their enrolment as members. However, no separate record of their membership is maintained by most of the parties. The only party which was able to provide an authentic figure of its women members was the Communist Party of India. It has a strength of 500 women members.

Though no separate figures of women members are kept, most of the political parties have women's sections or cells. The Congress party has a women's section in Punjab named as the Congress Women Front both at the state and the district levels. At the district level, the front is composed of 10 members with a convener and a joint convener. At the state level, it consists of 20 members with a convener and a joint convener. The women's section of the Congress is no doubt active during the elections but after that it exists in name only. There is no coordination between the women's section of the party and the women legislators. In the words of a former convener of this section, the Women's Front is not doing any constructive work and needs to be revitalized.

In the party hierarchy also women are accommodated. In the PPCC there are six women members out of whom three are coopted. In the executive of the PPCC also there is a woman member.

The Jana Sangh earlier had no separate section of women in Punjab. In 1973, it was established under the convenership of Lakshmi Kant Chawla, who is also a Municipal Commissioner of Amritsar. Ad hoc Committees with 11 members have been set up at Kapurthala, Patiala, Bhatinda, Phagwara, Jullundur, and Ludhiana. These Committees, besides carrying on the party directives, are engaged in issues such as rising prices, etc.

The Jana Sangh had so far not organized the women's section in Punjab. But now it has realised that more and more women members should be brought into its fold and being a cadre based party its emphasis is to train them right at the local level. The Executive Committee of the party has three women members. The convener of the women's section is an ex officio member of the Working Committee.

The Akali Dal has no women's section and the women do not find any place in the hierarchy of the party.

The Communist Party of India has a separate cell for women at all levels with a cell secretary. This cell is very active as the members of the cell are loyal and committed workers of the party. The members of the cell, besides vocally fighting on issues such as rising prices, higher wages, labour facilities, land movement, have taken up the cause of weaker sections of village women, and women labour who are exploited by their employers. For instance, recently in a semi-government concern where women labour force was employed without being given registration, leave, and medical cards, and were given less wages than men, the women party workers went there and organised the women labour force. They resorted to *dharnas* and *hartal* till their demands were conceded.

In the party hierarchy also, women are elected to the various bodies. The State council of the CPI, which is called the Sabha Committee, is composed of 101 members elected for three years, and it includes seven women members. The Executive of the State Council also has a woman member Vimla Dang, with 24 other members.

The District Council of the party is composed of 51 members, and the members are elected for three years. Most of the District Councils have women's representation; Jullundur has four, Amritsar two, Ludhiana one, Patiala one, Ferozepur two, Bhatinda two, Chandigarh two. The District Councils of Gurdaspur, Ropar, and Hoshiarpur have no woman member. Likewise, the ilaqa, block, and tehsil committees have women representation.

The party takes care to educate and indoctrinate its workers. Thus, 'party schools', also known as 'Marxist Schools', are organized by the education department of the party. Separate schools are held for women. So far two such schools have been organized at the State level in 1968 and 1974 at Chandigarh and was attended by 30 and 60 women respectively. At the first school, there were only 4-5 working class women and 15-20 educated women; but the second school had more of working and educated women. The purpose of this school is to educate the party workers and make them committed Marxists, acquaint them with the ideology of the party, its policies and programmes, national and international affairs. It is done through lectures, discussions, question-answer sessions, and through printed literature.

It is significant to note here that a separate party of Akali women has also been formed under the leadership of Rajinder Kaur (daughter of the late Master Tara Singh). Though it is a unique attempt, much success has not been achieved. It has a meagre following and has not made any significant contribution either to the cause of women or to the State politics.

In general, it may be observed that most of the political leaders interviewed favoured the inclusion of more and more women in their respective parties, and it was felt that women's participation was essential to stabilize the organization. Among the prominent women leaders in the Congress party is Sarla Prashar who began her career in the Communist Party but left it soon to join the Congress. Significantly, Nirlep Kaur of Akali Dal began her political career with the Swatantra Party and shifted to a regional party.

Women's Organizations

There are quite a few women's organizations in the State to espouse the cause of women. But the most active among these pressure groups are: The Punjab branch(es) of the All-India Women's Conference and the Istri Sabha.

The All-India Women's Conference branch was established in the erstwhile State of Pepsu in 1956 with 70 members. Soon after Pepsu's merger with Punjab, there were two branches, e.g., the south branch and the north branch with headquarters at Chandigarh and Amritsar respectively.

The organization has a membership of about 500 women. The General House which is represented by a representative of each branch, elects every two years two vice-presidents, one general secretary, one joint secretary, one treasurer, and six executive members. The Executive Committee also associates the members of 'Red-Cross', 'Child Welfare Board', and other such bodies.

This organization is mainly a middle class organization led by women from the families of the intelligentsia. The main spirit and life of the Punjab branch is Pritpal Kaur Wasu, who has been its general secretary ever since its formation. An advocate by profession, she is a leading Congress worker, who has been the convener of the Congress Women's Front for eight years and a member of the Legislative Council twice. In other words, the organization has a pro-Congress bias, if not completely controlled by the Congress. The North Branch, it may be observed here, is controlled by Jana Sangh sympathisers. Thus, the organization, though non-political, has political patronage.

The organization carries on with constructive centres in the service of women and children, such as maintaining creches, embroidery and stitching centres, and centre for war widows. It is also engaged in settling family disputes. At times, however, the organization has not remained confined to such work only but has raised its voice successfully against the attempts to whittle down the rights of the women.

The gains of this branch in the field of securing useful legislation and representation for women on public bodies can be briefly enumerated.

With the enactment of the Hindu Succession Act, women were given the right to hold property absolutely. But the landlords of Punjab did not accept this situation, and started to make sustained efforts to have it scrapped. The Akali government tried to bring about a law which would negative the right of woman to hold property.

The AIWC Punjab branch took up the issue and resisted the move of the government. Many demonstrations were held and deputations were led to higher officials in the State and at Delhi. Women were educated about their rights through public meetings and printed literature. A case was made in their favour, and it was circulated among the MLA's and MP's. Besides, the cooperation of all women's organizations in the states was sought in this regard. 'Women's Rights Day' was observed by the branches of the AIWC throughout India. Concerted efforts were thus made to safeguard the rights of women.

The branch has also carried out a dogged fight against the liberalization of excise policy of the Punjab government. The organization protested against it, and carried an agitation for reversal of this policy.

The branch also raised its voice against the proposal of the Central government to club the incomes of the husband and the wife for income-tax purposes.

In the field of securing representation for women on local bodies, the branch has played a significant role. It sponsored a move that in every municipal body there should at least be one or two women members. The Punjab government was successfully persuaded to enact a law whereby it was made incumbent upon every municipal committee to coopt at least two women members. To achieve this end, the branch put in hard labour for many days successfully. The representatives of the branch met the Chief Minister and the Minister concerned several times, and succeeded in persuading them to issue an ordinance for the purpose as the legislature was not in session and it was time for the elections to the local bodies to be held. So an Ordinance was issued. Later, the Ordinance took the form of an Act. The result is that all over the State, there are more than 200 women members of the various municipal committees at present. Likewise, there is women's representation in panchayats also.

The other organization which has been working for the women's cause is Istri Sabha, a broad-based organization which unlike the AIWC Punjab branch, is an organization working at the grass roots level among lower-middle class families, labourers, workers, and peasantry.

Istri Sabha is committed to the principles of secularism, democracy, and emancipation of women. It came into existence in 1948, when it was known as Lok Sabha. The founders of this organization were none else than the members of the Women's Self Defence League which had been established at Lahore (now in Pakistan) in the wake of the Second World War. After independence, the League was not revived; instead the Lok Sabha was formed at Amritsar with an 11-member body. The Sabha initially covered ten villages and had five units. Later on, it spread to other districts and the first conference was held in 1952, at Jallianwala Bagh in Amritsar where it gave the call for the emancipation of women.

The Lok Stri Sabha was affiliated to the National Federation of Indian Women in 1954, when it came to be known as Istri Sabha.

The organization has at present a membership of 5,000. The State Executive Committee is composed of 25 elected members. Its constitution provides for a president, two vice-presidents, one general secretary, two joint secretaries, and a treasurer. Elections are held every two years. The elections seem to be a mere formality for the office-holders have been the same persons for quite some time. In fact, the organization is in the hands of active members of the Communist Party of India. Its general secretary, Vimla Dang, is a member of the Executive Committee of the Punjab Subha Council of the CPI.

There are district committees and village committees also on the same pattern. The district committees are being activized now. The village committee for practical purposes has no distinct identity from the party unit in the village.

The organization, though open to all women holding any political conviction, works on the guidelines of the Communist Party of India. It supports and carries on all the programmes of the party. Thus, it has wider aims to serve and achieve. Though the Sabha fights for the cause of the women, it is not a purely feminist movement.

The primary aim of this organization is to strive for a socialist society where freedom and rights are secured to women, and the exploitation of women is rooted out. The society cannot change, according to this organization, unless women are secured their rights, that is unless the contradiction that now exists between the formal acknowledgement of women's equal rights and the actual inequality in their status is put to an end.

The organization, in the words of its general secretary, Vimla Dang, is of a 'militant nature'. The organization has not confined itself merely to protests and demonstrations to pressurize the government or any body in regard to their demands; it has invariably resorted to *dharnas*, hunger strikes, courting arrests, etc. Besides this, the organization arranges talks, discussions, mohalla meetings, debates, seminars, etc. to educate the women about their rights. It is interesting to note that at the mohalla meetings the topics of discussion range from rising prices to Diego Garcia.

The main issue for which it has struggled since its inception is the implementation of the laws concerning women. It has been struggling hard against the evil of dowry, arranged discussions and seminars to educate the people, launched mass signature campaigns, held demonstrations in the State capital as well as the Union capital. The members of the organization themselves also followed it by entering into inter-caste marriages without any dowry.

It has been consistently supporting the right of women to divorce and maintenance, and printed literature has been produced on the various rights of women to make them conscious about the existence of laws securing rights to women. The Sabha has even helped individual woman suffering from social oppression to take recourse to legal action.

The major issue on which the Istri Sabha along with the AIWC Punjab branch(es) launched a struggle was the Hindu Succession Act, which was proposed to be amended by the Punjab government. *Dharnas* were organized in front of the Secretariat. The leaders of the National Federation of Indian Women, to name a few, Aruna Asaf Ali, Hameeda Habibula Begum, sat in a *dharna* with other members of the Istri Sabha. Om Prabha Jain, the then Finance Minister of Haryana, also joined them. The literature in favour of the retention of the woman's right to property was also published by the organization.

The Sabha also made relentless efforts in securing for widows and old women the right to a pension, and in also getting it increased from

Rs.20 to Rs.50 per month. The Sabha has also been seeking civic amenities for women, the provision of more health and maternity centres. It has demanded the opening of more schools for girls, particularly in rural areas. The Sabha has also been consistently fighting against the rise in prices. On this issue it launched its first *satyagraha* in 1964. Since then, it has been pursued by the various units of the Sabha and have courted arrest in large numbers, many a time on this issue. Lately, the Sabha gave the call to its units to take the issue: 'food for all' and 'milk for every child'.

The Sabha also celebrates every year Women's Day on March 8, throughout the State of Punjab, and on this day it places a special slogan before the women.

Issues Which have Evoked Support/Opposition from Women since Independence

There are quite a few issues which have evoked support from women and their organized groups or organizations since independence. The prohibition of dowry is one issue which has evoked support from all sections of women. Likewise, the institution of monogamy has been supported. In 1968, the All India Women's Conference hosted by the Punjab unit at Chandigarh even favoured the adoption of the uniform civil code for the country. Not a single delegate at the conference opposed the theme of the conference, and it was resolved unanimously that Article 44 of the Constitution providing for a uniform civil code be implemented without delay in the interest of the nation. The divorce law and maintenance law have again found support among women.

On the language issue during the two movements in Punjab, namely the Hindi agitation and Punjabi Suba agitation, the women were divided. The Arya Samaj Mahila Samiti and the women of the Jana Sangh along with the women of Hindu religious bodies supported the Hindi agitation, whereas the Sikh women sympathized with the Punjab Suba demand and supported the creation of the Suba on linguistic basis. A large number of women participated in both the agitations, involving *morchas*, hunger strikes, and even arrests.

Another important issue which has got the support from the larger section of women is the right of the daughter in her father's property guaranteed under the Hindu Succession Act, 1956. During the Akali regime, however, the government intended to amend this act and thereby disinherit the daughter of the share in her father's property on the ground that it caused disruption of family properties and created family feuds. Among women the move was supported only by a few rich landladies on the plea that it caused disintegration of agricultural holdings of families besides estranging family relations.

But the move was opposed by the other sections of women. As already pointed out, the AIWC (Punjab) and the Istri Sabha both vehemently opposed the move. The president of the AIWC even threatened to launch an agitation if an amendment to the Succession Act was made.[14]

The amendment of the Succession Act by the Punjab government was not only opposed by the women from Punjab, but also by women throughout India.

Presently, the major issue which has been agitating the minds of women throughout the country is the issue of rising prices. The opposition has come not only through organized channels but indeed from every individual. Notwithstanding the fact that the per capita income of Punjab is the highest in the country, the scarcity and adulteration of goods and rising prices have evoked strong opposition from women.

General Observations

The study of the political role of women in Punjab warrants a depth study. The scope of the present study was restricted. Therefore, it was not possible for the writers to formulate and test any hypothesis. In general, however, it may be observed that the potential of women power has so far not been exploited by any political party. There has been a fair degree of women's participation in the electoral process in Punjab. It is sometimes argued that women do not make independent judgements or make independent decisions; and that they vote according to the advice of male family members. This of course needs to be tested for the input through the electoral process effects the output in the system.

What is perhaps true is that politically active women who wish to be deeply involved in political activities are few. The majority of them do not actively concern themselves with politics. They seem to think that politics is essentially suited to men, and the dominant male group in Punjab politics has not done anything to discourage this feeling.

Notwithstanding the limitations that emerge from the social structure and the value system, it still needs to be probed as to what are the factors that restrain women from entering the political life. One thing, however, is clear that if proper decorum is maintained in the discussions in both the Assembly sessions and party meetings, certainly more women are likely to be attracted to politics. The contention that there is a dearth of leadership among women and they lack capability is being eroded in Punjab, for women have been successfully managing their lands and have been successful doctors, lawyers, engineers, and teachers. There had been a more active participation of women in the political process, the entire spectrum of Punjab politics would have undergone a fundamental change. And yet the question is: why have women by and large remained dormant in regard to politics? This question needs an incisive analysis by political scientists.

References

1. 1971 census figures.
2. S.V. Kogekar and Richard L. Park, *Report on the Indian General Elections* (1957), pp. 135-150. Also see Bodh Raj Sharma, *Report on Elections in the Punjab,* 1951-52 (Jullundur, 1951), pp. 31-35.
3. Iqbal Narain (ed.) *State Politics in India* (1967); J.C. Anand, *Punjab Politics: A Survey (1947-65),* pp. 217-262. S. P. Varma, Iqbal Narain (ed.), *Fourth General Elections in India,* J.C. Anand, General Elections in Punjab, pp. 412-446. J.C. Anand, "Mid-Term Poll in Punjab, *Political Science Review,* 1971, Vol. 110.
4. B.S. Khanna: *Third General Elections in the Punjab (1962), Indian Journal of Political Science* Vol. 24, No. 1, 1963, p. 51(60).
5. *Studies in Fourth General Elections,* Indian Council of Social Science Research (1972), pp. 145-189.
6. *Ibid.* p. 149.
7. *Ibid.* p. 165.
8. *Ibid.* p. 168.
9. National Planning Committee Report: "Women's Role in Planned Economy", p. 39, Cf. Neera Desai; *Women in Modern India* (1957), p. 224.
10. Mrs. Jagdish Kaur contested as an independent candidate from two constituencies in the second General Election (1957). She, however, lost the election in one of the constituencies.
11. Refer to page 265 of this report.
12. Twenty-eight members were elected in the Mid-Term Election and one member was elected in a by-election.
13. See Pritpal Kaur Wasu, "Legislation for Women" *Tribune, 27 August, 1961.*
14. See *The Tribune,* 3 January, 1969, 3:3.

PROFILES OF WOMEN IN RAJASTHAN

Bhagwant Rao Dubey

Determination of the political status of women in a State like Rajasthan is a difficult task for a variety of reasons. Before the integration of the States and independence of the country, Rajasthan was divided into more than 20 princely states. These states had separate administrative systems, and progress in practically all fields was slow as compared to other parts of India. Political awakening among the people of these states was also slow as compared to their counterparts in other parts of the country. Gandhiji was of the view that the Indian rulers were supported by the British rulers and, therefore, he worked for the overthrow of the British rule. However, it was at Haripur Congress that a decision was reached to launch the Prajamandal movement in the princely states also. In the pre-independence days, except for Ajmer and Mewar, the then Rajputana was divided into the princely states. After that, Gandhiji did not visit any of the princely states of Rajputana and his visits to Rajasthan were restricted to Ajmer which he visited thrice. On 3 July, 1934, he addressed a meeting of women also.[1] Thus, in Rajasthan the masses could not be mobilized to the extent it was done in other parts of India under British rule.

Under the circumstances, it is useful to see the political status of women in a historical perspective. To a great extent the political status of women is determined or at least influenced by the general attitude of the society towards them. In the olden days whatever the political status of women in Rajasthan, the women were used as instruments in improving relations with enemy states. After defeating his royal enemies on the battlefield, Rana Kumbha, a celebrated ruler of Mewar, received their daughters in marriage, some came to him themselves, while others were presented by their guardians.[2]

With the contact between the Mughals and Rajasthan, an important development took place: it was the introduction of inter-religious marriage. In the context of Hindu-Muslim rivalry, it could not be a voluntary development. These marriages were, indeed, the outcome of political pressure on the one hand and a policy of expediency of the Rajput Rajas on the other.[3] Whatever the motives behind these marriages, this new relationship enhanced the position of the Rajput rulers in the Mughal court. These marriages were largely responsible for making the Rajputs active and also effective participants in Mughal politics.[4] These incidents prove that during the medieval period, marriage was thrust upon women for the political ends of the Rajas.

The birth of a girl was not welcome because of the dowry system and *neg* (money levied by charans on marriage) which made marriages expensive. In several instances, girls were killed soon after their birth.[5] Though polyandry was proscribed, there was no restriction on polygamy. The status of a man was so high that after the death of the husband the wife or wives committed *sati*. This practice was given religious sanction. The number of women committing *sati* on the death of Zorawar Singh, a former Maharaja of Bikaner, was 21.[6] Even when there was a doubt about the death of the husband, the wife would commit *johar*.[7]

The British rulers tried to put a curb on these practices and also successfully implemented the Acts connected with *sati* and polygamy. Though these social reforms substantially improved the social status of women, the political status of women continued to be a neglected field.

Many of these evils persisted till independence. The female infant mortality among Rajputs and Bhoumiyas continued to be practised in certain parts of Mewar and Shekhawati (Jaipur), though on a reduced scale.[8] Similarly, besides polygamous marriages, the Jagirdars and rulers, according to their status, maintained a number of men and women called Daroga, Chela, Ravana, Chakar, etc. In marriages, women from this class were also given dowry. Though the wives of the Darogas were legally married to someone else, the Jagirdar or the Rajput was permitted to have sexual relations with them.[9]

In 1917, Vijay Singh Pathik organized the peasants in Bijolia (Mewar) against the exploitation by Jagirdars. The peasants did not pay land revenue for four years. Gradually, this movement gained momentum and spread to other parts of the State. The important thing about this movement was the participation of women. Unhappy as they were at this development, the Jagirdars perpetrated a number of cruelties on the agitators. The Thakur of Ravarda (Begun), with a view to terrorizing the masses, had a woman dragged through the market. He also ordered a Bhil woman to be hanged and beaten.[10] Frightened peasants assembled at a place near Bijolia on Basant

Panchami in 1922 for the protection of the woman. In this assembly, the women also participated in larger numbers. The gathered agitators warned the Jagirdars to spare the women. In Bundi, the women agitating against bonded labour and high rates of revenue were injured by mounted police in 1922.[11]

The Neemuchana (Alwar) peasants protested against the enhancement of assessment by 50% at the time of the revised settlement of 1924. On 16 May, 1925, the Jay Pattan of the Alwar State beseiged the village from all the sides. When some of the villagers came out to get water, fire was opened in which nine persons including two women were killed.[12]

At the dawn of independence, an overwhelming majority of women were illiterate and backward. The higher caste women did not actively participate in public life because of the *purdah* system, and in the lower castes they were illiterate or were under the powerful influence of Jagirdars who did not like women to participate in public life. In fact, even in the freedom struggle women took part on a limited scale only. The context changed in 1950, when the Constitution of the Indian Republic was promulgated and equal rights were granted to both men and women. It was not surprising that in the first General Elections, when there were 160 Assembly seats only four women contested. None of them was elected and the security of all of these was forfeited.[13] It will, therefore, be quite interesting to know about the change that has occurred in the political status of women of the State. This will be broadly examined on the basis of the role of women in elections.

Vote Consciousness

During the fifth General Elections, the number of voters to the State Assembly was 13,823,457 (excluding Desuri constituency returing an unopposed candidate). Of these, 7,087,876 were males and 6,735,581 were females, that is, male voters were 2.5% more than the female voters. The margin being small, it can be said that the male and female voters were almost evenly divided. The number of male and female voters and percentage turnout in the past five elections is given in Table 1.

The figures given in Table 1 indicate that the number of women casting their votes has been steadily increasing except that there is no

TABLE 1

Election year	Total electorate '000			Turnout percentage		
	Persons	Male	Female	Persons	Male	Female
1952	7678	3997	3681	42.5	52.0	29.3
1957	8746	4868	3701	41.2	51.9	27.3
1962	10328	5374	4954	52.6	62.7	41.1
1967	12204	6306	5858	58.2	65.1	51.2
1972	13823	7088	6735	57.8	64.9	50.3

substantial change between the turnout percentage in 1967 and 1972. In the first General Elections, only 29.3% women voters exercised their franchise while in 1972 it was 50.3%. Thus, in the past 20 years, female voters showed an improvement of 21%. However, it must be noted with dismay that only 50% women came to vote in 1972, the other 50% choosing not to vote. Assuming that the non-voting was not deliberate, it could be attributed to educational backwardness and the prevailing socio-economic conditions. Male voters have all along been coming to vote in higher percentage than women. In 1952, 52% male voters exercised their franchise and in 1972, it was 64.9%, registering an improvement of about 13%. The corresponding figure for female voters is 21%. Women voters are far behind their target, and are even lagging behind male voters. Stationary figures for 1967 and 1972 raise a doubt that a kind of indifference is developing among female voters. It is only after the next elections that something can be said with certainty.

Data about the fifth General Elections are discussed in some detail below. Similar data in respect of previous elections are not available. Seventeen women candidates contested the elections, the total number of contestants being 875 for 183 seats. Of these, the women contested for 14 general, two scheduled caste, and one scheduled tribe seats. The number of voters in the constituencies from where women contested was 9.70% of the total valid votes polled, of which 17 women candidates claimed 323,945 valid votes. On the whole, women candidates secured 42.83% votes in the constituencies from where they contested. It is very interesting to observe here that on an average female contestants attracted more voters than their male counterparts.

Contestants

Having discussed the vote consciousness among the women, let us now turn to women's attitude towards contesting elections. In the five General Elections held so far, 76 women contested the elections and 36 were elected. Election-wise details are given in Table 2.

TABLE 2

Election	No. of seats	No. of women contestants	No. of women candidates elected	Percentage of women contestants elected	Remarks
1952	160	4	—	—	Two later returned in by-election.
1957	176	21	9	42.86	
1962	176	15	8	53.33	
1967	184	19	6	31.57	
1972	184	17	13	76.47	
Total		76	36	47.36	

For one thing there are fewer female contestants and about half of them are elected. Keeping in view the number of female voters, almost half of the seats should be filled by women members. The smaller number of female candidates shows that the females in the State are not politically very conscious.

In this context, it will be useful to know about the number cf women in other legislatures of the country. The Legislative Assembly of Jammu and Kashmir has no representation of women. In the contemporary assemblies of Mysore, Gujarat, and Kerala, there were nine, eight, and one women legislators respectively. On the basis of comparative figures, it can be said that the women in Rajasthan are not so backward.

District-wise Contestants

Within the State itself political awareness varies from place to place for a variety of reasons. In eight districts of Rajasthan, namely, Sawai Madhopur, Jhalawar, Banswara, Dungarpur, Sirchi, Bundi, Jaisalmer, and Jodhpur, no woman has contested. In the five elections held so far, district-wise number of women candidates contesting and elected are as given in Table 3.

TABLE 3

District	Contestants	Elected
1. Jaipur	14	4
2. Ajmer	8	6
3. Kota	6	3
4. Udaipur	6	2
5. Jhunjhunu	5	4
6. Churu	5	1
7. Alwar	4	2
8. Bhilwara	4	2
9. Barmer	4	2
10. Nagaur	4	4
11. Ganganagar	3	1
12. Bikaner	3	2
13. Bharatpur	3	1
14. Chittorgarh	2	1
15. Sikar	2	—
16. Jalore	1	1
17. Pali	1	—
18. Tonk	1	—
Total	76	36

In the fifth General Elections, 27 women candidates filed their nominations. Of these, nine withdrew, one was rejected and 17 contested the elections, and 13 were successful.

Party Affiliation

In Table 4, the number of candidates set up by the political parties, and the number of candidates elected in the last five General Elections are given, to give an idea of the popularity or otherwise of political parties among women.

The Congress was the only party from which women candidates were elected in good numbers in all the elections except the 1952 elections, when it did not set up any candidate. The Independents also contested all the elections except the first. However, only one

Profiles of Women in Rajasthan

TABLE 4

General Elections	KLP		JS		SOC.		Cong.		RRP		Swt.		PSP		Cong. (O)		Independent	
	C	E	C	E	C	E	C	E	C	E	C	E	C	E	C	E	C	E
1952	1	—	1	—	2	—												
1957							16	8							5	1		
1962							10	8							4			
1967							10	6			4	1			4			
1972			1	—			14	13							1	—	1	

C: Contested
E: Elected

candidate was elected in 1957. It may be mentioned here that only one woman candidate contested as an Independent in 1972. The KLP, Socialist, RRP, Swatantra, and Congress (O) set up women candidates only once in any one of the five elections. The Jana Sangh set up candidates only twice. With the exception of the Congress, only two women candidates (Swatantra and Independent) were elected for the State Assembly. There could be many reasons for the smaller number of women being elected from parties other than the Congress such as (a) the parties are not popular among the masses, (b) the women's wings of the parties are not well organized and/or are not active, (c) though the few parties are popular among the masses, the women do not like them, (d) the parties do not encourage women to compete with men on the same political ground, (e) there is dearth of keen, competent, and devoted party women workers who could be given party tickets, (f) the majority of women do not like joining the opposition parties which do not offer tempting official positions, etc.

As stated earlier, the number of women candidates contesting the fifth General Elections was 17. Of these, 14 belonged to Congress. The other three candidates belonged one each to Jana Sangh, Congress (O), and Independent. The Congress candidates together polled 322,427 votes. That is to say, on an average, every Congress woman candidate polled 23,030 votes. In sharp contrast to this, the Jana Sangh candidate polled 904 votes; the Congress (O) 388; and the Independent 226 votes.

Political Consciousness

Vote consciousness in any electorate depends both qualitatively and quantitatively, on its level of political consciousness. Do the electorate know how valuable their vote is? Do they vote under the influence of some one? Do they vote for certain principles, parties, individuals, or issues? Answers to these questions depend to a large extent on the political awareness of the electorate. These points have been examined to some extent in two election studies conducted in the State: (i) S.P. Verma and Iqbal Narain (*Voting Behaviour in a Changing Society*, Delhi, National, 1972) and (ii) C.P. Bhambhri and P.S. Verma (*The Urban Voter*, Delhi, National, 1973).

In both the studies referred to above, it was observed that between men and women the former were politically more informed and conscious than the latter. The majority of men were found to be highly informed about the contesting candidates for the municipal election, and their principal rivals along with their political affiliations, while the majority of women were not. The same was true about the names and political affiliations of the MPs and MLAs.[14] Similarly, majority of women expressed the desire to vote and also showed interest in election politics; in case of women, the reverse was the order. Even in matters of membership of political parties, men were far ahead of women.[15] Taking the participation in voting as an index of political consciousness and political mobilization, it can be said that women lag behind men.[16] The majority of women are neither definite about their intention of voting nor are they clear about the party or individual they want to vote for. Since the women usually follow the males in the family in their voting behaviour, the focus of political campaigns and mobilization for political parties is on the men, resulting in a continued neglect of the women.[17]

Female Considerations

Some characteristics have emerged from the election studies conducted in Rajasthan. The majority of women (44.5%) do not have any clear-cut idea about their criterion of voting; 19.5% considered the personality of the candidate as a factor; 8.3% considered the party as a factor; 5.5% thought the issues as a factor; and 22.3% thought the caste and family as a factor.[18] In the other study also a higher number of females were registered in the category, 'Does not know'. From the rest, a higher percentage of females were more candidate-oriented than party-oriented.[19] This also suggests that social considerations carry greater weight with women voters. However, it cannot be denied that the males in the family and the advice of village headman greatly influence the women voting in Rajasthan.[20]

Communication

Male voters were found to be highly exposed to mass media of communication. Radio and newspapers were more popular among men than among women. Very few parties or candidates employ women workers for campaigning, and door-to-door canvassing is restricted to men only. The majority of women do not have access to public libraries and because of illiteracy, difficult socio-economic conditions, and a heavy schedule of work, the women neither read the newspaper nor listen to the radio for news pertaining to elections. Thus, the only place where the women could discuss the elections was in the family or peer group.[21] Therefore, it has been rightly observed that men have an edge over women in their participation in the country's democratic politics as voters.[22]

Leadership

Leadership is an important aspect for determinating the political status of women. All the political parties, except Congress and Swatantra, do not have women workers who could be put in the category of leaders. This is despite the fact that all the parties active in Rajasthan have made explicit in their respective election manifestoes that they are opposed to discrimination on the basis of sex, and that they are for certain privileges being granted to women to bring them on par with men.

Among the women leaders in Rajasthan, Rajmata Gayatri Devi enjoys an enviable position. In the third General Elections, she secured 100,070 votes in the Lok Sabha elections. This was the highest number of votes polled by any candidate in the country. Coming from the Jaipur House, the Rajmata is very influential in that part of Rajasthan, which formed part of the erstwhile Jaipur State.

The Swatantra Party, to a great extent, owed its existence in the State to the Rajmata. The Rajmata has held key positions in the party hierarchy both at the State and the national levels. Keeping in view her popularity in the Jaipur region, the Rajmata was given a free hand in the selection of party candidates from Jaipur for the elections.[23] Her popularity suffered a serious setback when she was defeated from Malpura for the Assembly seat in 1967. The Congress is the only party forming a government in the State from the very beginning. It has women leaders both in the party and in the government. In the party hierarchy, Smt. Laxmi Kumari Chundawat has held very high positions. She was appointed president of the ad hoc committee of the Rajasthan State Congress,[24] a challenging job which Smt. Chundawat did extremely well. She is not only a political figure in the State, but also a social worker and literateur of repute. In only a few States has a woman held the highest office in the party hierarchy in the State.

Since the Congress has been forming the government, and there is a dearth of active women in politics in a substantial number, the women who showed some promise in party work were included in the Cabinet.

Rajasthan, after the integration of the States in 1948, has had six interim governments, and seven governments after 1952 when the Rajasthan Legislative Assembly was constituted.

In the interim governments not a single woman was included.[25] Since no woman candidate was returned to the Assembly, no woman was included in the first Cabinet formed by Jai Narain Vyas in November 1952. This Cabinet was expended twice in 1953 and 1954, but no woman was included. For the first time, a woman candidate, Smt. Kamla Benwal, was included as a Deputy Minister in the first Sukhadia Cabinet formed on 13 November, 1954.[26]

A review of the Cabinets of Rajasthan reveals that women have so far not been adequately represented in the Cabinets. It is very important to mention here that no woman has so far been given the Cabinet status in any of the Cabinets. This speaks of the inferior political status of women in the State.

Within the Assembly, Smt. Chundawat in the third and fourth assembly and Smt. Madan Kaur in the fourth assembly were included in the speakers' panel; Smt. Gauri Puniya was chairman of the Assurance Committee in the second Assembly; and Smt. Chundawat also worked as Chairman of the Public Accounts Committee. Thus, the women have been entrusted with responsible positions in the Assembly. In the discussions also their contribution has been significant.[27]

Privileges and Limitations

The Rajasthan Government wants an all-round development of women in the State. Since the independence of the country, the number of girls' schools and enrolment of girls at all levels of educational standard is steadily rising.[28] In the 1951 census, only 3% of the females were literate; this reached 5.84% in 1961, and 8.46% in 1971. It may be pointed out that there is a kind of lopsided educational development in rural and urban areas in the State. According to the 1971 Census, there are 29.69% females literate in urban areas while only 4.03% in the rural. Such a lopsided development is not unnatural because in the urban areas, where there is greater awareness in the people and age of consent is high, a large number of parents send their daughters to school. The Social Welfare Department and the Social Welfare Board are also working to raise the standard and status of women. In government service females are not discriminated against. Though they are not given preferential treatment in government service, relaxation in the upper age limit is granted to them. Despite this, there are very few women in higher posts in the administrative services; there is only one RAS, and about half a dozen IAS officers in the State. This speaks of the poor women's representation in administrative services. In education, medical and allied departments, however, the women are coming forward in larger numbers.

Appreciating the fact that women are backward in the State, the government has made a provision for nomination of women members in local bodies such as panchayats and municipalities. In the 26 districts of the State, there are over 232 Panchayat Samitis. Each Panchayat Samiti has village panchayats ranging between 15 and 51. In these panchayats, the number of women run into hundreds, but this consists mostly of nominated members, there being only 25 elected women in these panchayats.[29] Similarly, in the 66 municipalities of the State, there were only seven women members in a total of 851.[30] These figures indicate that politically the women of Rajasthan continue to lag behind men.

Members of high castes and classes are of the opinion that women should not be given difficult jobs. C.P. Bhambhri in his study has referred to the advice given to the returning officers not to appoint women as presiding and polling officers. These instructions were based on past experience. The ladies could not cope with the polling work successfully. Moreover, some of them committed serious irregularities.[31] This is not to suggest that ladies are not being given assignments in elections; wherever necessary, women polling officers were appointed to assist other polling and presiding officers.

Towards a Summing up

Before the integration of the States, women in Rajasthan got very few opportunities to take part in public life. The rulers of the princely states curbed the movements, and at some places the women taking part in the agitations were illiterate. In social life the status of women was poor, age of consent was low, dowry was prevalent, female infanticide was practised, widow remarriage and remarriages among higher castes were not permitted, polygamy was allowed, and women had no property rights, making the women absolutely dependent on men. At the time of the 1941 census, only 1.14% females were literate. A high percentage of scheduled caste and scheduled tribe people (according to the 1971 Census the former constitute 15.82%, and the latter 12.13% of the population of the State) makes the situation worse.

However, after the formation of Rajasthan substantial change has come about in the status of women: the constitution has provided equal rights to men and women. All the political parties agree to abolish the discrimination based on sex, concerted efforts have been made to spread literacy, equal rights have been granted in marriage and property matters (excluding the Muslims whose personal laws have not been amended), concessions have been granted for encouraging women to compete for government jobs, and reservations have been made in the membership of local bodies. Some of the women are holding, or have held, important offices in the party organizations or in the government. But these can be put in the category of special cases. They are not proportionately representative of the numerical strength or of the aspirations of the women folk of the State. In the past 22 years of public life after the introduction of General Elections in 1952, there has not been any woman to occupy the seat of the Speaker in the Assembly (though women have been included in the Speakers' panel), or a Minister of Cabinet rank. All the women ministers included so far in the Cabinet have been Deputy Ministers or Ministers of State. The women ministers have not only been few, but the same persons have been included in different Cabinets indicating the dearth of suitable candidates for the job. However, it is an encouraging trend that women party bosses in the Swatantra and Congress have never been opposed on the basis of sex. Smt. Laxmi Kumari Chundawat in Congress, and Rajmata Gayatri Devi of Swatantra have been respected figures in and outside their respective parties both inside and outside Rajasthan. However, the majority of women in the State are not aware of their rights and their strength. For the successful working of a democracy enormous work remains to be done among half the population of the State. Besides government efforts for improving the general status of women, the political parties can play a vital role in political mobilization of women, once the political parties give up their traditional approach to win over men only for the vote of the family.

References

1. Shobhalal Gupta, *Gandhiji Aur Rajasthan,* Rajasthan Rajya Gandhi Smarak Nidhi, Bhilwara, pp. 2-3.
2. G.N. Sharma, *Social Life in Medieval Rajasthan,* Laxmi Narain Agarwal, Agra, 1968, p. 114.
3. *Ibid.,* p. 115.
4. *Ibid.,* p. 117.
5. *Ibid.,* p. 115.
6. K.K. Sehgal, *Gazetteer of Bikaner,* Jaipur, p. 418.
7. G.N. Sharma, *op. cit.,* pp. 129-30.
8. Ram Naryan Chaudhari: p. 84
9. *Ibid.,* p. 82.
10. *Ibid.,* p. 91.
11. *Ibid.,* p. 104.
12. Bhagwant Rao Dubey, Neemuchana: Dyerism Double Distilled *proceeding of the Rajasthan History Congress* Second Session, 1968.
13. *Rajasthan Vidhan Sabha Ke 20 Varsha 1952-1972,* Vidhan Sabha Sachivalaya, 1972, p. 109.
14. C.P. Bhambhri and P.S. Verma, *The Urban Voters,* National, Delhi, 1973., pp. 63-64.
15. *Ibid.,* pp. 78-79.
16. S.P. Verma and Iqbal Narain: *Voting Behaviour in a Changing Society,* Delhi, National, 1972, p. 30.

17. *Ibid.*, p. 81.
18. C.P. Bhambhri and P.S. Verma, *op. cit.*, p. 149.
19. S.P. Verma and Iqbal Narain, *op. cit.*, p. 318.
20. *Ibid.*
21. C.P. Bhambhri and P.S. Verma, *op. cit.*, p. 85.
22. S.P. Varma and Iqbal Narain, *op. cit.*, p. 209.
23. C.P. Bhambhri and P.S. Verma, *op. cit.*, p. 58.
24. Nagendra Bala, *Vidhan Sabha Men Mahilaon Ka Yog Dan, Rajasthan Vidhan Sabha Ke Bis Varsha*, 1972, pp. 109-110.
25. *Ibid.*, pp. 162-163.
26. *Ibid.*, p. 164.
27. Nagendra Bala, *op. cit.*, pp. 107-111.
28. *Statistical Abstracts*, Rajasthan, 1958 onwards.
29. *Rajasthan Gazette*, September 11 and 18, 1965 and *Gazette Extraordinary*, September 11 and 18, 1965.
30. *Rajasthan Gazette*, August 4, 1966.
31. C.P. Bhambhri and P.S. Verma, *op. cit.*, p. 24.

PROFILES OF WOMEN IN UTTAR PRADESH

Indra Narayan Tewary

The purpose of this paper is to identify the political status of women in the State of Uttar Pradesh. In brief, it will focus on women as voters and as candidates contesting elections for the Legislative Assembly, and Parliament, their membership of State and Central Cabinets, and their place in positions of power and dignity, at the State, national, and international levels. It is difficult at this stage to identify their role in non-political fields. But right from the beginning of political activity in the country UP has been producing women who have national acceptability and international recognition.

The method of this study is a historical one based on the facts collected from documents released by the State and Central governments. In addition, other secondary sources have been used to substantiate the arguments of this paper.

The first fact one has to note is that the status of women in UP is determined by the poverty spread in the rural areas consisting of more than one lakh villages. The urban centres do provide more consciousness in terms of literacy and awareness as citizens. But, by and large, it is rural women whose conditions determine and, at the same time, indicate the political status of women in UP.

The second important factor that has influenced women's status in this State is the freedom movement and Gandhiji's leadership of the latter. The women of UP participated in a big way in the national struggle for freedom and joined the Indian National Congress in large numbers. Prominent among them were Swaroop Rani Nehru, Kamala Nehru, Vijya Lakshmi Pandit. Even otherwise, UP provided a national platform from where ladies from other States could participate in important national activities. These facts on the whole indicated a beginning of change. Political consciousness among women was aroused when Gandhiji requested them to join the Civil Disobedience Movement in 1930. He made a special appeal to women to leave their narrow domestic sphere and join the men in the freedom movement. A number of women from all over the State threw aside the conventions of centuries, and came forward to join the Civil Disobedience Movement. Many of them courted arrest and served prison sentences with an amazing fortitude. During the period when the movement was at its height, and the men were arrested in large numbers, the women carried on their work with remarkable endurance and displayed considerable powers of organizing activities at different levels.

But for all practical purposes, women of the state remained what they were. Only a few could have the financial resources, educational skill, and social climate to go ahead. While Gandhiji's call inspired many women to be brave, the majority remained confined to their narrow domestic affairs. This reflected the gap between their social role as envisaged by Gandhiji and their inextricable bondage in the society almost verging on slavery of women. The real situation is depicted by Gandhiji himself when he said "by sheer force of a vicious custom, even the most ignorant and worthless men have been enjoying a superiority over women which they do not deserve and ought not to have".[1]

However, when India became free, the Constitution guaranteed liberty and equality for women. For attaining the objectives set before the nation by the Preamble to the Constitution, certain fundamental rights and freedoms such as freedom of speech, protection of life and personal property, etc. are guaranteed. Article 14 ensured "equality before law" and article 15 "prohibits any kind of discrimination". Article 15(3) empowers the state to make any special provisions for women and children. Article 16(1) guarantees "equality of opportunity for all citizens in matters relating to employment or appointment to any office under the State". Specially article 16(2) forbids discrimination "in respect of any employment of office under the State" on the grounds of "religion, race, caste, sex, descent, place of birth, residence".[2]

As a result, nearly 15 million women in UP including the illiterates and the ignorant have the right to decide the nature of state power, responsible for the authoritative "allocation of resources" and values to the society, Community-wise, percentage distribution of these women is as shown in Table 1[3].

Let us see how these women voters are distributed in the different regions of the State. The percentage distribution as reflected in Table 2 shows unevenness.[4]

It is true that the maximum number of decision-makers or legislators are sent from eastern Uttar Pradesh, and the percentage of women voters in that region is also of some consequence. The western

TABLE 1

Hindu	83.76
Muslim	15.48
Christian	0.75
Sikh	0.42
Buddhist	0.05
Jain	0.14

TABLE 2

Hill region	4.3
Western region	35.6
Central	17.8
Eastern	39.4
Bundelkhand	4.9

region is also very significant in its voting power, though less in proportion to the eastern region. The central region balances between the two and the Hill and Bundelkhand regions are extremely insignificant in their voting power. However, it should be noted that in both the Hills and the eastern region, the women are concentrated in rural areas.

A fact that affects the quantity and quality of women's power in Uttar Pradesh is the severe imbalance between male and female population. The only district where women outnumbered men are in the backward regions. The sex ratio (women per 1,000 men) in these seven districts is: Tehri Garhwal 1,189, Garwal 1,118, Chamoli 1,061, Pithoragarh, 1,033, Almora 1,077, Pratapgarh 1,016, and Jaunpur 1,011. The distribution of population in the remaining 48 districts which include the more developed areas of the State shows preponderance of men over women[5]. In both urban and rural sectors women have lower birth rates than men. An examination of the statistics of birth rate in Uttar Pradesh brings out that for every 1,000 males born, the number of females born was 898 in rural areas, and 900 in urban areas in 1971. Death among the infant females (169.6) is also larger than males (154.5)[6] in rural areas. Nature, one may say, is opposed to women, and man has done little to arrest her influence.

Apart from these factors which affect the quality of voting power, what is more depressing is the quality of voting power. The spread of literacy in UP is indicated in Table 3.

TABLE 3

Sex-wise percentage of literacy since 1951[7]

Census	Population	Male	Female
1951	10.77	17.18	3.60
1961	16.65	27.30	7.02
1971	21.70	31.50	10.55

Regional variations in the spread of literacy also affects women's voting strength. It is true that rural women voters are not less articulate than the educated urban women voters. But, it is very difficult to minimize the role of education in making a woman qualitatively a different citizen who can weigh the power of her vote in deciding periodically the nature of state power itself. The level of literacy is very crucial. We use it as an indicator to assess voting power of the Scheduled Castes and Scheduled Tribes women in the context of general voting power of the upper castes. While Scheduled Caste males have also not reached the level of education prevalent in the upper classes, the depression of the women is much more intense, and is bound to affect their capacity for political participation.

TABLE 4

Percentage of literacy of the general population, Scheduled Castes and Scheduled Tribes in UP[8]

UP	General population	Male	Female
Total	21.70	31.50	10.55
Rural	18.13	28.02	6.99
Urban	43.63	52.08	33.33
Scheduled Castes			
Total	10.20	17.13	2.46
Rural	9.11	15.77	1.74
Urban	23.43	33.01	11.75
Scheduled Tribes			
Total	14.59	22.51	5.50
Rural	13.33	21.35	4.33
Urban	29.09	35.13	21.24

The extremely low level of literacy among women particularly in rural areas and among different groups such as Scheduled Castes and Tribes affects their awareness as voters. Proclamations of equality of opportunity remain meaningless in the face of this persistence of illiteracy which has proved to be the most effective barrier to any effective exercise of political rights.

Largely because of the above factors and the lack of resources, women in UP lag behind men in contesting elections. The will to contest is the essence of a representative democracy. But in a State of 90 million population, on an average there are only 45 women candidates in each General Election as indicated in Table 5.[9]

TABLE 5

General Elections	Total number of candidates	Women contestants	Percentage
1952	2,604	34	1.3
1957	1,711	42	2.4
1962	2,620	54	2.06
1967	3,014	45	1.4
1969	2,871	60	2.08

The inner dimensions of contesting power reveal some interesting facts. For example in the 1957 General Elections, there were 26 constituencies from which women contested and certainly the percentage of votes that they polled was similar to that received by male candidates. It is evident that in general voters in India have no specific consideration for women contentants.[10]

The intensity of contest faced by a woman candidate is on an average six in each constituency. It is to be remembered that mostly they face male candidates. Nearly one-fourth of the women candidates secured more than 50% votes; one-ninth received more than 40% of votes. Most of the winning women candidates secured less than 30% of votes. In reserved constituencies, women candidates won with very low percentage of votes. The low number of women contestants and the low percentage of votes secured by them require careful investigation. It may be interesting in this context to examine the pattern of women's voting itself.

While free India appears to have opened the gate for women to enter the legislative arena, they have not done too well and their numbers are very few. They, however, appear with a sense of regularity, capturing a few seats in the provincial legislature.

TABLE 6

Sl. No. of constituency	Intensity of contest	% of votes secured	Parties
11	Unanimous	100	Congress
22	12	18.23	Congress (SC)
22	12	17.34	Congress
39	3	52.74	Congress
40	3	36.60	Congress
43	5	43.85	Congress
52	2	52.02	Congress
31	5	34.10	Congress
142	5	21.49	Congress (SC)
166	9	19.40	Congress
168	4	50.90	Congress
191	4	51.00	Congress (SC)
197	3	50.21	Congress
250	14	26.65	Congress (SC)
251	11	46.37	Congress
253	5	34.00	Congress
259	4	47.00	Congress
262	4	25.00	Independent
268	5	24.35	Congress (SC)
282	3	30.99	Congress
285	6	23.04	Congress
294	15	10.35	Congress (SC)
301	2	56.00	Congress
306	3	44.00	Congress
311	6	22.60	Congress
325	8	25.00	Congress

TABLE 7

Number of Women in UP Legislative Assembly since 1952[11]

1952	11
1957	26
1962	20
1967	6
1969	18
1974	18

As mentioned earlier, the women representatives are very few. In a House of 430 members, almost regularly more than 400 seats are captured by male representatives from different political parties. If the

Legislative Assembly is to be a genuine instrument of state power, expressing the views of the majority of the people, then a more balanced representation of the sexes is essential.

The power of franchise has necessarily an implication of being represented in the different decision-making bodies. Since long effort has been made to give opportunities to women in UP for getting elected to the Legislative Assembly. The Montagu-Chelmsford reforms of 1919 which were put into effect through the Government of India Act of 1919, was an important step in this direction. This Act gave a limited extent of franchise to women, but they did not receive any special right to be elected as a member of the Legislative Assembly. It was the Government of India Act of 1935 that introduced an element of flexibility and provided opportunities for women to get elected to the provincial assembly. The UP Legislative Assembly under the Act of 1935 consisted of 228 members. The electoral system was based on the principle of communal, class, and interest representation. The representation of women and labour was not an integral part of the original decision of the Government of India, but an afterthought. The distribution of assets in the Legislative Assembly provided for a strictly unfavourable balance of representation against the women as is evident from Table 8.

TABLE 8

Composition of Legislative Assembly of UP according to the Government of India Act 1935 election held in 1937[12]

General	140 (including 20 seats for Scheduled Castes)
Muslims	64
Europeans	2
Indian Christians	2
Anglo-Indian	1
Commerce and industry	3
Land-holders	6
University	1
Labour	3
Women	6 (4 Hindus and 2 Muslims)

In an empirical study of 15 women legislators (1957), S.M. Sayed found that the majority of them were drawn from rural constituencies. Except one, out of eighteen, all the women legislators came from families actively associated with political activities at different levels and generally they entered politics at the instance of either their husband or father. Most of the women members of the UP State Legislature are Hindus and two belong to Muslim community. Educational standards of these members appear to be fairly high, as most of them were either graduates or M.A. s. The occupational pattern of the women members showed that they belonged to the middle and lower-middle class. Entry into politics seemed to be generally a planned one rather than an accident. Party affiliation of these members indicate that they belonged mostly to the Congress. Many of them did not enter politics through social service of any significance.

Most of the present women legislators attend the sessions of the Assembly religiously but seldom participate in the debates, except in the case of the Food Minister who has to make frequent statements on food policy. As compared to male members, women members seem to have little work in their constituencies and it is also true that constituents hesitate to meet them. Above all, women legislators appear to suffer from a sense of inferiority which inhibits their functioning in the governmental process.

The representative position of women from UP at the national level presents certain contrasts. On the one hand, UP has contributed some outstanding women legislators to Parliament and the national government including Indira Gandhi, Vijayalakshmi Pandit, Sucheta Kripalani and others. On the other, the membership of the Lok Sabha and Rajya Sabha indicates that women members from UP are only few in number and fulfil the demand for parity only at a formal level and has registered a decline in recent years.

TABLE 9

Membership of Lok Sabha and Rajya Sabha[13]

	Lok Sabha	Rajya Sabha
1952	4	3
1957	2	0
1962	6	4
1967	7	3
1971	6	N.A.
1974	6	Nil

The composition of the Council of Ministers decides the actual course of operation of political power in the State. It appears that right from 1950 up to the present day, the UP Cabinet has been by and large a masculine one. Except one, there have been seven male Chief Ministers in the past 28 years. The data given in Table 10 show that generally women were conspicuous by their absence. They are generally found in the rank of State Ministers and Deputy Ministers with peripheral portfolios.

TABLE 10

Distribution of membership of the UP Cabinet since 1947[14]

	Cabinet Minister	State Minister	Deputy Minister	Total
1947	11	0	8	19
1952	12	7	6	25
1957	10	4	16	30
1962	17	4	24	45
1967	11	2	0	13

The ministership for the women may be identified very distinctly. There has been only one woman Chief Minister, 2 Deputy Ministers, and one Cabinet Minister (Food) in the government in all these years. This shows that despite massive voting power of women for deciding the nature of operative State power, they are in a most disadvantageous position.

Almost the same story of conspicuous absence of women is repeated in the administrative hierarchy. UP Civil Service was composed of 565 members in 1965; 351 civil servants were functioning in 55 district headquarters; 20 were deputy secretaries; 82 held special posts; 45 officers were meant for substituting leave vacancies; 45 were kept for deputation services; and 22 were meant for training. This was all a male affair in 1966. Even today the situation has not changed much. A few women started appearing in the provincial service examination. Even if they are selected, they seldom obtain important posts. Till recently, the Chief Minister was very much opposed to the practice of introducing women to the administrative system. However, recent developments show that women have started taking some initiative for entering administrative jobs. But still the resistance from every corner persists.

It is a fact that like other progressive States, women in UP have also won some seats in the panchayat elections. But their relative position is only a marginal one. There are 72,265 village Panchayats spread over the 55 districts of the State[15]. The Gram Sabha electorate includes 50% of women. But in terms of articulation of power at the village level, their effectiveness is anaemic. Despite their membership of the Gram Sabha, only a few women are represented in the panchayat executive and as Pradhans of the Gram Sabha. It may be noted that panchayat politics is not as sophisticated as national or State level politics. Considering their level of education, women may be suitably given the opportunity to participate in the local power structure. Also attempts need to be initiated so that women belonging to the minority castes and other depressed communities should share and shape these institutions of power for the benefit of the community.

The role of the Block Pramukh in articulating the interest of the people is potentially enormous. They are directly elected for a term of five years. In a way the Pramukhship helps the local leaders to graduate themselves into State politics. But the elective system at this level also suffers from masculine totalitarianism. Among the nearly nine thousand Pramukhs, women are conspicous by their absence. In fact they do not contest elections meant for electing Pramukhs. Even if they made an effort to do so, the possibility of their not being elected is practically guaranteed. Thus, at the intermediate level of decision-making, women are not creative sharers in power and position – a situation which warrants some statutory provision for ensuring greater participation of women in the functioning of state power.

Hardly any municipal corporation of the State has significant percentage of women as members which obviously reflects the quantum of their participation in the civic affairs of the State. It may be recalled that the Municipal Corporations of Agra, Allahabad, Kanpur, Lucknow, and Varanasi, established in February 1960, consisted of councillors and eldermen with a term of office of five years. The councillors are elected by direct election on the basis of adult suffrage from various wards into which a city is divided. The eldermen are elected by the councillors. The maximum number of councillors prescribed in the UP Nagar Mahapalika Adhiniyam of 1959 is 190, but the State government has power to determine the number for each corporation. The five major cities do have 50% women voters, but hardly any of them are elected as councillors.[16]

In consonance with the ideological position of the Communist

Party of India, the State unit of the Communist Party believes that complete equality of women is not possible in the capitalist system. Only a socialist system can emancipate women from all types of exploitation. Women's role is vital for bringing about the desired social revolution. As stipulated in the Directive Principles of State Policy of the Constitution of India, the State Communist Party demands equal pay for equal work, removal of all restrictions on employment of married women, extension of maternity benefits to all employed women, and enforcement of social laws for improving their status. Although the party claims 5% women membership out of a few thousand members in the whole State, it has not been able to recruit sizable number of women members unlike the pattern of West Bengal, Andhra, and Kerala. Nor has the party fielded women candidates to fight the election in the State. The party has understood that no meaningful change in women's status is possible unless women become copartners in the productive system. In fact, in accordance with the policy of the national executive, the provincial executive has been demanding 20% reservation of jobs for women in industry.[17]

Almost all the political parties, according to their manifestos, are of the view that women belong to the backward section of the society. For bringing them at par with men, there is need to provide special privileges to them.

Accordingly, the Indian National Congress as originator of the present Constitution of India intends to implement the principles of the Constitution. Right from 1937, the Congress party has been emphasizing rapid uplift of Indian womanhood. The Uttar Pradesh Provincial Congress Committee as one of the biggest Congress units cannot shirk this obligation. As instructed by the national executive, the Provincial Congress Committee decided in 1957 to sponsor 15% women candidates for the 428 Assembly and 85 Lok Sabha seats, but so far it has not reached the stipulated target, though it is a fact that the Congress party sponsored the maximum number of women candidates and such candidates at times included invaluable women from minority and scheduled communities. Nor can it be denied that through the instrumentality of the Congress party, a number of women have been unfolding their brilliant political careers. But this is also true that in practice, barring a few occasions, the UPCC has been masculine in its composition and decision-making. Nearly 54 District Congress Committees have been negligent in ensuring the representation of women.

The Jana Sangh believes that a strong India cannot emerge without the advancement of women. The party seriously intends to remove social and educational disabilities to enable them to discharge their responsibilities to the family, society, and nation without disturbing the traditionally organized social order. According to the stipulations of the party constitution, it is mandatory that women should be members of the provincial executive and the district committees. Although such principles are also applicable for local committees, but it is difficult to get such representation.

In their discussion with the present author the members of the local party organization underlined the need to arouse national consciousness among women by increasing political participation, spreading civic and political education by removing the present trend in advertising and films which used female figures in a very vulgar manner.

The provincial wing of the Socialist Party understands, like the national leadership, that women suffer from social inequalities, economic and cultural backwardness. Accordingly, the party demands special opportunities for women to enable them to enjoy their constitutional rights The party has always made efforts to include a few women in the provincial executives. Invariably the Socialist Party has been putting up women candidates for fighting elections for the past 30 years. However, it has not been able to reach its desired goal. The local party leaders complain of the ignorance and indifference of women regarding the responsibilities and duties guaranteed under the Constitution of India. They feel that the average Indian woman is still a secondary citizen, but they believe that statutory provision for allocating seats for women at different levels of the legislative and executive bodies may lead to the emergence of a harmonious society.

Masculine Totalitarianism

A perusal of facts presented in the paper shows that four crores of women of UP are victims of masculine totalitarianism. Certainly the predominantly made Constituent Assembly guaranteed all kinds of theoretical rights to women. It is also true that women themselves are reluctant to leave their hearth and home in large numbers. But the conditions prevalent for the growth of personality is controlled, regulated and maintained by male members of the society. Unless women have a sense of creative partnership in them, India's own individuality cannot be identified. It requires serious effort at research and policy-making levels to create conditions, so that more women can participate in the general political processes, occupy positions of consequence, exercise power, undertake responsibility, and participate in meaningful decisions.

The composition of most high level power bodies are decided by men and, therefore, even women of sound qualifications and ability are kept away from the places of significance in policy-making. Statutory provisions are necessary to enable women to play a more effective part in the various elective and non-elective bodies. In UP, this would mean reservation of 200 seats for women in the State legislature and 40 seats in Parliament in proportion to their demographic position and share in the community resources of the State. Certainly, at lower levels of decision-making women of UP should have more than 50% seats as to begin with it would be easier for them to understand the intricacies of the political processes at this level. Services like education, communication system, and even transport could be managed by women. Such steps may correct the present masculine imbalance and create conditions in which principles of uniqueness of individuality and indispensibility of community function.

References

1. Mahatma Gandhi in *Young India*, 22, 1919.
2. Constitution of India.
3. D. M. Sinha, *Uttar Pradesh: A Portrait of Population* (Lucknow, 1972).
4. *Statistical Diary, 1973*, Uttar Pradesh, State Planning Institute, Economics and Statistics Division, UP (Lucknow 1973).
5. D. M. Sinha, *op. cit.*
6. *Ibid.*
7. *Statistical Diary, 1973, op. cit.,*
8. D. M. Sinha, *op. cit.*
9. S.M. Sayeed *"Women's Participation in U.P. Politics, A Study of Political Attitudes and Performance of Women Members of the UP Assembly", Indian Journal of Political Science*, Vol. 32 (April-June on the second General Election).
10. Government of India (New Delhi, 1957).
11. *Times of India, Directory and Year Book, 1965-66.*
12. M. Zaheer and Jagdeo Gupta, *The Organization of the Government of Uttar Pradesh*, 1966.

13. *Times of India, Directory and Year Book, 1965-66.*
14. *Statistical Diary,* 1973.
15. *Ibid.*
16. S. Zaheer and Jagdeo Gupta, *Op. cit.*
17. Author's observation after his interview with local party workers of Varanasi.

PROFILES OF WOMEN IN WEST BENGAL

Bangendu Ganguly

In Bengal, the dawn of the 19th century ushered in a new era in the history of women's emancipation. The impact of British rule, capitalist economy, and modern western culture produced here a great awakening – the Bengal renaissance – which aimed, among other things, to end social oppression perpetrated on women.

A new life was brought to the movement for the emancipation of women when the stream of the social reform movement merged with the struggle for political independence of the country. Vast masses of women participated in the freedom struggle, and it became clear even to women in the remote villages that independence was an essential precondition for the emancipation of women.

Participation in Elections

Starting from the first General Elections of 1952, only 26 women from West Bengal have contested elections to the Lok Sabha so far, while the corresponding number for the Vidhan Sabha is 149. Only ten women (38.46%) from West Bengal have so far been elected to the Lok Sabha and 57 (38.25%) to the Vidhan Sabha. The ratio between the contestants and the winners is almost the same in both the cases. During the four Vidhan Sabha elections since 1967, there were 4,308 contestants, and only 90 of them (excluding the one elected in a by-election) were women.

The number of women elected to the Lok Sabha from West Bengal varied between one and three, while those elected to the Vidhan Sabha varied between five and 14. If we calculate the ratio of the number of elected women to the total number of seats, it is found that out of the 40 Lok Sabha seats allotted to West Bengal, only one, i.e., 2.5%, was won by a woman candidate in 1971. Subsequently, another woman candidate was returned in a by-election, thus raising the percentage to 5. In the case of the Vidhan Sabha, there were only five women members in a House of 280 in 1971. In the 1972 election, the number of women elected and the percentage – 1.8 – remained exactly the same. The addition of a woman member through a by-election subsequently has raised the percentage to 2.1. It may be noted here that this percentage does not compare unfavourably with that in many western countries. Representation of women in the elected bodies of many countries in the west also is negligible – only 1.7% in France, 2.8% in Belgium, 2.9% in Great Britain, and 2.9% in Italy.[1] The actual number of women who contested and those who won the elections in West Bengal is, however, smaller than what apparently suggests, because in many cases the same persons have sought elections and have been elected more than once.

If we take into consideration the partisan affiliation of the candidates who have been victorious (Table 1), it becomes clear that West Bengal voters have positively shown their preference to candidates set up by political parties. Some women indeed contested the elections as independent candidates, but with the exception of one, all were defeated. The only independent candidate who won a Lok Sabha seat in 1967 was a well-known trade union leader who was backed by some leftist parties in the State.

Of the ten women candidates elected to the Lok Sabha from the State, five belonged to the Congress, three to the CPI, and one to the CPI(M). The proportion of the Congress candidates elected to the Vidhan Sabha was well over 60% – of the 57 women elected, as many as 37 belonged to the Congress. The CPI was able to send ten candidates to the Vidhan Sabha, while the CPI(M) was able to get five women elected. The Socialist Unity Centre had to its credit one seat each in 1969 and 1971. The remaining two legislators belonged to the Sevak Sangha of Purulia (elected in 1957), and the Bangla Congress (elected in 1969).

Though the political participation scores of women in West Bengal do not look very impressive in terms of the number of women who contested and those who won the elections to different elective bodies, such scores improve to some extent if we consider (a) the percentage of women who have exercised their franchise on different occasions, and (b) the number of women who have participated in the hundreds of pre-election meetings and in the election campaigns organized by different political parties.

In the Lok Sabha elections between 1957 and 1971 women voters to women electors in West Bengal varied between 33.38% and 47.62%. The highest percentage was recorded in 1962 and the lowest in 1971. In the case of the men voters also, the turnout was the highest

TABLE 1

Affiliation of women elected: Lok Sabha and Vidhan Sabha 1952-72

Party	Lok Sabha					Vidhan Sabha					
	1952	1957	1962	1967	1972	1952	1957	1962	1967	1969	1971	1972
Congress	0	2	1	1	1*	4	9*	13*	6	1	0	4*
CPI	1	1	1	0	0	1	1	1	2	2	1	2
CPI(M)	0	0	0	0	1	0	0	0	1	2	3	0
Socialist	0	0	0	0	0	0	0	0	0	1	1	0
Other parties	0	0	0	0	0	0	1	0	0	1	0	0
Independents	0	0	0	1	0	0	0	0	0	0	0	0

*One elected in a by-election

Source: Compiled from the *Reports of the Election Commission of India* and *West Bengal*, a periodical published by the Government of West Bengal.

in 1962 and the lowest in 1971. In each election the percentage of women voters to women electors was less than that of men voters to men electors.

It is a general truth that everywhere the percentage of non-voters is higher among women than among men. This has been established by researchers in the west also.

Voting Behaviour

A voting behaviour survey sponsored by the Indian Council of Social Science Research and conducted by the author in West Bengal in 1972 also shows that the percentage of abstainers was higher among women than among men. For the purpose of this survey, West Bengal was stratified into three regions on the basis of intra-State disparity in the levels of economic development: region A representing the highest level of development and region C showing the lowest level with region B standing in between.

According to official sources, the votes cast to the total electorate in West Bengal in 1972 was 60.43%[2]. In our survey, out of the 504 respondents interviewed, 432 voted and 72 abstained. If we assess this figure against our sample of 660, we find a turnout rate of 65.45%. There is thus only a difference of 5.02% between the external data and our survey data on turnout. When assessed against the figure 504, i.e., the number of actual respondents, the turnout rate looks much higher. It is thus seen that the proportion of voters to the respondents is much higher than the actual proportion of voters to the total electorate. This discrepancy is noted in most surveys.

It is against this background that we have to assess the voting figures of women in West Bengal. Of the 182 women interviewed by us, 33 (18.02%) did not vote while out of 322 male respondents only 39 (12.11%) abstained. For every non-voter, there were only 4.5 voters among women while among men there were 7.2 voters. A region-wise analysis also bears out this disparity. In region A, 18% women against 11.22% men did not vote. The corresponding figures are 23.07% women and 17.33% men in region B, and 26.47% women and 13.63% men in region C. We may thus say that the rate of abstention among women and economic development varies inversely.

The reasons for abstention among women merit special attention because the turnout among women may be, to some extent, determined by circumstances peculiar to them. In order to analyse these problems, we asked all our respondents the following question: "We find that some women are unable to vote. What do you think are the reasons for their being unable to vote?" Many respondents, both male and female, expressed the opinion that there was no particular reason. A large number stated only one reason, while many gave more than one. The maximum of two responses have been presented.

There seems to be a clear difference in the assessment made by male respondents and the female respondents. According to the responses given by the former, the three most important reasons for abstention among women are illiteracy, lack of awareness, and domestic responsibility, in that order. According to the responses given by female respondents, such reasons are domestic responsibility, lack of awareness, and illiteracy. It is interesting to note that both give the same reasons but in a different order. If we calculate on the basis of the responses given, we find that 25.91% of those given by male respondents pertain to illiteracy, 17.27% to lack of awareness, 12.62% to domestic responsibility, 6.31% to shyness, and 5.98% to apathy. Orthodox attitudes and distance of polling stations each covers 5.31% of the responses. But, of the responses given by female respondents, 32.50% relate to domestic responsibility, 19.37% to lack of awareness, 10% to illiteracy, 8.75% to shyness, and 6.87% to fear of violence. Female respondents do not appear to attach much importance either to the distance of polling stations or to the fear of teasing. Not a single one of them mentioned – as a probable reason for abstention – difference of opinion in the family, inconvenience due to shabby dress, or absence of separate arrangements for women.

It may be possible that abstention among women in West Bengal would decrease considerably if attempts were made to solve the problems of illiteracy, lack of awareness, and domestic responsibility. The first two are in a way related problems and the removal of the former might lessen the latter. Progressive measures may indeed solve both the problems and effectively increase the turnout rate of women.

Personal Influence

Researches on the part played by people in the flow of mass communication have revealed that in public affairs men played an important role in influencing the opinion and attitudes of women. It was also found that a very large majority of these men were members of the immediate families of the women concerned. For married women the most important male who exerted influence was their husbands.[3]

We tried to find out the opinion of our respondents on the question whether women should be guided by others in the sphere of partisan choice or whether they should vote independently. We asked each respondent, irrespective of sex, two questions: (a) "Do you think it is important for female members of the family to vote the same way as male members?" and (b) "Do you think it is important for a wife to vote the same way as her husband?"

The responses to the first question revealed that while 64 men and 63 women thought female members of the family should vote the same way as the male members, 256 men and 117 women held the opposite view. Thus, 79.50% of the male respondents and 64.28% of the female respondents wanted women to exercise independent partisan choice. Strangely enough, the percentage of people holding such a view was lower among women than among men. Perhaps this was partly due to the lower level of literacy among women.

In the 21-25 age-group, 76.12% of the male respondents and 75.86% of the female respondents were in favour of independent voting by women. A much higher percentage of both male and female respondents in the 36-40 age-group (86.04% and 81.25% respectively) held the same view. Those between 46 and 50 years, also conformed to the same pattern, for 87.09% of men and 80% of women had the same opinion. Among those who were above 60, only 28.57% women wanted that female members of the family should not necessarily vote in the same way as male members. Though a higher percentage of men in the same age-group held similar views, even that percentage was less than 50.

Support for independent partisan choice by women was much more prevalent among the highly educated than the illiterate. While only 57.14% of illiterate men and 42.85% of illiterate women wanted such independent choice, 98% of men and all the women in the category "college degree and above" subscribed to this view. Among those men who had college education but no degree, 90.90% held the same view. The percentage of similar-minded women in the same educational level, however, was much lower – 66.66%.

On this issue the Brahmin and the Vaishya men appeared to be much more conservative than the Kayasthas and the Vaidyas. But in the case of women it was just the opposite.

It is interesting to note that while all the unemployed men and all the men belonging to the category of professionals wanted women to vote independently, only 75% of the men working as executives thought that way. In the case of women, the position was different. Only one woman belonged to the category of unemployed and only three to that of executives, and all of them were in favour of independent partisan choice by women. Most of the women were covered by the category "others", which included housewives, and 64.90% of them favoured independent choice.

If we try to analyse the opinion of the respondents from the point of family income, we find that 70.45% of the men and 65.21% of the women enjoying a family income of Rs.50 and less wanted independent choice by women. But in the next higher category, the percentage of people of the same opinion was slightly lower: 67.03% in the case of men and 58.62% in the case of women. In the highest category, covering those with a family income of Rs.2,001 and above, the percentage of people supporting the above view was not very high: 66.66% in the case of women and 50% in the case of men. But in the next lower category, that is, among those enjoying a family income of Rs.1,001 to Rs.2,000, the percentage was much higher – 82.60% in the case of men, and 75% in the case of women.

An analysis of the views of the respondents classified on the basis of their self-image shows that the working class respondents were more conservative than the middle class, both among men and women. While 85.02% of the men and 73.53% of the women who placed themselves in the middle class wanted to vote independently, the same view was held by only 78.09% of the men and 60.00% of the women who belonged to the working class.

It is interesting to note that the number of both men and women who wanted the wife to vote the same way as her husband was somewhat higher than that of men and women who wanted female members of the family to vote the same way as the male members. We found that 69 men and 73 women wanted the wife to follow her husband in the sphere of partisan choice, while 251 men and 107 women held the opposite view. Here also, one male respondent had no opinion to express on the question and the opinion of three respondents could not be ascertained. Thus, 20.05% of the male respondents opposed the wife's independent choice, while 77.95% men and 58.79% women did not think that this was necessary.

Respondents in the 21-25 age-group were more conservative than those in the 26-30 age-group. While in the former group 74.62% men and 68.96% women wanted the wife to vote independently, in the latter group 84.09% men and 58.82% women held the same view. Those between 36 and 40 also were more liberal than the youngest group: 83.72% men and 75% women in the 36-40 age-group held that the wife need not necessarily vote the same way as her husband. The 46-50 age-group was even more liberal: 87.09% men and 80% women held the above view. People in the highest age-group were naturally much more conservative. In fact, they were even more so than the youngest voters. Among those over 60, 47.05% men and 28.57% women wanted the wife to exercise her right to vote independently of her husband.

The highly educated people were much more in favour of independent partisan choice by a wife than were the illiterate. Among the latter, only 50% men and 36.90% women favoured such choice. But among those who belonged to the category of "college degree and above" 98% men and all the women wanted the choice to be made independently. Those who had some college education but no degree were somewhat less liberal: 90.90% men and 66.66% women said that the wife need not vote the same way as her husband.

The Brahmin and the Vaishya men were more conservative than the Kayastha and the Vaidya men. While 86.36% Brahmin men and 85.29% Vaishya men wanted the wife to vote independently, the percentage was as high as 98.41% in the case of the Kayastha and the Vaidya men. In the case of female respondents, the picture was different in the sense that 75% Brahmin women and 82.14% Vaishya women wanted the wife's independence while 70.27% each of the Kayastha and the Vaidya women held the same view.

All the unemployed men and all those belonging to the category of professionals wanted the wife to vote independently. But only 75% of the executives favoured such independence. There were three women executives and one unemployed women, and all of them favoured independent partisan choice by the wife. Of the women professionals, 80% held the same view. As already noted, most of the women fell in the category marked "others" and of them 58.27% wanted the wife to vote independently.

Among those who had a family income of Rs.50 and less, 68.18% men and 43.47% women thought in the same way. In the next higher group the picture was only slightly different: 63.73% men and 50.98% women favoured the wife's independent choice. In the highest income group, there were very few respondents and only 50% men and 66.66% women supported this view. In the Rs.1001-2000 group, people were more liberal: 82.60% men and 75% women held that the wife should vote independently.

In this category also, the working class is more conservative than the middle class. Among those who placed themselves in the former class only 75.23% men and 54.28% women held that the partisan choice of the wife need not be the same as that of her husband. But among those who said that they belonged to the middle class, 83.98% men and 71.56 per cent women subscribed to this view.

Participation in Campaigns

Though the fate of the candidates in an election is finally decided on the polling day, the process of shaping that fate starts long before; part of that process is reflected in the numerous pre-election meetings organized by different political parties. A careful perusal of the newspapers from 1952 shows that on the whole women in West Bengal joined such pre-election meetings in considerable numbers. In addition to such participation, they attended meetings convened specially for women. Another notable feature of women's participation in West Bengal is that many women served as campaign workers for different political parties. A newspaper report on the first General Elections, for example, stated that there were as many women canvassers as men in the urban areas though in the rural areas most of the canvassers were men.[4] Another report on a rural constituency, however, showed that there were a large number of women volunteers who worked for different candidates.[5] A report on the mid-term poll of 1969 stated that it was strikingly all red in the CPI(M) poll offices in Calcutta and the surrounding areas, and women workers lent more colour with red cholies and red scarves around their necks.[6]

Local Government Elections

Lack of women's participation in panchayati raj institutions becomes obvious. When we add up the total number of women elected to gram panchayats in the different districts of West Bengal, we find only 359 persons in the field. This figure looks hopelessly insignificant when we calculate the ratio between the total number of gram panchayat members and the number of women members. In West Bengal, there are 19,662 gram panchayats[7], each having a membership varying between 9 and 15. The total number of women elected to anchal panchayats also is quite insignificant. There are only 52 of them in 2,926 anchal panchayats throughout the State. Among the 19,662 adhyakshyas of gram panchayats we find only 14 women. Only eight women are to be seen among an equal number of upadhyakshyas. There are just three women pradhans and one upapradhan among 2,926 pradhans and an equal number of upapradhans of anchal panchayats.

It is, however, impossible to construct any political participation index on the basis of panchayat election data in West Bengal, because panchayati raj has not been given a fair trial in the State. The West Bengal Panchayat Act 1957[8] was gradually brought into force in the whole of rural West Bengal, excluding the colliery areas of Asansol and the tea garden areas of north Bengal, during the period 1958-59 and 1964-65. The gram panchayats and anchal panchayats have been functioning without elections for quite a number of years. The age of the present panchayati raj institutions varies between 9 and 15 years though their statutory terms were limited to four years only.

The higher tiers of panchayati raj bodies – anchalik parishads at the block level and zilla parishads at the district level – were established in different areas in 1964-65. But these were subsequently superseded by the government.

A new Panchayat Act has recently been enacted, and it was expected that elections to different panchayati raj institutions will be held under the new Act by the middle of 1974.

If we add together the number of all the women who have fought the municipal corporation elections since 1952 we do not reach even a two-digit figure. Only two of the contestants have been elected: one was elected in 1961 on a Congress ticket and another in 1969 as a candidate of the Socialist Unity Centre.

Calcutta Municipal Corporation councillors, however, have since 1952 elected three women aldermen – one each in 1957, 1965, and 1969. More women have served on the committees of the Calcutta Corporation. Records of the Corporation show that 23 committees have had women members since 1952. This number, of course, includes the women councillors and aldermen. The others have served as associate members. We have to remember that the same woman has at times served on different committees concurrently. Moreover, the same person has served the committees in different years. In 1969-70, the Accounts Committee of the corporation was headed by a woman councillor. She also served as a member of the Standing Committee on Education in 1970-71. One woman councillor served as the deputy chairman of the Standing Committee on Education in

1961-62. In 1964-65, the same person served as the deputy chairman of a Borough Committee, and as the member of two standing committees. So if we count the actual number of women who have been associated with the committees the number comes down to nine.

Complete data on the number of women who have fought the electoral battles in the 86 municipalities in West Bengal are not available. But leaders of different organizations are of the opinion that the picture, so far as these municipalities are concerned, is not radically different from that in the other elective bodies.

Role of Religion

Though the number of women who have contested the elections in West Bengal is negligible, the level of consciousness of the women voters in the State does not appear to be very low. That is most probably the reason why religion or religious symbols are not generally used in the State for the purpose of eliciting the support of women voters.

One of the principles in the Code of Conduct laid down by the Election Commission of India on the eve of the 1972 election was: "There should be no appeal to caste or communal feelings for securing votes. Mosques, churches, temples or any other place of worship should not be used as forums for election propaganda." All the political parties in West Bengal agreed to abide by this principle and, on the whole, they kept their word. Even if religious feelings might have been fanned in isolated instances, these were never meant primarily for appealing to women voters. Women leaders of different political parties are unanimous on the point that religion did not play any significant role in determining voting behaviour of women in West Bengal.

It may be mentioned here that since independence the people of West Bengal have never chosen political parties which use communal slogans. This becomes evident from an analysis of the votes obtained by parties such as the Hindu Maha Sabha, the Jana Sangh, and the Muslim League since 1962. The Hindu Maha Sabha obtained 0.80% of the votes polled in 1962, 0.13% in 1969, 0.004% in 1971, and 0.02% in 1972. The Jana Sangh secured 0.45% of the votes in 1962, 1.33% in 1967, 0.83% in 1969, 0.68% in 1971, and 0.19% in 1972. The Muslim League's plight was only slightly better. It secured 2.59% of the votes polled in 1971. But the percentage came down to 0.94% in 1972.

The voting behaviour survey of 1972 shows that caste/religion did not play any significant part in determining either the turnout or the partisan choice.

Women in the Ministries

Though West Bengal had a woman Governor for a full decade, from 1957 to 1966, poor representation of women in the State legislature has been reflected in the composition of all the ministries since 1947. When in July 1947 the ministry for the western part of Bengal was formed under the leadership of Dr. P.C. Ghose, not a single woman was included.[9] The position, however, improved considerably after the first General Elections of 1952. In the new ministry formed then, Renuka Roy, a former member of the Constituent Assembly, was appointed a Cabinet member, the first woman to be appointed to this post in any State in India.[10] Apart from her, there were two women Deputy Ministers in the same Cabinet, one of whom was dropped after a reshuffle of the ministry.

Though the total number of women ministers remained the same after the second General Elections, no woman was given Cabinet rank. In the new ministry, one woman was a Minister of State and one a Deputy Minister. Some parliamentary Secretaries were appointed, but there was no woman among them.

The largest number of women ministers so far has been found in the ministry formed in 1962: two women were included as Cabinet Ministers and three as Deputy Ministers. But the situation changed in two years' time when the post of the Deputy Minister was discontinued. Only two women remained as Cabinet members till the fourth General Election.

When a United Front government was formed in 1967, West Bengal again got a ministry without any woman. Most probably the partners of the United Front government were, for obvious reasons, more interested in the representation of different political parties. When the United Front came back to power in 1969 with an obverwhelming majority in the Legislative Assembly two women were included in the ministry: one as a Minister with Cabinet rank and one as a Minister of State. The shortlived government of 1971 also did not have any woman minister.

Politics in West Bengal turned full circle in 1972 when there was a

Congress government. But the 28-member ministry formed after the election included only one woman – a Deputy Minister.

The number of ministers in West Bengal has varied from time to time. But if we look at the persons who have served as ministers of different ranks, we find only ten women.

Poor representation of women in the legislature is generally held to be the main reason for the small number of women in the ministries. But if we go deep into the reasons behind such poor representation, it becomes clear that male domination of political parties which set up candidates is largely responsible for this state of affairs. As we have already seen, people of West Bengal are not reluctant to elect women legislators. Votes in West Bengal are generally cast on a political basis. But political parties set up very few women candidates.

Political Parties and Women

Though each political party differs from others by a specific programme, the major political parties in West Bengal do not differ from one another in their goals on the basic question of the need for equality between men and women. But the political parties are concerned with all the aspects of the political process, and differ in their basic approach to a problem as well as in the matter of emphasis.

It is to be noted in this connection that almost all the major political parties in West Bengal today happen to be branches of broader party structures and the views expressed by the parties in West Bengal on the problems of women are not, therefore, different from those held by the party branches outside the State.

Though the election manifesto issued by the six-party United Left Front in 1971 did not specifically include in its programme the solution of the problems faced by women in general, it stated that the ULF stood by the commitments made in the 32-point programme of the United Front. The 32-point programme issued in 1969 stated: "The special problems of women will receive due consideration from the U.F. Government. Attempts will be made to expand the facilities of education and training for women, more jobs specially suited for them will be created."[11]

For a clear idea about the role of Communists in West Bengal we have to take into account the Naxalite movement. Some members of the CPI(M) broke away to form first the All-India Coordination Committee of Revolutionaries and later the CPI(M-L). The CPI(M-L) believes that in order to build a new society it is of the utmost importance to arouse the broad masses of women to join in productive activity. The draft programme of the party stated that the people's democratic state would remove all social inequalities and "guarantee equality of status to Indian womanhood".[12] The party's attitude towards women was expressed through some posters which, quoting Mao Tse-tung, pointed out that women were subjected to an additional form of domination – domination by men.[13]

The educational and social demands contained in the programme of the Revolutionary Socialist Party also cover the demand for "equal status and opportunities for women in all spheres of life including equal wages for equal work, and equality of economic opportunities and freedom for them".[14] In the opinion of the Socialist Unity Centre, India has not yet achieved national freedom in the real sense of the term because power is still in the hands of the capitalist class, and emancipation of women is dependent on the emancipation of the society as a whole. So without a socialist revolution there can be no real emancipation of women.[15] The manifesto of the Workers' Party of India does not specifically speak of the equality of the sexes. The manifesto, however, says that the party is a "Marxist-Leninist party".[16] It follows logically that the party upholds the ideal of equality between men and women.

The Forward Bloc believes that backwardness of women who constitute about half the total population hampers the progress of the whole nation. The capitalist system does not provide women at any level with any scope for self-reliance. Only a socialist society can solve all these problems. The party holds that the establishment of a socialist society as envisaged by Netaji Subhas Chandra Bose will enable Indian women to fulfil their proper role in society.[17]

Women in Party Hierarchy

As we have seen, all the political parties of any significance in West Bengal uphold the equality of men and women. It would, therefore, be natural to expect a considerable number of women in the ranks of the political parties. But the actual situation seems to be quite different.

According to a prominent leader of the Paschim Banga Pradesh Congress Committee, about 18% of the primary members of the

Profiles of Women in West Bengal

Congress in West Bengal are women. But most of them are inactive. There are indeed some women activists of the Congress in every district of West Bengal. In each District Congress Committee, except in Murshidabad, there are also one or two women. In the Pradesh Congress Committee itself – that is, the State executive – there are two women out of a total membership of 30.

The Pradesh Congress has set up a separate women's wing of the party, "Pradesh Congress Mahila Samiti", which in 1973 had a total membership of 3,500. The Samiti aims at raising the membership to 10,000 in 1974. It more or less corresponds to the women's subcommittee of the undivided Congress. After the party split, a women's cell was formed and subsequently, after the Bidhan Nagar Congress (held in December 1972), the Pradesh Congress Mahila Samiti was set up. It must be noted, however, that a member of the Congress can become a member of the Mahila Samiti only on paying an additional membership fee.

The Samiti believes that in order to secure effective political participation by women it is necessary to raise the level of their political consciousness. In the opinion of the Samiti, Indian women are socially exploited, especially in the rural areas.[18] So the Samiti seeks to extend its base mainly in the rural areas. Partial success has already been achieved in this sphere. This is borne out by the fact that on 22 January 1974 the Samiti collected 500 quintals of paddy from a village in the 24-Parganas in its effort to help the government implement its procurement programme.[19]

The Samiti has grown into a militant organization within the party. Recently, about 500 women of the Samiti gheraoed the leaders of the Pradesh Congress for hours and submitted a memorandum demanding regular supply of essential commodities at a fair price.[20]

The women leaders of the CPI feel that women have come to play a more significant role in the party after the Communist Party split in 1964. Though exact figures are not available, it appears that women do not comprise more than 3% of the total membership. In the Calcutta district, however, the percentage of women members is 6.25: of the 2,593 members in Calcutta, 162 are women. Apart from that, there are quite a few women sympathisers who participate in party activities on various occasions.[21]

The percentage of women in the undivided Communist Party in West Bengal was also about 3. This is implied by the fact that there were only ten women among 333 delegates who attended the special conference of the West Bengal Committee of the party held in January 1958. Of the 313 delegates who attended a conference of the same committee in April 1959, there were 9 women.[22]

The percentage of women members of the Communist Party in West Bengal does not look at all impressive when we compare it with the percentage of women members in some of the Communist parties abroad. Women constitute 20% of the Communist Party membership in the Soviet Union, 16% in Israel, 21% in France, and 13% in Cuba.[23]

There are, however, some women members in the different party committees in West Bengal. The State council has six women members out of a total of 70. In the State executive committee there are three women members including one member of the State secretariat. Out of 65 members of the Calcutta district council, six are women. After the Calcutta district conference held in 1968, one women's department consisting of seven women members of the district council was set up. This department established a 25-member party fraction to coordinate party work among women.[24]

In the opinion of the women leaders of the party, there is no resistance in the party to accept women in the leadership. The small number of women in the leadership is merely due to the fact that the movement has not thrown up a sufficient number of women leaders. It must be noted in this connection that when the Communist party split into two most of the noted women leaders of the undivided party in West Bengal joined the CPI.

The political-organizational report of the CPI(M) Central Committee to the eighth congress of the party (held in December 1968) frankly admitted that in West Bengal the party had not been able to activize working class women even in the trade unions though a small number of women were activized during strikes; nor had the party been able to draw in peasant women. Most of the party leaders and ordinary members in West Bengal did not take any interest in building up a women's movement and a women's organization. The party was bringing out a monthly women's paper with a circulation of about 4,000. Out of 16,000 members in the State, only about 500, i.e., about 3%, were women. It may be of interest to note here that in the whole of India the number of women party members would not exceed 1% of the total membership. The report also reveals that the Central Committee had earlier decided to pay attention to work among women as auxiliary to and apart of trade union, kisan, and middle class employees organizations, and to the task of recruiting them into the party.[25]

Many women participated in the Naxalite movement in West Bengal in both rural and urban areas. In the former, most of the women activists belonged to tribal families. In the urban areas the movement got an enthusiastic response mainly from young girls, junior under-graduate students, and senior school students. Many of these students joined the movement after being influenced by Charu Mazumdar's arguments as contained in a booklet, *On Student and Youth Movement*, based on one of his lectures. Though a number of young girls joined the movement because of the romantic thrill of clandestine activities, many of them also revolted against the existing system of education. Tribal women, some of whom actively participated in the 'annihilation' programme of the CPI(M-L), were actually up against those who were regarded as their 'class enemies'.

Though the movement initiated by the CPI(M-L) got the support of many women, the organizational leadership of the party was in the hands of men. Neither in the Central Committee nor in the West Bengal State Committee was there any women member. There were, however, some women in the party committees at the lower levels. As in the case of other political parties, male domination over the party machinery was clear in the CPI(M-L).[26]

There is no woman in the Central Committee, the State Committee or the Calcutta District Committee of the Revolutionary Socialist Party. It has to be noted, however, that about 14% of the delegates elected by the general members to attend the last Calcutta District Conference were women.[27]

The reason for the absence of women in the leading committees of the party lies in the active membership clause of the party constitution. Any member who has continuously and effectively worked for six months on any mass front for the party under its direct supervision and guidance, and is prepared to place his services and time completely at the disposal of the party, shall be entitled to become and active member of the party. Active members are entitled to be elected to any position in the party. The overwhelming majority of the active members are whole-timers. Because of family problems, it is difficult for women to make the declaration that they are prepared to place their services and time entirely at the disposal of the party. Some women members of the party, however, attend party committee meeting even at the top level as invitees.[28]

Though there are no women in the Central Committee of the Socialist Unity Centre, the Provincial Committee has one woman member and about 20% of the members of the Calcutta District Committee are women. In the local committees there are on an average as many women as there are men.

An analysis of the social background of the party members shows that the women belong mainly to the middle class, though some come from the working class and the kisan families. There are some Muslim women in the party, particularly in the villages of the 24-Parganas.[29]

The Workers' Party has a small membership and naturally the number of women members is not very large. There is one woman in the State Committee of the party.[30]

Like some of the other parties, the State Committee of the Forward Bloc has no woman member. There are, of course, a few women in the lower committees. The exact percentage of membership of women has not yet been ascertained. But there is a separate party cell for them.[31]

About one-fourth of the primary members of the Congress(O) are women. But most of them are inactive. There are, however, some prominent women leaders in the party including one former Cabinet member of West Bengal and one former Deputy Minister. The party organ *Yuger Dak* is edited by the woman leader who was formerly a Cabinet member. There is a party sub-committee on women. But it is virtually a defunct body.[32]

Interest Groups

In addition to the special women's units of the political parties, there are in West Bengal numerous associational groups which seek to protect the interests of women.

While some of these groups are primarily concerned with welfare activities and relief work, some others combine such activities with broader politically motivated efforts. Though these groups may not be formally affiliated to political parties, they are in many cases dominated by one or another political party. In such cases, the political organ of the party concerned sometimes publishes reports on the activities of the group that operates under its informal leadership. For example, the organs of the CPI, the *Kalantar* daily, the *Kalantar* weekly, and the *New Age* weekly, focus attention on the activities and achievements of the Paschim Banga Mahila Samiti. Likewise the

Ganashakti, the *Desh-hitaishi* and the *People's Democracy*, organs of the CPI(M), publish news about the activities of the Paschim Banga Ganatantrik Mahila Samiti.

The bulk of these groups in West Bengal are affiliated to two federations: the Women's Coordinating Council (WCC) and the West Bengal branch of the National Federation of Indian Women (NFIW). The most important part of the WCC is the All India Women's Conference (AIWC), and today it forms the most important part of the Women's Coordinating Council which has 82 organizations affiliated to it. This Council came into being in 1960 mainly as an agency for coordinating the work of women's organizations during emergencies and for certain other purposes where united efforts could be effective. The organizations affiliated to WCC keep their independent entities. The WCC acts through sub-committees and these sub-committees give us an idea of the nature and extent of the Councils' activities. The Emergency Relief Sub-committee and the General Relief Sub-committee, as their names imply, organize relief work during disturbances and natural calamities. The International Affairs Sub-committee acts as the liaison for contacts with the outside world and arranges meetings with eminent women visitors from abroad. The Educational Affairs Sub-committee organizes seminars on important national issues while the aim of the Information and Vocational Guidance Sub-committee is to set up an Information and Vocational Guidance Bureau to help young people find avenues of self-employment. The Family Welfare and Bustee Welfare Sub-committee seeks to look after poor women and children. The Handicrafts Sales Promotion Sub-committee has concretely helped organizations which have no marketing facilities by operating a sales counter at the Council office. An interesting feature of the WCC is the North Bengal Project Sub-committee which has helped in the supervision of two community centres.[33]

The Women's National Front was opened by the WCC in 1970 to activize women to take preventive measures against anti-social activities. In the same year the WCC set up a Youth Council which, in addition to cultural activities, sports, and relief work, undertook social service projects in the less developed areas. In recent times the WCC has realized the need for focusing attention on the alarming rise in prices and the widespread adulteration of essential food articles. As a result, in May 1973 it set up the Consumers' Action Forum with organizations interested in public welfare, in addition to the 82 organizations affiliated to the WCC. The main objective of the Forum is to coordinate the activities of voluntary organizations in building up a planned and sustained consumer movement with the housewife playing a key role in it.

The AIWC has naturally taken a leading role in all these efforts. Though constituted at the beginning to deal with the issue of women's education, the AIWC pays considerable attention to the basic civil rights of social justice, integrity, and equal rights as well. To attain these objectives the AIWC is pledged to work on non-violent and non-party political lines, and seeks to adopt the means, among others, of universal education, social services, and family planning.[34] After the attainment of independence, the AIWC intensified its lobbying for social laws and has been quite successful at that.[35]

All interest groups seek to utilize all the available communication structures. But some groups show preference for some specific access channels and the WCC as well as the organizations affiliated to it are more likely to articulate their demands through personal contact channels and through elite representation. The mass media are of course well utilized by them. From time to time the Consumers' Action Forum brings out leaflets, folders, and a bulletin of news.

It is of interest to note that the National Federation of Indian Women (NFIW) was constituted in Calcutta in 1954 under the auspices of the National Coordinating Committee of Women. This organization was established to coordinate the activities of various women's organizations working in different parts of India, inspired with the same objective of the emancipation of women and the welfare of women and children.

In Bengal, the Mahila Atmaraksha Samiti was set up during the Second World War. In 1943, the Samiti had organized a very big hunger march of starving women from the villages. The organization was, however, declared illegal in 1949, and 'had to take to the path of underground work from 1949 to 1951. After 1951 the samiti started functioning legally and the torn threads of the organization were put together'.[36] At its ninth conference held in 1959, the Samiti was renamed the Paschim Banga Mahila Samiti[37] which is today the most important constituent of the NFIW in West Bengal.

Thirteen associations are affiliated to the West Bengal branch of the National Federation of Indian Women which is about one-sixth the number of such groups affiliated to the Women's Coordinating Council. But this is not to say that the NFIW does not play an important part in the life of the women of West Bengal.

The members of the NFIW include women belonging to all religions, castes, and different political beliefs. The Federation declares that it is not a political organization and that its activities are not confined to feminist aims alone. Rather, its objective is to achieve national improvement with which emancipation of women is interlinked. The Federations avowed methods of work are: (a) constructive work centres such as adult literacy schools, children's nurseries and schools, and work centres for women; (b) agitation for demands affecting the lives of women and children, education of women in progressive ideas, and fight against superstitions and obscurantism; and (c) helping individual women who are victims of social oppression.[38] The Paschim Banga Mahila Samiti, an affiliate of NFIW, works for the equality of sexes and for the fullest social, economic, and political rights of Indian women. It seeks to promote women's health and educational and cultural development as well as child welfare. The Samiti tries to secure equal rights for women in the field of employment so that women can become self-supporting and can look after themselves and their families in the present situation of economic and social crisis. The Samiti holds that for the achievement of these aims it is necessary to secure the democratic rights of the Indian people and to have peace in the world. The Samiti carries on a relentless fight against the danger of war and for a nuclear arms ban.[39]

For the fulfilment of these aims the Samiti carries on a publicity campaign and a movement among the women through "just and legal means".[40] In addition to welfare activities and relief work, it holds meetings and demonstrations on various issues, including the issue of soaring prices, and arranges signature campaigns and deputations. The Samiti has actively taken part in the movement initiated by the Kisan Sabha for occupying land. Workers of the Samiti went to different villages to organize squads and *padayatra* (march) on this issue. On certain occasions they also actively helped the Kisan women in their fight against police oppression. It participates in the workers' movements and it also seeks to protect, in particular, the interests of women workers of factories and plantations.

An interesting feature of the Samiti's activities was that at the height of the politics of violence in West Bengal, its workers pinned badges on pedestrians with a slogan against fratricide inscribed on them. During the 1969 election, the Samiti sought to activise women voters. In 1971, when the leftist parties were divided into two main fronts, the United Left Front, under the leadership of the CPI(M), and the United Left Democratic Front, under the leadership of the CPI, the Samiti issued a statement in support of the ULDF candidates and actively participated in the election campaign. In 1972, though the Samiti did not issue any statement in favour of the Progressive Democratic Alliance, its workers in the different districts participated in the election campaign for a stable government in the State.[41]

In its attempt to strengthen the international solidarity of women, the Samiti took various concrete measures to help the Vietnamese women and children, the people of Bangladesh, and the victims of tyrannical persecution in different countries.

The activities of the 12 other affiliates of the West Bengal branch of the NFIW are very much limited. Like the Samiti, they take part in the literacy campaign, run various types of training centres for women, and undertake relief and welfare measures. Of these 12 groups, the most organized and disciplined group is the Mahila Sanskritik Sammelan. This organization takes part in all the movements initiated by the West Bengal branch of the NFIW.[42]

An analysis of the activities of the NFIW and its chief constituents reveals that the communication channel of physical demonstration is used by them much more extensively than by the WCC and its affiliates. On the other hand, the NFIW places much less reliance on elite representation. The Paschim Banga Mahila Samiti brings out in Bengali a quarterly journal called *Chalar Pathe*. It may be mentioned here that in the earlier days the Mahila Atmaraksha Samiti used to bring out a monthly magazine *Ghare-Baire*. During the years 1948-50, when the Samiti was banned, its organs – *Ghare-Baire, Jaya*, and *Muktir Pathe Nari* – were banned as well.

The Paschim Banga Ganatantrik Mahila Samiti can rightly be called a sister organization of the Paschim Banga Mahila Samiti, though the relationship between the two is not exactly cordial. As the Paschim Banga Mahila Samiti had been working mainly under the domination of the undivided Communist Party, the split in the party also brought about a division in the Samiti. But the two splits took place at different times. Even after the party split the Samiti remained undivided up to 1970. In 1970, however, the Samiti members whose sympathies lay with the CPI(M) broke away to form a new Samiti which also, for some time, was called the Paschim Banga Mahila Samiti and which became the Paschim Banga Ganatantrik Mahila Samiti in 1971. The Samiti which carries out organized activities in all the 16 districts of West Bengal has 121,632 members on its rolls.[43]

In order to achieve its aims the Samiti carries out a publicity campaign among women and seeks to organize them and tries to work in collaboration and in friendship with all the other organizations of women – workers, peasants, and middle class militant people upholding ideals similar to its own.

The activities of the Samiti included implementation of the laws providing for monogamy, equal rights in the fields of marriage and divorce, women's right of inheritance, for the abolition of the dowry system, equal pay for equal work, abolition of illiteracy, etc.

Though the Samiti is not formally affiliated to any federation, it maintains an informal, fraternal coordination with similar samitis in Maharashtra, Kerala, Tripura, Assam, Andhra Pradesh, and Tamil Nadu.[44] An analysis of the social background of the members of the Samiti shows that it is predominantly a middle class organization. Of the 469 delegates that attended the conference of the Samiti in April 1973, background data about 455 are available. It is found that as many as 408 of them belonged to the middle class, 26 to the working class, and 21 to the peasantry; and out of these 442 were literate (including 79 students) and 13 illiterate.[45]

The Banga Ganatantrik Mahila Samiti makes extensive use of physical demonstrations. Even if there may be some scope for utilizing personal connection channels, the possibility of passing on its message through elite representation does not exist. The Samiti brings out a monthly magazine *Eksathe*.

The Nikhil Banga Mahila Sangha, dominated by the Revolutionary Socialist Party, believes that the larger section of women in the present social system of our country exists as a part of exploited humanity. But women lack that class-consciousness which inspires the exploited people to organize themselves into powerful bodies and help social progress. The Sangha tries to rouse the class-consciousness of women and seeks to help women prevent the collapse of family life in a situation of economic crisis. Women are to be roused according to the Sangha, in the demand for better arrangements for maternity and child welfare. It is the aim of the Sangha to prepare the woman for her role as a nurse in the birth of the new society through class struggle and mass movement.[46]

The organization has a membership of about 5,000. Its activities are mainly confined to the districts of Calcutta, the 24-Parganas, Murshidabad, and Jalpaiguri.[47] The Sangha brings out a periodical *Angana*.

The Mahila Sanskritik Sangha is a mass organization under the leadership of the Socialist Unity Centre. It believes that women's problems cannot be solved merely through measures such as the sale of literature or running sewing schools. Economic freedom of women is the only solution and that can be achieved only after the socialist revolution. The Sangha, however, undertakes some relief work as well as cultural activities. It fights against obscenity and vulgarism in literature, films, and other cultural fields. The Sangha is active in Calcutta Birbhum, the 24-Parganas, and some of the districts of north Bengal.[48]

The objectives of the Agrani Mahila Parishad, dominated by the Workers' Party, are more or less similar to those of the women's organizations functioning under the leadership of the other leftist political parties in the State. The Parishad, however, is a small organization with a meagre membership of 300.[49]

The Paschim Banga Agragami Mahila Samiti, which in reality is a front organization of the Forward Bloc, was set up in 1959. Women have some problems of their own and they have to play the leading role in solving these problems. Thousands of women in the villages are still deprived of the opportunity of education though some middle class women in the urban areas have been educated. Particularly distressing is the condition of peasant and working class women who are still looked upon as persons whose main functions are to serve the family and to procreate. The Samiti seeks to build up public opinion against this state of affairs and to raise women's awareness. It seeks to carry on a campaign against child marriage and dowry. The Samiti undertakes relief work as well.[50]

It may be mentioned here that in May 1967, 22 women's organizations led by different left parties in the State came together through a convention in support of the United Front government and formed the Samjukta Mahila Samiti. The Samiti, however, languished when the leftist parties split.

Response to Important Issues

It is true that West Bengal has so far produced only a few women legislators and fewer women ministers. The women, however, are not apathetic to the problems around them. Their response to various issues makes this amply clear.

Soon after the attainment of independence, West Bengal women rallied together in an attempt to stop communal riots. To help stabilize peace in Calcutta, both Hindu and Muslim women participated in meetings and joined peace marches. In recent times also, they have demonstrated against fratricide, against the politics of violence, and against anti-social elements.[51]

One of the issues that have elicited enthusiastic response from women – both in the urban and in the rural areas – is the fight against soaring prices and ensure the regular supply of essential commodities and the demand for steps against hoarding and blackmarketing. Since the fifties, the women of West Bengal have participated in signature campaigns, meetings, demonstrations, hunger marches, and even in *satyagrahas* on these issues.[52] Peasant women of West Bengal have taken part in large numbers in the movement for land or for a better share of the harvest. On many occasions they have been joined by women from urban areas. The tebhaga movement which started on the eve of independence and the militant peasant struggle at Dongajora, Chandanpiri, Sankrail, Dubirveri, and Kakdwip could be cited as instances.[53] Women have likewise rallied on the occasions of strikes in factories and offices.[54]

The demand for more jobs, equal pay with men, better working conditions, more hospitals and schools, and extensive facilities for free and better education, adult literacy, and technical training have roused women in their hundreds.[55]

On numerous occasions the women of West Bengal have come together to demand legislation for ending social oppression. The most spectacular was the support given to the Hindu Code Bill. The proposal to give the right of inheritance and divorce to Hindu women had evoked a storm of opposition from conservative circles who made an attempt to create public opinion against the Hindu Code Bill. Women's organizations including the AIWC and the Mahila Atmaraksha Samiti united in a great campaign in support of the Bill.

Different women's organizations joined hands again to support the Dowry Bill. Besides holding meetings and demonstrations, they organized the despatch of letters and memoranda to the members of the second Parliament. In West Bengal, a memorandum signed by 25,000 people was presented to the Chief Minister, and one with 15,000 signatures was presented to the Prime Minister. Moreover, 5,000 postcards were sent from the State to the Union Law Minister in support of the Bill.[56] At the present moment also efforts are being made to build up public opinion against the outmoded custom of dowry which, instead of decreasing, has actually assumed larger proportions. Women's organizations are now demanding that the giving and the taking of dowry should be made a cognizable offence.[57]

The women of West Bengal have not remained indifferent to international issues. They have raised their voice against the murder of Patrice Lumumba and President Allende. They have risen to express solidarity with the people of Vietnam, Chile, and other countries. They have joined, in large numbers, demonstrations, meetings and conventions to condemn the U.S. blockade and bombing raids in North Vietnam.[58] Women in West Bengal were very active in the campaign for expressing solidarity with the people of Bangladesh and in helping the freedom fighters as well as the refugees. Many women's organizations joined to form a women's wing of the Bangladesh Mukti Sangram Samiti. They, as well as other women's organizations, arranged mammoth rallies to explain the issues connected with the Bangladesh struggle. Blood donations and financial contributions were collected and dispensaries were organized. It is true that many other calamities such as the riots in Assam and the floods in West Bengal, had evoked sympathetic response from the women, and they had helped generously in relief work. But their response on the occasion of the struggle in Bangladesh was not only massive but unprecedented as well.[59]

Laws That Protect Women[60]

Of the statutes adopted by the State legislature for safeguarding the interests of women, chronologically speaking, the first place was occupied by the West Bengal Maternity Benefit (Tea Estates) Act, 1948 (33 of 1948). This statute had to be amended twice within a few years: in 1950 and 1959, under the provisions of the West Bengal Maternity Benefit (Tea Estates) Amended Acts (Acts 12 of 1950 and 9 of 1959). But the Act subsequently became repugnant to a Central Act, the Maternity Benefit Act, 1961, and so was rendered void. In the fifties the State legislature had to adopt three more amendment Acts: the Bengal Nurses (West Bengal Amendment) Act, 1950 (21 of 1950), the Bengal Nurses (West Bengal Amendment) Act, 1951 (12 of 1951), and the Bengal Nurses (Amendment) Act, 1956 (5 of 1956).

Women in the State have benefited by the provisions of at least two more statutes adopted within a decade of the attainment of independence: the Lady Dufferin Victoria Zenana Hospital Act, 1955 (16 of 1955) and the West Bengal Panchayat Act, 1957 (1 of 1957). The first Act provided for the transfer of the Lady Dufferin Zenana Hospital in Calcutta to the State of West Bengal. The Act provided, inter alia, for the division of the cash assets including securities, of the Countess of Dufferin Fund, Bengal branch, into two parts – one part, being three-fourths of the whole of such assets, was to be utilized only within West Bengal. The income out of this part of the assets would be utilized 'mainly to provide for medical tuition including teaching and training in West Bengal of women as physicians, surgeons, hospital assistants, nurses and midwives, to provide for them during the period of tuition, hostels and residence under suitable control and to establish, endow and make provision benefit of women students and trainees towards studying or being trained to become physicians, surgeons, hospital assistants, nurses or midwives'. [Section 5(2) proviso]

The Panchayat Act stated that the functions of a gram panchayat would include those which the State government might assign to it in respect of 'rural dispensaries, health centres and maternity, and child welfare centres' [Section 32(1)(b)]. It may be stated here that the Act which has recently been adopted for reorganizing the village panchayats – the West Bengal Panchayat Act, 1973 (41 of 1973) – also contains the same provision [Section 20(1)(b)]. The new Act also provides for the nomination of women as members of the panchayat bodies. Section 210 of the Act says: 'The State Government may appoint two women to be members of any Gram Panchayat, Panchayat Samiti or Zilla Parishad: provided that (a) no such appointment shall be made if two women have been elected to such Gram Panchayat or Panchayat Samiti or Zilla Parishad, as the case may be, under the provisions of this Act; and (b) one such appointment shall be made if only one woman has been elected to such Gram Panchayat or Panchayat Samiti or Zilla Parishad, as the case may be, under the provisions of this Act.'

An important statute which seeks to safeguard the interests of some working women in the State is the West Bengal Shops and Establishments Act, 1963 (13 of 1963). The Act says that 'no woman shall be allowed or permitted to work – (a) in any establishment for public entertainment or amusement other than a cinema or a theatre, after 6 o'clock post-meridiam, or (b) in any shop or commercial establishment, after 8 o'clock post-meridian' (Section 10). The Act also provides for the maternity leave of women working in a shop or establishment in accordance with such rules as may be prescribed [Section 11(d)].

Any discussion on the West Bengal statutes which safeguard the interests of women would remain incomplete without a reference to a President's Act enacted in 1971: the West Bengal Employees' Payment of Compulsory Gratuity Act, 1971 (7 of 1971). The Act provides for a uniform scheme of retirement benefit for employees engaged in factories, plantations, or shops and establishments, and for matters connected with such benefit. While defining the term 'family' in relation to an employee, either male or female, the Act says that 'if a female employee, by a notice in writing to the controlling authority, expresses her desire to exclude her husband from her family, the husband and his dependent parents shall no longer be deemed, for the purposes of this Act, to be included in the family of such female employees unless the said notice is subsequently withdrawn by such female employee' [Section 2(g) *proviso*].

Towards a New Life

The legal status of women has indeed changed to a large extent. But, as Myrdal has correctly stated, 'only in the exceptional instance has there been any significant change in their actual condition...not much has changed, particularly in the rural areas, where 80 per cent of the people live'.[61]

The percentage of literacy among women has undoubtedly increased since independence. But the rate of increase is unfortunately not at all impressive. During the two decades following 1951, there has been an increase by only 9.69%. The status of urban middle class women has certainly improved and the urge for economic independence is fairly widespread today. But women agriculture workers are generally unpaid helpers of their families. Laws relating to the working conditions of women means little to them. The economic independence achieved by many urban middle class women is even today beyond the dreems of the vast majority of the women in the villages.[62]

In various other spheres women today suffer from numerous social and economic disabilities. Some remnants of feudal oppression still exist. As Jawaharlal Nehru rightly stated: 'A country's progress can best be judged by the status of the women in that country and the opportunities given to them. Law helps and is important, but something much more than legal changes are necessary to bring about basic social changes...We must remember that social changes must come from below and cannot be merely imposed from the top'.[63]

Since independence there has certainly been a stir of new life in West Bengal, but it has not broken out in manifold expressions in the case of women. Women belonging to various organizations have launched a conscious movement against different forms of oppression. The work of all these organizations has not always been confined to feminist aims alone, or to running constructive work centres. A beginning has indeed been made. But much still remains to be done. Women's organizations in West Bengal must raise the level of consciousness of women in general regarding their rights as women, citizens and workers. They have to fight for broadening the mental horizons of both men and women. They have to struggle hard for changing those feudal attitudes and beliefs which are still prevalent in society.

References

1. *Zhensochinv Mira V Borbe Za Sotsialniv Progress*, Moscow, 1972, p. 173.
2. *West Bengal*, A periodical published by the Government of West Bengal, Vol. XVII, No. 26, 15 April 1972.
3. E. Katz and P.F. Lazarsfeld, "Personal Influence" in H. Eulau et. al. (eds.), *Political Behaviour*, Amerind, New Delhi, 1972, pp. 249-251.
4. *Amrita Bazar Patrika*, Calcutta, 4 January 1952.
5. *Ibid.*, 9 January 1952.
6. *Ibid.*, 10 February 1969.
7. Government of West Bengal, *Statistical Handbook,* 1970, p. 118.
8. Though the Act was passed by the West Bengal Legislature in 1956, it received the President's assent in January, 1957, and was published in the *Calcutta Gazette* on 24 January 1957, as Act I of 1957.
9. *Amrita Bazar Patrika*, Calcutta, 3 and 8 July 1947.
10. Based on interview with Renuka Roy.
11. *Programme of the United Front*, 1969, paragraph 22.
12. *Ibid.*, paragraph 41 (g).
13. Based on an interview with a former associate of the (CPI(M-L).
14. *Proceedings of the All-National Conference of the Revolutionary Socialist Party*, Vol. 2, Report and Theses on Current National Political Situation, New Delhi, December 1972, p. 45.
15. Based on interviews with Gayatri Dasgupta and Menoka Basu Roy, leaders of the Socialist Unity Centre.

16. *India's Path: Socialist Revolution*, Manifesto of the Workers Party of India, chapter 8, paragraph 213.
17. Based on interview with Aparajita Goppi, leader of the Forward Bloc.
18. Based on an interview with Pratima Basu, Vice-President, Paschim Banga Pradesh Congress Committee and President, Pradesh Congress Mahila Samiti.
19. *Ananda Bazar Patrika*, Calcutta, 24 January 1974.
20. *Ibid.*, 17 January 1974.
21. *Report* of the Calcutta District Council of the Communist Party of India, Women's Department, 1971.
22. *New Age*, New Delhi. 9 February 1958 and 26 April 1959.
23. Communist Party of India, *Problems of Peace and Socialism*, Vol. 2, No. 3, March, 1974, pp. 54, 161, and Nadezhlla Tatarinove, *Women in the Land of Lenin* (Bengali edition), Soviet Desh Booklet, 1973, p. 78.
24. *Report* of the Calcutta District Council of the Communist Party of India, Women's Department, 1971.
25. *Political-Organisational Report* of the Central Committee to the 8th Congress of the Communist Party of India (Marxist), Cochin, December, 1968, pp. 304-05.
26. Based on an interview with a former associate of the CPI(M-L).
27. Based on interview with Mani Chakravarty, Secretary, Calcutta unit of the Revolutionary Socialist Party.
28. Based on interviews with Geeta Sengupta and Dr. Buddhadeb Bhattacharya, leaders of the Revolutionary Socialist Party.
29. Based on interviews with Gayatri Dasgupta, Menoka Basu Roy, and Subir Basu Roy, leaders of the Socialist Unity Centre, West Bengal.
30. Based on interview with Jyoti Bhattacharya, leader of the Workers Party.
31. Based on interview with Nirmal Bose, leader of the Forward Bloc.
32. Based on interview with a leader of the Congress (O).
33. Women's Coordinating Council, West Bengal, *Annual Reports*, 1970-71, 1972-73.
34. All India Women's Conference, *Souvenir, 1927-70*, pp. 19-20.
35. Based on interview with Renuka Roy, President, Women's Coordinating Council, West Bengal.
36. Renu Chakraborty, "The Women's Movement in India" in *Communism and Women*, Communist Party of India. New Delhi, August 1973, pp. 38-41.
37. Paschim Banga Mahila Atmaraksha Samiti, *Ninth Conference, Secretary's Report and Resolutions*, Calcutta, 1959.
38. Vimla Farooqi, "The National Federation of India Women – Its Aims and Activities" in *Souvenir*. The National Federation of Indian Women, 8th Congress, Calcutta, December, 1973.
39. Paschim Banga Mahila Samiti, *Constitution and Rules*.
40. *Ibid.*
41. Based on interview with Vidya Munshi and Paschim Banga Mahila Samiti, Fourteenth State Conference, Decmber, 1972, *Secretary's Report*, p. 12.
42. National Federation of Indian Women, 6th State Conference of the West Bengal Branch, November, 1970, *Secretary's Report*.
43. Paschim Banga Ganatantrik Mahila Samiti, 14th State Conference 1973, *Report and Resolutions*, p. 30.
44. Based on interview with Kanak Mukherjee, editor, *Eksathe,* organ of the Paschim Banga Ganatantrik Mahila Samiti.

45. Paschim Banga Ganatantrik Mahila Samiti, 14th State Conference, 1973, *Report and Resolutions*, p. 90.
46. Pledge form of the Nikhil Banga Mahila Sangha.
47. Based on interview with Geeta Sengupta, leader of the Revolutionary Socialist Party and the Nikhil Banga Mahila Sangha.
48. Based on interviews with Gayatri Dasgupta and Menoka Basu Roy, leaders of the Socialist Unity Centre and the Mahila Sanskritik Sangha.
49. Based on interview with Jyoti Bhattacharya, leader of the Workers' Party.
50. Based on interview with Aparajita Goppi, leader of the Forward Bloc and the Paschim Banga Agragami Mahila Samiti.
    Amrita Bazar Patrika, Calcutta, 21 September, 1947; Paschim Banga Mahila Samiti (new), 13th Annual Conference, March, 1970, *Report* p. 22; Paschim Banga Mahila Samiti, 14th Annual Conference, December, 1972, *Secretary's Report*, p. 10.
52. See for example *New Age*, New Delhi, 22 September, 6 October, 1957; 11 May, 5 October, 1958; 30 July, 20 August, 1967; *Ananda Bazar Patrika*, Calcutta, 6 March 1974; *The Statesmen*, Calcutta, 12 March 1974; National Federation of Indian Women, *Report to 8th Congress*, December, 1973.

Appendix

Extracts from *Towards Equality – Report of the Committee on the Status of Women in India*, Government of India, Department of Social Welfare, Ministry of Education and Social Welfare, New Delhi, December 1974.

1.03 The Preamble to the Constitution of India resolved to secure to all its citizens: Justice, social, economic and political; Liberty of thought, expression, belief, faith and worship; Equality of status and opportunity; and to promote among them all Fraternity ensuring the dignity of the individual and of the Nation.

1.04 To attain these national objectives, the Constitution guarantees certain fundamental rights and freedoms such as freedom of speech, protection of life and personal liberty. While these may be termed positive rights, the negative rights are the prohibition of discrimination or denial of equal protection.[1]

1.05 Indian women are the beneficiaries of these rights in the same manner as Indian men. Article 14 ensures "equality before law" and Article 15 "prohibits any discrimination". There is only one specific provision in Article 15(3), which empowers the State to make "any special provision for women and children", even in violation of the fundamental obligation of non-discrimination among citizens, *inter alia* of sex. This provision has enabled the State to make special provision for women, particularly in the field of labour legislation like the Factories Act, the Mines Act[2] etc. These special provisions in favour of women need not be restricted to measures which are beneficial in the strict sense, and therefore, the provision upholding that a man is punished for adultery but not a woman was regarded as not being distriminatory.[3]

1.06 Article 16(1) guarantees "equality of opportunity for all citizens in matters relating to employment, or appointment to any office under the State". And Article 16(2) forbids discrimination "in respect of any employment of office under the State" on the grounds only of "religion, race, caste, sex, descent, place of birth, residence or any one of them". The obligation not to discriminate in matters relating to employment or appointment to any office under the State has thus at least normatively ensured a significant position and status to Indian women. However, the Supreme Court recently dismissed *in limine* a writ petition of a women lawyer who challenged her being prevented from employment in the Judge Advocate General's office for a 5 year short service commission in the law branch. The reasons given by the Government for barring women from

---

[1]Basu, *Commentary on the Constitution of India* (3rd edition), p. 69.
[2]Infra Chapter V for details.
[3]Yusuf v. State of Bombay 1954 S.C. 398.

applying were that "they are required to travel by rail, road, and river, sometimes for long periods at a stretch; they will have to be present in Court Martial where judge, accused and witnesses will all be males, and that lady advocates are required to study life of soldiers (all males) in Army Units for several months". The Government failed to appreciate the fact that these same grounds would also apply to the nursing and medical corps of the Army where women are employed.

1.07 In this context we would like to mention that during the tenure of Shri Charan Singh as Chief Minister, and under his instruction, the Government of Uttar Pradesh attempted a direct violation of this constitutional provision. In reply to a question asked in the Uttar Pradesh Vidhan Sabha on 16 July 1971, the State Government admitted that "in June 1970, the State Government sent a letter to the Government of India stating that women officers should not be admitted to the Indian Administrative Service. If that was not possible, then at least they should not be sent to this State.[4]

Though this attempt did not succeed, it is a pointer that vigilance is necessary to ensure that the special provision permitted under Article 15(3) is not used to the detriment of women by legislative or executive action.

1.08 The Directive Principles of State Policy enunciated in Part IV of the Constitution embody the major policy goals of a welfare State. They concretize, together with the Chapter on Fundamental Rights, the constitutional vision of a new Indian socio-political order. The Directive Principles are declared as non-justiciable; but "nevertheless fundamental in the governance of the country", and the State is charged with "a duty ... to apply these principles in making laws" (Article 37). The Directive Principles were made non-enforceable in courts because it was felt that their fulfilment would be spread over a time-dimension of a few decades. The constitutional values embodied in the Fundamental Rights chapter needed immediate implementation; but in the case of the Directive Principles, this was not possible save at the cost of the viability of the State.

1.09 Juridically, the Directive Principles are a vital part of Indian Constitutional Law. Like the Preamble, they reflect high ideals of a liberal democratic polity; they are meant to be used by all agencies of the State as guidelines to action as major goals of policy; courts can use them as a body of values and standards of relevant to the act of judicial choice-making. But the Directive Principles confer no power or legislative competence; nor can they give rise to a cause of action for which remedy is available in a court of law. The principles in themselves do not confer power, bestow rights or create remedies. At the same time, they cannot be amended, save through the prescribed procedure. Some of them concern women indirectly or by necessary implication. A few are, as it were, "women-specific".[5] In the first category fall:

(a) the omnibus provision of Article 38 which in brief directs the State to

---

[4]Asha Goel v. Union of India.

[5]Baxi, Upendra, "Constitutional Provisions relating to Status of Women – an analytical examination", Paper prepared for the Committee.

Appendix

secure a just social, political and economic order, geared to promote the welfare of the people; Art. 39(b) (c) and (f) distribution of ownership and control of material resources of the community for the common good, prevention of concentration of wealth and means of production to the common detriment, and protection of childhood and youth against exploitation and moral and material abandonment; Art. 40 (organisation of village panchayats to promote self-government); Art. 41 (right to work, education and public assistance in cases of unemployment, oldage, sickness, disablement and other types of undeserved wants); Art. 43 (provision of work, a living wage, conditions of work ensuring a decent standard of life and full enjoyment of leisure, of social and cultural opportunities, and the promotion of cottage industries); Art. 44 (uniform Civil Code); Art. 45 (free and compulsory education for all children up to the age of 14; and Art. 47 (raising the level of nutrition and the standard of living of the people and improvement of public health).
(b) Directive Principles which concern women directly and have a special bearing on their status; these include Art. 39(a) right to an adequate means of livelihood for men and women equally); Art. 39(d) (equal pay for equal work for both men and women); 39(e) (protection of health and strength of workers – men, women and children – from abuse and entry into avocations unsuited to their age and strength); and Art. 42 (just and humane conditions of work and maternity relief).

1.10 As already mentioned, the Fundamental Rights and the Directive Principles are the instruments to attain our national objectives of Justice, Liberty and Equality. By adopting the principle of adult franchise, it seeks to establish a democratic republic by giving the adult population direct or indirect share in the Government.

1.11 The special attention given to the needs and problems of women, to enable them to enjoy and exercise their constitutional equality of status, along with other specific provisions relating to the hitherto suppressed sections of our society have led many scholars to describe the Indian Constitution as a "social" document embodying the objectives of social revolution. There is no doubt that the Constitution contemplates attainment of an entirely new social order by making deliberate departures in norms and institutions of democratic governance from the inherited, social, political and economic systems. In doing so the Constitution assigns primacy to law as an instrument of directed social change. It thus demands of the legislature, the executive and the judiciary, continuous vigilance and responsiveness to the relationship between law and social transformation in contemporary India.

*   *   *

Indicators of Political Attitudes

7.39 Relative differences in the political attitudes of men and women have been studied by various scholars and form a feature of most of our political literature since independence. Certain broad trends can be discerned, the most important of which are mentioned below. The point which emerges in the very beginning of our analysis is that there is no single homogeneous pattern. Levels of political awareness vary from region to region, from class to class and from community to community, and are conditioned greatly by the political culture of the area, the approach of the political parties to the women and quality of local leadership.

7.40 It is generally held that political awareness varies with the levels of modernisation in a given area, with concomitant factors such as literacy rates, education and exposure to urbanisation and mass media. This correlation however seems more apparant than real, as proved by studies in different regions.

7.41 We have already pointed out the distinction in the influence of literacy and education on awareness and participation. While the former is generally found to be an important determinant for both awareness and participation, education does not command a similar influence. While a correlation can be established between education and awareness, this does not always extend to participation. We have also noted that similarly, urbanization alone cannot be identified with high political awareness or participation.[15] In terms of urban rural variables, there is no significant difference in political awareness.

7.42 On an average, working women including professionals indicate a higher degree of awareness, but this is not necessarily reflected in their participation.[16] There is a uniform finding from different regions regarding the complaint of urban middle class women that they find their family responsibilities a handicap to political participation.[17]

7.43 There is no positive relationship between higher socio-economic status and degree of awareness. We may cite a few illustrations from Prof. Sirsikar's study – in Gujarat, the high income group women are less aware and participate less in the political process; in Maharashtra, the higher the socio-economic status – other factors being equal – lesser is the proportion of women who participate. This is further borne out by the apathy of professionals with high socio-economic status.[18] By and large, politics constitutes a peripheral interest for women from this stratum, though a significant number of women legislators come from an affluent background.

7.44 Most studies on political behaviour have so far held that women are considerably influenced by their husbands and family wishes in political matters. During the course of our tours, however, we received ample evidence that this pattern is beginning to change and many women now exercise considerable autonomy in using their right of franchise.[19] They emphasise their ability to do so because of the secrecy of the ballot. Many women told

---

[15]This is borne out by many of the State Studies.

[16]Narain, I, *op. cit.* "Women Voters and Mid Term Poll (1971) – A Study of Attitudes, Awareness and Commitments" by Upretti, N. and Mathur, D.B.

[17]*Ibid.* Also Sirsikar, *op. cit.*

[18]Upretti & Mathur, *op. cit.*

[19]This is corroborated by some of the State profiles of women in politics prepared for the Committee.

us that though their husbands still try to influence their judgement "they can't find out whom we have really voted for". In rural areas the influence of village elders plays an important role in determining political choice which also influence the women's behaviour. Even in this, however, it would not be correct to describe this as a universal rule.

7.45 In spite of such changes, it is still evident that there is a difference in the level of political information and perception regarding implications of the right of franchise, etc. between men and women, both quantitatively and qualitatively. Most scholars have attributed this to the lack of interest shown by political parties in improving the political knowledge of women. Some have also levelled this charge against the women's organisations and pressure groups. A study of urban voters in Rajasthan provides an illustration – 44.5% of the women did not have any clearcut idea about their criterion for voting, 19.5% considered the personality of the candidate, 22.3% caste and family as a factor, while only 8.3% and 5.5% considered the party and the issues respectively.[20]

7.46 All the State profiles indicate one common trend – that women are more concerned with problems that affect their day-to-day lives. The issues are price rise, non-availability of essential commodities, hoarding and blackmarketing, adulteration, unemployment and poverty. On several occasions during the last five years, women, have organised protest against these problems.

7.47 There are indications of a growing trend of disillusionment with the political process among women. This may be partly attributed to their reactions against the prevalence of corruption and inefficiency in political circles but a great deal of such attitudes is on account of their feelings of ineffectiveness in solving problems which affect their lives. According to a study conducted in West Bengal, about 25% of the respondents stated that having votes has not helped women and even men. About 8% stated that they would not vote on principle since it did not help in any way.[21] Another study done in Rajasthan in 1971 showed that 42% of the women interviewed including housewives and working women, supported revolution for social progress as opposed to the "ritual" of education.[22] The majority of respondents in this study felt that the problems of the country needing solution in order of priority were as follows: 1) employment and poverty; 2) rising prices; 3) corruption; and 4) law and order.

7.48 The freedom movement and the period immediately succeeding

---

[20]Bhambhri, C.P. and Verma, P.S., *The Urban Voter,* 1973, p. 149.

[21]Banerji, Nirmala, "Politicisation and Participation of Women in West Bengal" (Undertaken for the Committee).

[22]Upretti and Mathur, *op. cit.*

Note: As has been indicated, our findings regarding women in political attitudes are based mainly on our discussions with different groups of women during our tours and on the results of studies on political attitudes and behaviour in different parts of the country. Since such studies are a new development in India, they suffer from obvious limitations. Most of them are micro-studies limited to particular regions. Nor are such studies available for all States.

independence brought the involvement and commitment of women in the political process. However, the institutionalisation of this process resulted in difference in perception of goals and methods of achievement. The absence of a movement in the period after independence explains the low involvement of women in the political process. Such involvement is however always visible during national emergencies.

7.49 It was repeatedly brought to our notice that the unity between political, economic and social issues that characterised the freedom movement was one of the causes for women's high degree of participation. The divorce between social problems that affect women directly, and the political process, has been one of the major causes of women's lower participation in politics in recent years.

* * *

7.95 Our findings indicate that women's participation in the political process has shown a steady increase, both in elections and in their readiness to express their views on issues directly concerning their day-to-day life. But their ability to produce an impact on the political process has been negligible because of the inadequate attention paid to their political education and mobilisation by both political parties and women's organisations. The structures of the parties make them male-dominated and in spite of outstanding exception, most partymen are not free from the general prejudices and attitudes of the society. They have tended to see women voters and citizens as appendages of the males and have depended on the heads of families to provide block-votes and support for their parties and candidates.

7.96 The entire exercise of our Committee has indicated that in certain important areas and for certain sections of the female population there has been some regression from the normative attitudes developed during the freedom movement. Evidence of this has been given in Chapters III and V. Large sections of women have suffered a decline of economic status. Every legal measure designed to translate the Constitutional norm of equality or special protection into actual practice has had to face tremendous resistance from the legislative and other elites. Even after the promulgation of these laws, the protection enjoyed by the large masses of women from exploitation and injustice is negligible. As an example we would like to mention the cases of persecution of Harijan women that have increased in recent years. Among women themselves the leadership and the attitudes of the elites, social or political, have become diffused and diverse with sharp contradiction in their regard and concern for the inequalities that affect that status of women in every sphere.

7.97 We are, therefore, forced to observe that all the indicators of participation, attitudes and impact come up with the same results – the resolution in social and political status of women for which constitutional equality was to be only the instrument, still remains a very distant objective. While there is no doubt that the position of some groups of women have changed for the better by opening to them positions of power and dignity, the large masses of women continue to lack spokesmen who understand their

Appendix

special problems and be committed to their removal, in the representative bodies of the State.

7.98 From the point of view, though women do not numerically constitute a minority, they are beginning to acquire the features of a minority community by the three recognised dimensions of inequality: Inequality of class (economic situation), status (social position) and political power. If this trend is allowed to continue the large masses of women in India may well emerge as the only surviving minority, continuously exposed to an injustice.

7.99 The chasm between the values of a new social order proclaimed by the Constitution and the realities of contemporary Indian society as far as women's rights are concerned remains as great as at the time of independence. The right to political equality has not enabled women to play their role as partners and constituents in the political process, because we have forgotten Gandhiji's warning not to treat political rights as an end in itself but only as a means.

7.100 Instead, these rights have helped to build an illusion of equality and power which is frequently used as an argument to resist special protective and acceleratory measures to enable women to achieve their just and equal position in society. It is surprising that in spite of the special powers provided by Article 15(3) of the Constitution[35] almost no efforts have been made to redress the unequal status of women in different spheres. We have frequently heard the view that the greatest indicator of the status of women in this country is that it has been ruled by a woman for the last 9 years. We are compelled to disagree with this view because in our opinion this is not an indicator of the real status of women in this country.

7.101 Though at the public level there are a number of women who recognised and advocate the desirability of giving equal opportunities to women in economic and political spheres, the norms and attitudes regarding women's role in society remain traditional. In this sense, the new rights proved to be only concessional. Thus it is clear that despite certain legal and even institutional changes, the final legitimation for a successful reorganisation of society lies in a revolution in norms and attitudes in the minds of the people. The recommendations that we make are out of a desire to make the political rights of women more functional as required by the needs of a democratic system.

THE QUESTION OF RESERVATION OF SEATS FOR WOMEN IN LEGISLATIVE BODIES

7.102 Before we take up our recommendations we have to record our views

---

[35] Article 15(1), "The State shall not discriminate against any citizen on grounds only of religion, race, caste, place of birth or any of them ... (3) Nothing in this article shall prevent the State from making any special provision for women and children."

The only measures for the special protection of women taken up by Government since independence are in the field of labour laws. It should be noted that these were also recommended by various conventions of the International Labour Organisation.

on a suggestion to which we have given considerable thought. In the course of our tours we received a demand from groups of women in some States for a system of reservation for women in the legislative bodies in the States and in Parliament. We summarise their arguments below:

7.103 (A) The difficulties being experienced by women in obtaining adequate representation and spokesmen of their cause in these bodies, and the declining trend in the number of women legislations is the result of the reluctance of political parties to sponsor women candidates. The parties reflect the established values of a male-dominated society, which would be difficult to alter without certain structural changes in the socio-political set-up. The parties would continue to pay lip service to the cause of women's progress and the policy of "tokenism" by having a few women in the legislative and executive wings of government whose minority and dependent status offer serious obstacles of their acting as spokesmen for women's rights and opportunities.

7.104 (B) If this process continues over a period of time more and more women, losing faith in the political process to change their condition in life, may opt out of the political system and become either passive partners or rebels. In the present context in India the greater majority would undoubtedly follow the first path because most of them have not shaken off the feelings of subjugation and inferiority generated by centuries of subordination.

7.105 (C) A system of reservation of a proportion of seats for women in these bodies would provide an impetus to both the women as well as to the political parties to give a fairer deal to nearly half the population in the various units of Government. If women enter these bodies in larger numbers the present inhibitions that result from their minority position in these institutions may disappear faster and give them greater freedom to articulate their views.

7.106 (D) A system of reservation may also increase the women legislators' sense of responsibility and concern for the problems affecting women, thus ensuring the presence of a body of spokesmen of the women's cause in the representative bodies of the States. Such a system would also help to increase the degree of political modernisation of women both in the electorate and within the parties.

7.107 Support for reservation also came from a group of scholars who undertook an examination of women's role in the political process at the Committee's request. We summarise their views below:

7.108 (a) The process of Indian women coming into their own "politically" has been slow and halting because Indian political culture is a political, and the force of tradition has been particularly against participation of women in politics. Improving the political status of women in an integral aspect of the over-all problem of socio-economic change and "broadening the political elite structure". At a later stage of development changes in the socio-economic order may buttress changes in the political status of women but "it has to be the other wayround in present day India".[36]

[36]Narain, I., Political Status of Women in India – Introduction.

Appendix

7.109 (b) The failure of Indian society to "look upon women's participation with sympathy and understanding" is an exceedingly retarding factor in political socialisation of both men and women. A 30% reservation of seats in the legislative bodies for women will alter the very character of our legislature and will compel the political parties to change their strategies and tactics and induce them to given women their due. Reservation of seats for women cannot lead to their becoming "isolated pockets in the nation", because "women are not marginal to society as a majority group might be". It could, instead lead to increase in women's participation and motivate them to shoulder their political responsibilities.[37]

7.110 If "access to policy making powers and facilities is a component of social status" then the presence of more women in the legislatures will help to direct rate and type of changes in the position of women. Only a system of reservation, increasing the number of women representatives will help to broaden the base of women's representation in the legislative bodies.

7.111 Such a transitional measure to break through the existing structure of inequalities will not be retrogression "from the doctrine of equality of sexes and the principle of democratic representation" and may serve the long-term objectives of equality and democracy in a better manner than the present system where inequalities get intensified. As compared to the situation before independence when with a system of reservation women constituted 3.3% of the membership of the central legislature, the average proportion of women in Parliament since 1952 without reservation has been roughly 4%. The existing limitation on the role being played by this minority of women legislators may increase if their number declines further with the continuation of the already recognised trend in this direction.

7.112 We however received a strong opposition to the suggestion from representatives of political parties and most women legislators. They felt that any system of special representation would be a retrograde step from the equality conferred by the Constitution. There was also some resistance to women being equated with the socially backward communities as all women do not suffer from the same disabilities as these under-privileged groups. The representatives of some parties however did not have any strong objection to reservation of seats for woman in local bodies for which certain precedents were already existing.

7.113 Though we have to record that the problem of under representation of woman in the representative bodies of the State both quantitatively and qualitatively is a real one, after considering the matter very seriously we find ourselves unable to recommend and system of reservation to the State Assemblies and Parliament. Our reasons for rejecting the suggestion are summarised below:
(a) The woman's cause in India has always been championed by all progressive elements, men as well as women. A climate favourable for the betterment of women's status can best be created by their joint efforts.
(b) So far women have served as representatives of the people. Separate constituencies for women would narrow their outlook.

[37]Sirsikar, V.M., *Politicisation of Women in India.*

(c) There is a fallacy in the entire argument for separate representation for women. Women's interests as such cannot be isolated from economic, social and political interests of groups, strata and classes in the society. In point of fact the problems connected with status of women are linked with formulation, articulation and modalities of the realisation of other interests.
(d) Such a system of special representation may precipitate similar demands from various other interests and communities and threaten national integration.
(e) Experience has shown that the privilege of reservation once granted, is difficult to withdraw. This would amount to perpetuation of unequal status.
(f) Women have been competing as equals with men since 1952. They must continue to do so and stand on their own merits and intensify their political and social life. A departure from this equality now will be a retrograde step.
(g) The minority argument cannot be applied to women. Women are not a community, they are a category. Though they have some real problems of their own, they share with men the problems of their groups, locality and community. Women are not concentrated in certain areas confined to particular fields of activity. Under these circumstances, there can be no rational basis for reservation for women.

7.114 We do not think it would be proper for us to suggest such a major change in our political structure on the basis of the rather insubstantial evidence that we have received.

7.115 Even though we did not accept the suggestions for reservation for women in Parliament or the State Legislature, we find that in order to provide greater opportunities to women to actively participate in the decision-making process, it is imperative to recognise the true nature of the social inequalities and disabilities that hamper them. This can best be achieved by providing them with special opportunities for participation in the representative structures of local Government. The necessity to associate women representatives in local self-governing bodies is already accepted in this country and provision for reservation of seats for women through either election, co-option or nomination in these bodies exist in most of the State legislations that govern the constitution of these bodies.

7.116 It has been our experience, however, that this association, with the exception of a few areas is mostly regarded as a form of "tokenism". We feel that the time has come now to move out of this token provision for women's representation to a more meaningful association of women in the structure of local administration.

A second reason for this is the general apathy and indifference of these local bodies of women's development and change of status which has been reported to us by women's organisations and welfare and extension workers, particularly in rural areas. It may be noted that a large number of Mahila Mandals have been organised in both rural and urban areas through the initiative of welfare organisations like the Central Social Welfare Board and its State agencies, Ministry of Agriculture and Community Development and voluntary bodies like the Bharatiya Grameen Mahila Sangh. The status of these bodies is purely voluntary. Some of their members have acquired both experience and interest in developmental activities, but they are not representatives and their constitution does not result in associating or involving large majority of women in these activities. Nor do these bodies receive complaints of neglect and lack of funds for women's programmes from women workers throughout the country. This was confirmed by specialists working in the field of Community Development and Panchayati Raj.

7.117 We therefore recommend the establishment of Statutory Women's Panchayats at the village level to ensure greater participation by women in the political process. These bodies are not meant to be parallel organisations to the Gram Panchayats but should form an integral part of the Panchayati Raj structure, with autonomy and resources of their own for the management and administration of welfare and development programmes for women and children.

We recommend them as a transitional measure to break through the traditional attitudes in rural society which inhibit most women from articulating their problems or participating actively in the existing local bodies. An exclusively women's body would eliminate this difficulty and provide opportunity to more women to gain experience and confidence in managing their own affairs. Their enhanced legal status, we believe, will have a direct impact on the general status of women in rural society and their increasing experience and responsibility may be expected to improve women's keenness and capacity for greater participation in the political process. Lastly, the existence of such statutory bodies would help to ensure better co-ordination of various Government services and programmes for women at the level of implementation. Like the Panchayats, these bodies could be directly elected by the women of the village and should have the right to send their representatives to the Panchayat Samities and/or Zila Parishads. To ensure a viable relationship between the existing Gram Panchayats and the proposed women's panchayats, the Chairman and Secretary of both these bodies should be ex officio members of the other.

2. At the level of municipalities the principle of reservation of seats for women is already prevalent in certain states. We therefore recommend that this should be adopted by all states as a transitional measure.

We also recommend the constitution of permanent committees in municipalities to initate and supervise programmes for women's welfare and development.

3. We recommend that political parties should adopt a definite policy regarding the percentage of women candidates to be sponsored by them for elections to Parliament and State Assemblies. While they may initially start with 15%, this should be gradually increased so that in time to come the representation of women in the Legislative bodies has some relationship to their position in the total population of the country or the State.

4. We further recommend the inclusion of women in all important committees, commissions or delegations that are appointed to examine socio-economic problems.

NOTES OF DISSENT ON THE QUESTION OF RESERVATION OF SEATS FOR WOMEN

I do not agree with the first paragraph of the second recommendation regarding the reservation of seats at the level of municipalities in Chapter VII on Political Status for the same reason for which reservation of seats for women in Assemblies and Parliament was not recommended. I feel that women along with men form a part of society. Even if this reservation of separate seats for women is for a transitional period, in my opinion, it will not be of help in increasing women's participation as a whole. There is a possibility that reservation of seats will only help women of a particular class who are already privileged. It should be our aim to see that the masses of women of all classes become equal partners with men in all senses in society. Separate seats will weaken the position of women. They must come up on the strength of their own abilities and not through special provisions. It is only in this way that they will be in a better position vis-a-vis men and will be able to stand on their own as equal partners.

Apart from that, this type of reservation of seats might lead other communities/classes to argue for reservation of seats. This, to my mind, will encourage separatist tendencies and hamper national integration.

I feel very strongly that it is up to the leaders of the country, of all shades of political opinion and particularly women leaders who are already in positions of authority, to endeavour to see that women in large numbers are given seats and also to encourage women's participation. For this, it is absolutely necessary to provide facilities by which women may be prepared to take an active part in different elected bodies and also when elected, to function in a proper manner.

In municipalities, if seats are reserved for women, they represent the whole constituency and not only women. I agree that more women's participation in the municipalities and local bodies is needed. For that a well-thought-out system of education for women is to be planned and executed.

The sole consideration for selecting a representative must be seen from the viewpoint of efficiency as to who can serve the constituency better. It is not a question of representation of men or women. At the same time, in any elected body, even if the proportion of men and women is unequal, this does not prevent the elected body from functioning effectively or efficiently and also representing the entire society.

Women are an integral part of society. The provision of reservation of seats for women in municipalities will only serve to reinforce the separate identity of women rather than promote their representations and integration with the rest of society.

Phulrenu Guha

New Delhi
31 December 1974

* * *

Appendix

I am generally opposed to the system of reservation of seats in Legislatures and other elected bodies. It has no meaning, particularly in the case of women who constitute at least fifty per cent of the population. They have little representation in elected bodies, but giving them a nominal representation through reservation will not help them. It may even obstruct their progress as it may lead to complacency. Larger representation of women is essential in their own interest as well as in the interest of the society, but they should secure it by awakening women to their rights and responsibilities, and by creating public opinion in its favour. Efforts in that direction along with education to equip women to shoulder and discharge public responsibilities will prove of greater benefit to them than a few more seats secured through reservation.

Maniben Kara

* * *

As members of the pre-Independence generation, we have always been firm believers in equal rights for women. For us the recognition of this principle in the Constitution heralded the beginning of a new era for the women of this country. As we have never been supporters of special reservation or class representation in any form in academic discussions we had often criticised the system of reservation for Scheduled Castes and Scheduled Tribes, as a legacy of the colonial period which institutionalised the backwardness of certain sections of our population.

When we started out on this investigation, it had not even occurred to us to seek the opinion of the people about the system of representation provided in the Constitution. For us, it was a settled fact, embodying a principle of a democracy in which no change could be considered. This is why we never thought of including a question on this point in our questionnaire, nor did we think of asking this question of the people whom we interviewed during our early tours. Only when the problem kept being posed repeatedly before us by various groups of women in the course of our discussions did we become aware that a problem like this was real and very much in existence. The Committee has accepted the reality of the problem and our Report has presented both sides of the basic argument.

We regret our inability to agree with the Committee on the decision that was taken. While we, too, feel that our investigation and examination of this question was not adequate to recommend a major change in our system of representation, we consider that it would not be proper for us to turn our back on the pressing reality of the problem. A political system cannot be based on ideology alone, but must keep in touch with the actualities of the social situation and so adjust its operation as to achieve the desired goals of the society. The mechanics of a system, if they do not grapple with the needs of a society, can defeat the ultimate objective in the long run. It is for this reason that we are compelled to dissent from the Committee's decision on this point.

Our reasons for dissenting on this matter are consistent with the findings that ran throughout the Report, that despite progressive legal changes, the actual condition of life of the mass of Indian women has not changed much. The continuing under-representation of women prevents their proper participation in the decision-making process in the country. The success of a few in reaching positions of power and dignity may, to the uninformed eye, suggest the existence of full opportunity for such participation, but we have shown that this is far from so in the political process or in economic activity, in education and in general social status. The number of women elected to Parliament constitute less than 5% of the members. The proportion of women in the pre-Independence Central Legislature (elected under the Government of India Act 1935) was 3.4%. The infinitesimal gain of 1.6% in proportion over a quarter century (and the pattern has been a zig-zag one), when taken with the decline in the absolute number of representatives during the last ten years, is a sufficient indicator of the reluctance of our society to accept the principle of equal representation for women.

The second problem in a way stems from the inadequate representation of women in these bodies. The basic principle underlying universal franchise is the need to involve all classes and sections of the population in the process of decision-making so that the policy reflects the problems, needs, and aspirations of the whole of society, not of a limited group. Every democracy has to pass through this phase, when a limited group of persons, small in number as well as narrow in their class composition, acts as the voice of the people. The institution of universal franchise in the course of its functioning, should gradually expand the representative base of this group and alter its class composition. As Professor Sirsikar points out, this is already happening in the case of the male legislators in this country within the short period since Independence. In the case of the women, however, the story is quite different. More than 1/3rd of the women in Parliament belong to professional groups which means the urban middle class. Most of these members are college educated, and a fair number have overseas education as well. Quite a few of the women legislators in the States, as well as the Centre, belong to royal or zamindari families or have "agricultural interests" arising out of landed property. As compared to their male counterparts, the background of the women legislators is considerably narrower and represents mainly the dominant upper strata of our society.

Their restricted origin apart, Indian women legislators suffer from other inadequacies. A considerable number of them, as we were informed again and again, have not worked their way up in the political system from actual work among the people, but have been drafted into the system at different levels because of their contacts with persons in positions of power and influence. Our discussions with some individual members of this group revealed that they lacked enough awareness and understanding of the basic problems affecting the majority of women in our society. We were also told repeatedly that women members in the legislative bodies have not displayed adequate alertness and initiative in posing these problems before the Government, the legislatures of the people of this country. To cite a few examples, it is a regrettable fact, that in spite of the Law Commission's recommendations (15th Report of the Commission 1960) regarding the reforms needed in the Christian Law of Marriage and Divorce to ameliorate the disabilities of Christian women, the Bill was shelved without any dissenting voice from among the women members of Parliament. In the case of another recommendation of the Law Commission (41st Report – 1969), regarding reforms in the Criminal Procedure Code, to end the claim for maintenance to divorced wives, the law was passed, after specifically excluding Muslim women from this category. In this case, too, the women members of Parliament failed to register any protest against this injustice to a large section of women in our society.

In voicing our criticism we would not like it to be thought that we are merely condemning without understanding the difficulties under which our women legislators have to function. As we have pointed out, their small numbers and their dependence on the support of their political parties, which are all dominated by men, have aggravated their inhibitions and weaknesses in asserting righteous but unpopular causes. Most of us have had to experience the tremendous force of these inhibitions bred by cultural values over generations. It is far easier for a women to be outspoken when she is backed by a large group, than when she has to stand alone. We have also seen the courage with which some women have taken up the cudgels in defence of some unpopular causes, and the degree of social pressure, character assassination and social ostracism that they have had to face for such action. They deserve the admiration of the womenfolk of this country, but unless we can enlarge their ranks, it is our firm belief that the social revolution that Gandhiji had expected to be the end result of women's participation in the "political deliberations of the nation" will not be achieved.

The reasons given by our colleagues for rejecting the demand for reservation in the legislatures evade, in our opinion, the real issues and are based on an ideological principle which does not take into consideration the needs of women in present-day India. No one who has studied the history of the last 200 years would deny the signal contribution made by distinguished men to the women's cause. The greatest of them, however, always observed that the real cause of women's low status in this country lay "in men's interested teaching" and in women's acceptance of them. To believe that these champions of women's cause reflected the thinking of the majority of men in this country would be a travesty of history. If that had been the case, they would not have had to face the kind of social opposition that was unleashed on them at every step. It is certainly not expected that women alone will represent women; or progressive measures in their favour, just as men also do not do so. The fact that some men have managed to stand out in defence of women's rights shows that, with more women actively participating in the political process there will be more spokesmen with actual knowledge of women's problems. Larger numbers will also help to break the somewhat exclusive class composition of this group.

About the argument that the system of special representation might precipitate fissiparous tendencies, we cannot do better than quote Professor Sirsikar's answer. Anticipating this criticism, he observed: "women are not marginal to society as the minority group might be. They are not a dispensable part of the society – they are as essential as men for the very sustenance of the society." A system of reservation for women "would not create what is feared by the critics, isolated pockets... this may make exacting demands on women... but would motivate women to come forth to shoulder these responsibilities."

When one applies the principle of democracy to a society characterised by tremendous inequalities, such special protection are only spearheads to pierce through the barriers of inequality. An unattainable goal is as meaningless as a right that cannot be exercised. Equality of opportunities cannot be achieved in the face of the tremendous disabilities and obstacles which the social system imposes on all those sections whom traditional India treated as second class or even third class citizens. Our investigations have proved that the application of the theoretical principle of equality in the context of unequal situations only intensifies inequalities, because equality in such situations merely means privileges for those who have them already and not for those who need them.

Our colleagues did appreciate the reality of the problem of under-representation and the failure of the large majority of women to overcome social resistance to asserting their political and legal rights. This is implicit in the recommendations for the constitution of women's panchayats and for the reservation of seats for women in municipalities. We regret that they could not agree to the logical extension of the same principle to legislative bodies. We have been compelled to explain our decision at considerable length because we feel that the problem that we have posed requires careful consideration by all who strive for an eqalitarian and a just society.

Lotika Sarkar
Vina Mazumdar

31 December 1974

INDEX

Aaron, Gracy, 229
Adivasi women, 155, 210, 215
Adult franchise, 11, 12, 15, 16
Agarkar, Gopal Ganesh, 248
Agitational politics, 98, 102-3, 104-8, 210, 254
Agrani Mahila Parishad, 342
Aiyar, Mrs. Chandrasekhar, 5
Akhil Bharatiya Stri Shakti Sammelan, 258
All India Women's Conference, 3, 9-10, 11, 16, 213, 281, 284, 285, 287, 288, 289, 337, 338, 343
Alva, Smt., 225
Ammal, Rukmini, 182
Ammal, V. Kamalabai, 7
Ammukutty Amma, E., 227
Amrit Kaur, 17
Anand, J.C., 266
Anand Gram Society, 250
Anandabai, K., 183
Anandabai, T.E.S., 183
Anantagiri Panchayat Samithi, 188
Andhra Maha Sabha, 174
Andhra Mahila Sabha, 173-4
Andhra Pradesh Women's profiles, 173-90
Angelo, Mrs., Hannen, 8, 19
Arya Samaj Mahila Samiti (Punjab), 288
Asaf Ali, Aruna, 287
Assam Women's profiles, 191-9
Assam Mahila Samiti, 197
Ayesha Begam, 216, 217

Babar, Sarojini, 246
Baig, Tara Ali, 3
Balshastri, 248
Banerjee, Nirmala, 79, 140
Bengal, Vimalabai, 255
Bangladesh Mukti Sangram Samiti, 344
Benwal, Kamla, 300
Besant, Annie, 4, 5, 6
Bhagwat, Kamalabai, 246, 250

Bhambhri, C.P., 298, 302
Bharata Stree Mandal, 6
Bharatiya Mahila Federation, 254
Bhat, Yashodabai, 248
Bhatt, Urmilaben, 216, 218
Bhave, Vinoba, 258
Bose, Lady Abala, 5
Brar, Gurbinder Kaur, 278

Caste and politicization, 134-7, 140, 155
Chandramani, G.Y., 173
Chandrawat, Laxmi Kumari, 300-303
Chandrawati, 279
Charan Singh, 80
Chattopadhyay, Kamaladevi, 8, 19, 248
Chawla, Lakshmi Kant, 282
Cherian, Accamma, 230
Chinchalikar, Malatibai, 250
Chitambar, Mrs., 10
Chokhawala, Gordhandas, 213
Civil service
    Women members, 313
Committee on the Status of Women, 82
Communal Award (1932), 15
Constituent Assembly of India, 82, 316
Consumers' Action Forum, 338
Consumers' Guidance Society, 71
Cooption, 82
Cousins, Margaret, 4-5, 9, 11

Dandavate, Pramila, 246
Dang, Vimla, 283-287
Dange, Usha, 246, 250
Darji, Jhinabhai, 215
Dasappa, Yashodharamma, 221, 224, 225
Desai, Hitendra, 116, 212, 213, 216
Desai, Indira, 211
Desai, Morarji, 116, 201
Desai, Sonal, 211
Desh Sevika Sangh, 248
Deshmukh, Durgabai, 174, 190
Deshpande, Roza, 250, 255
Dolev, Lalit Kumar, 196, 198

Domestic pressures, 161-2
Dowager, Rani of Mandi, 10
Dowry, 167, 258-9, 292
Dubey, Bhagwat Rao, 291
Dubey, Swaroop Rani, 67
Dumasia, N.M., 6
Durgabai, 174, 178

Education and politicization, 128-30, 138, 140, 147-8, 165
Election campaign, 70-2, 99, 109, 200-1, 204, 230, 266, 267, 327
Election candidates, 32-41, 46-9, 67-8, 80, 88
    Andhra Pradesh, 177-80
    Assam, 191, 195-6
    Gujarat, 207-8
    Karnataka, 222-3
    Kerala, 232-7
    Maharashtra, 261-2
    Punjab, 270-6
    Rajasthan, 293, 295-7
    U.P., 309, 310
    West Bengal, 319
Election Commission, 26, 42, 72, 180
Eswaribai, 183

Faizi, A.A.A., 257
Family funds, 170
Family planning, 167
Female deities, 24
Female education, 5, 6, 9, 173, 200, 301
Female infanticide, 292
Forbes, Geraldine H., 3
Freedom movement
    Women's participation, 11-12, 24, 80, 174, 182, 226, 229-30, 248-9, 305-6

Gabhuru, Mula, 198
Gajawani, Nirmala, 214
Gandhi, Indira, 28, 33, 35, 41, 55, 63, 66, 68, 74, 116, 203, 258, 312
Gandhi, M.K., 11, 12, 14, 19, 20, 80, 115, 200, 201, 226, 229, 248, 291, 305, 306
Ganguly, Bangendu, 319
Gayatri Devi, 40, 41, 53, 59, 299-300, 303

Ghose, P.C., 330
Gill, Lachman Singh, 281
Goa liberation struggle, 257
Gokhale, Miss, 5
Gokhale, Avantikabai, 248
Gokhale, H.R., 211
Golvalkar (Guruji), 115
Gore, Mrinal 84, 250
Gouri, K.R., 227, 231, 240, 241, 242
Government of India Act (1919), 311
    Joint Select Committee, 6
Government of India Act (1935), 3, 268, 311
Gujarat
    Women's politicization, 79, 85-118
    Women's profiles, 200-20
Gujarat University
    Dept. of Political Science, 204
Gurnam Singh, 281

Hajrah Begum, 25
Hameeda Babibula Begum, 287
Hamid Ali, Mrs., 17
Hate, Chandrakala, 247
Hindi Agitation (Punjab), 288
Hindustani Sevika Dal, 248
Hingane Stri Shikshan Santha, 250
Home Rule League, 4, 6
Hospet, Kamlabai, 250
Husband/wife political differences, 127

Income and politicization, 148-9, 153-4, 165
Independent candidates, 33, 35, 39, 110, 191, 238
Indian Council of Social Science Research, 322
Indian Franchise Committee, 12-13, 15-16
Indian National Congress, 24, 25, 27, 33
    Fundamental rights resolution (1931), 12
    Support to women franchise, 6
Indira, D., 183
Inter-religious marriages, 291-2
Interest groups, 366-42
Iqbal Narain, 298
Istri Sabha (J & K), 71

Index

Iswari Amma, 229

Jacob, Lucy, 226
Jagdish Kaur, 275
Jaimati, Sati, 198
Jain, Lekhwati, 13
Jain, Om Prabha, 278, 279, 280, 281, 287
Jambhekar, 248
Jana Sangh Mahila Aghadi, 251-2
Janaki Amma, M.K., 229
Janaki Amma, P., 227
Jayaprada, B., 183
Jhaveri, Gangaben, 201
Jinaragadasa, Dorothy, 4, 5, 10
Johar system, 292
Joint Women's Action Committee, 254-256
Joshi, Dr. (Miss), 5
Joshi, Kumudben, 215
Joshi, N,M., 7
Jyoti Sangh, 213

K.K. Arts College, Ahmedabad, 211
Kala, Anasuya, 248
Kale, Anusayabai, 248
Kalichand, Ramnath, 256
Kallen, Matilda, 229
Kamadar, Ramiben, 248
Kamakshamma, Bathula, 173
Kamala Devi, M.K., 13
Kamala Prabha, 229
Kamalam, M., 227, 240
Kanakamma, Penaka, 173
Kantak, Prema, 217-248
Kara, Maniben, 248, 253
Karnataka
 Women's profiles, 221-5
Kartar Singh, Giani, 281
Kartyayani Amma, M., 229
Karve, Dhondo Keshav, 248
Kasturba Gandhi Memorial Trust, 197-8
Kasturba Mahila Ashram, 250
Kasturba Vidyalaya, Nellore, 173
Kelkar, Indumati, 246-250
Kerala
 Women's profiles, 226-45
Kerala Mahila Desa Savika Sangha, 230
Kerala Mahila Federation, 241-2
Khallat, Mrs., 227
Khanna, B.S., 266, 267, 276
Khedut Sangh (Gujarat), 211
Kogekar, S.V., 265
Kripalani, Sucheta, 41, 312
Krishnan, Devaki, 240
Kuktimalu Amma, A.V., 230
Kulkarni, Sumitra, 214
Kulwant Kaur, 279
Kumbha, Rana, 291
Kumudini Devi, Rani, 185
Kunhikvu Amma, C., 229
Kunhilakshmi Amma, 229
Kuruvilla, John, 230
Kuttimulu Amma, A.V., 227, 229, 231

Lakshamma, M.R., 221
Lakshmi Bai, Rani, 24
Lakshmibai, Sangam, 178, 182
Lakshmibayamma, Unnava, 173
Lakshmi Devi, 182-3
Lakshmikanthamma, T., 183
Lakshmipathi, Rukmini, 10
Language and politicization, 137-8, 155-7, 166
Lazarus, Mrs., 5
Leela Krishnan, C.K., 230
Legislative committees
 Women members, 183-4, 224, 299
Legislative measures
 Women's role, 280-1
 Assam, 192-4
 Gujarat, 201-2
 West Bengal, 344-6
Limaye, Anasuya, 246
Limaye, P.N., 119
Linlithgow, Lord
 Joint Select Committee, 16-17
Little Ladies of Brindavan, 173
Lok Sabha elections
 Women's participation, 24-50; Jaipur study, 51-66
Lok Stri Sabha, 286
Lokahitwadi, 248
Lothian Committee, 12-13, 15-16, 18

Madan Kaur, 300
Madhavi Amma, O.K., 227
Maha Gujarat agitation, 85, 203, 217
Maharashtra
    Women's politicization, 79, 119-39
    Women's profiles, 246-64
Maharashtra Rajya Shramik Mahila Samiti, 255-6
Mahila Atmarksha Samiti, 338, 343
Mahila Mudranalaya, 213
Mahila Sanskritik Sangha, 342
Mahishi, Sarojini, 225
Makwana, Shantaben, 214
Mann, Bhupendra Singh, 280
Mao Tse-tung, 332
Marriages, 167, 170
Mascarene, Annie, 230, 231, 238
Masculine totalitarianism, 316-17
Mass media, 82, 97, 106, 111, 299
Mathur, D.B., 51
Mattupalli panchayat, 185, 188
Maval Seva Mandal, 250
Mayo, Katherine, 17
Mazumdar, Charu, 335
Mazumdar, Shudha, 19
Mazural Huque, Mrs., 5
Mehta, Arunaben Sanat, 215
Mehta, Balwantrai, 216
Mehta, Hansa, 218-248
Mehta, Jivaraj, 216
Mehta, Pushpaben, 214, 217, 218
Menon, Laxmi N., 41, 227, 231
Menon, Leela Damodara, 227, 238, 240
Menon, P.K.K., 226
Mirjapur, Rani of, 174
Mistry, Roda, 181, 182, 183
Mofida Ahmed, Begum, 40
Montagu-Chelmsford Committee, 4-5
Montagu-Chelmsford reforms, 5, 311
Muni, S.D., 24
Municipal government
    Women's participation, 112, 183, 184-7, 202, 203-4, 231, 259, 301, 314, 328-9
Muslim Educational Society, 241, 242-3
Muslim Satya Shodhak Mandal, 257-8
Muslim Social Conference, 258
Muslim women

Political participation, 71, 81, 84, 94, 127
Myrdal, Gunnar, 346

Nagarathnamma, K.S., 224
Naidu, Sarojini, 4, 5, 6, 10, 12
Naik, Miss S., 5
Nair, K. Karunakaran, 226
Nathibai Damodardas Thakersey Institutions, 250
National Coordinating Committee of Women, 338
National Council of Women in India, 3, 9, 11
National Federation of Indian Women, 286, 287, 337, 338-9, 340
Nav Nirman Mahila Samiti, 211-12
Nav Nirman movement, 85, 108, 215, 217
Nav Nirman Yuvati Samiti, 211-12
Naxalite movement, 331, 335
Nehru, Mrs. Brijlal, 5, 10
Nehru, Jawaharlal, 19, 115, 346
Nehru, Kamala, 305
Nehru, Swaroop Rani, 305
Nikhil Banga Mahila Sangha, 341
Ninama, Hiraben, 214-218
Niranjan, Anupama, 221
Northeast India Women's Association, 197

Oral divorce, 257-8

Padia, Ritivatsala, 211
Panchayati raj
    Women's participation, 112, 187-9, 196, 204, 231, 259, 301, 314, 327-8
Pandit, Vijayalakshmi, 20, 42, 305, 312
Pankhurst, Mrs., 4
Pant, K.C., 211
Paranjape, Maltibai, 246
Paranjpye, Dr., 8
Parekh, Dhrulata, 209
Park, Richard L., 265
Parukutty, 227
Parulekar, Godawari, 246, 250
Paschim Banga Agragami Mahila Samiti, 342

Index

Paschim Banga Ganatantrik Mahila Samiti, 340-1
Paschim Banga Mahila Samiti, 336-7, 340
Patel, Chimanbhai, 210, 216, 217
Patel, Kamla, 213
Patel, Kamlaben, 211, 216
Patel, Maniben, 208, 214, 216, 217
Patel, Manjulaben, 216
Patel, Niruben, 215
Patel, Shantaben, 214, 215
Patel, Sushila, 250
Patel, Vallabhbhai, 115
Pathik, Vijay Singh, 292
Patwardhan, Indumati, 250
Pavamani, Margret, 229
Perin Captain, 248
Petti, Methuben, 200
Phule, Mahatma Jyotirao, 248
Pichchamma, Kalagara, 173
Pillai, T.K. Narayan, 231
Political awareness, 72-3, 75, 81, 145-7, 221, 249-50
    Jaipur study, 53-9, 63-4
Political discussions, 88-93
Political disillusionments, 162, 166
Political leaders
    Attitude towards women, 83
    Perception, 115-16
Political participation, 67, 80, 81, 86-7, 113
    Impact of education, 128-30
    Impact of religion, 132-4
    Institutionalization, 102-4
    State's responsibility, 83
    Suggestions, 82-3
    Gujarat, 85-118, 202-9
    Jaipur city, 59-60
    Maharashtra, 119-39, 247-50
Political parties, 81, 87
    Election manifestos, 68-70, 191-2
Political parties and women, 70-1, 88, 100-2, 112, 124-5, 198-9, 215-17, 221-2
    Gujarat, 201-2, 213
    Kerala, 236-40
    Maharashtra, 259-62
    Punjab, 282-4
    West Bengal, 331-6
Political preferences, 60-3, 64-5
Political socialization, 40-1, 87, 112-13
Politicization, 77-170
Polyandry, 292
Polygamy, 257-8, 292
Pon Morcha, 256
Prajamandal movement, 291
Prakash Kaur, 279
Prarthana Samaj (A.P.), 173
Prashar, Sarla, 278
Pressure groups, 209-12
Privileges and limitations, 301-2
Public meetings
    Women's participation, 90-1, 93-9
Puniya, Gauri, 300
Punjab
    Women's profiles, 165-90
Punjab Istree Sabha, 281, 286-7, 289
Punjabi Suba agitation, 288
Punnose, Rosamma, 240

Rajasthan
    Women's profiles, 291-304
Rajinder Kaur, 283
Rajput, P., 265
Rajwade, Rani, 16
Rajyalakshmi, 173
Ramabai, Pandita, 248
Ranade, Mahadev Govind, 248
Ranganekar, Ahilya, 250
Rao Mrs. Sanjiva, 5
Rashtriya Stree Sabha, 230
Rathbone, Eleanor, 17
Ravarda, Thakur of, 292
Ray, Amal, 221
Razia Sultana, 24
Reading habits and politicization, 157-8
Reddy, Muthulakshmi, 7, 8, 10, 13, 16, 17, 18, 19
Reddy, Sarojini Pulla, 185
Reddy, Sudha, 221, 225
Refinery movement (Assam), 197
Religion and politicization, 132-4, 138, 149-50, 165
Religious symbols, 262-3, 276-7, 329-30
Remarriages, 170
Round Table Conference, First, 10-11

Round Table Conference, Second, 12-13
Round Table Conference, Third, 15-16, 18
Rural women
    Politicization, 151-3

Sadalakshmi, T.N., 182, 183
Saikiani, Chandra Prabha, 197
St. Xavier College, Bombay, 249
Samajwadi Mahila Sabha, 252-3, 256
Samyukta Maharashtra movement, 257
Samyukta Stri Sanstha, 250
Sarabhai, Anasuyaben, 200
Sarabhai, Mrinalini, 201
Saraswati Amma, K.R., 240
Sarda Act, 9
Sarda Niketan, Guntur, 173
Sardesai, Krishnakumari, 248
Sarla Devi, 278
Sarojini, M.A., 227
Sati system, 292
Satya Deva, 267
Sayed, S.M., 311
Scheduled caste women, 40, 79, 81, 89, 94, 135-7, 138, 140, 155, 215, 258
Self-earning women
    Politicization, 130-2
Separate electorate, 15, 19
Seshamma, Balantrapu, 173
Shafi, Lady, 14
Shah, Mrs. Ahmen, 10
Shah, Arvind, 206
Shah, Ghanshyambhai, 216
Shah, Jayaben, 214, 216
Shah Nawaz, Begum, 11, 12, 15
Sharma, Bodh Raj, 266
Shauno Devi, 278
Shave, Mrs., 13
Sheth, Indumatiben, 213, 216
Shinde, Nalinibai, 246
Shukla, Dinesh M., 85
Simon Commission, 9-10
Sinha, Tarkeshwari, 41
Sirsikar, V.M., 79
Sita Devi, 278, 280
Social feminism, 20, 221
Social position and politicization, 159-60, 165, 167-70

Social taboos, 173
Social work, 250
Southborough Franchise Committee, 5-6
Sovani, Kusum, 248
Srivastava, Lady Kailash, 14
State politics, 171-349
Stree Matdata Sanstha, 71
Study circles, 108-9
Subbamma, Duvvuri, 173
Subbarayan, Radhabai, 11, 12, 18
Sukhtankar, Malini, 248
Support and opposition issues, 212-15, 256-9, 288-9, 343-4
Suramma, Jayanti, 174
Surat Grahak Mandal, 209, 212
Swaminathan, Ammu, 11

Taimur, Anowara, 194, 196, 198
Tara Singh, Master, 276
Tata, Lady Dorab, 9
Tata, Mithan, 6
Tata, Mrs. Terabai, 5-6
Tawale, S.N., 246
Tayyabji, Sharifa, 257
Tebhaga movement, 343
Tewary, Indra Narayan, 305
Thakur, Vimala, 217
Thayyil, Annie, 227
Tilakam, Bhanu, 183
Trade unions, 127, 158-9, 166, 200
Trikha, S., 67
Trivedi, Kantaben, 216
Tulpule, Malini, 255

Upreti, Nandini, 51
Urban women, 18
    Politicization, 150-1, 151-3, 206-7
Urbanization and politicization, 150-1, 165-6
Uttar Pradesh
    Women's profiles, 305-18

Vaghela, Gangaben, 214
Vaishya Seva Sadanam, 173
Vajpayee, Atal Bihari, 116
Veeresalingam, Kandukuri, 173, 189

Index

Verma, P.S., 298
Verma, S.P., 298
Vidyarthini Samaj (A.P.), 173
Vijaya Raje Scindhia, 40, 41
Vikas Gruha, 213
Voluntary organizations, 102
Voting behaviour, 26-7, 44-5, 70-4, 109-12
   Personal influence, 323-7
   Religion's role, 329-30
   Andhra Pradesh, 174-7, 180
   Gujarat, 204-6
   Karnataka, 222
   Kerala, 232-6
   Maharashtra, 260
   Punjab, 267, 268-70
   Rajasthan, 293-4, 298-9
   West Bengal, 322-7
Vyas, Jai Narain, 300
Vyas, Kokila, 213, 214, 215

Wasu, Pritpal Kaur, 278, 281, 284
West Bengal
   Women's politicization, 79, 140-70
   Women's profiles, 319-49
Women
   Social position, 167-70
Women as legislators, 3, 4, 41-2, 189, 200, 231
   Performance, 214-15, 223
   Andhra Pradesh, 180-4
   Punjab, 277-80
   U.P., 311-13
   West Bengal, 319-21
Women as ministers
   Andhra Pradesh, 182-3
   Assam, 199
   Gujarat, 216-17

Karnataka, 224-5
Kerala, 231
Maharashtra, 259
Punjab, 278-9
Rajasthan, 300
U.P., 313
West Bengal, 330-1
Women franchise, 3-23
   British women's support, 6
   First delegation (1917), 4-5
Women Graduate Union, Bombay, 6
Women leaders, 41-2
Women representatives, 60-6
Women students, 164
Women voters, 4
   Education level (Jaipur), 52, 63
   Mobilization, 26-32
   Andhra Pradesh, 174-7
   Punjab, 268-70
   U.P., 306-9
Women's Coordinating Council, 337
Women's Freedom League, 6
Women's Indian Association, 3, 4, 6, 8, 9, 10, 11, 12, 13-15, 16, 173
Women's International League, 6
Women's National Front, 337-8
Women's organizations, 3, 81, 102, 173, 240-3, 250, 284-8, 336-42, 347
Women's politicization
   Gujarat, 79, 85-118
   Maharashtra, 79, 119-39
   West Bengal, 79, 140-70
Women's Self Defence League, 286

Yagnik, Indulal, 115
Yodha, Charumati, 213

Zorawar Singh, 292

HQ1641 .M38X

a80365170800676c

WITHDRAWN
From Bertrand Library

DATE DUE

DEC 2 7 1984			
JAN 8 1991			
NOV 1 2 1991			
MAY 1 0 2007			
GAYLORD			PRINTED IN U.S.A